Genesis

Westminster Bible Companion

Series Editors

Patrick D. Miller
David L. Bartlett

Genesis

W. SIBLEY TOWNER

Westminster John Knox Press
LOUISVILLE
LONDON·LEIDEN

Table 1 is adapted from *The Hebrew Bible: A Socio-Literary Introduction* by Norman Gottwald, copyright © 1985 Fortress Press. Used by permission of Augsburg Fortress.

Table 2 is adapted from *Genesis* by George W. Coats, copyright © 1983 Wm. B. Eerdmans Publishing Co. Used by permission.

Lyrics from "Morning Has Broken" in *The Children's Bells* by Eleanor Farjeon. Published by Oxford University Press. Used by permission.

Verses from *The Torah: The Five Books of Moses: The New JPS Translation According to the Traditional Hebrew Text.* Copyright 1985 by the Jewish Publication Society. Used by permission.

Lyrics from "Great Is Thy Faithfulness" by Thomas O. Chisholm © 1923. Renewal 1951 Hope Publishing Co., Carol Stream, IL 60188. All rights reserved. Used by permission.

Lyrics from "Out of Deep, Unordered Water" by Fred Kaan © 1968 Hope Publishing Co., Carol Stream, IL 60188. All rights reserved. Used by permission.

Lyrics from "Am I My Brother's Keeper?" by John Ferguson © 1969 Stainer & Bell Ltd. Admin. by Hope Publishing Co., Carol Stream, IL 60188. All rights reserved. Used by permission.

Excerpt from "God Marked a Line and Told the Sea" by Thomas H. Troeger, © Oxford University Press. Used by permission. All rights reserved.

Excerpt from "The Apocrypha and Pseudepigrapha of the Old Testament," ed. R. H. Charles, © Oxford University Press. Used by permission. All rights reserved.

Portions of chapter 3, "The Fall," first appeared in "Interpretations and Reinterpretations of the Fall" in *Proceedings of the Theology Institute of Villanova University*, 1984. Used by permission.

Excerpt from *Come Sweet Death: A Quintet from Genesis* by B. Davie Napier. Used by permission B. Davie Napier.

Excerpt from *The Creation of the World and Other Business* by Arthur Miller. Copyright ©1972, 1973 Arthur Miller and Ingeborg M. Miller, Trustee. Used by permission.

Excerpts from *The Old Testament Pseudepigrapha*, ed. James H. Charlesworth, copyright © 1983, 1985 by James H. Charlesworth. Used by permission of Doubleday, a division of Random House, Inc.

Verses from *Biblical Limericks* by Donald R. Bensen. Copyright ©1986 by Donald R. Bensen. Reprinted by permission of Ballantine Books, a Division of Random House, Inc.

Book design by Publishers' WorkGroup
Cover design by Drew Stevens

First edition

Published by Westminster John Knox Press
Louisville, Kentucky

This book is printed on acid-free paper that meets the American National Standards Institute Z39.48 standard. ∞

PRINTED IN THE UNITED STATES OF AMERICA

01 02 03 04 05 06 07 08 09 10 — 10 9 8 7 6 5 4 3 2 1

Library of Congress Cataloging-in-Publication Data
Towner, W. Sibley (Wayne Sibley), 1933–
    Genesis / W. Sibley Towner.
        p. cm. — (Westminster Bible companion)
    Includes bibliographical references.
    ISBN 0-664-25256-7 (pbk.)
    1. Bible. O.T. Genesis—Commenaries. I. Title. II. Series.

BS11235.3 .T69 2001
222'.11077—dc21   00-053454

Contents

Series Foreword

This series of study guides to the Bible is offered to the church and more specifically to the laity. In daily devotions, in church school classes, and in listening to the preached word, individual Christians turn to the Bible for a sustaining word, a challenging word, and a sense of direction. The word that scripture brings may be highly personal as one deals with the demands and surprises, the joys and sorrows, of daily life. It also may have broader dimensions as people wrestle with moral and theological issues that involve us all. In every congregation and denomination, controversies arise that send ministry and laity alike back to the Word of God to find direction for dealing with difficult matters that confront us.

A significant number of lay women and men in the church also find themselves called to the service of teaching. Most of the time they will be teaching the Bible. In many churches, the primary sustained attention to the Bible and the discovery of its riches for our lives have come from the ongoing teaching of the Bible by persons who have not engaged in formal theological education. They have been willing, and often eager, to study the Bible in order to help others drink from its living water.

This volume is part of a series of books, the Westminster Bible Companion, intended to help the laity of the church read the Bible more clearly and intelligently. Whether such reading is for personal direction or for the teaching of others, the reader cannot avoid the difficulties of trying to understand these words from long ago. The scriptures are clear and clearly available to everyone as they call us to faith in the God who is revealed in Jesus Christ and as they offer to every human being the word of salvation. No companion volumes are necessary in order to hear such words truly. Yet every reader of scripture who pauses to ponder and think further about any text has questions that are not immediately answerable simply by reading the text of scripture. Such questions may be about historical and geographical details or about words that are obscure or so loaded with meaning that one cannot tell at a glance what is at stake. They may be about the fundamental meaning of a passage or about what connection a particular text might have to our contemporary world. Or a teacher preparing for a church school class may simply want to know: What should I say about this biblical passage when I have to teach it next Sunday? It is our hope that these volumes, written by teachers and pastors with long experience studying and teaching Bible in the church, will help members of the church who want and need to study the Bible with their questions.

The New Revised Standard Version of the Bible is the basis for the interpretive comments that each author provides. The NRSV text is presented at the beginning of the discussion so that the reader may have at hand in a single volume both the scripture passage and the exposition of its meaning. In some instances, where inclusion of the entire passage is not necessary for understanding either the text or the interpreter's discussion, the presentation of the NRSV text may be abbreviated. Usually, the whole of the biblical text is given.

We hope this series will serve the community of faith, opening the Word of God to all the people, so that they may be sustained and guided by it.

Introduction

Without a doubt, the book of Genesis is one of the five or six most important books of the Hebrew Bible. The book of Job is another, because of its sensitivity to human suffering; Psalms, too, because of its exquisite ability to seize human experience like a harp and strum on every one of its strings. The book of Exodus also belongs high on the list because of the model of God the liberator that it sets forth; and so do Isaiah and Jeremiah. Genesis rates near the top not only because of the burning importance of the material of antiquity with which it deals, but also because of the rich array of modern issues it raises.

Cosmology is here—the story of the creation of the world long ago. Because Genesis starts with this matter, it immediately triggers in us the modern problem of how that biblical account should be given its voice alongside the scientific models of the origin of the cosmos, in some of which we also believe. The latter are more in flux and more open-ended now than they have been at any time since Newton, so the opportunity for dialogue with our theological treatment of the matter is particularly ripe.

Anthropology is here—the story of the creation of the human creature in antiquity and the essential nature of that creature. In the very first chapter of Genesis, we hear that we are made in the image of God, which is a big truth claim about human nature. For one thing, it says that we can never talk about human nature apart from God's nature, and that, from the biblical point of view, all anthropology is also theology.

Indirectly, at least, *evolution* is here—that map of the slow and ancient emergence of human beings from the general pool of life. Genesis engages science with theology at this point as well, for it pushes us to affirm that the process was guided from start to finish by the hand of God. On this topic, Genesis quarrels with the creationists who believe the creation of Adam and Eve to be a special act of God unrelated to any that preceded or followed it. Genesis also quarrels with the strict Darwinians, who believe that evolution occurs randomly and without any purpose other than the enlargement of life itself.

The battle between the sexes is here—the element of ambivalence that inheres in the smallest of all human communities, woman and man. Genesis sets this issue in the context of the most primeval realities of human life, affirming that from the beginning we have belonged together and that we have always experienced strife and trouble in being together.

The grim reality of sin is here—not from the very beginning of the story, but already evident by the third chapter. Is there a "Fall" in scripture, an account of a bad afternoon in the garden when human nature was once and for all perverted from a state of innocence and purity to one that is totally depraved? Whether we answer that question Yes or No, it is clear that Genesis means to hold up our picture before us with shadow fully visible.

The issue of the elder and the younger brother is here—always imbedded in the larger story of family relationships and always reappearing in every generation. Though Cain and Abel, Isaac and Ishmael, and Joseph and his many brothers are figures of the ancient past, the psychological issues of rivalry, justice, vocation, and violence that they raise are with us still today.

The issues of the treatment of the vulnerable, the disenfranchised, and, above all, of women are raised in this book—explored not only with Eve but also with Sarah and Hagar, with Rebekah and Leah, with Rachel and Tamar. Lethal love is here, just as it is among us today.

The saga of family is here—the story of a single family with a destiny that is threatened by every tragedy of human experience: barrenness, greed, lying, hatred, murder. It is a family that triumphs in the end, and so gives us hope that families even today can accept God's covenant and pursue their callings with a measure of integrity and success.

A different type of issue is here as well—the issue of how we got our Bible. Did various hands give us this precious book, or is it all the work of one inspired mind? Is this, for example, really the book of J (see below), or are the traces of the hand of that brilliant but hypothetical theologian of the past finally submerged in the form of the book as it has been received by the synagogue and church? We have to watch the rich growth and elaboration of tradition in this book and constantly ask how different the process that brought us the first book of the Bible really is from the process by which scripture is proclaimed and elaborated upon each week in the pulpits and classrooms of our own time.

We have here stories that have always been so beloved by children and adults alike that they have given rise to new stories in their turn, new renditions in art and music and film and video. In short, the text has a foreground as well as a background. With Genesis there is a rich history of interpretation that, even though it can never be comprehended in a single book or perhaps even by a single person, ought to form part of our immersion in this book.

ANCIENT NEAR EASTERN MYTH AND GENESIS

The religions of ancient Mesopotamia (Sumer, Akkad, Babylon) and Egypt had rich mythic traditions, that is, stories about the gods at work creating and recreating the world. They also had wisdom traditions: stories of wise courtiers, collections of proverbs, and manuals for reading omens and interpreting dreams. Ancient Israel did not emerge out of nothing. Far from starting from scratch, its storytellers, theologians, and writers—inspired in their work, we believe, by God—found much of this rich lore useful. They kept no "myths" as such: They did not concern themselves with what Yahweh and the heavenly court may have been doing on their own before time began. They kicked all the gods out except one, and concerned themselves only with lining out the beginnings of the I-Thou relationship that exists between God and God's human creatures. They recast myth into saga in order to speak in their own way about the beginnings of the world, the creation of humankind, sin and punishment, the deluge, and the wonder that a man of humble origins such as Joseph could rise by virtue of his wisdom to prominence in the court of a foreign king.

From time to time, this commentary will, by way of comparison, cite texts from the religious traditions of the ancient Near East. Readers who wish to explore these parallel texts more fully can find extensive English translations of them in James Pritchard's reference work, *Ancient Near Eastern Texts Relating to the Old Testament.* For the record, the texts usually regarded as most relevant to Genesis, either because of their content, their genre, or their historical references, are the following (adapted from Gottwald, 52):

Table 1

Ancient Near Eastern Text	LanguageComparable	Genesis text
Creation Epic (Enuma Elish)	Old Babylonian	Genesis 1–2(Creation)
Akitu (New Year Festival)	Old Babylonian	Genesis 1–2
Enki and Nihursag (Paradise)	Sumerian	Genesis 2–3 (Creation and Fall)
Adapa Myth	Old Babylonian	Genesis 3(Fall)
Dumuzi and Enkimdu	Sumerian	Genesis 4 (Cain and Abel)
King List	Sumerian	Genesis 5 (Genealogy)
Ziusudra Myth (Flood)	Sumerian	Genesis 6–9 (Flood)
Gilgamesh Epic, XI (Flood)	Akkadian	Genesis 6–9
Atrahasis Epic (Flood)	Old Babylonian	Genesis 6–9
Tale of Sinhue	Egyptian	Genesis 12–50 (Family saga)
Nuzi Tablets	Akkadian	Genesis 31:19–42 (Theft of household gods)
Story of Two Brothers	Egyptian	Genesis 39 (Joseph and Potiphar's wife)
Tradition of Seven Lean Years	Egyptian	Genesis 41 (Seven lean years)

THE PROCESS OF ORAL TRANSMISSION AND ITS MEDIA

Before any word of the text of Genesis was set down in writing, there was, we believe, a rich oral tradition of stories about God the Creator, the founder and providential preserver of Israel, and about the heroes and heroines of that people. This lore was handed down from earliest times, from parent to child, from tribal storyteller to student, from one generation to the next. Much of this tradition was gathered up into the first written version of Genesis, but not all of it; perhaps some of it never was incorporated into our canonical biblical text. Many of these traditions, such as the stories of the patriarchs and matriarchs, traveled independently from each other in the beginning and were treasured around the towns and sanctuaries associated with the name of a particular founding family—Abraham and Sarah at Hebron, Isaac and Rebekah at Beer-sheba, Jacob and Rachel at Bethel. They grew together into a continuous account only secondarily, as the various Canaanite tribes that came to make up the new people Israel gathered for festivals and covenant ceremonies at central sanctuaries, and shared with each other their most hallowed traditions. Perhaps the plot—promise moving toward a fulfillment—that now guides the entire story of the father and mothers was given to these traditions only when the theological giants who first set them down in writing gave them their final form. To these great writers also may well be given the recognition for attaching as a prologue to the stories of Israel's beginnings (Genesis 12–50) another large and rich cycle of oral traditions about the beginnings of the whole world (Genesis 1–11).

How can one say very much about oral tradition, since by definition there are no written records of it? One must argue backward from the written forms, drawing at the same time from such evidence of practices and techniques as can be garnered elsewhere from oral cultures, both ancient and modern. Certain simple principles do seem to apply everywhere. For example, as stories are repeated orally they tend to fall into standard patterns or genres of narrative designed to facilitate memory. The presence of a large number of stereotyped, often-repeated patterns of narrative in a text like Genesis means that it had a prior oral phase.

A second principle follows immediately from the first. Specific formulas or genres belong to specific social settings, so that the way people speak in a tavern can be distinguished from the way people speak in a sanctuary or to their children.

We are familiar with these two principles from our own experience with the remnants of orality in our own literary culture: "Once upon a time" means that a fairy tale is about to begin; "Oyeh, oyeh" means that the bailiff has come into court to introduce the judge; "Extra, extra, read all about it" is the cry of a newspaper boy; "May the Lord bless you and keep you" means that the church service is almost finished. Apply the verbal clues about institutional setting, speaker, and audience to the full-sized narratives of Genesis, and you can say some cogent things about the form and content of the oral tradition prior to the introduction of Hebrew writing around 1000 B.C. and to the subsequent reduction of the sacred tradition to writing by the first great Israelite theologians.

Table 2, adapted from George Coats, shows ten of the most common oral genres found in Genesis. Some of these are long (saga), and some are usually short and to the point (blessing, etiology). Individual narratives may show features of more than one of these typical patterns of story-telling.

Table 2

Genre	Description	Examples
Blessing	Stylized wish in subjunctive or imperative mood, designed to increase power in recipient. Curse is the opposite.	Gen. 3:14–19 27:27–29 49:2–27
Etiology	Explains the origin of a custom, natural reality, place, or name.	Gen. 2:23 9:13–17 32:2
Genealogy	A list of family members, arranged in a line or showing branches.	Gen. 5:1–32 10:1–31 11:10–32
Cult legend	Explains the foundation of a sanctuary or altar.	Gen. 28:10–22
Legend	Story about a virtuous hero.	Gen. 22:1–19
Myth	Story about the gods at work in the divine realm bringing about things that impinge on us.	Gen. 6:1–4
Novella	A long narrative with literary features of plot and characterization. Probably originated as written text.	Genesis 37–50 (The Joseph story)
Saga	A long prose story about heroes and events of old. May include subgenres. Primeval saga: Genesis 1–11; Family saga: Genesis 12–50	Much of Genesis
Song	Poem to be sung, often for the purpose of boasting	Gen. 4:23–24
Popular tale	Short narrative with simple plot	Gen. 4:1–16 16:1–16

Students of oral tradition believe they can show which elements of a story tend to be the most subject to change during the course of transmission and which tend to be the most fixed. They can also demonstrate that the traditioners were remarkably accurate in passing on the text as they received it from their predecessors. Of course, any reconstructions of the earlier forms, earlier meanings, and institutional settings (sanctuary, court of law, teaching setting) in which the Bible originated must remain hypothetical. At best, they can throw light upon the form of the text that stands in the Bible that we now have; in some instances these studies can even help clear up questions about the precise meaning of a particular text. We do not preach or base our moral decisions on a hypothetical "original" form of any Bible story, however, but only on the form in which it now stands before the whole church.

EARLY THEOLOGIANS OF ISRAEL
AND THEIR LITERARY LEGACIES

Scholars of the Bible share widely the conviction that the hands of several individual theologians or "schools" of thought of ancient Israel can be discerned in the book of Genesis and throughout the Pentateuch. These "sources" or layers of redaction can be discerned by characteristics typical of each: the name or names of God employed, special vocabulary used, clues about the historical setting of each author or school, distinctive theological emphases. Without attempting to teach the reader how to do original source analysis, here in broad strokes are the results of a century and a half of work down this line:

1. The Yahwist (J, from the German spelling, *Jahwe*) worked in tenth-century B.C. Jerusalem during the period of the United Monarchy. Calls God by the proper name *Yahweh* (translated in NRSV by "LORD")

2. The Elohist (E) worked in the ninth century B.C. in the northern kingdom of Israel. Calls God by the generic name *Elohim* until Ex. 3:15.

3. The Deuteronomist (D) worked in seventh-century B.C. Jerusalem, not long before its fall to Babylon (little attestation in Genesis)

4. The Priestly writers (P) worked in the sixth century B.C., during the Babylonian Exile or shortly afterward. Probably a succession of individuals or a "school." Provided the final narrative framework of the Pentateuch.

Table 3

Section of Genesis	J	E	P
The story of Creation	Gen. 2:4b–4:26 (Garden, Fall, Cain, Seth)		Gen. 1:1–2:4a (Seven days of creation)
Adam to Noah			Gen. 5:1–32
The Flood	Gen. 6:5–8; 7:1–23; 8:2–13; 8:20–22; 9:18–27 (Flood and promise)		Gen. 6:9–22; 7:11–24; 8:1–5, 13–19; 9:1–17; 28 (Flood and covenant)
Table of the nations	Gen. 10:8–19, 21, 24–30		Gen. 10:1–7, 22–23, 31–32
The Tower	Gen. 11:1–9		
Noah to Abraham			Gen. 11:10–32
Abram moves	Genesis 12–14 Mixed J and P		Mixed J and P; Gen. 14:1–24? (War of the kings)
Covenant	Genesis 15–20 (mixed J, E, and P); 16:1–16 (Hagar and Ishmael); 18:1–33 (angels visit); 19:1–38 (Sodom)	Gen. 20:1–8 (Sarah and Abimelech)	Gen. 17:1–27 (Covenant rite)
Birth, marriage, and death	Gen. 21:1–6 Birth of Isaac (mixed J, E, and P); 25:1–33; 27:1–45 (Isaac stories)	Gen. 21:8–21 (Hagar and Ishmael); 22:1–24 (sacrifice of Isaac); 26:10–22 (Jacob's dream at Bethel; mixed with J)	Gen. 23:1–20 (death of Sarah); 25:7–20 (Abraham's death, birth of Esau and Jacob)
Jacob and Laban	Gen. 29:1–31:55 (marriage to Rachel, their children, flight and covenant with Laban)	Elements in chaps. 29–31	
Jacob and Esau	Gen. 32:22–32 (Jacob wrestles); 33:1–17 (Jacob meets Esau)	Gen. 32:13b–21 (Jacob prepares to meet Esau)	Gen. 32:3–13a (Jacob prepares to meet Esau)
Miscellany	Gen. 34:1–31 (rape of Dinah) Gen. 38:1–30? (Tamar and Judah)	Gen. 35:1–20 (return to Bethel and birth of Benjamin)	Gen. 35:27–37:2 (lists and genealogies)
Joseph and his brothers	Gen. 37:3–50:26 (complex intermingling of J and E, with many parallel versions of stories)		

The particular literary features and theological emphases of each of these sources were firmly established by 1865 with the publication in Germany by Julius Wellhausen of his *Prolegomena*. Table 3 gives a hint of the complex intermingling of written sources in the first of the "five books of Moses." Many of these results, particularly with regard to dating, are challenged from time to time, however, even by scholars who accept in principle the existence of Pentateuchal sources. The current state of the discussion is summed up well by Antony F. Campbell and Mark A. O'Brien in their *Sources of the Pentateuch*.

HOW THIS COMMENTARY WILL HELP YOU

An important servant of the gods of ancient Greece was Hermes, the little figure portrayed by artists with wings on his shoes. His job was to bring messages from the gods to mortals. Though we have dispensed with the messenger, his name remains imbedded in the technical word for an interpretive approach, a *hermeneutic*.

As you probably have gathered by now, the hermeneutic at work in this volume is a historical-critical one. This method attempts to locate the text of Genesis in the world of ancient Israel where it first arose. Another aim of this interpretive method is to help a reader of scripture solve problems: What is the plain meaning of an obscure text? What ancient views of the physical world are at work in this text that might need to be translated into modern understandings? How will the views of God and humankind expressed in this text be modified by the full canon of scripture as they make their way into our own theological confessions?

Some of the older historical-critical commentaries considered their work completed when they had resolved problems with the Hebrew text, commented on the semantics of key words, done their historical studies, made relevant comparisons with texts from other ancient Near Eastern religions, analyzed the structure and literary nature of the passages, and, in the end, offered a careful restatement of the message of the text. All of this work is important; Hermes could not do better in bringing the message from Olympus. This small study will from time to time go a final step beyond these good observations, however. In the name of a hermeneutic of contemporary faith enrichment, it will offer suggestions about how the original communication of the text might intersect our lives as they are actually lived at the beginning of the twenty-first century.

Take these "applications" with grains of salt, however. They are meant only to point out directions for your further reflection. The conviction that underlies this entire commentary is that sincere readers of the Bible, when they have hurdled the barriers to understanding that individual texts present, will draw their own valid conclusions that direct and empower godly living. That is what the "priesthood of all believers" means when it is applied to the study of the Bible. May God always bless the church and the synagogue with such readers!

Part 1: The Beginnings

1. Creation by God's Word
Genesis 1:1–2:4a

Biblical exposition done by and for the whole person would lead us to study texts with the Bible in one hand, the hymnal in the other, and great artistic renditions of the biblical stories projected on the wall. You will have to provide the art to accompany this commentary, but, in the case of Genesis 1, the music at least is ready at hand. The index of *The Presbyterian Hymnal* (1990) lists eleven hymns that echo the first chapter of the Bible (and, no doubt, other hymnals can add more). That is a greater number of hymns than accumulate around any other passage of the Old Testament, including the beloved Psalm 23. Anyone who doubts that creation theology, with its essential concerns for the environment and the integrity of other creatures, is a big issue in our time needs only to look at that fact. People want to sing about the great themes of Genesis 1 as well as talk about them. We want to throw our whole selves into a spirit of wonder and gratitude as we contemplate the first words of God to us in scripture. We want to sing, "Let All Things Now Living," "God of the Sparrow," "I Sing the Mighty Power of God," or the hymn by Eleanor Farjeon:

> Morning has broken
> Like the first morning,
> Blackbird has spoken
> Like the first bird.
> Praise for the singing!
> Praise for the morning!
> Praise for them, springing
> Fresh from the Word!

The Bible begins with the affirmation that all the great creations of God spring "fresh from the Word." People living at the beginning of the fourth millennium since Genesis was written seek answers to many other questions: How did God go about the work of creation? Was there a Big

Bang? How did life begin on earth? Did God call on an asteroid laden with amino acids or even with living cells from Mars or Krypton or some other corner of the universe? Is there life elsewhere in the cosmos as well?

The creation story in Genesis is not equipped to answer questions such as these because it is not a scientific treatise. Instead, it is a theological work in narrative form. It comes to render to us a picture of the author of our existence at work. It says, "God did it; God commanded it."

The hymn affirms that "every day" recapitulates the events of Genesis 1. Every day you can see what the first dawn saw, the awakening of light and life. That points to the *etiological* function of mythic stories like these, that is, the function of explaining how we got the dawn and why it seems so secure and so good. Furthermore, in the notion of "springing fresh from the Word," or re-creation, it points to the memory of Genesis 1 that operates in later *eschatological* (= end-time) texts. Since the days of the great German scholar Hermann Gunkel (1862–1932), scholars have demonstrated the truth of his teaching, "Primeval time is recapitulated in End-time." The dawn of the first day already anticipates the dawn of a new age. Even as at the beginning God had to struggle against chaos in order to create a cosmos, even as in the beginning God created an Eden and put an Adam and Eve to till the garden and keep it, so also in the end we are led to expect a new heaven and earth to emerge out of God's cosmic struggle with evil and chaos. Then will appear on earth a new Eden, a New Jerusalem, to be ruled by the Messiah of God, who is the new Adam and Eve.

Genesis 1:1–2:4a is the first of two distinctly different creation stories preserved in the library of the Bible. The second follows it immediately in Genesis 2:4b–25. Based on the distinctive vocabulary, the absence of the proper name of God (Yahweh), and the culminating event of Sabbath, this narrative has long been assigned by scholars to the latest of four sources of the Pentateuch, the Priestly source (see the introduction). The Priestly writers are thought to have worked during or shortly after the Babylonian Exile. A guess at the date of this written record of an older oral tradition would put it at about 550 B.C. This source-critical understanding of Genesis 1:1–2:4a makes the first creation story a narrative frame for the entire story of the Pentateuch, from the beginning of the world to the emergence of Israel as a people poised to possess a land and have a king in their own right. In the larger context of the full canon, it is the introduction of the larger story for which the re-creation of the world in the book of Revelation is the conclusion.

DAY ONE: CREATION OUT OF SOMETHING
Genesis 1:1–5

1:1 **In the beginning when God created the heavens and the earth,** ²**the earth was a formless void and darkness covered the face of the deep, while a wind from God swept over the face of the waters.** ³**Then God said, "Let there be light"; and there was light.** ⁴**And God saw that the light was good; and God separated the light from the darkness.** ⁵**God called the light Day, and the darkness he called Night. And there was evening and there was morning, the first day.**

[1:1] The great creation account of Genesis 1 opens with the famous phrase, "In the beginning . . ." Problems emerge immediately: there is no "the" in the Hebrew text. Why, then, did the NRSV translators not render the phrase, "In beginning . . . ," that is, "When [God] began to create"? In fact, they offer precisely that alternative in the footnote. (They also offer the King James standby, "In the beginning God created [the heaven and the earth]." By putting a period at the end of verse 1, the King James Version [KJV] led readers to understand Gen. 1:1 to be a headline for all that followed).

Not to put too fine a point upon it (as Mr. Snagsby used to say in Dickens's *Bleak House*), does this detail make a difference?

Perhaps not by itself. If, however, verse 1 is not a complete sentence, but is a subordinate clause of temporal character (NRSV: "In the beginning *when* . . ."), suddenly it is clear that the main clause is elsewhere than in verse 1. The NRSV places it in verse 2, which describes the condition of the earth "in the beginning"; other modern translations take verse 2 as a parenthetical remark, which describes the circumstances that prevailed when God's action began. They locate the main clause in verse 3. For example, the translation of the Jewish Publication Society reads as follows:

When God began to create the heaven and the earth—the earth being unformed and void, with darkness over the surface of the deep and a wind from God sweeping over the water—God said, "Let there be light"; and there was light.

Though these two modern translations construe the syntax or structure of verses 1–3 in slightly different ways, they are both closer to the mark than the KJV was. It seems likely, therefore, that the Priestly writers of Genesis 1 thought that the first act of creation was light. That would mean that the creative activity of God in the beginning of cosmic time and history was not to produce a world out of nothing (*ex nihilo*). Instead, it was to take the dark and swirling chaos that was already there and to put it into life-supporting, fruitful order. That suggests, in turn, that the Priestly school did not consider it a challenge to God's omnipotence to suggest that something coexisted with God from eternity. (Other biblical writers apparently did regard this view as unacceptable; by New Testament times *creatio ex nihilo*—creation out of nothing—seems to have become the normative view [see Rom. 4:17; Heb. 11:3] and so it has remained in our dogmatic formulations down to this century.)

Call it matter, call it freedom, call it chaos, call it being itself, the opening verses of Genesis picture God as a great artisan taking up the raw material that was at hand and fashioning a beautiful cosmos, beginning with light out of darkness. Such an understanding of the sense of Genesis 1:1–3 opens the door to fresh dialogue with the scientific cosmologies that securely lodge in the other halves of our twenty-first-century brains, for they too postulate the existence of unformed matter and energy prior to the formation of our present universe. Such an understanding opens new possibilities for understanding the relation of the star dust of which all things are made to the Maker's own self. If God is the Ground and Source of all being and we too share in that being, perhaps we and all the rest of the creatures of God are in some way fundamentally bound to our Maker (though not part of God or godlings in our own right), just as light is bound to the source from which it emanates.

One other detail about verse 1 deserves some close attention. Unlike our previous discussion, which centered on the *syntax* (the structure) of the sentence, this is a detail of *semantics* (the meaning of the words). The Hebrew verb for "create" that is used here is *bara*. Though a number of other verbs were available (such as "to make," "to fashion," "to form"), the writers carefully chose this one for the simple reason that God is the only subject the verb *bara* ever has. The objects of this verb in the Old Testament range from the entire cosmos (here and Gen. 5:1) and new heavens and earth (Isa. 65:17) to something as small and personal as a new heart (Ps. 51:12). In every case, these are things that only God can make. God's sovereignty is expressed in projects both massive and minuscule, all of which are, however, of utter importance to God's creatures. This means that each one of us creatures of God is a unique specimen of God's handiwork, neither self-generated and autonomous, nor a mere speck of matter accidentally floating in space. As the Bible understands it, we are the objects of God's special action of *bara*.

[2] Part of the problem of understanding how to visualize the "wind from God [that] swept over the face of the waters" (if, indeed, a wind can be visualized at all!) is semantic. The same Hebrew word can mean both "wind" and "spirit," and the whole phrase can also be understood as a form of the superlative—"a mighty wind." Perhaps the best translation would be

"God's wind"—a wind that is not part of the chaos but comes from outside to exercise creative power over the chaos. Even before creation began, God expresses divine care and sovereignty over the chaos. For its part, the chaos has no divine potency (as was the case in the polytheistic mythic world of Babylon, where the hostile salt water was the dragon, Tiamat, whom the creator had to overcome). It has potential that only God can draw out, a raw material waiting to be worked by the divine artisan.

The picture can be better understood if we penetrate its underlying metaphor. To do that involves the Hebrew verb that the NRSV translates "swept." The same word is used elsewhere to mean "hover," as an eagle does over its brood (Deut. 32:11). One is led, then, to imagine that the Priestly writers pictured God as a mighty bird sweeping over the chaotic surface of the abyss. Such a cosmological metaphor is not the same as the Egyptian creation myth that taught that the first thing to emerge out of the watery chaos in the beginning was the hill of Memphis on which a giant egg was perched. When that egg hatched, out sprang the first of the gods.

The picture in verse 2 of the God-wind is not so much a picture of a nurturer or even an egg fertilizer as it is a picture of a divine observer preparing to do a creative act. If "spirit" is used, it should not be capitalized as it was in the KJV and RSV, for the Priestly writers knew nothing about the Holy Trinity. Yet this is a wind or spirit from God, preparing for the first creative act. Such an act means life and light, creation and new creation. We can forgive the English poet Gerard Manley Hopkins (1844–1889) for his capitalization, for he captures the metaphor of Genesis 1:2 very well when he concludes his poem "God's Grandeur" with these words:

> And for all this [human struggle], nature is never spent;
> There lives the dearest freshness deep down things;
> And though the last lights off the black West went
> Oh, morning, at the brown brink eastward, springs—
> Because the Holy Ghost over the bent
> World broods with warm breast and with ah! bright wings.

The cosmos was "a formless void," says the NRSV, replacing the RSV's "without form and void." The two Hebrew words, *tohu wa-bohu*, used here are an almost comic-sounding cliché, with a single meaning such as "formless void," or perhaps simply, "chaotic." But the watery waste has a name here too—"the deep" (*tehom*)—that seems to echo the name of Babylon's hostile deity of the salt sea, the dragon Tiamat.

[3–5] The "then" with which the next sentence begins in the NRSV, makes clear the temporal sequence between the condition of the cosmos in verses 1–2 and the first creative act in verse 3: Chaos came first, followed by light. The light that sprang up from no particular source but simply from God's creative word was good in the sight of God (v. 4); its existence made possible the distinction between Day and Night (v. 5).

Before we leave this first and very weighty unit of Genesis, three issues that it raises deserve further exploration.

Creation from Nothing

Traditional theology has always insisted that God created the world from nothing; it did so in order to protect the unrivaled sovereignty of God, with no challenge even from inert water or matter. No one wanted to admit that there might be something out there that was, if not coequal, at least coancient with God. In the seventeenth century, the Westminster Confession talked about creation squarely within the notion of *creatio ex nihilo*:

> It pleased God the Father, Son and Holy Ghost, for the manifestation of the glory of his eternal power, wisdom, and goodness, in the beginning, to create or make of nothing the world, and all things therein, whether visible or invisible, in the space of six days, and all very good (4:1).

Appended to this teaching are proof texts: Genesis 1:1–3; Exodus 20:11; Psalm 104:24; Jeremiah 10:12; John 1:2–3; Colossians 1:16; Hebrews 1:2; 11:3. On closer inspection, most of these texts really do not say "from nothing." In fact, nowhere does the Bible specifically say that God created the world "from nothing." (Even the text in which the idea is supposedly first mentioned, 2 Macc. 7:28, is ambiguous.) A number of texts (especially Pss. 18; 19; 24; 29; 33; 68; 93; 95; 104; see also Wisd. Sol. 11:17) actually speak of God's struggle to bring chaotic and formless matter into shape. In so doing they retain a remnant of the mythological tradition of cosmic warfare and divine victory at the beginning.

By putting *ex nihilo* aside and allowing for a medium in which God the Creator could work fruitfully, modern theology is rediscovering a neglected dimension of the biblical witness on this matter. For example, the Russian theologian Nicholas Berdyaev argues that there was something into which God projected the creation, namely, freedom. He treats freedom almost as a substance. When God creates something in and of the medium of freedom, that thing that comes into being is neither inert nor dependent but is able to stand up and walk and look out for its own interests and even, in some cases, sin. In other words, God gave up some sovereignty in creating a world that is admixed with freedom. This freedom can be depicted, as the first chapter of Genesis does, in the metaphor of chaotic water, but the effect is still the same: God draws creation out of a medium that still forms part of our physical and spiritual persons, and still remains for us a reservoir of right relationships and life, but also a threat of chaos and death. The baptismal hymn "Out of Deep, Unordered Water" by Fred Kaan seems quite comfortable with this view of the work of the creator, who is also re-creator:

> Out of deep, unordered water
> God created light and land,
> World of bird and beast and, later,
> In God's image, woman, man.
> There is water in the river
> Bringing life to tree and plant.
> Let creation praise its giver:
> There is water in the font.

Christian theology also is revisiting the doctrine of creation in order to enhance dialogue with current scientific cosmologies. British theoretical physicist Stephen Hawking, for example, does not believe in a Creator because he no longer finds a place for a creation. In *A Brief History of Time*, he argues that the cosmos has always existed. Movements of the heavenly bodies are simply like dots on a balloon being blown up; they were not disseminated from an original starting point by a Big Bang. Of course, other scientific cosmologies do assume a Big Bang; some also believe that the universe not only expands but also contracts. In any case, with all such scientific theories, a biblical doctrine of "creation from something" is a more congenial partner in conversation.

In *Religion in An Age of Science*, Ian Barbour says that we have moved from a modern to a postmodern science. Recent postmodern scientific thinking is characterized by two major shifts: (a) a new openness to chance, and (b) relational ontology, by which he means that scientific models of the birth of the cosmos now want to stress relationships. Each of these has a bearing on our understanding of Genesis 1.

Randomness and Order

The shift in science toward more open systems allows a place for randomness and chance, those "aberrations" that were anathema to the clockwork regularity assumed by Newtonian physics. The new discipline of "chaos studies" comes in at this point. Our inability to predict what subatomic particles will do either reflects our lack of enough scientific tools to control all the variables or else it shows that particle behavior really cannot be predicted. Barbour and many scientists are more inclined to say that the latter is the case. The new recognition in science of the presence of chaos in the order of things demonstrates that unpredictabilities occur both in small systems and in big ones.

Physicist-theologian Frederic Burnham has followed these developments in scientific cosmologies and their implications for theology. In his article "Maker of Heaven and Earth: A Perspective of Contemporary Science," he discusses the seminal importance of studies in meteorology for the emerging discipline of chaosology. One such study involves the "Lorenz pattern" in weather advanced by meteorologist Edward Lorenz. Lorenz observed that instead of returning to the same starting point, weather patterns return to a nearby point within the same slowly rotating figure-eight configuration. The weather never leaves this pattern; it never becomes a figure nine. Neither does it ever repeat itself.

Just at that moment when you approach a starting point and think you are going to repeat but do not, you are at a moment of infinite potentiality, where order and chaos intersect. Why does this randomness creep into natural systems? Who knows? The variables are so limitless as to make control of them all quite impossible. The butterfly offers a famous example. If a butterfly flaps its wings in Tokyo, the weather in New York will be affected a few weeks later—infinitesimally so, but affected nonetheless. No one could predict that the butterfly would flap its wings at that moment. No one expected its effect. So the philosophical question "Which should be taken more seriously, predetermination or randomness?" is now being answered "Both/and." Some sectors of modern science are looking at the physical world as a work of supple character, open to the future.

Genesis 1 pictures God in the beginning at work bringing order out of chaos. Indeed, God is the great Orderer; however, that work is not finished in Genesis 1. All through the rest of the Bible God is at work bringing order both in the cosmic reaches of creation and in the midst of the chaos of human affairs. God can never stop struggling. The order is never absolutely fixed; chaos (or should we call it freedom?) is always in the background. The windows of the vault of heaven could be opened again (7:11). Freedom is the shadow side of creation with which God has to contend. The mythmakers of old tended to see this chaos-freedom as evil, an enemy of God. However, God knows—just as we have learned about our own shadow sides—that this freedom is not evil but is a dynamic source of energy that needs to be harnessed. The book of Job raises the burning question, How can really bad things happen to a really good person if the world is in any kind of moral order? The Lord's strategy in answering Job (Job 39–41) is to redescribe the creation in such a way as to show that orderly freedom exists in the created order as a pre-condition for truth and beauty. If there were no freedom in this creation, no touches of disorder, no open ends, then moral choice, creativity, and excellence could not arise. The world would be a monotonous cycle of inevitability, a dull-as-dishwater world of puppets and automatons. Do you see why creation is not, cannot be, *ex nihilo*, and why the Priestly writers of Genesis 1 were so insightful in picturing God working with chaos? God does not banish chaos utterly, but effects within it that which is ordered and beautiful and very good.

Ideal human behavior, too, can be described as orderly freedom. We cannot get beyond the boundaries that God established for us, although, as space travel and oceanography and the study of subatomic particles and brain science have now shown, those boundaries are far more gener-ous than we had ever supposed. Yet within those bounds there is mar-velous suppleness and space for human initiative. That is why a reading of Genesis 1 that celebrates God's greatness at bringing order out of chaos not once and for all but as an ongoing process is not only exegeti-cally justified but quite timely for a religious community that wants to make common cause with science in the building of a better world.

Relationships

Ian Barbour speaks not only of a new stress in science on the openness of natural systems, but also about what he calls "relational ontology"—the fundamental importance of pairs and symmetries in the created order. If one smashes an atom, certain paired particles fly off in opposite direc-tions. Two weeks later, if the spin on one of these particles reverses itself, the other one—now far removed from its mate—reverses its spin without ever being touched. Such phenomena are leading physics as well as the other sciences to a new appreciation of fundamental, natural relation-ships. This perspective is very much open to dialogue with the biblical account of creation that, as we see especially with the culminating account of the creation of humankind (1:26–28), turns out to have a lot to do with relationships.

DAYS TWO THROUGH FIVE: MOVING TO CULMINATION
Genesis 1:6–23

1:6 **And God said, "Let there be a dome in the midst of the waters, and let it separate the waters from the waters."** [7] **So God made the dome and sep-arated the waters that were under the dome from the waters that were** above the dome. And it was so. [8] God called the dome Sky. And there was evening and there was morning, the second day.

[9] And God said, "Let the waters under the sky be gathered together into one place, and let the dry land appear." And it was so. [10] God called the dry land Earth, and the waters that were gathered together he called Seas. And God saw that it was good. [11] Then God said, "Let the earth put forth vegetation: plants yielding seed, and fruit trees of every kind on earth that bear fruit with the seed in it." And it was so. [12] The earth brought forth vegetation: plants yielding seed of every kind, and trees of every kind bearing fruit with the seed in it. And God saw that it was good. [13] And there was evening and there was morning, the third day.

[14] And God said, "Let there be lights in the dome of the sky to separate the day from the night; and let them be for signs and for seasons and for days and years, [15] and let them be lights in the dome of the sky to give light upon the earth." And it was so. [16] God made the two great lights—the greater light to rule the day and the lesser light to rule the night—and the stars. [17] God set them in the dome of the sky to give light upon the earth, [18] to rule over the day and over the night, and to separate the light from the darkness. And God saw that it was good. [19] And there was evening and there was morning, the fourth day.

[20] And God said, "Let the waters bring forth swarms of living creatures, and let birds fly above the earth across the dome of the sky." [21] So God created the great sea monsters and every living creature that moves, of every kind, with which the waters swarm, and every winged bird of every kind. And God saw that it was good. [22] God blessed them, saying, "Be fruitful and multiply and fill the waters in the seas, and let birds multiply on the earth." [23] And there was evening and there was morning, the fifth day.

[1:6–8] On the second day, the Creator separates the chaotic waters above the earth, which earthlings recognize in the blueness of the sky, from the chaotic water on the earth. An apparently transparent "dome" or "firmament" is the divider. This ancient cosmology assumes that the universe is turtle shaped. A flat earth, covered by a dome, is supported over a nether world (Sheol) by pillars (Job 9:6; Ps. 75:3). As science, this account is of no use to us, though to ancients it explained much of what they saw around them in sky and sea. As theology, it is vital: God is the creator of night and day and sky, and they are all good. Good! In the world around us there is no admixture of evil, just as there is none in God. There is no cosmic dualism out there, no evil rival to God, no degenerate and corrupting matter. Evil and sin have to wait until a creature with independent choice comes along. The dualism of good and evil is moral, not cosmic, and its roots are in freedom.

[9–13] The account of God's work on the third day also explained several things to the ancient Israelites and early Christians: the origin of dry land, the confinement of the chaotic salt water to its proper boundaries (hurricanes and tidal waves are out of order), and the creation of plants. Special emphasis is placed on spermatophytes (seed-bearing plants) as opposed to algae, fungi, ferns, and other simultaneously created "vegetation." One can assume that this achievement prepares the way for the most significant act of creation yet to come, the creation of humankind. The seed-bearing plants are going to be the staff of life for the earth creatures and their companion animals (1:29–30), and as such are the plants of greatest interest to the oral traditioners and the Priestly writers.

The real subject of the first creation story in Genesis begins to emerge. The story is about God and us. Theology and anthropology go together in the Bible, right from its first chapter, and the linkage is never broken. We human beings are who we are because of God. We know nothing about the divine realm and the divine mind except what has to do with us. We got our means of sustenance from God and not from random chance. God, in turn, was thinking of us and our welfare from the very beginning. Texts such as Proverbs 8:22–31, Sirach (Ecclesiasticus) 24:1–12, and Wisdom of Solomon 7:22–8:4 introduce into the business of creation a third party, Dame Wisdom (*Sophia* in the Greek Old Testament). She is God's companion in creation, but she is also an intermediary between God and humankind. Even in these texts, then, the creation of the world is a theological event, the primary significance of which is to provide a setting for the human race.

[14–19] Now the origin of the celestial lights of day and night is explained. The order is puzzling, given that day and night were the work of the first day of creation. Where did the light come from before sun and moon and stars were created? The narrator does not say. Perhaps ancient cycles of worship underlie these verses. The appearances of the sun and moon at their appointed hours are signs "for seasons and for days and years," and as such they tell us mortals when to pray, when to take a sabbath rest, when to celebrate the annual festivals. Once again, God makes provision for the ordering of human life, even before humans are created.

[20–23] With the introduction of the sea creatures and the fowl, we also hear the words of God's first blessing. All creation is good, but the living, ambient creatures are given the special graces of sexuality and fecundity: "Be fruitful and multiply." Etiology is at work here, offering an explanation for why the ancient skies and seas teemed with life. Esthetics may play a small part here too: God gave us many wonderful companion creatures to admire and enjoy. An anthropological concern may also underlie the account. God is making long-term provision for the feeding of the thousands of human beings who will one day fill the earth.

DAY SIX: BEASTS AND EARTH CREATURES
Genesis 1:24–31

1:24 **And God said, "Let the earth bring forth living creatures of every kind: cattle and creeping things and wild animals of the earth of every kind." And it was so.** 25 **God made the wild animals of the earth of every kind, and the cattle of every kind, and everything that creeps upon the ground of every kind. And God saw that it was good.**

26 **Then God said, "Let us make humankind in our image, according to our likeness; and let them have dominion over the fish of the sea, and over the birds of the air, and over the cattle, and over all the wild animals of the earth, and over every creeping thing that creeps upon the earth."**

27 **So God created humankind in his image,**
in the image of God he created them;
male and female he created them.

28 **God blessed them, and God said to them, "Be fruitful and multiply, and fill the earth and subdue it; and have dominion over the fish of the sea and over the birds of the air and over every living thing that moves upon the earth."** 29 **God said, "See, I have given you every plant yielding seed that is upon the face of all the earth, and every tree with seed in its fruit; you shall have them for food.** 30 **And to every beast of the earth, and to every bird of the air, and to everything that creeps on the earth, everything that has the breath of life, I have given every green plant for food." And it was so.** 31 **God saw everything that he had made, and indeed, it was very good. And there was evening and there was morning, the sixth day.**

[1:24–25] As the sixth day of creation dawns, God populates the dry land with "wild animals" and "cattle" or domestic animals, plus creepers. Their significance will emerge in the verses to come, when they become subject to the "dominion" of the human beings (vv. 26, 28–29).

[26–27] The final and climactic act of creation is expressed in a long and deceptively simple sentence that abounds in theological issues. First, God says, "Let *us* make . . ." Why is the plural used? It is true that when the generic Hebrew word for "god" refers to Israel's God, it is usually plural in form—*Elohim*. However, this word is routinely treated as if it were singular, serving as the subject of singular verbs and the like. In this verse, for example, *Elohim* is the subject of a singular verb, "he said." No, God does not say "us" out of grammatical supercorrectness.

Is God using the "plural of majesty," and speaking in the manner of the queen of England or the pope? Not likely! If anyone has the right to make self-references in the plural (especially considering that God is, at least from a Christian point of view, a Holy Trinity), it would surely be God. However, this plural usage happens again only very rarely (e.g.,

Gen. 2:22; 11:7; Isa. 6:8). Surely, if God were thinking majestically, the plural would be used more consistently than that.

We are left, then, with the heavenly council as the only likely way of explaining this use of the plural in verse 1:26. Even in the latest hand to contribute to the final form of the Pentateuch—the Priestly writer—we come smack up against the feeble remnants of polytheism. God is speaking for the entire divine court: the "sons of God" (6:2), the "host of heaven" (1 Kings 22:19) of which God is Lord, the seraphim that surround the divine throne (Isa. 6:1–8), the great angels Gabriel and Michael (named for the first time in the latest book of the Hebrew Bible—see Dan. 9:21; 10:21; 12:1), and even the satan himself (Job 1:6). But the polytheistic background of this motif is only a remnant and the myth is faded. The heavenly beings surrounding God have no potency or role of their own here. They do not even speak; God speaks for them. However, they form a plurality, a community, juxtaposed to the new human community that is now going to come into being *in their image*.

Are we human beings created in the image of the angels then? Can we be created in the image of both God and the angels at the same time? Let us not make too much of this point. The meaning of "image" is, of course, crucial (see discussion below) and the intention of the writer is to forge a link here between the divine and the human realms. However, the writer remains vague about exactly who among the divine council is the model and prototype for the human creature. Gerhard von Rad puts it most delicately when he says, "The extraordinary plural ('Let us') is to prevent one from referring God's image too directly to God the Lord. God includes himself among the heavenly beings of his court and thereby conceals himself in this majority" (von Rad, 57).

A second issue introduced by verse 26 is the meaning and identity of *adam*. Note that the familiar "Let us make man" of the older English versions has given way in the NRSV to "Let us make humankind [*adam*]." Surely this is correct. The word *adam* is not really a proper name, but a generic name for the human species. When used this way, it is collective or implicitly plural in number. Moreover, its gender is not grammatically crisp. In one fell swoop God makes *adam* both male and female (v. 27). Apparently both genders are implicit in the collective word.

In Hebrew, the usual way to make a noun feminine is to add the letters *ah* to the shorter masculine form. The word *adamah*, however, which looks like the feminine form of *adam*, means "earth." Is the earth the spouse or the mother of this creature that is God's culminating achievement? Deep in the mythic background of the story, in the creation accounts of other cultures, humankind and the earth are related in some such way. Nothing much is made of the grammatical phenomenon here—*adam* is simply actualized as male *and* female. The grammatical tie between the two words, however, has led some contemporary scholars to prefer to render the term *adam* as "earth-creature," at least until it becomes explicitly male and female (in v. 27 and again in the second creation story, in 2:22–23).

Another key issue in verse 26 is the meaning of the Hebrew word that the dictionary defines as "image, likeness, or resemblance." What was an "image" in the Old Testament? Most of the evidence suggests that it was a three-dimensional object fabricated to resemble something else, like a statue or an amulet (see 1 Sam. 6:5; 2 Kings 11:18; Ezek. 16:17). In modern Hebrew the word has come to mean "photograph." Though a few occurrences of the word seem abstract, for the most part it refers to something concrete and physical. Is Genesis 1:26 teaching us that we human beings bear a family resemblance to God? Perhaps the Priestly writers had in mind the practice of ancient kings of placing statues of themselves in every corner of their dominions. God, the King of kings, has statues representing the divine self in every corner of the world, but unlike the immobile marbles of the kings, God's statues walk and talk. This is why God does not need any idols or portraits (Ex. 20:4–6; Deut. 5:8–10). God already has living images in the world, and they are a lot smarter than wooden or stone or plastic replicas. Furthermore, unlike dumb idols and amulets, living images like these can love their Maker and enter into relationships with their Maker.

"Image" is, of course, a motif drawn from the world of myth. Even if ancient Israel once entertained the idea, we no longer seriously believe that any human being, even Jesus Christ, whom Christians affirm to be the Son of God, looks like God. We have no idea what God looks like; God is spirit, and spirit possesses no legs or arms or hair. "Image" has to be taken as metaphor. But a metaphor for what? Once again, we discern in verse 26 the powerful anthropological interest of the first creation account. The Bible puts a great premium on human beings. We are not simply pieces of tissue or masses of electrons clinging to a speck of dirt that floats in the cosmic spaces. No, we are walking representations of God. Whatever "image" literally intends to say about God, it certainly means that the Priestly writers felt that human beings are of signal importance and exquisite value.

The metaphor of image is fruitfully explored by Douglas John Hall in his book *Imaging God: Dominion as Stewardship*. He divides the many proposals for understanding the meaning of the phrase "image of God" into two broad categories: "substantialist" understandings and "relational" understandings. Substantialists perceive the image of God in us to be embodied in some physical, emotional, or spiritual attribute, some substance or endowment, such as physical appearance, rationality, immortality, or freedom. A relational approach, on the other hand, like that of Barth, "conceives of the *imago* as an inclination or proclivity occurring within the relationship" (Hall, 98). Hall supports this relational under- standing because, as he correctly notes, all the basic notions of biblical belief (shalom, justice, righteousness, love) are relational ones. They exist only between beings. The whole burden of Hall's exploration of the theme of *imago dei* is to demonstrate that a right relationship with God yields a right relationship with the rest of the creatures of the world. "Relationship," says he (107), "is of the essence of this [human] creature's nature and vocation."

Jane Parker Huber expresses this idea poetically in her hymn "God, You Spin the Whirling Planets":

> We, created in your image,
> Would a true reflection be
> Of your justice, grace, and mercy
> And the truth that makes us free.

The visual metaphor of the image of God in humankind is that of a polished mirror with no cracks. Calvin speaks of "the faculties . . . in which man excels, and in which he is to be regarded as a mirror of the divine glory" (*Institutes*, 1.15.4). We are created to reflect back to God God's own justice, grace, and mercy. When Adam and Eve "fell" and sin entered the human experience, what happened to the mirror? Was it smashed? Was it fogged? Was it distorted like the mirrors in a fun house or the mirror of the Hubble telescope before they fixed it? The Calvinist tradition tended to speak of the image as "utterly defaced": The mirror was shattered and could never be renewed. Surely that notion has to be put behind us now, for it is clear that all human beings possess generous, altruistic characteristics that live alongside their universal capability for hatred and violence. Perhaps for us today a more meaningful analogy for the image of God in human beings would be the holograph. In it, the original image is visible in certain lights and from certain angles, but at other times appears to be defaced. There will be more to consider on this subject in chapter 3.

We cannot consider our work with verse 26 complete until we con- front the thorny issue of "dominion." For a number of years now, critical scholarship has been in general agreement that the "dominion" over all the creatures of land, sea, and air that God assigns to the first tiny human community flows from the image of God that God places within the earth creature, *adam*, and him/her alone. Let us follow that insight out.

Imbedded between the first two clauses of the crucial verse 26 is the lowly Hebrew conjunction, *waw*. Because this is a kind of all-purpose linking word, translators (including, in this instance, the NRSV) often simply render it with our English coordinating conjunction "and." However, this same particle also serves as a subordinating conjunction in Hebrew. In this verse, there is good reason to believe it should be construed that way, and that the second clause should express purpose: "Then God said, 'Let us make humankind in our image, according to our likeness, *so that they may* have dominion over the fish of the sea.'" Do you see what a difference that makes? It means that God's image in us is expressed or manifested in "dominion." When you are a living statue of God you are more than just another pretty face! You also have powers and capacities that have implications for all other living creatures.

This reading of the claim of Genesis 1:26 runs counter to the convictions of many modern ecologists (for example, the Canadian David Suzuki) that one of the worst culprits in the present struggle to get control of environmental degradation is the biblical concept of dominion. These writers charge that the notion of dominion has always led to human arrogance and exploitation. No doubt it sometimes has. The picture of Adam and Eve in the garden with the animals gathered around in a happy fellowship would be, on this reading, only another wistful reminiscence of a lost innocence. Yet the dominion presented here is subordinated to the image of God in human beings, and, for what it is worth, is followed not by the strong and adversarial Hebrew preposition *al* ("over, against") but by the simpler *be* ("on, among"). In short, the picture presented need not be understood as one of rape and pillage, of power and lordship, but one of husbandry and nurture.

The etymology of the verb *radah*, which we are taking to mean "to have dominion," has a disturbing relationship to a cognate Arabic word meaning "to trample." This warns us not to be too quick to dismiss the traditional understanding of the clause as warrant to exercise power over the other creatures, be it in the clear-cutting of forests, suburban development, or in the shooting of buffalo for sport. However, power need not be exercised in the mode of trampling. If any hint of that root idea still remained with the word when the Priestly writers took it up, they placed it in a context in which the exercise of power is modified in two directions: on the one side, by the source of the power that derives from the God-given image in humankind; and on the other, by the responsible and nurturing mode in which the power is to be exercised. The same issue arises again in verse 28, where we confront not only "dominion" but also the additional imperative verb "subdue it" (i.e., the earth). Given the fact that the ancient writer could not have imagined "subduing" the whole globe, and given the probability that dominion is to be exercised in subordination to the Creator's image, the sense of the word "dominion" here may simply be "domesticate it."

In summary, then, in Genesis 1 the "dominion" exercised by the creatures made in God's image is to be marked by a high sense of responsibility toward the things that God loves. Like Joseph to Pharaoh, we are God's viziers in the world. To other creatures we wear the very image of God. They should feel secure, however, for our lieutenancy means that we recognize limitations on our power. We know we have no right to play God with other creatures, or to commit genocide or "specicide." To be God's vizier is to serve at God's pleasure and to preserve that which belongs to God. It is to serve as mediator and conduit of goodness and health between the source of all goodness and the good creation. In short, the name of the mode and style in which the old narrative tradition of the Bible understands human dominion to be exercised is *stewardship*.

[28] Another major motif, mentioned in connection with lower animals in verse 22, now emerges in connection with humankind. "Blessing" has a history of its own in the Bible. This history is different from salvation history, the "history of the mighty acts of God," which reaches a crescendo in the story of God the Liberator in the book of Exodus. The history of God's blessing starts as soon as life emerges and it continues steadily, quietly, providentially. It continues because God wills that it continue. Blessing is not something that is earned by individuals or peoples, but is simply part of God's care for the world: "[God] sends rain on the righteous and on the unrighteous" (Matt. 5:45). Furthermore, this history of the blessing of humankind begins in Genesis 1:28 with, of all things, sex! Sexuality is not connected directly with the image of God, which, though it is manifested in both males and females (v. 27), is not manifested in fecundity. No, God's gift of fruitfulness through sexuality is reserved for the special blessing of verse 28. According to the Priestly story of creation, the most original truth about human beings is that they were created for fellowship with each other and with the God in whose image they are created. Sexuality is the second truth given by God to this tiny elemental community. Note this well: it is a *blessing*; it is not part of any fallen or broken state.

Taken as a whole, Genesis 1:1–31 nuances our relationship with other creatures past and present by placing us all in the same framework of divine creative activity. However, the text also proposes an ascending sequence of value and importance. The culminating effort of God's creative work is not the sun and moon and stars, wonderful as they are. Those are the means by which something more important could come about. Anthropology was on the writers' minds. They and you and I were on their minds. We human beings are the culminating achievement of God, the top of the hierarchy of the creatures, as the biblical writers understood reality. Alone of all the mammals, alone of all the plants, we are invited into personal relationship with God. Alone of all the creatures, we are said to be made in God's own image, a concept that we can now affirm has to do with a living, articulate relationship. We are capable of rejoicing and growing in that relationship. That is the biblical witness.

Of course, we must immediately reiterate that primacy and preeminence do not confer on us a primacy of power to be used to meet our own ends. Raw use of power is not consistent with the biblical witness. Dominion is exercised in stewardship. But primacy yes. It is no use trying to worm around that.

DAY SEVEN: SABBATH
Genesis 2:1–4a

> 2:1 **Thus the heavens and the earth were finished, and all their multitude.** **2 And on the seventh day God finished the work that he had done, and he rested on the seventh day from all the work that he had done. 3 So God blessed the seventh day and hallowed it, because on it God rested from all the work that he had done in creation.**
>
> **4 These are the generations of the heavens and the earth when they were created.**

[2:2–3] After working six days at creating the universe, God rests. Like everything else in the primeval history, this idea itself is not completely new. In the Babylonian creation story *Enuma Elish*, which also knows of a primeval week of creation, the gods spend the seventh day resting and celebrating. Presumably this mythic tradition set the stage in Babylon, as it did in Israel, for a day of cultic observance.

As always, however, Israel makes its own independent witness. God finishes the work, looks back over it all and finds that it is fit and good, and then blesses the day, the seventh day, the hallowed day. The implication is that this is a day for looking back and out over the good world. Notice that God does not go to church nor raise the matter of worship. The noun "Sabbath" does not even occur here, but only the verb *shabat*, "to cease."

In his Genesis commentary, Gerhard von Rad says of this passage: "One should be careful of speaking of 'the institution of the sabbath,' as is often done. Of that, nothing at all is said here. The sabbath as a cultic institution is quite outside the purview" (von Rad, 60). The point is underscored in the fourth commandment in Exodus 20:8–11 and Deuteronomy 5:12–15, where once again no mention is made of worship. Instead, the seventh day is to be "made holy" or sanctified, that is to say, set apart from all other days. It is not a taboo day exactly, for the word *taboo* implies danger and bad luck. It is simply a day unlike all other days, a day of rest and remembrance.

It is true that the Priestly writers are speaking of a rest that, because it is God's rest, becomes a part of the very makeup of the cosmos. It provides a rhythm in time that separates the original act of creation from all subsequent acts, thereby indicating the finality and perfection of the original. At the same time, it is probable that the Priestly writers were also looking toward the Israelite worship practices of their own time. About the time that Genesis 2:1–4a is thought to have been written, the leading Judeans were living in Babylonian exile. There they had made certain practices hallmarks of Israelite life, means of marking off the distinction between Israel and its pagan neighbors. Circumcision, perhaps synagogue, certainly Sabbath observance, were among those hallmarks. The Priestly writers, who lived in an environment in which Israel alone observed a weekly Sabbath as a day of cessation and perhaps a day of worship, grounded that custom in the very fabric of creation.

The earlier Yahwistic source (J) locates the institution of Israel's Sabbath ordinance in the wilderness. According to Exodus 16:29–30, the Sabbath rules were first articulated in connection with the manna: "'See! The LORD has given you the sabbath, therefore on the sixth day he gives you food for two days; each of you stay where you are; do not leave your place on the seventh day.' So the people rested on the seventh day."

This very different Yahwistic etiology of Sabbath observance agrees with Genesis 2:1–4a in one respect, namely, that the seventh day should be set apart from all the rest as a time of cessation. For J, the reasons for doing so are historical ones, however, and not cosmological ones. By grounding Sabbath in history, it allies itself with the motive for Sabbath observance in the version of the Sabbath commandment found in Deuteronomy 5:12–15. Here, too, the reason for resting is not cosmological but historical. You shall rest because you were "a slave in the land of Egypt, and the LORD your God brought you out from there . . . ; therefore, the LORD your God commanded you to keep the sabbath day" (Deut. 5:15).

In the version of the fourth commandment found in Exodus 20:8–11, the priestly ideal of a cosmic Sabbath is firmly linked with specific human behavior. The essential commandment is brief and to the point: "Remember the sabbath day, and keep it holy." There follows, however, a motive clause that echoes the priestly etiology of Sabbath given in Genesis 2:1–4a: "For in six days the LORD made heaven and earth, the sea, and all that is in them, but rested the seventh day; therefore, the LORD blessed the sabbath day and consecrated it" (Ex. 20:11).

Of course, the assertion that the cosmic God rested on a holy day had historical implications for Israel. Whatever form Sabbath observance may have had prior to the composition of the first account of creation by the Priestly writers, it was bound to have been reshaped by their notion of God's primeval rest. Sabbath rest came to be conceived of more and more as a divine ordinance that undergirds the creation from the beginning and continues into eternity as part of the permanent constitution of things. The practices of rest and worship by which human beings responded to what God did on the seventh day took on more and more the character of participation in the cosmic and divine order. Later, the saints began to view the Sabbath as a memory of the way things were in Eden, the best of all possible worlds, and as a preview of things that are to come. That spirit animates reflection on the meaning of the Sabbath in the early Christian community: "So then, there remains a sabbath rest for the people of God; whoever enters God's rest also ceases from his labors as God did his. Let us therefore strive to enter that rest" (Heb. 4:9–11).

2. Creation from the Dust
Genesis 2:4b–25

The second creation account, thought to have come from the hand of the Yahwist, is replete with delightful and significant theological issues. Particularly notable among these themes is that of the limits God has placed on human autonomy, signified by the tree of the knowledge of good and evil. Thomas H. Troeger explores this theme in his hymn "God Marked a Line and Told the Sea":

> God set one limit in the glade
>   Where tempting, fruited branches swayed,
> And that first limit stands behind
>   The limits that the law defined.
>
> The line, the limit, and the law
>   Are patterns meant to help us draw
> A bound between what life requires
>   And all the things our heart desires.
>
> We are not free when we're confined
>   To every wish that sweeps the mind,
> But free when freely we accept
>   The sacred bounds that must be kept.

In *Creation and Fall*, a meditation on Genesis 2 and 3, Dietrich Bonhoeffer understood that the tree marks the limit beyond which the first couple cannot go in their search for God. We know they will not honor this limit; we, their kith and kin, could not have, either. It did not take long for the man and woman to say, "We will know more (i.e., "good and evil") than you have given us to know." Then there was no limit. There was only confusion and pain, until God took a new Tree into a new garden, the anti-Eden called Calvary, and said once again, "You cannot go beyond this limit to know me."

To look at the tree in the garden as a limit may enable us to consider it not as an unfair temptation placed there by God, not as a threat to human happiness, but simply as a metaphor for a painful truth that is inherent in the very nature of things. That truth is that human beings live within a network of orders and limitations and these must be honored if we are to live in harmony and equilibrium (i.e., *shalom*) with the world around us.

In medieval paintings of the crucifixion, one often sees a skull situated underneath the cross. Though some art historians have understood this simply as a way of identifying the place as Golgotha, "the place of the skull," others believe that this is a graphic depiction of an ancient legend that when Adam died, his son Cain placed a seed of the tree of the knowledge of good and evil under his tongue. That seed grew up to be the very tree that was cut down to make the cross of Jesus. In this way did the older artistic commentators affirm the connection of these two trees. Perhaps it remained for our generation to discern in the two of them *limits* given by God for our wholeness and happiness.

THE HUMAN VOCATION ACCORDING TO J
Genesis 2:4b–9, 15–17

2:4b In the day that the LORD God made the earth and the heavens, 5 when no plant of the field was yet in the earth and no herb of the field had yet sprung up—for the LORD God had not caused it to rain upon the earth, and there was no one to till the ground; 6 but a stream would rise from the earth, and water the whole face of the ground—7 then the LORD God formed man from the dust of the ground, and breathed into his nostrils the breath of life; and the man became a living being. 8 And the LORD God planted a garden in Eden, in the east; and there he put the man whom he had formed. 9 Out of the ground the LORD God made to grow every tree that is pleasant to the sight and good for food, the tree of life also in the midst of the garden, and the tree of the knowledge of good and evil. . . .
15 The LORD God took the man and put him in the garden of Eden to till it and keep it. 16 And the LORD God commanded the man, "You may freely eat of every tree of the garden; 17 but of the tree of the knowledge of good and evil you shall not eat, for in the day that you eat of it you shall die."

[2:4b] In this verse for the first time God is called "the LORD." English language readers should know that this is a translation not of what is written—YHWH (always without its vowels in Hebrew), the proper name of God—but of what is pronounced. "The Lord," *adonay*, is the standard biblical substitute for the name that is above every name. This name change, among other considerations, has led modern commentators to propose that beginning with verse 4b a different, and in fact earlier (about 950 B.C.), writer offers a different account of creation. Because of the divine name, this great anonymous theologian is known as the Yahwist, or J (after the German spelling, *Jahwe*).

[4b–7] The syntax at the beginning of this J creation account resembles the situation in Genesis 1:1–3 in the P account. Verses 4b–5a are subordinate clauses of temporal character: "In the day that the LORD God made the earth and the heavens, when . . ." They are followed in verses 5b–6 by a parenthetical remark, set off with dashes in the NRSV. Only in verse 7 is the main clause reached.

What is the effect? The Lord's *first* (not last) act of creation, according to the Yahwist's version of the story, is to make *adam*, "humankind," from *adamah*, "the dust of the ground." It (not yet "he" because the rib is still within it; "he" and "she" are only implicit now) can truly be called the "earth creature." Even though *adamah* looks like the feminine form of the noun *adam*, the earth or ground is neither the fruitful wife nor the nurturing mother of human being, as is true so often elsewhere in the mythic traditions of other cultures. The primeval person of the Old Testament neither inseminates his earth wife through fertility rites designed to ensure a successful harvest, nor rapes his earth mother by putting her to the plow. No, for the Yahwist, *adam* is a creature drawn out of the very soil that will provide nurture to the human community and *adam* must remain in a right relationship with the *adamah* if the latter is to treat the former kindly.

The syntax of verses 4b–7 helps clarify the proper relationship of *adam* and *adamah*: Until the earth creature was formed out of the earth, the earth could not produce anything sufficient to sustain the life of creatures. The wilderness called Eden could not attain its garden-like beauty without the employment of *adam* as gardener. Conversely, without *adamah* the earth creature would soon starve. In other words, the human creature is born with a vocation. He-she is created so that the order the Lord intends for the world could be set in motion.

Harmony (*shalom*) and modest symbiosis exist from the beginning. A theology of blessing will be erected on this grammatical link between *adam* and *adamah* that we will see recurring throughout the opening chapters of Genesis.

[10–14] The four rivers that flow from Eden ought to help us locate the place. Certainly Tigris and Euphrates suggest a Mesopotamian venue; unfortunately, however, neither the names nor the locations of Pishon and Gihon correspond to any known rivers. Perhaps the mention of the lands of Havilah (Arabia?) and Cush (Ethiopia?) is intended to suggest that the rivers surrounded the entire known world. They are all rivers of paradise, however, and as such they may be the ancestors of the river of life that, in later biblical literature, springs from the throne of God (Ps. 46:4; Zech. 14:8; Ezek. 47:1–12; Rev. 22:1–2).

[15–17] "These three verses together provide a remarkable statement of anthropology. Human beings before God are characterized by *vocation*, *permission*, and *prohibition*" (Brueggemann, 46). *Adam* is placed in the newly planted garden of Eden "to till it and keep it." Thus does the earth creature assume the vocation for which he-she was created. And lo and behold, with the vocation also comes a divine word of permission and command. All trees are given for the pleasure and nourishment of the human being except one. One tree, the most interesting one, one of two planted right in the middle of the garden (see 2:9 and 3:2), is placed off limits. (The tree of life, also planted in the midst of the garden, is not fenced about with a prohibition, though apparently it too was a no-no; see 3:22). In fact, the prohibition is enforced with a threat: "in the day that you eat of it you shall die."

A limit in the very middle of life! Here we confront the issue of the limits with which God invests the created order. The tree of knowledge of good and evil is not the only one, of course. The world is full of orders that determine the viability of life itself, as well as the possibility of living together in community. The tree in the middle of the garden serves as a kind of metaphor for all of these inviolable orders.

The dangerous tree gets more play, but word about the job to be done is surely at least of equal theological importance. People say, "What am I here for? Why am I alive?" Genesis 2 (and, for that matter, Genesis 1 as well) offers an answer. We are here so that we can join the cause! We belong to a cause that is bigger than ourselves. The news that it is possible to transcend the self is the good news that people have been wanting to hear. We had a sense all along that this must be true. Even the earth creature, the first human being who ever was, must have taken it as good news that there was more to be done than just sitting around and picking fruit. He-she is to be the gardener of Eden. Now the task of caring for the good earth has come down to us.

THE TRUE NATURE OF SEXUALITY
Genesis 2:18–25

2:18 Then the LORD God said, "It is not good that the man should be alone; I will make him a helper as his partner." 19 So out of the ground the LORD God formed every animal of the field and every bird of the air, and brought them to the man to see what he would call them; and whatever the man called every living creature, that was its name. ²⁰ The man gave names to all cattle, and to the birds of the air, and to every animal of the field; but for the man there was not found a helper as his partner. ²¹ So the LORD God caused a deep sleep to fall upon the man, and he slept; then he took one of his ribs and closed up its place with flesh. ²² And the rib that the LORD God had taken from the man he made into a woman and brought her to the man. ²³ Then the man said,

"This at last is bone of my bones
and flesh of my flesh;
this one shall be called Woman,
for out of Man this one was taken."

²⁴ Therefore a man leaves his father and his mother and clings to his wife, and they become one flesh. ²⁵ And the man and his wife were both naked, and were not ashamed.

[2:18] The long-awaited division of *adam* into man and woman is about to take place. God takes the decision to move this way neither in the interest of sexuality nor in the interest of progeny, but in the interest of community. God meditatively remarks, "It is not good that the man should be alone" (a fate reserved for lepers [Lev. 13:46], other sufferers [Job 7:16–19] and sinners [Gen. 4:14] in ancient Israel). So God says, "I will make him a helper as his partner." Other English versions understand that the woman was created from the rib of adam to be a "help meet for him" (KJV), a "helper fit for him" (RSV), a "fitting helper" (JPS), a "helpmeet suitable for him" (JB), a "partner suited to him" (REB). You can see the problem with which translators struggle: What was the J writer's intention in juxtaposing the man and woman in this particular way here? By this phrase the woman's human relationship to the man is contrasted with that of the animals. She is the only creature that "fits"!

J is not talking anatomy here. J is talking about the emergence out of one creature of two creatures who can enter into relationship with each other. J is talking about soul mates, people of equal standing, equal merit, and yes, equal pay! J is affirming what was affirmed at a later time by the Priestly writer(s) in Genesis 1:26, for whom the truest things that could be said about human beings are these things: They are made in the image and likeness of God, and they are male and female. *Vive la différence*, indeed, but *vive la correspondence* as well. Some of the most recent translations, including the NRSV, have surely got it right when they use the word "partner." The primal people are a proud and perfect pair, probably prepared to propagate, but primarily present for each other as partner. And though they are not identical, they complete each other (an insight J had centuries before Plato and millennia before Jung).

But beyond that, the woman will also "help." Woman, too, has a vocation, and it requires her to enter into community with the man, and so to look beyond her own self. Her relationship with the man is not one of subordination, only chronology. "It" (adam) got created first and then "she" emerged out of what then was left as "he." Both possess the same dynamic capacity for change and exchange, for mutuality and maturation. They can transcend the point at which they began; they can "help" each other to live in companionship. To be a "helper" is no small dignity. Even God is called, from time to time, "helper"—Hebrew, *ezer*—as in the name *Eliezer* ("God is [my] helper," Ex.18:4) or in the prayers of the psalmists (e.g., "God is my helper; the Lord is the upholder of my life," Ps. 54:4).

To tend God's garden thus constitutes the pristine function of woman and man, in the view of the J writer. It is a role inseparable from human existence itself, a vocation that calls human beings out of the den of animal instinct that snarls in self-protection into the full light of day, where brute self-interest can be transcended and a social contract of mutual care within the tribe can emerge. Such a reading of the most basic reality of human nature resonates with modern discoveries of possible altruistic tendencies in early humankind, such as, for example, the 50,000-year-old skeleton of a Neanderthal adult male in the Shanidar cave of Iraq. One of this man's arms had been amputated above the elbow in his youth; evidently he had been cared for by the tribe for many years afterward (Dubos, 46).

[19–20] The Lord creates other earth creatures "out of the ground" and brings them to *adam* to be named. This is tantamount to giving *adam* a junior partnership in the creative process itself, for to name a thing is to identify its place in the scheme of things. In this way, the J writer acknowledges the human hegemony on the earth that the P writer named "dominion" (1:26). Yet the rule that *adam* bears over the other creatures is not a tyranny. The touch is a gentle one; *adam* only christens them.

[21] None, however, will do as a "partner" and "helper." So now the Lord mercifully sends a "deep sleep" (*tardemah*) onto the earth creature so that he-she will be anesthetized while surgery is performed. The state of sleep referred to here occurs elsewhere in the Hebrew Bible, usually in connection with encounters with the holy, or theophanies. (In the Greek Old Testament, the Septuagint, the word is often translated with *ekstasis*, "trance" or "ecstasy.") In Genesis 15:12, for example, it is the kind of sleep that descends upon Abram before he hears God's promise of progeny and land sealed by the smoking pot that passes eerily between the pieces of the sacrifice. In 1 Samuel 26:12, the sleep that allows David to escape from Saul's camp is identified as "a deep sleep from the LORD"

(compare Isa. 29:10). It is during a *tardemah* that Job's friend Eliphaz has his revelatory dream (Job 4:13), a possibility also acknowledged by friend Elihu (Job 33:15). Daniel receives from the angel Gabriel the interpretation of his vision of a ram and a he-goat while in a "trance" of this sort (Dan. 8:18). In short, for the Old Testament writers, this kind of dream is one of the instruments God uses to effect the divine purpose. Who knew that better than Jonah, who falls deeply asleep in the hold of the ship during the raging storm (Jonah 1:5)?

[22–23] The Lord "builds" the woman from the rib of the earth creature. Perhaps "fabricate" best captures the sense of this term. In chapter 1, God created simply with a word; in chapter 2, however, God is pictured as an artisan with the stuff of life (dust of the ground in v. 7 and now a rib from the earth creature itself). When the now subdivided earth creature sees the woman, he immediately recognizes her as his true partner. She is everything he is—the hard, strong stuff ("bone") and the warm, yielding stuff ("flesh"). The intimate bond between these two original human beings is underscored by *adam*'s last act of naming, which now is not an act of hegemony, but an acknowledgment of kinship and partnership: "this one shall be called Woman [*ishshah*], for out of Man [*ish*] this one was taken." This so-called "etymological etiology" explains to ages to come why the words for man and woman look so similar in Hebrew and English alike. It is because the creatures that they signify come from the same stock and will always belong together. They may still be known by their significant "proper" names, Adam and Eve (after 3:20 at least), but now they are the proud bearers of genuine human generic names, man and woman.

[24] A man "clings to his wife" (or as the KJV quaintly puts it, "cleaves to his wife"). From the Hebrew word translated "cling" here is derived the Hebrew noun for "glue." One does not want to conclude from this that the Bible encourages husbands to stick to their wives like glue! (Were that the case, women might think the primeval curse began in Genesis 2 rather than Genesis 3!) Actually, "embrace" or even "link up with" might be even better and less "codependent" sounding translations of the term. No doubt the verse was intended as an etiology of marriage. The linking word "therefore" may base marriage on the close interrelationship indicated by the words "woman" and "man" themselves, or it may reach back to the entire story of the creation and presentation of the "partner." The writer of Ephesians, of course, considers this an adequate metaphor for describing the relationship of Christ to the church (Eph. 5:31–32).

[25] The Hebrew word for "naked" (singular: *arumm*) sounds like the word "crafty" (*arum*), found one verse later in Genesis 3:1. A play on

words may be underway here, but the root meanings are unrelated. The nakedness of the first couple in chapter 2 is not evidence of superior wisdom in their "unfallen" state, but, as the word "unashamed" makes clear, of their innocence and naturalness.

Yes, they are as innocent and natural as children. In Genesis 2, the beautiful wild couple in the beautiful wild garden are participants in a lifestyle more simple and primitive than anything Brooke Shields and Christopher Atkins ever conjured up in *The Blue Lagoon*. Here is enshrined the ancient conviction that the natural person—exemplified in our collective Euro-American consciousness by the Native American—is able to teach us a humble sense of appropriateness as we take our place among the other wild creatures that inhabit the world. This first couple was created with a vocation to follow. They will trim bushes and transplant saplings. Some of the creatures that *adam* named will be domesticated (the distinction in v. 20 between "cattle" and "animal of the field" already implies that); indeed, some soil will be broken with the plow, some woodlands may even be burned off from time to time. In the garden, however, there will be modesty and respect for the wild things, both for what they can do for humankind and also for what they are in themselves. There will be stewardship, the proper mode in which human beings were meant to exercise their preeminent role in the world.

3. Humanity Goes Awry
Genesis 3:1–24

It is difficult to find a hymn in many of our modern hymnals that suitably accompanies Genesis 3, because the category "sin" has been abolished. It is instructive that the hymns that seem to deal most with "original sin" (if not Genesis 3 specifically) tend to be nineteenth-century gospel hymns, and predictably gloomy ones at that—hymns such as "There Is a Fountain Filled with Blood," "O Jesus Thou Art Standing," and "Just as I Am." But many of these are not used much any more. Apparently we do not want to sing about sin now. Even the serpent has lost out musically, though there appears to be a passing portrait of him in the still occasionally used hymn of Saint Andrew of Crete (A.D. 660–732), "Christian Dost Thou See Them":

> Christian, dost thou hear them,
>   How they speak thee fair?
> "Always fast and vigil?
>   Always watch and prayer?"
> Christian, answer boldly,
>   "While I breathe I pray!"
> Peace shall follow battle,
>   Night shall end in day.

Genesis 1 and 2 fulfill the etiological function of myth, though strictly speaking they are not myths (stories about the gods in their own realm) but more like sagas (stories about early human beings of heroic proportions; see introduction). They explain why things are the way they are, what gave rise to the sun, moon, animals, human beings, marriage, and the like. Genesis 3, too, looks like "faded myth," for it is a narrative laid in the fabled setting of Eden, and it offers etiologies for the serpent's lack of legs, women's labor pains, and the drudgery of men.

41

However, for the big question, "Why does sin exist in a good world made by a good God?" it has no answer. It offers no etiology of evil! Instead, it functions like a paradigm of human experience and behavior. With a sad and tender, almost humanistic, touch, it presents the plight of those who have to grow up and leave the garden. That is to say, it tells the story of us all.

TEMPTATION AND "FALL"
Genesis 3:1–7

3:1 **Now the serpent was more crafty than any other wild animal that the LORD God had made. He said to the woman, "Did God say, 'You shall not eat from any tree in the garden'?"** 2 **The woman said to the serpent, "We may eat of the fruit of the trees in the garden;** 3 **but God said, 'You shall not eat of the fruit of the tree that is in the middle of the garden, nor shall you touch it, or you shall die.'"** 4 **But the serpent said to the woman, "You will not die;** 5 **for God knows that when you eat of it your eyes will be opened, and you will be like God, knowing good and evil."** 6 **So when the woman saw that the tree was good for food, and that it was a delight to the eyes, and that the tree was to be desired to make one wise, she took of its fruit and ate; and she also gave some to her husband, who was with her, and he ate.** 7 **Then the eyes of both were opened, and they knew that they were naked; and they sewed fig leaves together and made loincloths for themselves.**

[3:1] The word "crafty" (*arum*) has an ambiguous history elsewhere in the Hebrew Bible. Apart from its use to describe the serpent in Genesis 3:1, its ambivalent use by Saul to describe the fugitive David—"I am told he is very cunning" (1 Sam. 23:22)—and a smattering of occurrences elsewhere, it appears most frequently in the wisdom literature. In the book of Proverbs, to be "crafty" or "clever" is always a good thing and comes highly recommended by the sages: "The clever do all things intelligently,/ but the fool displays folly" (Prov. 13:16; see also 12:16, 23; 14:8, 15; 22:23; 27:12). But, to offer an axiom, any asset is a virtue until it is turned into a vice. Other sages recognize that people can be too clever for their own good. Job describes God who

> frustrates the devices of the crafty,
>   so that their hands achieve no success.
> He takes the wise in their own craftiness;
>   and the schemes of the wily are brought to a quick end.
>   (Job 5:12–13)

Apparently serpents, too, can be too clever for their own good. The serpent is "crafty," and craftiness is not all right by us. We view it as excessive cleverness used to questionable ends. Yet, at the royal court of David or Solomon, where the stories of Genesis were probably first set down by the J writer, there must have been circles of sages who would admire a wise courtier like Joseph. What the serpent sought to inculcate, namely, knowledge of good and evil, was exactly what the sages were hired to pass on to the king's children. Craftiness, as wisdom, is not an inherent fault in this or any serpent. After all, in Greek mythology, the serpent was wise and good and brought healing to mortal beings—a tradition still enshrined in the twined serpents that make up the symbol of Aesculapius used by your neighborhood pharmacist even to this day. It was what the serpent of Eden did with its gift that moved it from beneficence to evil. By New Testament times the serpent's cunning was evil altogether (2 Cor. 11:3). In Genesis 3, one senses that the serpent's asset of wisdom could have gone either way, just as the English word *clever* can. Does the story of the temptation and "fall" in Genesis 3 contain an oblique polemic against some in the courtly wisdom circles surrounding the J writer, who might also have used their riches of learning and rhetoric to mislead others and see to their own greater glory?

The serpent is not Satan; therefore, being clever is not tantamount in this story to being satanic. Please note that there is no hint here of any of the dark, deep dragon-like dimensions that this creature acquired in subsequent reflection on the origin of evil. The perpetrator of paradise lost is just one of three poor saps who get it in the end. Its cleverness was meant to be ambiguous, and so it remains to this day.

At the end of verse 1, the serpent opens up what Bonhoeffer called the first theological conversation in history. It was a theological conversation because it was addressed not *to* God, as in prayer, but to one another *about* God and God's word (Bonhoeffer, 71–72).

[2–3] The serpent's misstatement about which trees God placed off limits is corrected by the woman. Genesis 2:9 made clear, of course, that there were two significant trees "in the midst of the garden." Yet according to 2:16–17, it is not the tree of life that is protected from human molestation by the threat of death, but the tree of the knowledge of good and evil. In 3:3 the woman acknowledges the threat. The reader's sense that she could have avoided the death threat altogether by eating first of the unprotected tree of life is lost on her. The human couple do not touch the tree of life in all of this narrative. Even though the tree of life is better known in ancient Near Eastern literature (in, for example, the Mesopotamian Gilgamesh Epic), in this story the J writer has given primary importance to "the tree in the middle of the garden" (only in 2:9 and 17 is it "the tree of the knowledge of good and evil"). An analysis of the plot of this story reveals that the rising tension between the serpent and the woman reaches a climax in verse 6, the eating of the fruit of the tree of the knowledge of good and evil. The tree of life, on the other hand, is placed at the end of the story in a very anticlimactic position, like an afterthought. All of this suggests that what is at stake in Genesis 3 is not immortality (tree number 2) but the things bound up with tree number 1—rebellion, maturation, and knowledge.

[4–6] Denying the truth of God's word about the penalty of violating the tree of knowledge (v. 4, which refers back to 2:17), the serpent tells the woman that she will not die. One of the dramatic ironies of the story is the fact that the serpent was right—the man and woman do not die right away as a penalty for their disobedience. In their state of innocence, they would have died as other creatures do, going gentle into the good night, perhaps curled up in final peace under the tree of life. Of course, once they broke through the barrier of disobedience they had to be kicked out of Eden so that they would not attain that means of immortality (v. 22).

In verse 5 the serpent pursues the virtues of eating of the fruit of the off-limits tree. Instead of dying, they will become "like God," or even better, "godlike." Because the Hebrew generic term for God or gods is usually expressed in the plural form, *elohim*, the statement could also mean that the woman and the man would attain divine attributes in their own right. They could become little "gods" (see NRSV footnote). They could learn what grownups know: good and evil, joy and sorrow, perhaps even the plusses and minuses of human sexuality. The serpent functions as a kind of Hebrew Hermes. Like the little figure of Greek mythology who had wings on his shoes and who brought messages from the gods to mortals, it offers the woman access to everything she needs to know to live in freedom. It offers her power, for such knowledge is power indeed.

The advantages of independent, although disobedient, action come home to the woman. She sees dangling before her on the tree nutrition, aesthetic pleasure, and, above all, wisdom. And what is wrong with wisdom, after all? The Hebrew verb used here, "to make one wise," is not the ambivalent term used to characterize the serpent as "crafty" in 3:1. No, this verb gives rise to nouns that mean such things as "enlightenment" and "wise persons." The latter are praised repeatedly in Proverbs (e.g., 16:20; 17:2), lauded in the Psalter (e.g., Ps. 14:2; 36:4; 41:2; 53:3), and idealized in Daniel 1:4. In fact, the writers of

Daniel, who no doubt counted themselves among the "wise," believed them to be the very people who would enjoy deliverance in end times (see Dan. 11:38, 12:3, 10). No doubt the wisdom circles in the courts of David and Solomon out of which the J writer may have emerged valued "wisdom" more than most people. So why shouldn't the woman have found that the fruit that would give her access to all this "was to be desired"?

The answer must be, of course, that though wisdom is good, obedience to the word of God is better. Wisdom linked with disobedience yields such things as deceit, cunning, conspiracy, and gas chambers. Perhaps the J writer had reason to drive this point home to his own community.

It is noteworthy that in verses 1–6, the woman is the strong and interesting character, the one who envisions a bigger world and who takes risks in order to get there. The man merely does what he is told. The Western artistic tradition captures this narrative detail; from Renaissance to modern times, the woman with the beautiful strong body is shown reaching out for the fruit, acting decisively, while the often skinny man is shown scratching his head or with his back turned to the painter. As Phyllis Trible notes, "His presence is passive and bland. The contrast that he offers to the woman is not strength or resolve but weakness" (Trible, 113). Perhaps the older artists and commentators intended by this to put the blame on the woman, and if so they missed part of the story's point— all three of the characters are responsible for what happens. However, they do capture the difference in the characterization of the two human protagonists, the woman and the wimp!

[7] Open eyes mean knowledge, not yet of good and evil, but of nakedness. This knowledge seems matter-of-fact enough, and is unaccompanied by tittering or embarrassment or sex play. If anything, it brings an awareness of vulnerability. It leads the couple to fashion makeshift "loincloths" out of fig leaves. (The Geneva Bible of 1560 called them "breeches," and that early English version was known as the "Breeches Bible" ever after.)

CONFRONTATION AND CURSE
Genesis 3:8–19

3:8 **They heard the sound of the LORD God walking in the garden at the time of the evening breeze, and the man and his wife hid themselves from the presence of the LORD God among the trees of the garden.** 9 **But the LORD God called to the man, and said to him, "Where are you?"** 10 **He said, "I heard the sound of you in the garden, and I was afraid, because I was naked; and I hid myself."** 11 **He said, "Who told you that you were naked?**

Have you eaten from the tree of which I commanded you not to eat?"
[12] The man said, "The woman whom you gave to be with me, she gave me
fruit from the tree, and I ate." [13] Then the LORD God said to the woman,
"What is this that you have done?" The woman said, "The serpent tricked
me, and I ate." [14] The LORD God said to the serpent,
>   "Because you have done this,
>   cursed are you among all animals
>   and among all wild creatures;
>   upon your belly you shall go,
>   and dust you shall eat
>   all the days of your life.
>   [15] I will put enmity between you and the woman,
>   and between your offspring and hers;
>   he will strike your head,
>   and you will strike his heel."
[16] To the woman he said,
>   "I will greatly increase your pangs in childbearing;
>   in pain you shall bring forth children,
>   yet your desire shall be for your husband,
>   and he shall rule over you."
[17] And to the man he said,
>   "Because you have listened to the voice of your wife,
>   and have eaten of the tree
>   about which I commanded you,
>   'You shall not eat of it,'
>   cursed is the ground because of you;
>   in toil you shall eat of it all the days of your life;
>   [18] thorns and thistles it shall bring forth for you;
>   and you shall eat the plants of the field.
>   [19] By the sweat of your face
>   you shall eat bread
>   until you return to the ground,
>   for out of it you were taken;
>   you are dust,
>   and to dust you shall return."

[3:8–13] Scarcely any narrative time passes before the woman and the man
are confronted by their disobedience. It happens as God takes the cus-
tomary divine stroll in the garden. The climatological perspective here is
Palestinian, not Mesopotamian. Anyone who has lived in an area with a
Mediterranean climate knows how pleasant it is when the sea breeze flows
in to replace the hot air rising off the land at the end of the day. Yahweh
apparently found it so as well. The delightful anthropomorphic description of God's stroll fits well with the humanistic flavor of the entire story.

Suddenly the man and the woman no longer feel it appropriate to meet the Maker while they are naked. Something has moved the child-like man and woman away from simple unawareness to an embarrassed need to cover up. The man covers up because he is afraid—he has violated a taboo. Thus is the paradigmatic character of the story revealed once again; back in our faces is mirrored our own behavior. Nurture takes over from nature at a certain point with our own children and they react in the same way. To run around unclothed is to violate a cultural taboo, there and then, here and now, and most everywhere in between.

The Lord knows all about it (v. 11). God lets the excuses flow on, however, until all the characters of the story have fully implicated themselves and each other (vv. 12–13). Only then does God announce the sanctions.

[14–15] Of the three protagonists, only the serpent is specifically "cursed" by Yahweh. Losing his legs is bad enough, but even worse is the sentence of everlasting alienation and conflict between serpent and human beings. Much has been made of the sentence, "he will strike your head and you will strike his heel" (v. 15). Since the time of the early Christian father Irenaeus (ca. A.D. 135–202), verse 15 has been understood as a prophecy of the struggle between Christ ("offspring" or "seed" of the woman) and the great serpent, Satan ("offspring" of the serpent). This allegorical messianic interpretation caused this passage to be known as the *Protoevangelium* ("Pre-gospel"). It is a favorite theme in Christian art down to the twentieth century. One can still see the Virgin Mary crushing the dragon's head in a huge ceiling mosaic over a side altar at the National Shrine of the Immaculate Conception in Washington, D.C., the largest Catholic church in the United States. This interpretation exceeds the plain meaning of the text on two counts, however. First, the word "seed" or "offspring" is collective in meaning; it means "humankind." Second, the genre of verses 14–19 is a judgment, a sentence, even a curse, but not a promise or a prophecy.

[16] The woman's punishment is twofold: pain in childbearing (in antiquity, frequent death as well), and submission to the husband's rule. These sentences are etiological in function because they explain to the Yahwist's readers how the realities of the life they lived came about in the first place. Overly narrow readings of the statement "he shall rule over you" have caused women (and men) much grief over the millennia. Remember that this sentence is not found in Genesis 1—2, which describe the way things were meant to be, but in Genesis 3, which describes the way things came to be after human relationships with God and each other experienced brokenness and alienation. The life courses of both man and woman are warped by this judgment, for with a stroke

the simple and equal relationship of partners is ended. As the "ruled over" one, the woman's horizon is reduced and focused on the man. As the "ruler," family responsibility is thrust upon him—something many men have tried to get out of ever since.

[17–19] The punishment of the man is hard labor. Now the right relationship between the man (*adam*) and the ground (*adamah*) that existed in the beginning and that resulted in nurture for the earth creature (2:7) is broken. Instead of nurture, the ground will yield thorns and thistles. In the end, the ground will reclaim the creature made from its own chemicals and particles. The memorable slogan with which the man's judgment ends sums up the inexorable destiny of all humankind: "you are dust, and to dust you shall return." The words are echoed in the traditional service of committal: "Unto Almighty God we commend the soul of our brother departed, and we commit his body to the ground; earth to earth, ashes to ashes, dust to dust." One can almost hear the clods of earth striking the coffin lid.

PARADISE LOST BUT GRACE REGAINED
Genesis 3:20–24

> 3:20 **The man named his wife Eve, because she was the mother of all living.** 21 **And the LORD God made garments of skins for the man and for his wife, and clothed them.**
> 22 **Then the LORD God said, "See, the man has become like one of us, knowing good and evil; and now, he might reach out his hand and take also from the tree of life, and eat, and live forever"—**23 **therefore the LORD God sent him forth from the garden of Eden, to till the ground from which he was taken.** 24 **He drove out the man; and at the east of the garden of Eden he placed the cherubim, and a sword flaming and turning to guard the way to the tree of life.**

[3:20-21] Death is not the last word. When the word of judgment is finished, the man and the woman have to get on with their lives. First, Adam names his wife. He does so with a pun. Her name, Eve (*hawwah*), resembles the word for "living thing" (*hayyah*). This etymological etiology explains all at once the significance of her name and establishes her relationship with all human beings that follow. She is the mother of us all.

Nakedness had been the couple's newfound shame, the badge of their vulnerability. Yahweh understands this sensitivity, and knows that the fig leaf loincloths will not meet the need. The "garments of skins" should therefore be understood as an act of reconciliation from God's side. It is the first of three such acts that will follow three such falls and punishments. Adam and Eve, Cain, and the generation of the Flood all sin in escalating degrees, and receive more and more severe sentences. Each, however, receives a gracious token of the Lord's continuing care for them—a way out, as it were, from their doom. Only the last group, the greatest transgressors of them all, the builders of the Tower of Babel, are dealt a terrible punishment and receive no gift from God. (See "Reflections on Human Alientation" in chapter 8.)

[22–24] It is a pity that the design of this commentary series excludes illustrations, because the artistic tradition has done wonders with this passage. Tiny cringing figures make their way out of a beautiful garden over a stony path to the east of Eden, while brilliant light manifests the presence of the guardian cherubim with the flaming sword. The artists felt their pain for sure, for it is the pain of all of us who want to get back to the garden. The expulsion is motivated not so much by their disobedience and the danger of their newfound knowledge as it is by the danger that they would eat of the other tree—the tree of life, which has played such a minimal role in the story. Of course they would have; we know this because we would have. Then their deification would have been complete.

Can a creature that lives forever be truly human? Can such a creature really bear rule in a world full of other creatures that are made of the earth? No doubt the writer of Genesis 3 wanted us to look on the loss of Eden and its magic tree as a disaster for humankind. Nevertheless, there seems to have been a gentle irony in that writer's thinking. Perhaps the irony emerged only after the earlier Yahwistic source was given the new introduction of chapter 1 by the Priestly writers. However it arose, we are led to consider how the the first couple were ever going to fulfill their calling to "fill the earth and subdue it" and to have dominion in the earth if they just stayed forever in the garden. We learn that ourselves in our journey from childhood to maturity. If you are ever going to complete your destiny, you have to get out of paradise!

SOME FURTHER THOUGHTS ON "THE FALL"

It is appropriate that a Protestant theologian (and a Calvinist) should discuss the Fall, since we Protestants have been prone to assume countenances as bleak as the rain-drenched craggy moors of Scotland when contemplating all the dire consequences unleashed upon humankind by our disobedient first parents. We Protestants did not establish the normative Christian way of thinking about the Fall, however, but Augustine of Hippo (A.D. 354–430) did. Augustine believed that human nature was fundamentally changed that fatal afternoon in the garden and that this change was transmitted by Adam and

Eve to their descendants forever. Before the Fall, human nature was tranquil, happy, and obedient. Afterward, it was wholly disposed to evil and misery.

Augustine identified the sin that led to the Fall as rebellion, a "despising of the authority of God." The fuse that lit that fire of rebellion was lust. Augustine could prove that because the first couple became ashamed of their nakedness only *after* their sin. Human sexuality, thus, was implicated in the Fall, and human beings ever after sought to cover their private parts:

> Consequently all nations, being propagated from that one stock, have so strong an instinct to cover shameful parts, that some barbarians do not even uncover them in the bath. (*The City of God*, 14. 17)

All of this came about because of Satan, the fallen angel who was envious of the unfallen man and woman. The serpent was not itself Satan, according to Augustine, but was Satan's mouthpiece. Satan also employed his knowledge of human nature to attack the woman first because she was, "the weaker part of that human alliance" (14. 11).

Satan promoted sin, which is by definition assertion of autonomy against God, and post-Fall humanity suffers sexual shame and pain in childbearing as a consequence, as well as the curses of hard labor and death. No human being can escape this universal blight, for the new sinful fatal anthropology is inherited with the father's sperm and the mother's egg.

Ever since Augustine, this view of the Fall has been normative in the confessions, catechisms, and dogmatic treatises of Catholics and Protestants alike. In the past century or two, however, believers and unbelievers alike have begun to hold as nonsense the notion that a genetic mutation in human nature could have been derived from a single act on a single afternoon by a single pair of human beings, or that they were motivated in their transgression by Satan in the guise of a snake. Several factors may have led to this reassessment. No doubt secularism, with its rebellion against the notion of inexorable predetermination and its emphasis on human freedom, has played a role. So also have modern psychological models. They have given us new maps of the human mind that see rebellion against parental authority and struggle against the threat of death as inevitable and necessary aspects of human experience.

From within the religious communities, critical reading of scripture has contributed to rethinking of the idea of the Fall and the attendant notions of total depravity and original sin as they have been traditionally described in confessions and dogmatic statements. As the discussion of this chapter has suggested, Genesis 3 simply does not provide the data needed to support the full Augustinian notion of a prelapsarian (pre-Fall) and postlapsarian anthropology. Nothing genetic is said to have changed in human nature, nor are sin and guilt laid at the door of the descendants of the first couple. Sexuality is not implicated, and death is not the penalty. (After all, they had not eaten from the other tree, which would have made them immortal.) Nor is the serpent

Satan. It is not even the female temptress, the night hag Lilith (Adam's jealous first wife, according to rabbinic legend), whose head it so often wears in medieval paintings of the scene. It is just a snake, more clever than any other animal, so clever, in fact, that it can talk and launch the first recorded theological discussion in history. Although entire edifices of theology have been erected upon it, this fascinating but minimal story by no means answers the big questions that are put to it: Where did sin come from? How did human nature come to be capable of evil?

True, Christian orthodoxy has also had to deal with Paul's transformation of the story in Romans 5:12–21. By the time of the apostle, there had been an extended tradition of reflection on Genesis 3 in Judaism, as evidenced by 2 Esdras 7:118: "Oh, Adam, what have you done? For though it was you who sinned, the fall was not yours alone, but ours also who are your descendants."

In line with this tradition, Paul attributes all sin to one man and all death as the consequence of that one sin (Rom. 5:12). However, a critical reading of Paul on the Fall shows that the point of his entire discussion of what happened in the garden is to create an exact contrast between the guilt and death that flow from Adam's trespass and the gifts of grace and life that flow from Christ's obedience. In other words, for Paul, the story of Genesis 3 is necessary to develop a Christology. Paul sums up his argument in the famous verse: "Therefore, just as one man's trespass led to condemnation for all, so one man's act of righteousness leads to justification and life for all" (Rom. 5:18). One can only assume that Paul is serious about this parallel and about the word "all." His purpose in establishing the solidarity of all humankind with the fallen Adam is to justify establishing the solidarity of all humankind with the obedient and triumphant passion of Christ. Paul is not trying to explain where evil came from, nor to discuss the role of Satan in the beginning. Paul is not speculating on what human nature was like before the Fall. His only purpose is to place the redemptive work of Christ against the universal background of human sin and failure. That background no one can or should deny. In fact, one should take it more seriously than if one simply says, "What can we do? Adam started it all and we inherited it from him." The universal human experience of sin and failure is all the more powerful if one recognizes that people have a choice not to sin and fail and it is that they might make that choice rather than the other that Christ came to work among us.

How could we have gone so far afield from what is taught in Genesis 3? That question is heightened when one realizes that Eastern Christianity never has viewed the afternoon in the garden as a disaster of universal, tragic import. Irenaeus saw the Fall as a movement from childish innocence toward adult maturity. The Fall did not spoil the divine image in human beings; that image abides in us. The disobedience in the garden was indeed a sinful act by frail creatures, but at the same time, it was a "fall upward." God's work of blessing in the world is of course delayed and made complicated by human sin everywhere. At the same time, however, innocent children could not have fulfilled their role to fill the earth and subdue it and have dominion in it had they only just stayed within the peaceful and trouble-free perimeter of the garden.

Scarcely any of the great modern interpreters of scripture or particularly of Genesis 3 read it in the Augustinian mode. Modern creeds and confessions do not speak of an altered anthropology, even though they recognize the post-Holocaust profundity of the human capability of sin. They simply never imagine there was a time when human beings were not capable of hurting one another and rebelling against God. Among the great commentators, both Karl Barth and Dietrich Bonhoeffer take the Fall not as a historical fact, but a prototypical one. It is not a story of cosmic dualism pitting God against Satan, not an account of the origin of evil, which it never was intended to be, and not a proclamation that at a certain moment in time humanity was fundamentally changed from its original innocence. Instead, the story plays back every person's sad experience of making autonomous will superior to obedience as the guiding principle of life.

In his book *The Serpent Was Wiser,* Richard S. Hanson argues along the lines of Irenaeus that the tree of the knowledge of good and evil means simply, "the tree of growing up. . . . Its fruit will wean one away from his parents" (Hanson, 39). Genesis 3 is not a Fall narrative but a story of maturation, of risk-taking and adventure, of the willingness of the youthful Adam and Eve to leave the safety of the garden and to fulfill the vocation given to them, to subdue the earth and have dominion over it. "The notion of a fall becomes necessary only when one begins with a concept of the perfect man," argues Hanson (39). But that notion is foreign to the Old Testament. It belongs to what Hanson calls the "orphic world of thought," something like a gnostic view, which links the notion of a fall to the concept of pure spiritual perfection trapped in imperfect and inadequate material nature. "But the Genesis story which we are considering does not begin with such a perfect creature. It begins with a real specimen, a child of the earth . . . who must await the realization of his potential." "Only the future can reveal the perfect man" (41). Indeed, Paul claims that in Christ the future did reveal the new Adam who was the perfection of all of us. Hanson even advances a kind of esthetic argument in appreciation of the sin of Adam. The grasp for the fruit of the tree of knowledge was necessary if human beings were ever going to grow up and realize their potential: "Call it the rebellion of man, the rise of man, or better still, the story of man's discovery of himself" (41). Though the crunch on the forbidden fruit was in direct violation of God's express command, it was an inexorable part of coming of age. It was tragic not because it introduced death, but because it introduced the fear of death. Without that "fallen" knowledge, however, there could be no ambition, no raising of monuments, no need to create children or novels, no "rage against the dying of the light" (Dylan Thomas)—in short, none of the other virtues that flow from the knowledge of death. Hanson finds Genesis 3 not the story of a fall, but of a profound dilemma, namely the mounting consciousness that rebellion against the yoke of authority is both an inevitable and, in fact, a necessary element in human growth.

Two poets, one Muslim and one Christian, have reflected upon the situation of the imperfect human creature standing before the perfect God. Hear first the bitter and heroic words of Omar Khayyam, the mystical Islamic poet:

> O Thou, who Man of Baser Earth didst make,
> And ev'n with Paradise devise the Snake,
>   For all the Sin wherewith the Face of Man
> Is blackened—Man's Forgiveness give—and take!
>
>   (Edward FitzGerald, *The Rubaiyat of Omar Khayyam*, 58)

Faced with the dilemma of living freely, responsibly, and heroically, and yet inevitably sinfully, Omar Khayyam proposes to forgive God for creating this double bind.

A contemporary biblical scholar and poet, B. Davie Napier, voices similar ideas:

> *You* are the problem, God.
> You *force* us into disobedience—
> If disobedience it really is,
> and that's a matter simply of perspective.
> The theologians want to call it pride
> or even by the stronger term, rebellion.
> The pious make the charge apostasy
> and hypocrites will cry idolatry.
> But this is nonsense, God. It is our nature
> (you ought to know, who mixed the hot ingredients)
> to spurn the docile role of subjugation;
> to be not merely creature, but creator;
> to stand alone; to cherish in ourselves
> all requisite resources for renewal;
>   to mount with wings as eagles
>   to run and not be weary
>   to walk and not to faint.
>
>   (Napier, 27)

Perhaps these quotes enable us to sum up this discussion of Genesis 3. There is no Fall in this chapter, if by Fall one means the doctrine of the shattering of the divine image in humankind, the loss of immortality at an early moment in human history, and the inexorable transmission of original sin through human genes ever after. What Genesis 3 gives us is a paradigm, a story about every human being rebelling against the commandments of God and thus discovering alienation and despair. It is a powerful, primitive rendition of a reality all of us know full well—the truth that life is a pilgrimage from innocence to maturity through a land fraught with the dangers of loving and hating, growing powerful and cowering in humiliation, living and finally dying. It is a story about God too, whose name is not only Yahweh, but also

Emmanuel, and who will not leave his beloved creatures to their fates even when they defy him to his face or thrust a spear in his side. Genesis 3 is a story of growing up, and grow up we must now, in a hurry, for we live in a world in which the instruments of death and evil and overpopulation and biodegradation cannot be left in the hands of adolescents. If this world is not hopelessly fallen, though, then grow up we can, and cope we can.

4. The Family Goes Awry
Genesis 4:1–26

Genesis 4 is the story of many firsts. Enshrined in this legend of primeval history are the first human conception of children, and the first mention of agriculture, the first mention of sacrifice and offering to God. Not all of these firsts are happy ones: The first case of sibling rivalry leads to the first case of fratricide. It is not the first story of sin and consequent punishment, nor does it contain the first divine act of grace to follow. All of those occurred in the previous chapter when the parents of Cain and Abel had their own crisis of disobedience, their own curse of expulsion and alienation, and their own experience of an act of divine grace in being clothed with skins. But the repetition of the triad of sin, punishment, and grace here marks an escalation over the first and points directly toward the greater escalations that lie ahead.

The story of Cain's murder of Abel seems to be an expansion upon a basic genealogy that includes 4:1–2 and 17–26. That it is really a story about Cain is demonstrated by the big attention given to the meaning of his name and the slight attention given to Abel's name and to Abel himself. Furthermore, the details of the murder are barely mentioned, and the major action of the story is in the dialogue between Cain and Yahweh. The story is based on a motif common in folklore—the rivalry between brothers (e.g., Romulus and Remus, Seth and Osiris; numerous examples from ancient literature are offered in Westermann, 315–17). The close parallels that it shows with Genesis 3 suggest that while the relationship between a woman and man might lead to mutual sin and resulting expulsion, the relationship between brothers is even more dangerous. It can lead to quarreling, enmity, and even murder.

In 1 John 3:12, the two brothers are presented as the yin and yang of good and evil: "We must not be like Cain, who was from the evil one and murdered his brother. And why did he murder him? Because his own deeds were evil and his brother's righteous." Genesis 4 itself does not actually attribute Cain's act to "the evil one." That would indeed have made it an idealized struggle of polar opposites, an intrinsically right- eous man versus an intrinsically evil man. Instead, what the narrator gives us is a story about two brothers, both potentially normal people whose lives could have gone in other ways than they did. One became a victim, and the other became a victimizer, a villain, and a fugitive. The one who became the fugitive is our prototype. The man named Cain is Everyman.

CAIN AND ABEL
Genesis 4:1–16

4:1 Now the man knew his wife Eve, and she conceived and bore Cain, say- ing, "I have produced a man with the help of the LORD." 2 Next she bore his brother Abel. Now Abel was a keeper of sheep, and Cain a tiller of the ground. 3 In the course of time Cain brought to the LORD an offering of the fruit of the ground, 4 and Abel for his part brought of the firstlings of his flock, their fat portions. And the LORD had regard for Abel and his offering, 5 but for Cain and his offering he had no regard. So Cain was very angry, and his countenance fell. 6 The LORD said to Cain, "Why are you angry, and why has your countenance fallen? 7 If you do well, will you not be accepted? And if you do not do well, sin is lurking at the door; its desire is for you, but you must master it."

8 Cain said to his brother Abel, "Let us go out to the field." And when they were in the field, Cain rose up against his brother Abel, and killed him. 9 Then the LORD said to Cain, "Where is your brother Abel?" He said, "I do not know; am I my brother's keeper?" 10 And the LORD said, "What have you done? Listen; your brother's blood is crying out to me from the ground! 11 And now you are cursed from the ground, which has opened its mouth to receive your brother's blood from your hand. 12 When you till the ground, it will no longer yield to you its strength; you will be a fugitive and a wanderer on the earth." 13 Cain said to the LORD, "My punishment is greater than I can bear! 14 Today you have driven me away from the soil, and I shall be hidden from your face; I shall be a fugitive and a wanderer on the earth, and anyone who meets me may kill me." 15 Then the LORD said to him, "Not so! Whoever kills Cain will suffer a sevenfold vengeance." And the LORD put a mark on Cain, so that no one who came upon him would kill him. 16 Then Cain went away from the presence of the LORD, and settled in the land of Nod, east of Eden.

The story naturally falls into two parts. Verses 2–8 describe the rising enmity and the culminating action of murder interrupted by an impor- tant speech by Yahweh that provides much of the theological substance of the passage. Verses 9–16 contain rather different materials. First, the Lord indicts Cain for his sin and pronounces a curse even over Cain's objection. A promise of divine protection for Cain then concludes that passage. It is worth noting that the only real interaction in the entire story is between Cain and the Lord; the latter acts as judge, executor of punishment, and also savior of Cain. The reader is left with these questions: Why did Abel have to die? Why was Cain allowed to live?

[4:1–2] The man knew his wife, Eve. The Hebrew verb "to know" carries many connotations, ranging from skill through recognition through cognitive knowledge to sexual relations. In the basic sense of the usage here, "to know" means "to experience." A physiological event has taken place to be sure, but "to know" bears the added overtone of a personal encounter between husband and wife. Had the man not "known" his wife prior to this? Surely he knew her as a fellow gardener in Eden and a fellow sinner at the base of the tree of the knowledge of good and evil. Apparently, however, it is only after the expulsion from paradise that he knows her sexually as a woman. This means, as has been noted before, that sex is neither the cause nor the result of the transgression in the garden.

The result is predictable. She "gets" or "acquires" a son "with the help of the LORD." Lest anyone think that a virgin birth is involved here or a mating of human and divine beings, the phrase, "with the help of" probably has the sense of "just as." The woman is proud to say, "Like Yahweh, I too have produced a man," thus setting the procreation of the human community firmly within the realm of human possibility without denying the claim of Genesis 2 that humanity originated in a prior creative act of Yahweh.

Another issue in Eve's cry of joy is the verb that she chooses: I have "produced" (or "acquired") a man. As the NRSV note points out, in Hebrew the word translated "Cain" (*qayin*) sounds as if it were derived from the verb "to produce" (*qanah*). Cain's name seems to have arisen from more than just a wordplay on the root "produce," however. In 2 Samuel 21:16, the word *qayin* means "spear," a sense that can be explained by reference to cognate words in other Semitic languages that mean "metal worker" or "smith." Smithing is in fact the very vocation of Tubal-cain in Genesis 4:22. However, the Cain of our story is not a smith, but a farmer.

Others have seen a link between the name Cain and the tribal group, the Kenites (Num. 24:21–22), who were particularly associated with Moses' father-in-law, Hobab or Jethro (Judg. 4:11) and therefore with the mountain of God at Sinai. Some scholars think that Israel learned to worship Yahweh at Sinai from priests and custodians of that sanctuary who were members of the Kenite tribe. All of this suggests that Cain's very name brings with it hints and dim memories of a fuller tradition about this primeval human.

In verse 2 we learn of the birth of a second son, named Abel, possibly a twin of Cain. (Notice the similarities to the account of the birth and naming of the twins Jacob and Esau in 25:24–27.) His name, too, is meaningful, though the meaning is not explained to the reader as was Cain's name in verse 1. The Hebrew term *hebel* means "emptiness" or "ephemerality." It is the same word that is used so often in Ecclesiastes: "Vanity of vanities, all is vanity, says the Teacher" (Eccl. 1:2). That's a surprise, isn't it? If names are commentaries on the individuals, then the second son, who has always enjoyed good press because he was an innocent victim, is also acknowledged to be the son born in vain. He plays no further part in the genealogy of verses 1–2 and 17–26 into which the story of the fratricide is inserted. Though he was an innocent victim, it was not he but Cain who was the elect one, in the sense that he and his line survived. The great story of the Bible is the story of the return to Eden from whence our first parents were expelled. The first stage in that long, long search for the way back to the garden will pass not through the innocent Abel but through the violent sinner Cain. (Humanity, it should be noted, is descended not from Cain but from Seth, through Noah, according to Genesis 5.)

We learn that Abel was a shepherd and Cain was a farmer. As has been pointed out in the commentary on chapter 2, humankind was created with a vocation. That vocation was spelled out in Genesis 2:15; "The LORD God took the man and put him in the garden of Eden to till it and keep it." In the second generation of primeval humankind, a division of labor is manifested. There may be no greater significance to the division of labor than that these two vocations—that of the nomadic shepherd who raises flocks on the steppe and that of the farmer who grows crops in the fertile and irrigated lower lands—are the natural, original divisions of human labor for the production of food. With division of labor, however, also come turf wars, barbed wire fences, struggle for preference and for markets, and all the makings of competition and conflict. It is not the division of labor, however, that points in the direction of fatal controversy. It is the Lord's arbitrary preference!

[3–5a] In the course of time, each son of Adam and Eve brings an offering of his produce to the Lord. We hear of no prayers accompanying these two simple offerings, nor of any altar upon which they are placed, nor of any fire or ritual slaughter. Even the very term for offering that is used, *minhah*, is in this early text a general word for any kind of offering (in 43:11 it simply means "a present"). In short, there is no reason to see this story as the beginning of the sacrificial cultus, which in later times became a complex and elaborate system in which the term *minhah* meant a cereal offering. It seems clear here that the original farmer and the original herdsman simply intend to thank the author of their success in agriculture for blessing them with produce.

The Lord, who apparently has always liked the smell of barbecue, smiles more favorably on Abel's meat offering than on Cain's vegetables. (When "the LORD smelled the pleasing odor" of Noah's post-Flood sacrifice, things took a turn for the better then, too [8:21]). The scene of these two offerings from act 3 of Arthur Miller's 1972 play, *The Creation of the World and Other Business*, is delightful. Abel's bloody side of lamb is gloated over by the Lord:

GOD: Young man, this is undoubtedly the sweetest, most delicious, delicate, and profoundly *satisfying* piece of meat I have ever tasted since the world began.

ADAM:Boy, this is our proudest moment. . . .

CAIN: Lord, There's still my corn. You haven't tasted my corn.

GOD: Oh, I can see it's very nice. You have done quite well, Cain. Keep it up. *With which he walks into the light with Adam, and Abel following behind.*

EVE, *beckoning:* Cain? *Seeing his shock.* Darling, he loved your vegetables. Come. (Miller, 90–91)

We have no idea why Abel's offering is preferred over Cain's. Perhaps the story points to the prestige enjoyed by nomadic shepherds over settled farmers. Even today in the Arab world, the nomadic Bedouins are respected by many people for the purity of their culture and their language, to the disfavor of the effete city dwellers and peasants who work the land. Common sense also suggests that a flesh offering, which requires that an animal be butchered, would be regarded, especially by poor people, as a more serious gift. Although there is no hint that this story is intended to account for the origins of the sacrificial system that had come into use by the time Solomon built his temple, it is significant that offerings in which an animal was burned stood higher on the list of sacrifices and were intended to cover more serious transgressions or express more serious thanks than cereal offerings did. It is not possible to say that in some way Cain's offering was defective whereas Abel's offering was not. Abel brought what was supposed to be brought for an animal offering, and as far as we know Cain did the same with his agricultural produce. Also, we do not know anything about the relative attitudes of the two brothers that would suggest that Cain's offering was grudging. In short, we do not know why God preferred Abel's offering to Cain's, nor do we learn how Cain became aware of this preference. We have no choice but to stay within the terms of the story itself and take Cain's reaction to the rejection of his offering as a test of his ability to handle provocation and jealousy.

[5b–7] When it becomes clear that the Lord prefers Abel's offering, Cain gives physical evidence of his displeasure. The Hebrew says, "[his nose] burned to Cain very much and his faces fell." (Aren't we fortunate that our modern English translations render the Hebrew in the idiomatic English that we actually speak? Otherwise, our sacred word would be unintelligible at times.)

Perceiving the frustration of the elder brother at the preference shown the younger, the Lord addresses Cain directly with a rather cryptic sentence (v. 7) in which he likens sin to a beast lurking at the door. Note that it is "sin" and not "Satan" or some such cosmically evil thing that crouches. Were it the latter, the Lord could hardly have uttered the profound and evidently general principle that "its desire is for you, but you must master it" (v. 7b). A different translation of the same verb would be permissible grammatically and preferable in sense: "You can master it." Cain will not be able to shift the blame for his actions to anyone else.

From a theological point of view, verse 7 seems to be the key to unlocking the entire story: "If you do well, will you not be accepted? And if you do not do well, sin is lurking at the door; its desire is for you, but you must master it." The text is difficult in Hebrew, but the NRSV translation reflects the general consensus about its meaning. The sentence opens with the phrase "If you do well . . ." Walter Brueggemann explicates what "doing well" between brothers means by linking this passage closely with Jesus' radicalization of the sixth commandment against murder in the Sermon on the Mount (Matt. 5:21–26). The only viable alternative to fury against a brother or sister is reconciliation. If one comes to the altar with furious rage against one's sibling, the offering makes no sense until the furious rage has been replaced by peace and reconciliation. Similarly, in 1 John 3:11–17, where Cain is explicitly mentioned, an echo of the Sermon on the Mount is present: "All who hate a brother or a sister are murderers, and you know that murderers do not have eternal life abiding in them" (v. 15). In contrast, where reconciliation has taken place and love replaces anger and hate, "We know that we have passed from death to life because we love one another" (v. 14). Thus the ultimate issues of new life and resurrection are inescapably linked to the way we get along with the persons closest at hand, including our brothers and sisters. As Brueggemann puts it,

The issue of the brother is made the ultimate theological crisis. . . . Most days, we would choose death (cf. Deut. 30:19) rather than to face the brother. But the gospel is uncompromising. The promises are linked to the brother and will be had no other way. It is a mystery that the gift of new life is so close at hand, present in the neighbor. So close at hand, but so resistant. We do not readily embrace such a mystery. Perhaps that is the reason sin waits so eagerly. (Brueggemann, 64)

The other key element in this verse is the last clause. The beast lurking at the door is always present and "its desire is for you, but you must (alt.: can) master it." Yahweh tells Cain that his future is open. The sin of anger and violence that lurks at the door of Cain is something he can deal with if he chooses to do so. He is not a helpless victim but a human being who is capable of taking charge of his life. The news that sin is lurking at the door comes to no one as a surprise, for it crouches at the very door inside of which you are reading these words. Like the legendary Cain of long ago, we twenty-first century persons have no choice but to confront that opportunity for mayhem and murder, rape and crookedness, and either succumb to it or overcome it. No one else can be invoked as the cause of one's failure to master the beast at the door. You cannot say, "The devil made me do it." You cannot even say, "My depravity made me do it."

The Lord's remark to Cain in verse 7 thus proves to be a general principle about the opportunity for moral growth that temptation offers. Angry thoughts indicate a point in Cain's life and, generally, in our lives in which some work needs to be done. We need to understand ourselves better. The sin lurking at the door is like a little red light that warns us we have some peace to strive for, some reconciliation to achieve. By itself, anger is not an occasion for grief or guilt or fear. The sin that lurks at the door is itself morally neutral. If it is properly recognized it could lead Cain into personal growth and push him toward intimacy, forgiveness, and reconciliation; if it is not recognized and adequately dealt with or "mastered," it could lead to murder.

John Steinbeck recognized all of this in his treatment of the Cain and Abel story in *East of Eden* (1952). One of his characters explains that when he looked at Genesis 4:7b, he saw neither a promise ("Thou shalt rule over him," KJV) nor an order ("Do thou rule over him," American Standard Version). Instead he saw "Thou mayest rule over sin." Neither obedience nor predetermination are in view here, but only responsible human choice. Whether we like it or not, the Lord leaves Cain's choice up to him. The God who in a troubling way is the cause of Cain's anger is also independent of Cain's choice. "God presents himself not quite enemy, surely not friend, certainly not advocate, finally leaving it fully 'up to us'" (Brueggemann, 60).

[8–12] Cain does not master the beast. Abel innocently obeys when Cain says (according to the Greek Old Testament, which supplies the missing sentence), "Let us go out to the field" (v. 8). There Cain murders his brother. Just like that! The Lord is not deceived about this for one minute. God says to Cain, "Where is your brother Abel?" Cain replies with one of the best known sentences in the whole Bible, "I do not know; am I my brother's keeper?"(v. 9).

Contrary to the usual intuition, the correct answer to the rhetorical question posed by Cain is "No" (Riemann). This can be known in part from the fact that No is the usual response in the Hebrew Bible to a positively stated rhetorical question. More definitive, however, is the fact that in the Hebrew Bible, only the Lord is the subject of the verb "to keep" when the object is a free human being: "He who keeps Israel will neither slumber nor sleep" (Ps 121:4). God can keep people secure and safe, but only human beings keep prisoners, slaves, or sheep. Cain is not his brother's keeper. Cain is his brother's brother. That is a far more profound responsibility than simply to provide safe haven for a flock.

In the aftermath, the truth enshrined in John Ferguson's hymn "Am I My Brother's Keeper?" becomes fully manifest:

> "Am I my brother's keeper?"—
> The muttered cry was drowned
> By Abel's lifeblood shouting
> In silence from the ground.
> For no man is an island
> Divided from the main,
> The bell which tolled for Abel
> Tolled equally for Cain.

When one is one's brother's brother and one violates that filial love, the victimizer is also victim of his own folly. The deed produces its own destiny—we know that from our own lives. In the Genesis 4 account, however, there is nothing automatic about reward and punishment. Yahweh puts Cain on trial (Brueggemann) and, after determining his guilt (vv. 9–10), pronounces a terrible sentence (vv. 11–12). Cain is alienated from the ground (*adamah*).

This is the appropriate time to pick up once again (see commentary on 2:4b–7) the evolving play on the word *adamah*, "ground," and the apparently related word *adam*, "humankind," that runs throughout the first chapters of Genesis in the Yahwistic source. By examining the way in which the relationship between *adam* and *adamah* oscillates, one can discern the movement between curse and blessing that is at the heart of the primeval history.

As has been noted, in the beginning the ground is not fruitful (2:5). Water and the husbandry of a farmer are necessary to make it fruitful, a perception that is early and essentially accurate. In order to remedy the fruitlessness of the *adamah*, *adam* is created and the ground becomes fruitful (2:9). Thus does an ecology of the J source begin to emerge. A close, harmonious relationship ought to exist between humankind and the earth. That harmonious relationship is spoiled only to the mutual destruction of the two.

In Genesis 3:17, in the aftermath of the disobedience of the first couple, the ground is cursed. The primitive and original state of blessing that existed between ground and humankind is spoiled and now sustenance can be wrested out of the soil only with much effort. Nevertheless, a deep relationship continues to exist between *adam* and *adamah* as Genesis 3:19 and 23 suggest. The *adam* was taken from the *adamah* and returns to it, for the latter is the fundamental medium out of which life comes.

The story before us, Genesis 4, begins on an upbeat note. In verses 2–3, the ground yields the "fruit" brought in by Cain. It seems that an adequate nurturing relationship still exists. Then this too is interfered with by human sin. In verses 10–11, the very ground that received the blood of innocent Abel cries out a curse upon Cain. Although verse 12 ("When you till the ground, it will no longer yield to you its strength") parallels the thought of Genesis 3:17 ("Cursed is the ground because of you; in toil you shall eat of it all the days of your life"), now the curse is even worse. The ground will no longer yield the strength necessary to maintain life.

Genesis 5:29, however, sets up a promise and fulfillment scheme. When Noah (= "rest, comfort") is named, his father Lamech says, "Out of the ground that the LORD has cursed this one shall bring us relief from our work and from the toil of our hands." However, human sin postpones that hope for relief and the Lord vows, "Every living thing that I have made, I will blot out from the face of the ground" (7:4). Only after the terrible punishment of the Flood is the nurturing relationship between *adam* and *adamah* restored. In Genesis 8:13, the first sign of this recovery is the face of the "ground" drying off from the flood. The restored relationship is affirmed in 8:21, when the Lord says, "I will never again curse the ground because of humankind, for the inclination of the human heart is evil from youth." This oscillation of the right and wrong relationship between *adam* and *adamah* then moves out of the primeval history and into the history of the fathers and the mothers of Israel. Abram is given the promise that through his blessing all the families of the *adamah* will find a blessing (12:3).

In summary, then, the shifting relationships between the ground—the source of human life, the medium out of which human flesh is made, and the recipient of the dead—and humankind continue to mark moments of human sin and divine punishment as well as moments of God's restoration of God's people. This constantly shifting relationship between wholeness and brokenness continues down to the very end of the Hebrew Bible (for example, Gen. 19:25; 28:14–15; Josh. 23:13, 15; Isa. 30:23; Dan. 12:2). Indeed, it is a prime topic in our discussions of theology and ecology to this very day.

[13–16] Not only is Cain alienated from the ground, the very source of sustenance, but his penalty involves expulsion from his farm. He is sentenced to being a refugee, a landless fugitive. Such a person was and is today among the marginal persons of society, always vulnerable to oppression and misuse and even massacre. Remember the Cherokees' "Trail of Tears"? Remember the starving Armenians? Remember the Palestinian refugee camps in Beirut, Sabra, and Shatillah? Remember Auschwitz? Cain knows his vulnerability and cries out, "Anyone who meets me may kill me" (v. 14).

It is then that the act of grace occurs. God puts the mark on Cain, the mark both of guilt and protection. It will ward off anyone who would take vengeance on Cain. Anyone who would snap the link between the Eden of the past and the Eden of the future, or who would cut off human evolution before it can begin will be warned and deterred. What was this mark? The narrator gives us no clue, except that it was designed to protect a single individual who stood accused and condemned. Perhaps he had in mind an identifying tattoo like those worn even to this day by the various Bedouin tribes. Perhaps the Kenites/Cainites had their own tattoo that distinguished them as they moved from pasturage to pasturage and that protected them against being treated as simple lost persons. There is no basis for claiming the sign was dark skin, as was so foolishly asserted by some of our forebears in the American interpretive community who also happened to be slaveholding Protestant Christians. Whatever the narrator understood the mark to be, it was a mark of mercy for Cain and for all his descendants who survived because of it.

In the end, Cain "went away from the presence of the LORD" to the mysterious land of Nod (v. 16), a word that means "wandering." Nod and "wandering" are, of course, no more outside the Lord's hegemony than Jonah's Tarshish (Jonah 1:1), nor even the psalmist's Sheol (Ps. 139:8). The very next unit shows the writer firmly reinserting Cain into the saga of God's creative purposes.

CAIN'S FAMILY TREE
Genesis 4:17–26

Genesis 4:17–26 is the first of many genealogical tables to be found in the book of Genesis. As has been noted, perhaps this genealogy should include 4:1–2, inasmuch as it carries the human community from Adam and Eve down several generations. This genealogy is the work of the Yahwist, a writer who normally does not devote much attention to this kind of material. Priestly writers are the ones who use genealogical material as a major structural element in their narrative of the beginnings of the human community. We will have an opportunity to look at a Priestly genealogy in the next chapter. The function of 4:17–26 in the hands of the J writer is to explain certain social structures that existed in his own context many centuries later. In other words, there is an etiological function to this material: It tells how certain things came to be the way they are. Social structures are organized under the general rule of kinship. They are derived from a common ancestor, and they are horizontally related to one another. In this text, nomads, musicians, and smiths end up brothers and cousins—just as in real life.

Two types of genealogy can be found in the Hebrew Bible; indeed, these same two types are found to this very day in traditional literatures everywhere. The first is the branched or segmented genealogy in which a father and a mother give rise to children whose own children then branch out further and further through several generations. We usually call this a family tree. The second type is the linear genealogy in which the ancestry of a single person (or in the case of the Bible, the person who stands for a whole tribe or nation) is traced backward in a single direct line to some ancient origin. Each of these serves a specific function. The branched genealogy can help establish a pecking order within a community, as for example, in the account of the twelve tribes of Israel in Genesis 29:31–30:24 and 35:16–20. In this account of the origin of the twelve tribes, different tribes are assigned to different mothers, though obviously all are sons of Jacob/Israel. The tribes descended from Rachel stand at the apex of prestige and importance, whereas those derived from Leah fall lower in the pecking order. Those derived from slave women fall even lower. This arrangement seems to mirror the relative standings of the tribes in the later literary traditions of Israel.

Genesis 4:17–26, which includes elements of both of these types, is a linear genealogy running through six generations from Cain to Lamech. At Lamech's generation the writer pauses to discuss the wives and the sons of Lamech, thereby creating a branched genealogy. In the end, he returns to the second generation and adds the new son, Seth, to the nuclear family of Adam and Eve, thereby creating a branched genealogy for the first couple. The exact purpose of this J genealogy is a little obscure in that the kinship groups listed are not entirely expected. Jabal certainly represents two of the major segments of the early Israelite community, nomads and shepherds. The other two sons, however, would not seem to represent major segments, though perhaps the mention of metalworking should be viewed as an acknowledgment of a stage in the early development of Israel that brought it into the bronze and iron ages.

The goal of genealogical research in our culture is to develop family trees that are as historically accurate and flawless as possible, down to the exact dates of births, baptisms, marriages, and deaths. That is not at all the way in which genealogical tables function in the Bible. These traditions are marked by fluidity. As they moved from oral to written stages, later traditioners felt free to rearrange the order of names, to derive descendants from different ancestors, and, in short, to use the genealogical tradition to create various maps of community life and kinship relationships. Genealogies could even be shaped to support an overarching theory of history (see commentary on chap. 5).

[4:17] From early times, interpreters have had many interesting questions to ask about Adam, Eve, and their descendants. Some of these have centered around the ancient problem of where Cain got his wife. Not only did the Pharisaic scribes and rabbis of the first centuries of the common era speculate on this matter, but so did Christian commentators, including the Reformers. Luther, however, was sure of one thing: "It is certain that Cain married his sister." Luther did wonder, though, what kind of woman would marry the first murderer of all time:

> The young woman who married him certainly deserves great praise. Adam must have been an eloquent orator to be able to persuade his daughter to follow him who was cursed and so severely punished for his sin. It may be that God blessed Cain and his descendants on account of his wife, who took her bloodthirsty brother in sincere faith and out of obedience to God and her parents. (Luther, 111–12)

Having acquired a wife from nowhere in particular, Cain proves himself to be a city builder, not a fugitive and wanderer. Enoch, the city Cain named in honor of his eldest son, was the first human community larger than four persons. When they announced the mandate given to the first human couple to "be fruitful and multiply" (1:26), the Priestly writers may have reflected the consciousness of their later, more sophisticated generation of theologians that population growth leads directly to urbanization. Not so here. The J writer merely recounts the events, though the events do build toward the crisis of overpopulation that J will bring forward in chapter 6.

Is building a city a bad idea? Is Cain's decision to build a city what one would expect of a man of sin, given that desire and culture go together (Brueggemann, 65)? Is the movement from nomadism and agrarianism into the huddled mass of the city another manifestation of Cain's fall? Is it bad to want to be part of a critical mass of people who can support symphony orchestras and office towers, Burger Kings and Pizza Huts? Perhaps the root cause of urbanization is the desire of people to be with their own kind, to get together for the purposes of mating and painting, music and murder. Whatever the cause, rather than accept the lonely life of the scattered nomadic tribe, the man who has just murdered his brother now builds a city.

Surely this city of Enoch was no Brasilia, constructed in empty wilderness according to some ideal plan. If archaeology can be our guide, the city would probably have been a population center with an infrastructure of small houses, shops, streets, and the defensive structure of a city wall. (At Jericho, a massive twenty-five-foot-high circular wall-tower with an interior stairway was built by a people who had not yet learned to make pottery. From earliest times, sad to say, cities had to protect themselves from those who would sack them of their treasures if they could.) As soon as we talk about architecture and economics, we are talking about culture. To build the first city is, therefore, a shorthand way of describing the founding of civilization.

In his book *Beast or Angel? Choices That Make Us Human*, René Dubos discusses the beginnings of civilization in the Cro-Magnon culture of China some 50,000 years ago. Those early human beings preferred to live crowded together in caves in groups of about 250 persons (just about the population of the average Presbyterian Church [U.S.A.] congregation). There was plenty of room in China in those days. There was no pressing geopolitical reason why 250 shaggy, unbathed persons had to crowd together in a single cave. (One can get the feel if not the smell of the cave from the opening scene of the compelling 1981 Jean-Jacques Annaud film about the dawn of humanity, *Quest for Fire*.) But cluster up they did, in a cave here and a cave there with plenty of space in between. They preferred caves elevated somewhat above the valley floor from which they could enjoy the view of the empty space and the other caves. Obviously there were defensive values in this lifestyle, but, in the opinion of Dubos, the principal reason for this behavior was so that human beings could enjoy companionship, help each other, and get on with the business of making the cultural choices that would make them more and more human.

Evidently the J writer was on the right track. He knew that human beings want to cling together. He skips the slow process of cultural evolution that we have learned about from science. He presses past the caves toward the kind of communal expression of civilization that he knew from his own experience—the city.

It may be the case that oral storytellers who gave us the Cain of Genesis 4:17–26 simply drew upon a different cycle of tradition about this founding father and pre-Flood hero than did the narrator(s) of 4:1–16. As the stories now stand juxtaposed in the context of scripture, however, the contrast between the two Cains is either too stark to be comprehended or else the two were united in the mind of the J writer along some such axis as that described above—Cain, the builder of a city, the innovator of culture and civilization, is also the man who once failed to master sin's desire (v. 7). If so, in the Yahwist's view, sin and city would have always to be bundled together for the purposes of theological reflection.

[18–22] Further descendants of Cain are enumerated in the ensuing verses. Isn't it odd that the name of Cain's wife, that precious, elect woman through whose body the first generations of humankind were channeled, is never given? One would have thought her name to have been more important than the names of Adah and Zillah, the two wives of Cain's great-great-great grandson, Lamech (v. 19). Perhaps those estimable ladies are named because of their maternal ties with three important aspects of human culture other than urbanization itself: nomadism and animal husbandry (through Adah's son Jabal, v. 20), music (through Adah's other son, Jubal, v. 21), and metallurgy (through Zillah's son, Tubal-cain, v. 22; see the discussion at Gen. 4:1 for the association of the name of Cain with metalwork). Zillah also bore a daughter (v. 22), whose excellence endures only because of her name, Naamah, "pleasant, lovely."

Biblical writers prefer concreteness and vividness; if a name can be given, it is. If a skill can be named, it is. Few abstractions or generalities are to be found. Instead of gushing on about the ancient heroes and heroines who brought culture from heaven to humankind, the J writer gives us "real people," the mothers of the shepherd, the piper, and the smith. The crucial importance of the shepherd and the smith to the material culture of later ages is self-evident. The importance of the player of the lyre and pipes may be linked with the very transmission of culture through the act of recitation of the epic tradition. The practice of singing poetry to the accompaniment of stringed instruments is well attested in traditional cultures everywhere, including ancient Israel (see, for example, 1 Sam. 16:16, 23; 1 Chron. 15:16–29; Ps. 150; Amos 6:4–7).

Obviously such recitation would be seriously hampered for a bard who tried to accompany his own song on a flute or reed instrument. Jubal must also be the ancestor of the backup combo as well!

The intertestamental Jewish book of *Jubilees* does for the Israelite tradition what Greek mythology does for the Hellenistic world: It gives a more detailed account of how various gifts were brought to human beings from the heavenly realm.

[In the days of Jared (the great-great grandson of Seth)] the angels of the Lord descended on the earth, those who are named the Watchers, that they should instruct the children of men. . . . And in the eleventh jubilee Jared took to himself a wife and her name was Bâraka, the daughter of Râsûjâl, a daughter of his father's brother, in the fourth week of this jubilee, and she bare him a son in the fifth week, in the fourth year of the jubilee and he called his name Enoch. And he was the first among men that are born on earth who learnt writing and knowledge and wisdom and who wrote down the signs of heaven according to the order of their months in a book, that men might know the seasons of the years according to the order of their separate months. And he was the first to write a testimony, and he testified to the sons of men among the generations of the earth, and recounted the weeks of the jubilees, and made known to them the days of the years, and set in order the months and recounted the Sabbaths of the years as we made (them), known to him. (*Jub.* 4:15–18, Charles edition)

All we have in the canonical Bible is this one little passage, verses 20–22, in which the origins of three human trades are singled out for mention.

[23–24] The seventh person in descent from Adam in the Cainite genealogy of the J writer is Lamech. In such a significant position he gets special attention. In his boastful little song, Lamech tells his wives that he killed a man who had assaulted him. Lamech probably claims only one victim; the "young man" and the "man" of verse 23b are one and the same victim, mentioned in parallel clauses. Hebrew poetry is structured neither by rhyme nor rhythm but by parallelism. A typical line of poetry will say the same thing a second time using different words. (Attention to this point about Hebrew poetics might have saved the writer of the Gospel of Matthew the embarrassment of picturing the Messiah riding into Jerusalem on Palm Sunday mounted on two donkeys at once [compare the poetic prophecy in Zech. 9:9 with Matt. 21:5].) God had protected Lamech's ancestor Cain with a threat of sevenfold vengeance against his would-be murderer (v. 15). The elevenfold multiplication of this threat by Lamech may just be traditional braggadocio (compare the taunts exchanged between David and Goliath in 1 Sam. 17:10, 36, 43–46), or perhaps the figure is a hint that with increasing population and urbanization, human relations were becoming more complex and dangerous.

Is Jesus alluding to the overweening wrath of Lamech when, in Matthew 18:22 he charges Peter to forgive an offender not seven but seventy-seven times? If so, his teaching undoes Lamech's claim that in extravagant vengeance wrongdoing is overcome. Not in violence but in extravagant forgiveness is wrongdoing overcome, according to Jesus. Even before New Testament times, of course, the Old Testament recognized that uncontrolled vengeance was a threat to the fabric of the human community. The *lex talionis*, "eye for an eye, tooth for a tooth" (Ex. 21:24), was a principle actually intended to restrain violence, especially by the powerful against the weak. Through the Deuteronomist, the Lord taught "Vengeance is mine, and recompense" (Deut. 32:35; see also 12:19). The Psalter too stresses that justice and retribution properly belong to the Lord (Ps. 94:1–3). In Lamech's poem, the speaker acts on his own initiative to effect what he considers justice; in contrast, in the psalm, the worshiper calls upon God to take revenge upon God's enemies. Clearly, uncontrolled vengeance is a matter of great political and social importance. The city that Cain now builds will need to find ways of handling and defusing the need for vengeance if it is to survive!

[25–26] In any event, Lamech's reference to Cain rounds out the story of Cain and his descendants. Now the Yahwist introduces the "afterthought" son, Seth, who will substitute for the murdered Abel. The ensuing linear genealogy of one son, Enosh, is short, but it is a sufficient peg onto which the Priestly writers can hang an entirely new table of descent of the human race that will eradicate the blood of Cain from all our veins forever (see commentary on 5:1–32). The freshness of this start after Cain's line sinks into oblivion is underscored by the meaning of the name Enosh—"humankind."

The chapter closes with the much-discussed sentence, "At that time people began to invoke the name of the LORD." This sentence seems to run counter to the understanding of Exodus 3 that Israel learned the name of its deity only at Sinai after Moses' encounter with the burning bush. However, the stress here should be laid upon the verb "to invoke" (or "to call" or even "to worship"). The Yahwist apparently wants to affirm that Israel came to know the proper name of the deity. Worship is a general, worldwide human phenomenon rooted in primeval history, but although peoples everywhere use many names for the deity, Israel knows that all true worship ultimately is directed to Yahweh alone.

The phrase "at that time" might be taken to mean that prior to the birth of Enosh, no one worshiped the Lord or invoked the name of Yahweh. A distinction has been made between those who were created at firsthand (Adam from the ground, Eve from his rib, Cain, Abel, and even Seth born "with the help of the LORD") and those ensuing generations who emanated from their ancestors and heard about the Lord second-hand. Such a distinction seems forced, however. The best understanding of verse 26b may simply be that with Enosh, whose name means "humankind," a universal propensity to religion came into being and it is from that predisposition that all subsequent religion derives, including the faith of Israel.

5. The Human Family before the Flood
Genesis 5:1–32

Chapter 5 of Genesis is one of those genealogical tables that Christian readers of the Bible, Sunday school teachers, and preachers alike love to skip. Yet we do so to our own loss. Earlier generations of interpreters understood how important these periodic reckonings of time were for the biblical writers themselves. The book of *Jubilees* took this chapter extremely seriously as part of its overall effort to show that time from the beginning is significant for the other great events of history and that it took exactly fifty jubilees, or 2500 years, to bring history from the creation of the world to Israel's entry into the promised land. (The jubilee year was the fiftieth year, after the passage of forty-nine, or seven times seven, years; see Lev. 25:8–17.) Josephus found great interest in biblical chronology, as did Luther and Sir Isaac Newton. Perhaps best known to us are the calculations of the mid-seventeenth-century archbishop of Armagh in Ireland, James Ussher, who announced that the creation of the world took place on Sunday, October 23, 4004 B.C. Most people take Archbishop Ussher's figures as foolishness now, and even the most traditional editions of the Bible do not put his dates in the margin until at least chapter 11 of Genesis. Geology, the traditions of other cultures, and astrophysics have all contributed to our own realization that as factual history the figures of Genesis 5 and the other Priestly genealogies in Genesis have no value. However, as conveyors of ideology and theology about God's purposes, these chapters continue to have merit. It is to discern that merit that we now examine Genesis 5:1–32.

[5:1–2] Lest anyone doubt that the genealogy that follows picks up the Priestly story of creation in Genesis 1, these verses should dispel that doubt. As Genesis 1:26 makes clear, God created humankind in God's own "likeness" (the similar word "image" does not appear here) and both male and female share in that divine likeness. Verse 2 makes clear that the blessing of sexuality that Genesis 1:28 announces is now to be manifested in the descent of the generations from the marriage of the original male and female. One detail not mentioned in Genesis 1:27–28 is added here: God names them "Humankind" when they are created. As we know, in scripture to name something is to establish a certain authority over it. By naming humankind, God demonstrates God's sovereignty over the human community and over the process of generation that will now tie Adam to Noah and thence on into the future. This great process of elaboration of humanity happened under the sign of unity. They are all one family and they are all blessed. What a positive note on which to trace the enlargement of the human community! It is a note as important to our understanding as are the themes of rebellion, punishment, and fratricide that were announced in chapters 3 and 4. One final clue that this text emanates from Priestly circles is that the table is called a "list." The Hebrew word used here is *sefer*, "book." Whether it is correct or not to assume that the writer is working with a written record, at least the attempt is being made to establish its authority as a historical archive.

[3–32] At least four things are noteworthy about the genealogy itself.

1. It is a linear genealogy. It connects Adam with Noah in a straight line through a series of ten generations. In each of the ten generations, only the eldest son is mentioned by name, for these are the children of destiny.

2. The genealogy is purely a Sethite one. The line of Cain is now completely abandoned. We can assume that Irad, Mehujael, and Methushael of 4:18 are equivalent to Jared, Mahalalel, and Methuselah of chapter 5, and that Cain's own name may be repeated in Kenan (5:9), who is the son of Enosh ("humankind"). With the added observation that both Enoch and Lamech appear in the genealogy, we can safely assume that the Priestly writer has simply merged the Cainite genealogy into the Sethite one. This demonstrates the fluidity of genealogy in biblical tradition. There is a willingness to reuse materials in a different order, placing descendants in different generations as children of different parents. It also suggests that a theological interest is at work. By making all subsequent descendants not of Cain but of Seth, the Priestly writers free us from the onus of Cain's fratricide and his mark.

3. The pre-Flood worthies all live to very great ages. In fact, the average life span of these ten generations of patriarchs, through Noah, is 857.5 years. Adam was still alive when Noah's father, Lamech (his great-great-great-great grandson), was a boy. Modern readers find these life spans incredible, and so they are, although they are moderate compared to the life spans of the heroes prior to the flood in Mesopotamian tradition. That tradition was known from ancient times through the writings of Berossus, who wrote a history of Babylon in Greek in about the third

century B.C. He too had ten generations before the deluge. The combined total of the reigns of his kings came to 432,000 years. He was interpreting to his generation a much older tradition based on the Sumerian king list that detailed how the first king ruled 28,800 years, the second, 36,000, and so on, for a total of 241,000 years before the flood swept away habitation on the earth.

So perhaps the surprise is not how old Methuselah, Jared, Noah, Adam, and the others are, but how young they are by comparison to the rival accounts. From birth to birth the figure of 1556 years plus the added hundred years to the Flood (7:6) yields a figure that was no doubt intended to be significant. (Significant also is the fact that for the first time since Adam, no ancient ancestor was still alive at the time the Flood occurred.) A different significance must have been intended by the Greek Old Testament (Septuagint), which has the Flood occurring in 2242 A.M. (= *anno mundi*, or years of the world's existence). The Samaritan Pentateuch, an ancient Hebrew version rediscovered in the sixteenth century A.D., places the flood in 1307 A.M., a date agreed with by the book of *Jubilees*.

4. All of this betrays the great interest in chronology typical of the Priestly writers. That interest shows itself again in Genesis 11:10–26 where the ten generations between Adam and the Flood are matched by ten generations between the Flood and Abraham. We can only assume that the Priestly writers meant these figures to be taken literally, that for them a year was a year, that Methuselah did live to be 969 and that the Flood did occur 1656 years after creation. In other words, the writer was not speaking metaphorically or figuratively.

After encountering other cultures that have their own stories of creation and time lines from the beginning, as well as geological evidence that places the beginning of the world billions of years in the past, we twenty-first-century believers are quite right in rejecting these figures as an accurate historical chronology. However, we have to take seriously the theology implied in this genealogical account. There is a scheme here. Ancient Israel wants to carry us back to absolute zero in our understanding of who human beings are. God's purpose for humanity expressed in his words to Adam at the beginning of the human experience is the original legitimization of humankind, the original empowerment of humankind with the vocation of stewardship. God extends that vocation through time in significant segments such as ten generations. The divine design, however it may develop, binds us together with Adam, Eve, Cain, Seth, Noah, Abraham, Jesus, and all the saints who have gone before.

[22–24] The account of Enoch given in chapter 5 lays the basis for the great legendary expansion of this figure in later Jewish tradition. Bearing in mind that not until the very end of the Old Testament period is there any notion of life after death in the Bible, some persons were nevertheless thought to have moved from the earthly realm to the heavenly council. "Enoch walked with God; then he was no more, because God took him" (5:24). This sentence may simply mean that Enoch died, but it has been taken by interpreters through all the ages to mean that he was assumed into heaven. It is no surprise, then, that a vast Enoch literature should have arisen. In the Ethiopic book of *Enoch*, this worthy is presented as an apocalyptic figure returning at the end of time with accounts of heavenly journeys and disclosures of heavenly mysteries. In the Priestly account, Enoch is not the first but the significant seventh generation. He also ceased to exist on earth at the youngish age of 365 years, far earlier than any of the other pre-Flood heroes. The figure of 365 suggests some link of Enoch with the solar calendar. It is not surprising that in the extra-canonical book of *Enoch* a solar calendar is very strongly advanced.

[28–31] Lamech plays a very different role in the Priestly genealogy than in the Yahwistic one. There he was the boastful, vengeful killer (4:23–24). In this chapter he is known only for having named his son Noah (from the Hebrew verbal root meaning "rest") because he prophesied that Noah would bring relief from the curse that had been placed upon the ground at the murder of Abel (see commentary on 4:8–12).

[32] As was the case in the Yahwistic genealogy of 4:17–26, the Priestly genealogy ends its linear movement with a sudden branching. Noah is mentioned as having only sons, and only in Noah's case are the names of more than one son mentioned. This branching will lay the basis for an explanation in chapters that lie ahead of various clans of humankind.

REFLECTIONS ON BIBLICAL CHRONOLOGY

In his booklet *Biblical Chronology: Legend or Science?* James Barr points out that it is impossible to reconstruct a coherent biblical chronology that reaches from the beginning of the Old Testament through the New and that corresponds to history as we know it from secular sources. One of the paradoxes is that the portion of the Old Testament that seems to care most for detailed historical accuracy, the history of the kings of Judah and Israel, does not correlate well with what we know from secular accounts from the period of time between the accession of Solomon in about 962 B.C. to the end of the monarchy and the destruction of the temple in 587 B.C. If one adds up the figures given in the book of Kings for the lifetime of the temple, it comes to 430 years, exactly the same amount of time between the promise of land given to Abraham and the covenant at Sinai (Gal. 3:17, in which Paul follows the Septuagint version of Ex. 12:40, which makes clear that the figure of 430 included both the patriarchal period and the time spent in Egypt).

Such a coincidence suggests that even in that portion of the Old Testament in which exact chronology seems most possible and most desirable, some kind of scheme was at work. In other words, in giving dates and chronologies, the writers of the Old Testament were obliquely expressing theological convictions. It is interesting that the figures at the beginning of the biblical chronology seem much more exact than those that appear later on. (For example, it is impossible to construct any chronology of the Persian period; the New Testament gives very little attention to chronology as well.) The numbers given in Genesis are purely legendary in character, part of the storytelling program designed to convince the reader of the unity of humankind, of our descent from Seth and not Cain, of the priority of the Hebrew account of the origins of humankind to all other accounts, and of the reality that God has a plan that those who have eyes to see can find somewhat obliquely manifested in genealogy.

Barr suggests that two other motives may also be involved in the chronological schemes of Genesis and the rest of the Bible: (1) protology, interest in the beginning of time, and (2) eschatology, interest in the end of time. The genealogies in Genesis are written from the point of view of God looking from year zero forward. That point of view is totally foreign to the traditional Western worldview, derived from Christianity, in which time is divided by a great center point into B.C. and A.D. and in which history gets more diffuse the farther one goes backward from the center point. The Genesis genealogies are written from an *anno mundi* standpoint, preserved to this day in the traditional Jewish calendar, which starts at the beginning and comes forward to the year in which these words are being written, 5760 A.M.

What this makes possible is a schematization of history like that of Archbishop Ussher. By Ussher's time it had been accepted that Jesus was born in 4 B.C., the year of Herod's death. Ussher's figures led him to conclude that creation was four thousand years before the birth of Jesus and the completion of the temple about three thousand years later, leaving one thousand years from the temple to the birth of Jesus. Such calculations are open to projection in the other direction—toward end times. One certainly may question Ussher's figures (though he was a remarkably careful student of these matters and by no means the first—Luther's study of biblical chronology was one of his best known and most widely read works). However, he probably captured one of the purposes of biblical genealogy, namely to establish for those readers who care to do their own addition the idea that history was divided by God into great segments. In all of these segments—be they of one thousand or four thousand years, or segments of ten generations or seven generations—God's hand was at work bringing forth turning points in human affairs at God's appointed times. It is a notion that becomes highly explicit again in biblical apocalyptic texts in which all things occur on the timetable that God set for them in the beginning.

6. Genetics Goes Awry
Genesis 6:1–9:29

The lengthy story of the Flood is prefaced by a passage (6:1–8) in which the Yahwistic writer offers two discernible motivations for God's wrathful judgment. Angel marriages and their bizarre progeny are the topics of verses 1–4; the pervasive human tendency to do evil and Yahweh's regret at having made creatures capable of such behavior are the subjects of verses 5–8. Of these two motivating narratives, the mythic and cryptic subject of human-divine mating is more immediately intriguing; however, the narrator's daring in revealing to us the thought life of God in verses 5–8 proves to be of enduring interest as well.

TWO CAUSES FOR THE FLOOD
Genesis 6:1–8

6:1 When people began to multiply on the face of the ground, and daughters were born to them, 2 the sons of God saw that they were fair; and they took wives for themselves of all that they chose. 3 Then the LORD said, "My spirit shall not abide in mortals forever, for they are flesh; their days shall be one hundred twenty years." 4 The Nephilim were on the earth in those days—and also afterward—when the sons of God went in to the daughters of humans, who bore children to them. These were the heroes that were of old, warriors of renown.

5 The LORD saw that the wickedness of humankind was great in the earth, and that every inclination of the thoughts of their hearts was only evil continually. 6 And the LORD was sorry that he had made humankind on the earth, and it grieved him to his heart. 7 So the LORD said, "I will blot out from the earth the human beings I have created—people together with animals and creeping things and birds of the air, for I am sorry that I have made them." 8 But Noah found favor in the sight of the LORD.

[6:1–4] Diverse factors are involved in the crisis that leads to the Flood. In verse 1, the earth begins to groan under the burden of human population. People are multiplying, and an unusual stress is put on the birth of "daughters" who are perceived to be the generative engine of population growth. (At the root of the sexual double standard that exists in most traditional societies may be the consciousness that the reproductive capacity of women is limited by age and quantitative factors. We now know that only four hundred to five hundred eggs are produced during a woman's thirty to forty childbearing years, yet those ova are vital to the future of the society. Unlike with simpler creatures, who can afford to waste most of their eggs, the regeneration of humankind is a relatively precarious business. The traditional solution is therefore to surround women with the protective barriers of taboo and moral stricture so that the precious product of their wombs can be made to serve the greater social good. Men, on the other hand, are a dime a dozen when it comes to their role in reproduction, and little prevents them from sowing oats wild or domestic. In fact, often when men have gone on the rampage and tried to destroy the roots of another culture, they have used rape as a weapon, as happened in Bosnia in the 1990s.)

It seems possible, then, that the ancient tradition understood overpopulation to have necessitated the Flood. Overpopulation also provides a very good explanation for the Lord's cryptic remark that "My spirit shall not abide in mortals forever, for they are flesh; their days shall be one hundred twenty years" (v. 3). In light of the life spans of the pre-Flood generations given in Genesis 5, this decision seems very prudent. Post-Flood genealogies such as Genesis 11:10–26 slowly begin to reflect this revised life span, though the patriarch Noah, already a spry six hundred years of age at the time he built the ark (7:6) gets "grandfathered in" for an additional 350 years afterward (9:28–29). It is really not until after the death of Joshua at 110 (Josh. 24:29) that the life expectancy of biblical heroes settles into something like the normal "threescore years and ten."

Not only are the rabbit-like multiplication and extreme longevity of the pre-Flood human community significant problems, but so also is the pollution of that bloodline by an extraordinary infusion from an unexpected source. The daughters produce hybrid offspring, not because they were raped by enemies but because they were seduced by "the sons of God" (v. 2). These "sons of God" are not sons of Yahweh; they are angelic members of the heavenly court that surrounds God (see Gen. 28:12; 1 Kings 22:19–22; Job 1:6; 38:7; Ps. 29:1; 82:6; 89:7).

Is this myth? A myth is any story of the gods in their own realm, out of the sight of human witnesses, creating realities with which we human beings are familiar but that require an explanation. Because myths have to do with divine creative activity, they are often set in primeval times when the world itself was just beginning. The little story of Genesis 6:1–4 meets most of these criteria, and we can label it "mythic" or even "faded myth." It seems to preserve a fragment of some wondrous Near Eastern tale about ancient demigods.

As it now stands, however, it does not function as myth at all, but has become part and parcel of Israel's lengthy saga of human origins. The community is no longer being asked to give credence to a once-upon-a-time incident of human-divine mating, or even accept the existence in the past of larger-than-life heroes. Now the story has been pressed into greater service, namely, to justify the ways of God to God's people, and to serve as part of a literary motivation for the Flood so compelling that readers through all the ages will say that God was right to destroy that ancient human world.

We have reason to believe that at some time and at some level this story did exist in Hebrew tradition in order to explain a fabulous feature of the past, namely, the presence of giants and demigods on the earth. The best evidence that this was an ongoing and larger tradition is the puzzling allusion in verse 4 to "the Nephilim," who may or may not be the same as the "heroes that were of old, warriors of renown." The latter two terms have military overtones; the first, "Nephilim," has been traditionally understood to mean "giants" (see KJV). (It is not absolutely clear from v. 4 that these creatures were, like the "heroes" and the "warriors of renown," the products of the divine-human liaisons.)

Like other traditional cultures, the ancient Israelites seem to have imagined that the aboriginal people were bigger and stronger than anyone around in their own time, and that they were hostile figures. (Even our "cave man" movies, such as the 1981 film *Quest for Fire,* tend to present the ancients as great hulks, when in actual fact Neanderthal and Cro-Magnon skeletons are much smaller than ours.) The Hebrew verbal root of Nephilim is "to fall," and some interpreters have therefore understood them to be bad angels, or "fallen ones." However, other references to the Nephilim in the Hebrew Bible suggest that they were thought to be a subspecies of humankind still to be seen around the edges of the land in historical times. According to Numbers 13:33, the Nephilim—or, if Deuteronomy 1:28 has it right, their oversized descendants, the Anakim—terrified the twelve men sent by Moses to spy out the promised land. They were finally exterminated within the sphere of Israelite settlement by Joshua (Josh. 11:21–22).

What is wrong with having a demigod in the religious closet? After all, don't we Christians have a God-man at the very heart of our faith, one who, "conceived by the Holy Spirit," was born of a human mother? Surely it was delicacy on this issue that led the early Christians to speak of virgin birth rather than divine-human mating.

From the Israelite perspective, out of which the Christian sprang, everything was wrong about such a notion. A half-god/half-human being pollutes both categories. It would have had about the same status of purity as a crab has when compared to scaly fish, which is to say, no purity. Fish are supposed to have scales and fins; a crab looks more like a bug and has no scales. Of course, we now know that a crab is a maritime spider, and we can accept it as such today. For the ancient Hebrews, however, a crab or a shrimp or even an oyster was an extraordinary sea creature, and was out of order. All things have their proper place and belong to their proper order. On the ground, dirt is fine. It is even "clean" in a ritual sense, because it is in its proper place. On the dining room table, however, dirt is unclean because it is not in its proper place. Furthermore, when a creature shares the features of two distinct orders, that creature is out of order and "unclean." Assumptions such as these underlay the biblical rules about clean and unclean animals, edibles, and even behavior.

It goes without saying, then, that a half-god/half-human creature would be inappropriate and evil from square one. God belongs up there and we belong down here and if the two get mingled, a disorderly cosmos results.

Even here in the earliest Pentateuchal source one sees in the dim outlines of the faded myth a much larger story. To get the larger story, one has to more forward a thousand years to a section of the great Jewish extracanonical work, the book of *Enoch*, that can be dated to about 200 B.C. Though this book was written by Jews and is quoted as scripture in the New Testament (Jude 14–15), it fell into disfavor in the fourth century A.D. and was all but forgotten in western Judaism and Christianity until manuscripts of the work were found in Ethiopian monasteries and brought to Europe in the eighteenth century. Even now it is known in its entirety only in Ethiopic manuscripts, though Greek and Latin fragments exist and Aramaic fragments of all but one section of it have turned up among the sacred scrolls at Qumran by the Dead Sea.

To make a long story short, the book of *Enoch* knows all about these children of the sons of God and the daughters of men:

> In those days, when the children of man had multiplied, it happened that there were born unto them handsome and beautiful daughters. And the angels, the children of heaven, saw them and desired them; and they said to one another, "Come, let us choose wives for ourselves from among the daughters of man and beget us children" . . . [The names of many "angels"

then follow.] And they took wives unto themselves, and everyone (respectively) chose one woman for himself, and they began to go unto them. And they taught them magical medicine, incantations, the cutting of roots, and taught them (about) plants. And the women became pregnant and gave birth to great giants whose heights were three hundred cubits. These (giants) consumed the produce of all the people until the people detested feeding them. So the giants turned against (the people) in order to eat them. And they began to sin against birds, wild beasts, reptiles, and fish. And their flesh was devoured the one by the other, and they drank blood. And then the earth brought an accusation against the oppressors. (*Enoch* 6:1–2; 7:1–6, Charlesworth edition, Vol. 1)

Is this witness to the story of the divine-human unions merely the speculations of later teachers expanding on the hints of Genesis 6:1–4, or is this more like the full story that was there all along and was only displayed in a faded form in the canonical text? Apocalyptic texts such as *Enoch* are given to great elaborations of mythic traditions not acknowledged elsewhere in the sacred tradition or else known only in much simpler forms (for example, the creation stories). The apocalyptic task, after all, is to prepare for a new "deluge" and a new creation, using the stories of primeval times as prototypes. Even apart from apocalyptic literature, the tension between official faith and popular faith is always present. For the most part, scripture articulates only the official faith; however, we are sometimes able to extrapolate from biblical polemics and occasional extrabiblical sources the things that people actually may have believed. Perhaps before the oral tradition was reduced to writing some Israelites were willing to speak so anthropomorphically about God that they could even imagine God presiding over a whole passel of sexy sons!

The intertestamental book of *Jubilees*, also found in its entirety only in Ethiopic (with Hebrew fragments now available from Qumran), also takes up the tradition preserved in Genesis 6:1–4. *Jubilees* is thought to have emanated from early circles of Pharisees even before the time of Christ; it takes the form of a running paraphrase of Genesis. Its version of Genesis 6:1–4 is as follows:

And when the children of men began to multiply on the surface of the earth and daughters were born to them, that [*sic*] the angels of the Lord saw in a certain year of that jubilee that they were good to look at. And they took wives for themselves from all of those whom they chose. And they bore children for them; and they were the giants. And injustice increased upon the earth, and all flesh corrupted its way; man and cattle and beasts and birds and everything which walks on the earth. And they all corrupted their way and their ordinances, and they began to eat one another. And injustice grew upon the earth and every imagination of the thoughts of all mankind was thus continually evil. (*Jub.* 5:1–2, Charlesworth edition, Vol. 2)

Like the writer of Enoch, this writer has no doubt that the "sons of God" were angels, though the biblical text itself does not require that translation. The *Jubilees* version is a much more conservative rendition of the tradition than that of *Enoch*, but it too hints at a much larger memory of the sons of God and daughters of men. For one thing, predation was rampant—everyone ate everyone else!

[5–8] A rather different motivation for the Flood is offered in the next two verses. A contrast is offered here between the evil heart of human beings and the broken heart of God. God is forced to change the divine mind. We should not be too fastidious about speaking anthropomorphically about God, at least if we wish to remain consonant with Old Testament language. In the Hebrew tradition God is presented as having to cut losses and change course.

In verse 7, God vows to blot out not only human beings, but also the rest of the ambient creatures of the world, concluding with the fatal words, "I am sorry that I have made them." Why would the wrath of God against humankind extend also to the birds and the bees and the fish and the gazelles? Is God simply taking away the gifts of animal companionship and nurture that were given to humankind in Genesis 2? Did the curse brought down upon the ground (*adamah*) by the earth creature (*adam*) extend also to all the other animals that drew their sustenance from that accursed source? Did the fall of humankind automatically mean the fall of all animals? Or did the creatures sin in their own right? Perhaps this puzzle can be solved by the simple observation that the storyteller could think of no way God could blot out all human life without sweeping other life-forms away in the process? But then why did plants get off so easily?

Certain texts of scripture suggest that the rest of the creatures are corrupted by human corruption, and that the release for which they long and groan is release from bondage to our decay (see Rom. 8:19–21). A view that attributes animal demise to our corruption is surely preferable to one that claims that they have behaved in a way that brings punishment from God down upon them. From a modern ecological standpoint, human corruption manifested in rape of nature can lead and has led to disaster for other creatures. Perhaps the most we can say about verse 7 is that human corruption leads to disaster for all.

Even in this third and so far most terrible "fall" and subsequent punishment of humankind, however, God sounds a note of grace. Almost an aside, one human being is singled out of the mass of doomed creatures: "But Noah found favor in the sight of the LORD" (v. 8). The reader instantly senses that this tiny figure will be the link to the future. (See the discussion of the four falls of Genesis 3–11 in the commentary on 3:20–21.)

Gerhard von Rad helps us really see what we are looking at in Genesis 6:5–8. He argues that in these verses for the first time we have the actual words of the Yahwist, the great theologian who gave us the oldest Pentateuchal source. Before this point everything has been older tradition. Paradise (chap. 2), the tragedy in the garden (chap. 3), Cain and Abel (4:1–16), the genealogy of the Cainites (4:17–25), even the angel marriages (6:1–4) are all narratives that came to the Yahwist from the people's tradition. The Yahwist's achievement was to weave them together into a coherent narrative of human origins and sin and divine grace.

What follows in the story of the Flood, too, is traditional saga. In the short unit of 6:5–8, however, the theologian injects a personal note, not to add another story, but to offer "a communication about God's judgment on man and hear of a decision in the divine heart" (von Rad, 112). As such, the verses sum up the Yahwist's theological evaluation of the beginnings of humanity, placed in God's own mouth. Not only has human sin spread; it is endemic, it is continual, it is from the human heart. That affliction touches the heart of God too. In the Old Testament,

> the "heart" . . . is the seat not only of the emotion but also of the understanding and the will. The statement comprises, therefore, the entire inner life of man. "The thoughts of his heart"—the imagery of the expression is vivid! It means even the reflections of fantasy, the rising and freely formed movements of the will, were "only evil continually." In daring contrast to what is said about the human heart there follows a word about what takes place in God's heart: grief, affliction, and disappointment in man. Precisely in this way, by reference to the Creator's bewilderment, he has communicated something of the incomprehensibility of this incursion of sin. (von Rad, 113–14)

Two theological themes present themselves in this second introduction to the story of the Flood in Genesis 6:5–8.

Human depravity. "The LORD saw that the wickedness of humankind was great in the earth, and that every inclination of the thoughts of their hearts was only evil continually" (v. 5). Taken by itself, we might conclude that the Lord had reached the decision that the creation of humankind was a great error and that the creatures themselves were hopeless because of their inability to conjure up just and moral decisions from their evil hearts. Indeed, the nearly total obliteration of the human race that follows supports that reading of this verse.

Two considerations, however, keep us from saying that God regarded the human creatures as utterly corrupt, depraved, and incapable of any good whatever. First, among the masses of human beings, God found Noah "a righteous man, blameless in his generation" (6:9) and his family—his wife, three sons and three daughters-in-law—to be people who could become the progenitors of a new human community. If depravity were genetic and inescapable, then not even eight persons could be found to escape that universal plague. Second, the fact is that even after the Flood is over, God recognizes that "the inclination of the human heart is evil from youth" (8:21). The Flood did not eliminate the human ability to make the rotten choice to do evil. Even the descendants of the righteous man, Noah, and his family could do that.

What are we to conclude from this then? In the narrative context of this theme, we are driven to say that the writers recognize the profound truth about the human experience, namely, that in our freedom, when confronted with choices between good and evil, inevitably, universally, inescapably, we will from time to time choose evil. Holocausts of warfare and death can pour forth out of inhumanity to humankind into the horrors of death camps. Indeed, whole generations can become so profoundly corrupted that a Flood is required to rectify the situation. These things are true and the legend acknowledges that truth. It also acknowledges, however, that God loves this creature of God's own creativity and will not reject it forever. God will find ways to tease out of the human propensity to choose evil new episodes of the saintliness and new examples of the righteous living of which human beings are also capable.

God's flexibility. "And the LORD was sorry that he had made humankind on the earth" (6:6). In these early narrative reports that God experiences regret and has changes of mind, we encounter the phenomenon of anthropopathism, that is, the attribution to God of human emotions. We get off the track of biblical interpretation when we start bringing up such abstract notions of divine omnipotence and omniscience. Such doctrines have their place in an adequate systematic theology, of course. That is not the framework, however, in which the Hebrew Bible speaks about God. The narrators have to talk about process. God has to react to what is going on. Because God's human creatures really are free to make evil choices (and do so continually), even God does not know what might happen and has to be prepared to innovate. God is God, of course, and is Lord of all places and times (Num. 23:19 and 1 Sam. 15:29 even deny that God ever has a change of mind). However, God is not immutable in all respects. God goes with us on our pilgrimage through time and takes some of the kicks and blows that we experience. Nothing demonstrates this fact more clearly than the cross. There the evil inclination of the human heart caused God once again to bring to an end the world as it had been. This time it happened neither by water nor by fire, but by the heroic act of the Son, who bore in his own body the wounds inflicted by a humankind full of hatred and rage.

Ludwig Koehler provides a helpful perspective on God's change of mind. He says that the meaning of the many human descriptions of God in the Old Testament

> is not in the least to reduce God to a rank similar to that of man. To describe God in terms of human characteristics is not to humanize Him. That has never happened except in unreasonable polemic. Rather the purpose of anthropomorphisms is to make God accessible to man. . . . They represent God as person. They avoid the error of presenting God as a careless and soulless abstract Idea, or a fixed Principle standing over against man like a strong silent battlement. God is personal. He has a will, He exists in controversy, ready to communicate Himself, offended at men's sins yet with a ready ear for their supplication and compassion for their confessions of guilt: in a word, God is a living God. (Koehler, 24–25)

THE FLOOD
Genesis 6:9–8:19

The Flood is the story of how God undid creation. The writers draw this reversal of Genesis 1 with wonderful artistry. The deluge occurs (7:11) because the upper and lower waters separated at creation (1:6–7) are reunited. The cycle of nature established in Genesis 1:14 is set aside so that the Flood can destroy life; the cycle is reestablished in 8:22. The ark is a kind of floating garden of Eden where animals and human beings live together in harmony. Noah, the tenth generation after Adam and the first man born after Adam's death (a fact available to those with patience to add up the figures in 5:3–29), is a new Adam, for he is the father of all subsequent humanity. Like the first Adam, he has three sons, one of whom turns out badly. The blessing of fecundity that the Lord pronounces over Noah in Genesis 8:17 and 9:7 is a direct quotation of the similar blessing pronounced over Adam and Eve in Genesis 1:28. Ten generations separate Noah from Abraham, the father of Israel, just as ten generations separate Noah from Adam, the first father of humankind.

Like two of the other great legends of primeval history (Adam and Eve in the garden, Cain and Abel), the Flood story involves the classic triad of sin, punishment, and gracious renewal. It also follows a coherent story line: (1) God instructs Noah on how to build the ark and Noah follows the specifications meticulously (6:9–22); (2) the deluge is then unloosed (7:1–24); (3) the deluge ends at God's command (8:1–14); (4) God commands Noah and all the other passengers of the ark to go forth and inaugurate a new world order (8:15–19). The story is followed by two sequels (8:20–22, J/E; and 9:1–17, P) in which God looks ahead and covenants with humankind never again to do such a thing.

For all its literary and theological coherence, the Flood story that we have shows signs of more than one writer's hand. J (combined with E to form what is sometimes called the "older epic source") supplies a coherent and sequential narrative, but P too is a narrative source and offers a parallel tale that tends rather consistently to elaborate and enrich the original Flood story.

The thoroughness with which the two sources have been blended together is demonstrated in this schematization of the usual source analysis of Genesis 6:9–9:17. To hear the story as each source told it, try reading each column in the order given in Table 4:

Table 4

Older Epic Source (J/E)	Priestly Source
6:9–12, 13–22	
7:1–5, 7, 16b, 8–10, 12, 17b, 22–23	7:6, 11, 13–16a, 17a, 18–21, 24
8:6a, 2b, 3a, 6b, 8–12, 13b	8:1–2a, 3b, 4–5, 7, 13a, 14, 15–19
8:20–22	9:1–17

If you read the texts in the left-hand column in the order given there, you will hear the Flood story in the probable form in which it first reached the stage of writing during the United Monarchy of David and Solomon. If you read the right-hand column, you will hear the narrative framework supplied by the last editor or compiler of the Pentateuch, at the end of the Babylonian Exile. You will find that the two columns disagree in many details. Is this a problem? If one insists on knowing exactly what really happened historically at the time of the Flood, it is a problem. However, if one begins with the recognition that these chapters are not written history as we know it, but are theological writing in narrative form, then the heightening of the Flood story that took place during the four or five centuries between J/E and P becomes more understandable. Preachers and storytellers, perhaps drawing on various traditions, also elaborated in order to underscore certain aspects of the tradition. They did what preachers and teachers always do, and thus manifest again the incarnate nature of the word of God. That word reflected on itself and grew. The technique of analyzing the Pentateuch into sources becomes a blessing then, not an offense, for it enables us to explain discrepancies in the story as evidence that the story is not a static record but a living, composite witness that grew over many years.

Before proceeding to a detailed discussion of the story itself, yet another piece of background information deserves mention. Even before the early theologians of Israel assembled the epic story of the Flood and set it down in writing, there existed cycles of oral tradition about a deluge that went back into deep antiquity (see introduction). The relationship of Israel's account of the Flood to these other accounts, particularly those from Mesopotamia, is a subject of keen interest.

As its name implies, Mesopotamia is a land prone to flooding because it lies between two great rivers that bring the melting snow and the spring rains down from the mountains of Anatolia into the alluvial plain of Sumer and Akkad. Archaeology has discovered evidence of inundations in about 2900 B.C. at Kish and elsewhere in Iraq. The present-day Iraqi site called Fara, the ancient Shuruppak, shows evidence of devastating flooding too. This is particularly interesting because Shuruppak was the home of Utnapishtim, the hero of the flood story in the Gilgamesh Epic.

The story of a great flood is found in Mesopotamian tradition in four different versions. The earliest is the Atrahasis Epic, which is a history of humankind from the beginning to the deluge and immediately afterwards. There is also an early Sumerian flood narrative. The flood episode is given in its fullest form on the eleventh tablet of the Babylonian Gilgamesh Epic, though it appears to be an addition to that story. A third-century-B.C. Babylonian priest named Berossus retold the story in Hellenistic times from the Sumerian version. In that version, the hero of the flood is another king of Shuruppak, Ziusudra, whom Berossus rendered in Greek as Xisuthros. Besides the four extant Mesopotamian versions, no one knows how many other deluge legends lie behind the biblical account.

Whether or not they knew them in written form or even in their indigenous Mesopotamian forms at all, it seems very likely that the ancient Israelite community drew on these traditions. Since there is no evidence of ancient flooding in Israel's own land, we can assume that borrowing is how the Hebrew Bible came to include a deluge.

In all of the stories, the flood is a divinely ordained turning point within the larger history of humankind, and humankind's future is assured only through the actions of a hero. Beyond these commonalties, however, the various flood stories display very different characteristics. In the Mesopotamian versions, the gods set out to destroy all humankind. One group of human beings survives only because of the treachery of one of the gods against the others. In Atrahasis and Berossus, the savior of the human race is a hero famed for integrity and piety; however, Utnapishtim, the hero of the Gilgamesh Epic, is not distinguished in this way. The reason the deities decide to end the human community is not given in the Gilgamesh Epic or in Berossus, but in the old Atrahasis version, a reason is given: The gods are fed up with the noise and tumult of the human community.

In contrast to the precise chronologies given in the Genesis account, the duration of the flood differs in the various Mesopotamian accounts. In these stories, the heroes bring onto their vessels crews to assist in sailing as well as various passengers and relatives; in contrast, in the biblical account all humankind after the Flood is descended from the single family of Noah. In the biblical account, Noah's utter dependence on God is stressed; he acts exactly as God commands him. In Genesis 7:16, God even shuts the door of the ark and Noah and family do not leave it until God says, "Go out" (8:15). In Genesis, God speaks directly to Noah seven times; in the Mesopotamian tales, the human community and even the hero are kept in the dark. In the biblical account, God is completely in control at all times. It is God's decision to send rain for forty days and forty nights (7:4). It is God's decision to end the flood and make a wind blow over the earth that would cause the waters to subside (8:2; compare the original wind of God in 1:2). This contrasts interestingly with the confusion of the gods in the Gilgamesh Epic, where according to Utnapishtim, once their flood started, the gods "cowered like dogs crouched against the outer wall; Ishtar cried out like a woman in travail."

In summary, then, while it is clear that Israel drew upon a deluge tradition that was well known in the ancient Near East, it put its own distinct literary and moral stamp on the story and used it as a way both to vindicate the power and holiness of God and the obedience of one in whom God was pleased and through whom God purposed to save the human community.

[6:9–8:19] The Flood story is best taken as a whole, with notations on the seams where legends of different generations have been pieced together. As is typical of it, the P source is keenly interested in chronological and geographical detail, even though it was a half-millennium removed from the purported time of the deluge. In Genesis 6:14–16, for example, the Priestly source preserves in considerable detail God's blueprint for the building of the ark. The word *tebah*, "ark," is used of a craft only in these chapters and in Exodus 2:3–5, where it describes the box in which the infant Moses was set adrift in the Nile. The coincidence is not accidental. The description given here is of a box-like vessel made of otherwise unknown gopher wood (cypress?) caulked with pitch, 450 feet long, 73 feet wide, and 45 feet high, displacing 43,000 tons, laid out on three decks divided into "rooms" or stalls (6:14). No means of navigating the box is mentioned; therefore, no crew is needed. The occupants are utterly at God's mercy and will survive and go ashore only at God's behest.

In the Priestly account, the waters crest at 15 cubits (22.5 feet) above the highest mountains (7:19–20). In due course the ark runs aground on "the mountains of Ararat" (8:4)—probably not today's 17,000-foot Mount Ararat that rises at the junction of the borders of Turkey, Iran, and Armenia, but the tableland kingdom known as Urartu in Assyrian texts and mentioned in 2 Kings 19:37, Isaiah 37:38, and Jeremiah 51:27.

When they combined their version of the deluge with that of the older epic source, however, the Priestly writers allowed discrepancies to remain. In P, for example, the bird sent out by Noah was a raven. This raven apparently went in and out of the ark over many days, perhaps feeding, as ravens do, on vegetation and carrion alike (8:6–7). In contrast, the older tradition had a dove go forth, return once with an empty beak, return a second time with an olive branch, and then not return at all from its third outing (8:8–12). These differences in detail are insignificant, really; they probably simply reflect different streams of tradition. One wonders, however, why, if the Priestly writers were working with the older, well-known tradition in front of them, they would have allowed such discrepancies to remain: A modern editor surely would not have. This problem has led some to propose that even P was not the final editor of the Pentateuch, but that a redactor made a subsequent combination of the sources, treating them both as if they had the status of Holy Writ and could not be altered.

In a case like this, one can always be literal and say that Noah sent out both a raven and a dove, and that the raven was the less faithful of the two birds. However, the discrepancies get stickier in other areas. Substantive but differing claims are made, for example, about the number of animals taken onto the ark. J/E remembers that there were seven pairs of all clean animals and one pair each of unclean ones on the ark (7:2). P, on the other hand, remembers only one pair of each kind (6:19). (Cleanness or uncleanness refers to the ritual status of animals and birds [see 8:20], that is, their suitability for sacrifice, and not to their dietary acceptability [see 9:2–3].)

Different also are the figures on how long the flood remained. J/E states that "the rain fell on the earth forty days and forty nights" (7:12), and that fourteen more days passed before the nonreturn of the dove indicated that independent life on land was possible (8:10–12). For P, there was no rain as such. The waters that in the P creation account in Genesis 1:6–8 were divided into upper and lower parts by the dome called Sky, here simply pour out onto the land from both directions. In other words, the second day of creation was undone. From the time the "fountains of the great deep burst forth, and the windows of the heavens were opened" (7:11) on the seventeenth day of the second month of Noah's six-hundredth year, to the time it was possible to exit from the ark (8:13a, 14–15), apparently one year and eleven days elapsed (i.e., it was Noah's year 601, month 2, day 27). For anyone interested in the history of the Flood, these are not small differences!

Except for the number of pairs of animals on the ark, the P source is the more elaborate and detailed account. A tendency toward elaboration is one of the rules of oral transmission of tradition—stories get bigger and better as they are told and retold over the centuries. The same contrast between the older epic tradition and the P source can be seen in the account of the crossing of the Sea of Reeds in Exodus 14: It is P, not J, who has Israel pass through the sea between walls of water that are opened and closed by waves of Moses' staff (Ex. 14:21a, 22, 26, 29). In J, in fact, the Israelites do not cross at all. They merely find the dead Egyptians on the shore the next morning (14:30).

Neither the older epic tradition nor the P account of the Flood comes to us bearing news of a natural disaster in the spirit of a historical account or with the eyewitness accuracy of a network newscast. How could they? After all, we are quite certain that there never was a worldwide deluge, at least during the time that human life has existed on the earth. The real meaning to be grasped in this story is from the theological truth claims being made. In the older epic source, the flood comes as a direct answer to the evil inclination and sin of human beings. In the P account, however, over Noah and his charges the Lord casts a shield of protection. They are the passive recipients of God's grace. In P, the operative concept seems to be that out of the renewed primeval chaos of the flood a new world order was created, just as one had to be created out of the original chaos of Genesis 1:2. This time, however, God enlists a human participant, Noah, in the cocreation of a new sacred order in which mechanisms will be put in place to ensure the continuation of a right and wholesome world. In Genesis 8:16–17, P reports to us the charge that God gives to Noah as he leaves the ark and to the animals that are under Noah's dominion: "Be fruitful and multiply on the earth" (see 1:28).

NEVER AGAIN! GOD'S FIRST COVENANT WITH NOAH
Genesis 8:20–22

8:20 **Then Noah built an altar to the LORD, and took of every clean animal and of every clean bird, and offered burnt offerings on the altar.** ²¹ **And when the LORD smelled the pleasing odor, the LORD said in his heart, "I will never again curse the ground because of humankind, for the inclination of the human heart is evil from youth; nor will I ever again destroy every living creature as I have done.**
²² **As long as the earth endures,**
   seedtime and harvest, cold and heat,
summer and winter, day and night,
   shall not cease."

[8:20–22] In the J conclusion to the Flood story found in these verses, God acknowledges that the problem of the moral evil that lingers in the human heart cannot be solved by floodwaters or any other punitive act. In a magnificent donation to the world order, the Lord forswears any repetition of world destruction as an act of punishment and unilaterally commits to a providentially maintained framework within which life can exist forever (v. 22).

God's providential order will work no matter what the human response proves to be. There will be blessing in the regular cycles of life just as much as in God's mighty acts of salvation. Nevertheless, it is appropriate that people express their deep gratitude to the Lord for the continuation of life. God can and will be pleased with obedient and prayerful hearts, even as God was on this occasion of the first recorded sacrifice offered to God. This is the explanation of God's reaction to Noah's offering of "every clean animal" and "every clean bird" (v. 20) upon the fire altar. That "the LORD smelled the pleasing odor" does not mean that God anticipated a lip-smacking barbecue well prepared to satisfy a holy hunger. In the Gilgamesh Epic, the gods were practically starved for the food and drink for which they depended upon humankind. After the flood, when they smelled the pleasing odor, they "crowded like flies around the sacrifice." In the ritual acts of the Hebrew Bible, the expression "the LORD smelled the pleasing odor" has come to mean simply that God accepts the sacrifice as a sincere act of worship and thanksgiving (see also Ex. 29:18, 25, 41; Lev. 26:31).

A beloved hymn that captures the providential spirit in the promises that follow the deluge in both the J/E and P sources is "Great Is Thy Faithfulness," by Thomas O. Chisholm. God's covenant with Noah is echoed in verse 2:

> Summer and winter, and springtime and harvest,
>   Sun, moon, and stars in their courses above
> Join with all nature in manifold witness
>   To Thy great faithfulness, mercy and love.
> Great is Thy faithfulness!
>   Great is Thy faithfulness!
> Morning by morning new mercies I see;
>   All I have needed Thy hand hath provided;
> Great is Thy faithfulness, Lord, unto me.

Change the speaker from an individual to the people as a whole, and you have a response appropriate to the promises that God makes both in Genesis 8:22 (J/E) and in Genesis 9:11–17 (P). The theological term for the kind of ceaseless and unstinting care for the world promised by God here is providence, and providence is predicated upon God's faithfulness. For evidence of God's faithful, providential care we are referred both in the Flood story and in this hymn to the natural orders—the turning of the seasons, the certainty of planting and harvesting, the sun, moon, stars, and the never-failing rainbow in the sky. God's promises after the flood are among scripture's best witnesses to the reality of divine providence, ranking alongside the tradition of the manna. In Exodus 16:4, that miraculous sustenance given Israel by God in the wilderness is also described as a test of Israel's obedience. They are not to gather manna on the Sabbath but are to trust God to double the collection of the sixth day. Israel flunks the test on week one, but God never flunks the test. Through murmuring and rebellion, sin and apostasy, the manna keeps coming until they reach the borders of the Promised Land. That too is providence at work. "Great is thy faithfulness, Lord, unto me."

The world that God upholds by providential care is a world with no surprises, a dependable world and—because it is fruitful and nurturing—a blessed world in the best Old Testament sense. Nature working its cycles and seasons mirrors the peace of God that passes understanding and yet that is felt and understood in the very inmost cells of all living things. In God's providence we encounter a grace that moves even beyond the forgiveness of sin. Here is an answer to our deep dread of annihilation. Never again! The Creator brought the world into being out of chaos and nonbeing and the Creator will not allow chaos to reclaim it. It is the will of the sovereign and providential God that there be a human community alive and well and able to praise God from its fruitful home "while the earth remains."

WILL IT BE FIRE NEXT TIME?

They called old Norah a foolish man,
Oh! didn't it rain!
'Cause Norah built the ark upon dry land,
Oh! didn't it rain!

When it begun to rain,
Oh! didn't it rain!
Women and children began to scream,
Oh! didn't it rain!

It rain all day and it rain all night,
Oh! didn't it rain!
It rain 'til mountain top was out of sight,
Oh! didn't it rain!
God told Norah by the rainbow sign,
Oh! didn't it rain!
No more water but fire next time,
Oh! didn't it rain!

Judgment Day is a coming,
Coming in the Prophet's way;
Some folks say they never prayed a prayer,
They who will pray that day.

In this folk hymn, the link is made straightway between the great act of judgment of Noah's day and the coming judgment by fire. The knot was already tied in the New Testament:

They [the scoffers] deliberately ignore this fact, that by the word of God heavens existed long ago and an earth was formed out of water and by means of water, through which the world of that time was deluged with water and perished. But by the same word the present heavens and earth have been reserved for fire, being kept until the day of judgment and destruction of the godless. (2 Peter 3:5–7)

In the Yahwist's conclusion to the story of the Flood in Genesis 8:20–22, God explicitly vows never to destroy the world a second time. Yet the principle of "primeval times are recapitulated in end times" is at work. Biblical writers and Jews and Christians ever since have tended to see in the stories of creation prototypes for the future, both for the Judgment Day and the New Creation.

This tendency has practical implications for our time. In discussions of peacemaking and peacekeeping issues, church members have been known to say, "Maybe nuclear bombs are God's instruments for inflicting punishment on this sinful generation. After all, doesn't scripture say it will be fire next time?"

Well, yes, but that is not the conclusion to be drawn. First, the question accepts the notion that the modern governments and peoples who created the nuclear menace are incapable of undoing it. Events since the decline of the communist bloc have shown the fallacy of that argument.

Second, this argument suggests that scripture commits God to a future destruction of the world. While it is true that certain apocalyptic texts envision such a thing, we see that in one of the conclusions to the story of the first judgment, the watery one, God explicitly disavows any such possibility. Even granting that some texts imagine a second judgment drawn on analogy to the first (though by fire), they still place that instrument and that hour squarely in the hands of God and God alone. Any firestorm of human making can only be called sin magnified to its grossest proportions. That fire is ours, not God's. While it is true that in scripture God acts in history through the agency of human servants of God, such agents are commissioned by God to act. Furthermore, the perspectives of history and prophetic hindsight are required before the consensus can be reached that in this agent and not that one God was indeed at work. To justify the use of nuclear weapons by saying, "What can we do? God allows it, so this must be the 'fire next time,'" is both unscriptural and patently absurd.

OVER THE RAINBOW: GOD'S SECOND COVENANT WITH NOAH
Genesis 9:1–17

9:1 God blessed Noah and his sons, and said to them, "Be fruitful and multiply, and fill the earth. 2 The fear and dread of you shall rest on every animal of the earth, and on every bird of the air, on everything that creeps on the ground, and on all the fish of the sea; into your hand they are delivered. 3 Every moving thing that lives shall be food for you; and just as I gave you the green plants, I give you everything. 4 Only, you shall not eat flesh with its life, that is, its blood. 5 For your own lifeblood I will surely require a reckoning: from every animal I will require it and from human beings, each one for the blood of another, I will require a reckoning for human life.

    6 Whoever sheds the blood of a human,
        by a human shall that person's blood be shed;
    for in his own image
        God made humankind.

7 And you, be fruitful and multiply, abound on the earth and multiply in it."

8 Then God said to Noah and to his sons with him, 9 "As for me, I am establishing my covenant with you and your descendants after you, 10 and

with every living creature that is with you, the birds, the domestic animals, and every animal of the earth with you, as many as came out of the ark. ¹¹I establish my covenant with you, that never again shall all flesh be cut off by the waters of a flood, and never again shall there be a flood to destroy the earth." ¹²God said, "This is the sign of the covenant that I make between me and you and every living creature that is with you, for all future generations: ¹³I have set my bow in the clouds, and it shall be a sign of the covenant between me and the earth. ¹⁴When I bring clouds over the earth and the bow is seen in the clouds, ¹⁵I will remember my covenant that is between me and you and every living creature of all flesh; and the waters shall never again become a flood to destroy all flesh. ¹⁶When the bow is in the clouds, I will see it and remember the everlasting covenant between God and every living creature of all flesh that is on the earth." ¹⁷God said to Noah, "This is the sign of the covenant that I have established between me and all flesh that is on the earth."

[9:1–3] The Flood is over and God has already commanded the remnant of humanity as well as the rest of life to be about the business of repopulating the earth (see 8:15–19). Now the Priestly writer reiterates (v. 1) the command to fecundity that was first issued as a divine blessing on human sexuality in Genesis 1:28. Fecundity after the Flood has a difference, though, in that the "dominion" over the rest of the created order originally delivered to the first man and woman now explicitly includes permission to slaughter animals for food (v. 3). Reproductive energy will now be enhanced by lamb chops and chicken giblets.

[4–7] The new order comes with stipulations, however. In Genesis 8:22, the unilateral gift of providential protection that God offers through the J writer is perpetual. As the P writer understands it, the post-Flood renewal and enlargement of life has strings attached. God hands us a list of things that we must do. Human beings are responsible for maintaining their minimal side of a bilateral covenant arrangement. Bracketed by the far from onerous responsibility to "be fruitful and multiply" (vv. 1, 7), human beings must now honor the prohibitions against eating the blood of animals (v. 4) and shedding human blood (v. 6). The latter ban is motivated by reference to the Priestly concept of the divine image in humankind (1:26).

In Genesis 9:1–7 we see P's full statement of God's work of reconstruction. All the orders of life are put in place. The picture is consistent with P's conviction elsewhere that if the temple is in place, worship is conducted, sacrifice is offered, and the people honor God's commands, then the world is secure. The new privilege of eating meat involves a ritual act, for the carcass must be drained of blood (v. 4), which is its life. It would be possible to read verse 5 as saying that even animals will be held accountable for blood needlessly shed. With human beings, the special retaliatory sanction of verses 5–6 is put in place—when a human being sheds the blood of another, the killer's blood, too, shall be spilled.

In short, P not only elaborates the story of the Flood, but also brings it into line with his own vision of an ordered world in which obedience to God's will will insure a vital and viable human community. Note, by the way, that this entire story deals with humankind as a whole, and not just with Israel. Therefore, the covenant with Noah contained in chapter 9 is addressed to all the peoples of the earth. It has always been understood in Judaism that God holds all human beings accountable to this Noachic covenant, with its simple rules against eating blood and shedding human blood.

[8–17] God's unilateral promise that secures the world for human habitation is set forth in these verses. God undertakes to refrain from ever again destroying all life by a flood (v. 11), and puts the rainbow in the sky as a sign to all that this covenant is everlasting (v. 16).

The rainbow is the culmination of the passage. God can see it, and so can all of us. The story of the Flood ends by touching everyone's life. The rainbow signifies the everlasting assurance that God has given all human beings. We have space and time in which to live! In its own way, the rainbow also promises the comfort of the humdrum, of quiet, ordinary existence—the very kind of peaceful and stable life that the Priestly writers hoped to secure through the establishment of order in public and cultic life.

Before we leave Genesis 9:1–17, one more detail should be noted. In verse 16 God says, "When the bow is in the clouds, I will see it and remember the everlasting covenant between God and *every living creature* of all flesh that is on the earth." God's promise also touches the lives of the nuthatches and the hippopotami, it seems. They have a future too. It was not their sin that brought them ruin in the Flood, but ours. So also their future will be deeply intertwined with ours. God enters into an everlasting covenant with alligators as well as human beings, and guarantees their place within the providential order.

If you ask, How big is God's commitment to the future of the earth? the answer is, It is everywhere this way and everywhere that way, for all creatures and forever. God's providential care is both universal and eternal. God enacts it in the time of rain, which is beneficent moisture, and offers a public confirmation of this providential arrangement in the sign of the rainbow (vv. 8–17). All this is given in order to provide space for the proliferation of humankind (vv. 1–7).

This primeval narrative relates beautifully to the abiding Priestly concern for stability and order. The rainbow is the sign that all is well. The temple is another sign from a different era that all is well, and that God's presence abides in the midst of God's people. In the temple, God is manifested as light ("glory"). Is the rainbow another kind of "glory" of God that appears in order to show God's abiding presence in the great outdoor temple we call the earth? The only thing that keeps the beneficent rain from turning destructive is God's choice to be gracious. In fact, it is "amazing grace" alone that keeps the earth habitable at all for living creatures.

We are left at the end of Genesis 9 with questions such as these:

Is there any earthly order that is not established against the background of chaos?

How does this story prefigure end times, on the principle that "primeval time recapitulates end time"? Must destruction precede new life? Will it be fire next time, since God has forsworn water (9:11, P)? Or will there be no destructive end time, but providential care "as long as the earth endures" (8:21b, J)?

Is God the source of all things, both good and evil? The Flood that killed all but eight people in the world looks pretty bad to us, and yet it is described here as punishment for human sin. Christian doctrine has traditionally held that God is only good, but that human beings are capable both of good and of evil. In other words, ours is a theological monism and an anthropological or ethical dualism. Human beings, not God, are the source of evil. The Flood is not, therefore, an evil act, though from the human point of view it is a terrible and tragic one. As Genesis understands it, it is the appropriate and expected response by God to human sin—it is a destiny that the human community unleashed on itself. The story of the Flood is normative only in the sense that it says that sin brings consequences. It is not intended to teach that all floods and natural disasters are punishments for human sin.

An ancient people gave us a story about a universal catastrophe. Perhaps they did so because they were aware of the precariousness of existence. Therefore, an eternal (and worldwide) covenant is all the more wonderful a gift of God. Have we come full circle, and once again, under the shadow of the nuclear cloud, become keenly aware of the precariousness of existence? Once again an eternal covenant awaits its articulation, giving us the basis both for hope and for action. Surely it will have to include in its terms the same profound connection between the divinely commanded respect for human life and the possibility of blessed fruitfulness that, in its own way, this passage—the Noachic covenant—demonstrated long ago.

NOAH AND HIS SONS
Genesis 9:18–29

Ungainly texts abound in the book of Genesis. They involve the most elemental human passions, and they make no pretense that our spiritual ancestors were pure as the driven snow when it came to experiencing these elemental passions. Think of these texts: Cain commits fratricide against his brother Abel, the sons of God mate with the daughters of men and produce giants, Abraham tries to pass his wife off as his sister to save his own neck, Jacob deceives his father by making his hands hairy like Esau's, Joseph has to fight off the advances of Potiphar's wife. This text, Genesis 9:18–29, ranks with the others in ungainliness. Even though the world has been newly purified by the extinction of all but a select few creatures and human beings, no sooner has the land dried off than Noah and his sons are involved in drunkenness, sexual perversion, and anger. So it goes!

[9:18–19] The pericope provides a link between the single human family who survived the flood and all of the human community that sprang from them. The link is through the three sons of Noah—Shem, Ham, and Japheth. The writer of the saga does not, however, merely name names, but inserts right into the very fabric of things an evaluation of the relative merits of these earliest human clans. In short, this passage is also etiological in function in that it shows that the origins of later realities (those known to the Yahwist in his own time) are rooted in the beginnings of things.

[20] Here is the etiology of viniculture and its attendant evil, drunkenness. Noah, described here for the first time as a "man of the soil," plants a vineyard as his first act toward the restoration of agriculture. He then makes wine, gets drunk, and lies "uncovered" in his tent—that is to say, his genitals were exposed. The uncovering of the private parts was taboo in Israelite religion from beginning to end. (See, for example, Lev. 18:6–19; 20:17–21. In 1 Maccabees 1:14–15, the hellenized Jews of the second century B.C. surgically removed the marks of circumcision in order to run naked in the gymnasium with the gentiles.)

Ham, the father of Canaan, then sees "the nakedness of his father." In itself, this might have been an unavoidable incident. He blunders into the patriarchal tent and is shocked to see the old man sprawled out there. Or perhaps there is more to it than that. Perhaps he intentionally violated the taboo or even engaged in some kind of incestuous homosexual act. As the later prophetic writings make clear, Israel deemed Canaan capable of such things constantly. The Canaanite fertility religion, with its rites of sacred prostitution, orgiastic worship, and so on, led the prophets to inveigh against Israelite participation in Canaanite cultural norms (see, for example, Hos. 4:12–14). No doubt the same thing was true in the time of the Yahwist. So it is that the Yahwist projects back into antiquity the perfidy of Canaan and provides an occasion at the very beginning of history for Noah, the ancestor of us all, to relegate Canaan to the status of a cursed people. Shem and Japheth, who are the traditional ancestors of the Semitic peoples—including Israel itself and the Europeans—come off better. Having learned from Canaan of their father's plight, they contrive to cover his nakedness without ogling him in his drunken state.

[25–29] The rewards and punishments appear in the anathema and blessings that Noah pronounces upon his sons when he awakens and learns of their behavior. Shem comes out as number one, with Japheth as a guest or resident alien in the tents of Shem. Canaan is condemned to the role of slave to his brothers. As in the case of the curses pronounced against Adam, Eve, and the serpent, readers are left with the conclusion that all the peoples of the world have been given permanent statuses relative to one another by virtue of the behavior of single individuals in deep antiquity.

ISRAEL AND CANAAN

Imbedded in our biblical tradition are texts that, if not properly understood, have the potential to create terrible problems. Such texts cry out to be seen against the background of the historical realities of the community that wrote them, lest they become a pretext for oppression or injustice against peoples long after the time of their origin. This text is one of these. In fact, it was used as a basis for enslaving Africans. Ancient religious and ethnic hatreds can be provided with holy authority by those who would misuse scripture. Each in their own way, Bosnian Serbs, Croats, and Muslims appeal to ancient precedents to relegate their rivals to inferior status and even to drive them away or murder them. In the United States, the same was done to slaves and Native Americans. This text reflects the rivalry between ethnic communities in Israel of the early monarchical period. Israel had had to struggle to maintain its identity as it emerged slowly into existence in Canaan. No doubt many of the Israelites of the tenth century were in fact descendants of Canaanites of the twelfth and thirteenth. In that awful struggle to move from the extreme margin of being a nonpeople or an incipient people into the full status of nationhood (albeit as a small and somewhat vulnerable nation), Israel staked out its claim to precedence over the other tribes with which it shared the land of Canaan.

That Israel was born and survived and gave us the lofty ethical teachings of the prophets and the messianic hope that laid the groundwork for Christianity are facts for which we believers can give thanks to God. To the degree that texts such as this one, ungainly and even tragic as they may be, contributed to that survival, they played a role in the divine economy. We must not say this facilely, however. This text has the potential to lead to bigotry and prejudice and no doubt has done so. Let it do so no more. Let there be no judgment among the peoples that by primeval decree one group is inferior to another. But let us also acknowledge the torturous path and the great risks that God took in electing to effect the divine purpose in history in an incarnate way, using human agents and human communities. From a start as slow as this one, God moves us toward the day when all the peoples of the earth will acknowledge that they are the children of one Creator and that they belong to one worldwide human community that can live in shalom.

7. The Human Family after the Flood
Genesis 10:1–32

Before the digression of the drunkenness of Noah (9:20–28), the story of the Flood ended with these words: "[Shem, Ham, and Japheth] were the sons of Noah, and from these the whole world branched out" (9:19, JPS). Chapter 10 is the story (for, in fact, a genealogy is a type of narrative) of that branching out. It happens before our very eyes, like a computer graphic of exponential growth. Human regeneration occurs. It occurs not by magic or by special acts of the gods, but by the normal process of birth, generation by generation. Chapter 10 is a branched or segmented genealogy, as is appropriate for a story of branching out (see the discussion on biblical genealogies at Gen. 4:17–26). The intention of the genealogy is not to carry the reader to an important person at the end of the series of generations but rather to establish kinship relationships among a whole table of descendants. This chapter has to be taken alongside Genesis 11:10–32, which is a retelling of the genealogy springing from Shem that introduces the chronological element that is missing in chapter 10. Between these two genealogies is the brief legend of the Tower of Babel (11:1–9), which rises up as an explanation of the greatest calamity that ever befell the cause of human unity—the separation of the languages and the ensuing impossibility of communication.

Chapter 10 is a table of nations that contains the names of seventy people. There are many difficulties with this list. For example, Sheba and Havilah are said to be descendants both of Cush (v. 7), the son of Ham, and of Joktan, the great-grandson of Shem (vv. 28–29). Language is mentioned as a factor in the list, but does not seem to have affected its organization because Canaan, a people that spoke a northwest Semitic tongue very similar to Hebrew, is classed as one of the Hamitic peoples along with Egypt. (This is necessitated, of course, by the polemical treatment of Canaan in 9:18–27, and his association with Ham there.) The Elamites, on the other hand, are included among the Semites (10:22), though their language was not a Semitic one. Cush seems to mean at least two different things in the list in that some of the Cushites are African peoples (vv. 6–7) and others are Mesopotamian (vv. 10–14).

A number of the names in this list are given in the plural form (v. 16), making clear that they are not individuals but whole groups. Many of the other names are those of name-giving ancestors—Egypt, Canaan, Tarshish, Kittim, and probably most of the rest. So it is not really a family tree but rather a collection of the names of peoples and their associated cities. The fact that it contains seventy names indicates that the writers intended to suggest an absolutely comprehensive figure. The figure seventy elsewhere in the Bible suggests the totality of a community (see 46:27, the household of Jacob that went down to Egypt). In other words, everybody is here. Because it is written from an Israelite perspective, it is organized so that the least interesting and important branches of the family are given first. It then moves toward the historically and geographically more contiguous groupings. The same pattern is followed in Genesis 4:17–25, where the dead lineage of Cain gives rise in chapter 5 to the living lineage of Seth. Similarly, in Genesis 25:12–18, Ishmael's lineage, which goes nowhere of interest, is cleared out of the way before the really interesting lineage of Isaac is set forth.

The chapter falls, then, into the following pattern: v. 1, opening summary formula; vv. 2–5, Japheth; vv. 6–20, Ham; vv. 21–31, Shem; v. 32, concluding summary formula. With each of the major blocks, Japheth, Ham, and Shem, there is a closing mention of territory and the acknowledgment of the families, languages, and nations that spring from these stems. Here and there are annotations and expansions, such as the lengthy discussion of Nimrod (vv. 8–12) and the shifting occupation zones of the Canaanites (vv. 18b–19). Overall, the impression is of a highly schematic table designed to give a comprehensive and prioritized account of all peoples originating in kinship relationship with one another and remaining in essential unity under one sovereign creator.

[10:1] The last verse prior to my discussion of Noah's drunkenness (9:19) spoke of the branching out of the descendants of Noah over the earth. This verse identifies the branching out as occurring in the time after the Flood. In the Bible, as in other Near Eastern texts, the time after the Flood begins to take on more of the character of real history. We will see the other evidence of that in the greatly reduced life spans of the post-Flood communities in Genesis 11:10–32.

[2–5] The Japhethites live in an arc described across the map of the ancient world north and west of Israel. In other words, they are the ancestors of the people of Europe and Asia Minor. Without attempting to identify all fourteen of the nations derived from Japheth, some are worth noting. Gomer, or the Cimmerians, were a people of the Caucasus who made incursions into Asia Minor in the eighth and seventh centuries B.C. Magog has not been located geographically, but its association with Gog in Ezekiel 39:1 and elsewhere points to Asia Minor. Gog may be identified with King Gugu, known from cuneiform sources as a king of Lydia and predecessor of Croesus. Madai seems to refer to the Medes who inhabited the mountainous country on the east of the Tigris-Euphrates valley, now in northwestern Iran. Cyrus, the founder of the Persian Empire in the sixth century B.C., was of Median origin. He got his start by becoming the king of the Medes and defeating his contemporary, the Lydian Croesus. He is, of course, the hero of the liberation of the Jews from Babylonian captivity (see Isa. 45:1–7). Javan is the Hebrew name for Greece, and is a corruption of the word Ionia. The descendants of Gomer include Ashkenaz (originally a people of Indo-European origin in the region of the Caspian and Black Seas, but later identified by the Jews with eastern Europe and Germany) and Togarmah (which Ezek. 27:14 and 38:6 associate with Asia Minor). When taken together, the impression that these are peoples to the north and to the west of Israel is strengthened.

The descendants of Javan also inhabit western areas. Tarshish is usually identified with Tartessus on the Iberian Peninsula and with Spain itself—essentially the westernmost locale on the horizon of ancient Israel. (The "Tarshish type" ships mentioned in 1 Kings 22:48 would be long distance haulers.) Kittim originally referred to inhabitants of Kition on Cyprus, but in time it came to mean the entire island of Cyprus. It was inhabited originally by Minoans, then by Mycenaeans, then by Greeks. In the Dead Sea Scrolls, the Kittim seem to be citizens of the then-prevailing world empire, Rome. Finally, the Dodanim, or as the NRSV reads, Rodanim, following ancient versions, probably refers to the island of Rhodes. The link, then, of these descendants to "the maritime nations" (JPS) or the "coastland peoples" (NRSV) is quite apparent.

[6–20] The Hamites inhabit an area described by an arc reaching from Mesopotamia across Egypt and down into Sudan. Put (sometimes rendered Libya by the Septuagint; see Ezek. 27:10; 30:5), gives rise to no further descendants. Cush and Canaan, on the other hand, are downright prolific. In the Bible, Cush is usually associated with Egypt and particularly with Nubia in upper Egypt, north of modern Sudan. Such an identification fits at least that descendant of Cush called Havilah. According to Genesis 2:11–12, one of the rivers of the Garden of Eden, Pishon, wound its way through the land of Havilah, "where the gold is." The primary source of gold for Egypt was Nubia ("the gold of that land is good," 2:12). Seba is also linked with Egypt and Cush in Isaiah 43:3 and

45:14. Other names among the descendants of Cush mentioned in verse 7 seem more associated with northern Arabia. On the other hand, the Cush who became the father of Nimrod (v. 8) is not Nubian at all, but clearly is associated with the Mesopotamian region. Some have identified this other Cush with the royal city of Kish, where, according to the Mesopotamian flood story, kingship resumed after the flood. This Cush bore Nimrod, a great man and the founder of all the greatest cities of Mesopotamia mentioned in verses 10–12—Babel, Erech, Accad, Nineveh, and others. Various attempts have been made to identify Nimrod with one of the early Mesopotamian kings, such as Naram-Sin of Akkad, who ruled for fifty years during the third millennium B.C. Micah 5:6 shows that the biblical tradition consistently identified Nimrod with northern Mesopotamia or Assyria. The interesting thing about him here is that the narrator offers a proverbial saying, "Like Nimrod a mighty hunter before the LORD" (vv. 8–9). Whoever Nimrod was, he was not outside the interests of Yahweh. In the view of the Priestly genealogist, he lived out his life of greatness by the grace of the creator of all peoples.

The peoples (all names given in the plural) affiliated with Egypt in verses 13–14 are largely unknown with the exception of the Caphtorim. Cognate terms in neighboring languages suggest this name refers to the island of Crete. According to Deuteronomy 2:23, Caphtorim settled in Gaza, which as other texts show was the major center of the Philistines during the period of the Judges. If we link the Caphtorim with the Philistines, everything falls into place except the tie with Egypt. The general assumption is that the Philistines were sea peoples who were part of the great migration of Macedonian or Hellenic peoples to the east during the fourteenth century B.C. They had no ethnic connection with the Egyptians, though Egypt may have controlled Crete and certainly controlled Gaza during many periods. The NRSV corrects the Hebrew text to make explicit the link of the Caphtorim or Crete with the Philistines.

Canaan should not be linked with Ham because the Canaanites spoke a Semitic language. In fact, there is reason to believe that they contributed significantly to the makeup of the population of the emergent Israel during the period of the Judges. However, Canaan was under Egyptian control from the Middle Bronze Age down to the simultaneous appearance of Israel and the sea peoples and again at many other times in history. Furthermore, it was in the interest of this writer to keep Canaan separate from the clan of Israel itself. So Canaan becomes a Hamitic tribe.

The peoples listed as descendants of Canaan begin with Sidon. During the fifteenth through the eleventh centuries, Sidon, the dominant seaport in Phoenicia, is often synonymous with that land (Deut. 3:9; Josh. 13:4, 6). Only by the tenth century B.C. was it displaced by Tyre in importance. Heth, the other child of Canaan mentioned in verse 15, no doubt is the ancestor from whom the Hittites derive their name. They actually inhabited an area in Asia Minor and northern Syria and had neither linguistic nor ethnic ties with the Canaanites. The other tribes and peoples mentioned include "the Amorites," almost a generic term for west Semitic peoples, who, beginning about 2000 B.C., infiltrated the entire Fertile Crescent. Others are little known, though the references in verses 17–18 to the Arkites and others refer to five Syrian cities north and east of the present city of Tripoli, Lebanon. After verse 18 says that "the families of the Canaanites spread abroad," verse 19 gives a more restricted territorial description of the Canaanite area. However, it does not correspond to other biblical accounts of the extent of Canaan. No other biblical text ever gives Canaan the city of Sidon, for example, but these texts suggest that the writer was very aware that Phoenicia, the larger area, and Canaan, the more restricted one, shared many cultural similarities.

[21–31] From the writer's point of view, the last section of this table of the nations is the most important because it is the line that gave birth in time to Terah (11:27), who was the father of Abram, who was the founder of Israel. The twenty-six nations that descend from Shem include thirteen largely affiliated with Mesopotamia. Eber is singled out as the descendant of Shem, that son of Noah whose children will be most important, and because his name can easily be understood as equal to "Hebrew." Indeed, as Genesis 11:10–26 makes clear, it is through Eber that the first people actually called Hebrews—Abraham, Isaac, and Jacob—descend. Thirteen nations or places are also affiliated with Joktan, the son of Eber (10:26–30). Many of these can be linked with Yemen and the Hadhramaut region of southern Arabia (mentioned in the Hebrew word *hazarmavath*, v. 26). With this closing segment of the table of nations, Israel acknowledges its immediate kinship with the Arab peoples, even as it denies immediate kinship with the Canaanites.

[32] The table of the nations closes with a formula summarizing the expansion of Noah's family over all the earth.

The genealogical record of Genesis 10 comes as good news to Jews and Christians who want to know how far and over whom the sovereignty of God extends. The answer given here: Everywhere and over everyone! The seventy peoples listed in this table are meant to tell the reader that no place and no tribe lies beyond the bounds of the Lord's care. Almost as a further emphasis of the point, Cushite Nimrod is presented as a Yahwist, for he is called "a mighty hunter before the LORD" (v. 9). Readers should bear in mind that listed among the seventy nations are all of those against whom Israel struggled most desperately during the course of its history: Egypt, Assyria, Babylon, and especially, Canaan. Yet never did Israel require a ruling from the high priest that the Moabites, Edomites, Hittites, or Arabs were real people and not beasts of some kind (unlike the Spaniards, who sought from the pope a ruling on whether the native people whom Columbus encountered in Hispaniola were real people or not). Chapter 10 makes clear that the Priestly writers understood that from its beginning the human race was a large family with kinship relationships. The disunity that will result in chapter 11 from the sin of the generation of the Tower of Babel will disrupt that unity but will never destroy it. What ultimate peace will require is nothing more than a reunion of that which was from the beginning one large, diverse, and increasingly interesting family.

8. Human Solidarity Gone Awry
Genesis 11:1–9

The story of the Tower of Babel explains a number of things. It tells about the origins of the many languages of the world. It also gives the meaning of the proper name Babel. It explains why towers, some lying in ruins, dotted the Babylonian landscape. It offers a theological critique of human self-assertion, of people making their own name great. It may even explain why nations, ethnic groups, and individuals are alienated from one another. It tells why humankind is scattered everywhere.

Generally we have been taught that this story is directed against human pride above all, and that it condemns the attempt by people to storm heaven. Should we now reassess the Tower of Babel legend to take it as a polemic against urban culture and technology? Perhaps it is an attack on the imperialism of the greatest power of the world, whose very name, Babel, in the mind of ancient Israel was synonymous with oppression.

How shall we decide among these many meanings of the story of the Tower? Must it have only one meaning? Why not all of these? Are all of these possibilities aspects of a full meaning of the story? Are some of these possible meanings more important than others? Is there an independent, external test of some kind that would establish the correct line of interpretation for this story? Or has the story undergone a constant enrichment of meaning as it has moved from its original oral, independent form, on into the Yahwist source, then into the setting of the Pentateuch, and finally into the canon of scripture as a whole?

If, as one suspects was the case, this story was originally intended to explain why there are so many languages, it very quickly ceased to work at that level. Such a teaching will not pass the truth test—a tower incident is not why there are so many languages. We know that; ancient Israel probably knew it too. In the course of time they put the story to better, more profound use.

Before we plunge into a close examination of the text, however, a simple question needs to be asked: Could a monument to successful collective human effort such as the Tower of Babel ever actually have stood in ancient times? In fact, there was an impressive one in Palestine itself, though its date is so ancient that it seems unlikely that any memory of it lingered on in ancient Israel. This is a twenty-five-foot-tall defensive tower with an interior circular staircase found near the bottom of the mound of buried Jericho by the British archaeologist Dame Kathleen Kenyon in the 1950s. The burned timbers of a house adjoining the tower can be dated to about 7000 B.C. Here was a "primitive" community that did not yet know how to make pottery or communicate in writing, yet was socially organized enough to build a massive tower as a defense against some evidently well-organized enemy. A more nearly contemporary tower mentioned in scripture was at Shechem, and was allegedly large enough to shelter the one thousand men and women who were trapped there by Abimelech, the son of Gideon (Judg. 9:46-49). Doubtless towers crowned the defensive perimeters of Jerusalem and many other cities of ancient Israel and of its enemies (including Thebez, from the tower of which Abimelech was brained by a millstone dropped on him by a woman of the place). Each of these represented a significant collective effort, each represented the claim of a *name*, each signified an effort by a people to secure themselves against dispersal and destruction.

No towers were more famous and no ruins more dramatic, however, than the ziggurats of ancient Babylon. Not only did they testify to the wealth and social cohesion of their respective city-states, but as cultic installations they offered to the kings of cities such as Babylon, Erech, Eridu, and Ur the possibility of holding intercourse with the gods. They were the doorways to heaven. Extensive remnants of them still survived in the time of the Yahwist and may have served as confirmation to the tale coming down by word of mouth from the preceding generations in Israel. The general wisdom of modern scholars is that one of these was the tower that served as the model for the primeval structure of Genesis 11:1-9.

11:1 **Now the whole earth had one language and the same words. 2 And as they migrated from the east, they came upon a plain in the land of Shinar and settled there. 3 And they said to one another, "Come, let us make bricks, and burn them thoroughly." And they had brick for stone, and bitumen for mortar. 4 Then they said, "Come, let us build ourselves a city, and a tower with its top in the heavens, and let us make a name for ourselves; otherwise we shall be scattered abroad upon the face of the whole earth." 5 The LORD came down to see the city and the tower, which mortals had built. 6 And the LORD said, "Look, they are one people, and they have all one**

language; and this is only the beginning of what they will do; nothing that they propose to do will now be impossible for them. ⁷ Come, let us go down, and confuse their language there, so that they will not understand one another's speech." ⁸ So the LORD scattered them abroad from there over the face of all the earth, and they left off building the city. ⁹ Therefore it was called Babel, because there the LORD confused the language of all the earth; and from there the LORD scattered them abroad over the face of all the earth.

[11:1] The story of the Tower of Babel begins by asserting that the whole earth had "the same words." Though the Hebrew has also been understood to say that the whole earth had "a few words"—as if the tower were built during a primitive stage of social development when speech consisted of grunts and "ughs"—the notion of a single vocabulary that allowed for free communication among all peoples is vital to the sense of the story. This is not early anthropology. Instead, it offers a wistful vision of a human solidarity that ought to have existed at the front end of the rainbow: No alienation resulting from misunderstanding speech interrupted the vast human cooperative effort about to get underway here. The simple, folkloristic style of the narrative, well established by this opening remark, shows that this story is cast in the genre of legend—a story about human origins set in primeval times.

[2–3] This early, unified human community moves "from the east" to the "land of Shinar." The footnote in the NRSV, "migrated eastward," shows that the Hebrew text itself is not clear about the direction of this migration. In any event, from the Jerusalemite point of view of the writer, all these things happened far toward the rising sun in the legendary lands of Eden, Ararat, and Shinar.

The writers of the Old Testament generally affiliated Shinar with Babel and other sites near today's Baghdad in central Iraq (see 10:10). Late in the Hebrew canon (Dan. 1:2) Shinar and Babylon become synonymous, and the Greek Old Testament (Septuagint) translates "the land of Shinar" in Zechariah 5:11 simply as "the land of Babylon." As verse 4 shows, however, the Shinar/Babel/eastward connection, while certainly the stuff of legend, is not without a basis in historical and geographical knowledge.

For example, the story says that they used "bitumen" (tar, pitch) for mortar to bind together the mud bricks of the tower (v. 3). In an era before oil wells, would it have been possible anywhere in the world to obtain pitch right off the earth's surface? The answer is Yes. Though the oil table appears to have dropped worldwide, in prehistoric times, even in North America, great pools of crude oil sat on the surface. The La Brea tar pits in California, for example, were natural traps for saber-toothed tigers and woolly mammoths. What was true of California was even more true for the Middle East. The Latin name sometimes employed for the Dead Sea by Josephus and Pliny was *Mare Asphaltitis*, suggesting that pitch had come to the earth's surface in the Great Rift Valley, which at the Dead Sea lies some 1292 feet below sea level. As we have already seen, the ancient Greek historian Herodotus claimed that clumps of asphalt floated down the rivers of ancient Mesopotamia. In Genesis 11, then, we have a memory of an authentic phenomenon of the ancient world of the Bible, a memory that was doubtless communicated by word of mouth over many generations to Judeans living far away from the scene of the story.

[4] But this is no longer really a story about ancient towers and clumps of tar, if that was ever its primary intention. With the speech of the people in verse 4 the point of the story begins to emerge for the first time. The purpose of the collective effort of those who begin to build on the plain of Shinar is not to erect a glorious work of architecture and not to storm heaven. The purpose is more desperate and daring than that: "Let us make a name for ourselves; otherwise we shall be scattered." The people want to become a self-sufficient elite who are free from any need to answer to others. They want to make a name so that they can say to their challengers, "Who are you?" A great reputation is a self-defense mechanism comparable socially and spiritually to what the tower itself would have been militarily. One would have thought that the South African government might willingly have disposed of Nelson Mandela during the years of his imprisonment. Why didn't they? No doubt it was because his name was so well known. It appears from verse 4 that the purpose of this entire tower project is the building up of the greatness of the *name* of the human community to the point that God could not touch it without risking a major scandal on earth and in the heavenly places alike.

Even making a great name is not a deed done for its own sake, however. It is only a means to an even more fundamental end, namely, that human solidarity be secured forever—"otherwise we shall be scattered abroad upon the face of the whole earth." The great cooperative social effort of building the city and the tower leads to the establishment of a high sense of group identity for the human community. Isn't that in fact what a great reputation accomplishes? Strong group identity in its turn serves as a bulwark against self-interest, factionalism, ethnicity, and all else that divides and weakens the human community. No socialist of our time could have expressed the vision of human cooperation and collectivity more simply than did the builders of the tower so long ago!

[5] "The LORD came down to see." Does verse 5 suggest that God is nearsighted? It seems more likely that a delicious irony is intended. From

up there wherever the house of God is, the mighty work of human hands is a nearly invisible speck! The Great Wall, built to secure China from its enemies to the north, is said to be the only human structure visible from the surface of the moon. Maybe God can see the Great Wall from afar, but this tower, designed to secure human autonomy and solidarity against all opponents, could be seen by the King of the Universe only upon much closer inspection. How is that for putting things in perspective! One is reminded of the words of Psalm 2:1–4:

> Why do the nations conspire,
>   and the peoples plot in vain?
> The kings of the earth set themselves,
>   and the rulers take counsel together,
>   against the LORD and his anointed, saying,
> "Let us burst their bonds asunder,
>   and cast their cords from us."
> He who sits in the heavens laughs;
>   the LORD has them in derision.

[6–7] Verses 6–7 suppose that the Lord has returned to the divine council to give a speech that no human being could have heard. Once again God uses the plural ("let us go down," v. 7) to address this heavenly assembly (see commentary on 1:26–31). Surely we have here elements of a myth (a story about primeval events that occur in the divine realm outside the universe of real human experience [see introduction]). However, the myth is not told fully for its own sake. Unlike other ancient peoples, Israel preferred not to speculate on the activities of the divine beings in heaven. Though the ancestors of the stories of Genesis 1–11, including the story of the tower, may once have done so, they no longer do. Now they are "faded myths." The things that the heavenly beings did and said that day in the divine council are no longer of importance, and God's own words are reduced to a spare minimum. The transactions of God within the divine realm have here been incorporated into the lengthy saga about human beginnings, human frailty, and the divine-human relationship.

The terrible response of God and the divine council to the human effort to achieve unbreakable solidarity is to "confuse their language . . . so that they will not understand one another's speech." The fundamental basis of unity is undercut at a stroke, and the most profound source of alienation, disunity, and strife is put in place by the simple device of rendering the spoken words of one person unintelligible to another. One senses that the confusion involves more than the simple introduction of diverse languages. Not understanding the speech of another might even include not understanding the speech of one who speaks the

same language; in short, it might include not really listening, not com-
prehending, not really caring to get it. Walter Brueggemann elaborates:
"Not listening is related to death in a relationship. To fail to listen
means declaring the other party null and void. A society that suffers
failed speech, as in our text, not only cannot build towers, it cannot
believe promises, cannot trust God, cannot be human" (Brueggemann,
103). "I hear you, but I can't make out a word you're saying." In that
hostile remark is summed up the essence of alienation.

[8–9] When the Lord's decision turns to action, chaos results. God
kicks the anthill over and the little creatures are now forced to run in
every direction. From God's point of view, the chaos is not all bad. After
all, the fact that they are scattered abroad "over the face of all the earth"
fits with the original divine plan that human beings should "be fruitful
and multiply, and fill the earth and subdue it" (1:28). One of the scrip-
tural environments that now gives the story of the Tower of Babel fuller
meaning is the theme of the spread of humankind over the known world
after the Flood. That theme is clearly sounded in the verse just preceding our story: "The nations spread abroad on the earth after the flood"
(10:32). They are now going to be pioneers, pushing ever outward into
uncharted reaches of the world (and, in our time, the cosmos). As
Brueggemann puts it, "The scattering God wills is that life should be
peopled everywhere by his regents, who are attentive to all parts of creation, working in his image to enhance the whole creation, to bring 'each
in its kind' to full fruition and productivity" (Brueggemann, p. 99). They
could never have done that had they all withdrawn into the single city
and clustered around the mighty symbol of human solidarity.

But the punishment wrapped in the chaos is that they cannot (or will
not) understand each other anymore. Had they been willing to march
forth as God's pioneers in obedience to God's purpose to fill the earth
and till and keep it, they might have done so in peace and in a true unity
that could have handled even their dispersion. But no, they have to be
driven out, away from their obsessive obelisk to autonomy. Therefore,
they can neither work together nor trust each other anymore. No angel
with a flaming sword is even necessary to guard the way back to the
building site; now they are alienated, and cannot bear to be together
again. They had said, "Come, let us build . . . and let us make a name for
ourselves." In perfect antithesis to this human attempt to solidify a position of impregnable autonomy and power, God said, "Come, let us go
down, and confuse their language there." The result was a permanent
crippling of human autonomy and power, the setting of group against
group, the inauguration of a human history full of Vietnams and
Lebanons and Northern Irelands and Yugoslavias. The devastating judg-

ment rendered at Babel is still with us. Our languages our still confused, we still do not listen to each other. Each ethnic group now busies itself building its own little minitower to secure itself from its little neighboring group. Little Babels pop up everywhere.

In verse 9 we encounter another explanation of a name. Through the play on the words *balal* ("confuse") and *Babel*, the writer links to Babylon and its tower the origin of diverse human languages and, with it, the origin of confusion, disorder, and alienation within the human race. The etymology is not linguistically valid; nothing would encourage an "L" to turn into a "B" over many years of usage of the word. The name *Babel* actually means something like "entrance (*bab-*) of God (*el*)." The place was probably called Babel first, and then, as this legend emerged in Israel's theological account of human origins, a secondary significance was assigned to the name. For the Jewish and Christian traditions, however, the meaning of Babel was henceforth and forever linked with the babble of voices that give daily reminder of that most awful judgment handed down by God upon the human community in the beginning of time. The sentence is this: No longer will we be able to act together with singleness of purpose because we do not comprehend each other's meaning and do not trust each other.

REFLECTIONS ON HUMAN ALIENATION

Of the several possible meanings of this story suggested at the outset, the theme of alienation has emerged as paramount. At its most profound level, this story places back in primeval times the beginning of our tragic human propensity not to get along with each other and with God. This meaning will turn out to be a major feature of the plot of the book of Genesis and indeed of the Bible as a whole. It also points to one of theology's most abiding issues. Three theses support these claims.

Fall, punishment, grace. The first thesis is derived from the Genesis commentary of German scholar Gerhard von Rad. No matter what independent origin in the realm of myth each of the legends of the primeval history might have had, as ordered and retold by the Yahwist they now form an intelligible sequence that "is characterized on the human side by an increase in sin to avalanche proportions" (von Rad, 148). There is not one "fall" in Genesis 1–11, but at least four, each more serious than the former (see commentary on 3:20–21). The disobedience in the garden is followed by fratricide, only to be followed by the angel marriages that preceded the Flood and finally by the human attempt at the Tower of Babel to achieve autonomy from God.

Each of these crises is followed by God's punishment, and, as the chasm between God and the human community grows wider, each punishment is more severe than the last. Expulsion from Eden is followed by the banishment and homelessness of Cain that is followed in turn by the drowning of almost

all living things and finally by the most terrible punishment of all—the disso-
lution of human unity and the consequent alienation of all people. But with
each "fall" and each judgment there is also an act of grace, a providential move
by God to preserve the human race. Adam and Eve are clothed against the
harshness of life outside of Eden; Cain receives his mysterious sign of divine
protection; a tiny community of people and animals floats above the Flood and
starts life anew when the waters recede. Only in the case of the tower is there
no evident act of grace, no move by God to restore the shattered relationship
with humankind. Does this positioning of the story of the tower not suggest
that the Yahwist intended us to see it as the climactic crisis, and the reality of
alienation it portrays as the most serious threat to human happiness? At the
end of the primeval history we are left with these questions: "Is God's relationship to the nations now finally broken; is God's gracious forbearance now
exhausted; has God rejected the nations in wrath forever?" (von Rad, 149).

The answer to these questions is, of course, No. But the act of grace that
responds to the tragedy of the tower is disclosed only after we leave the
primeval history altogether. In God's call to one pagan of Haran named
Abram to go and become a focal point of reconciliation in the world (12:1–3)
is the humble act of grace by which hope for the future is disclosed. A discussion of this tiny answer to the huge sin of Babel will be the proper subject matter of our commentary on those verses.

The quest to put things right again. The rest of the Bible is the story of how
the human community may finally overcome the curse of Babel and get back
together again. For years, Christian preachers and exegetes have understood
that the story of the birth of the church at Pentecost told in Acts 2:1–13 holds
forth the promise that the confusion of tongues and the consequent alienation
of people from one another is not a permanent blight on humankind. When
the devout Jews from every nation heard the spirit-filled apostles speaking in
other languages, they were amazed and they asked,

> Are not all these who are speaking Galileans? And how is it that we hear,
> each of us, in our own native language? Parthians, Medes, Elamites, and
> residents of Mesopotamia, Judea and Cappadocia, Pontus and Asia,
> Phrygia and Pamphylia, Egypt and the parts of Libya belonging to
> Cyrene, and visitors from Rome, both Jews and proselytes, Cretans and
> Arabs—in our own languages we hear them speaking about God's deeds
> of power. (Acts 2:7–11)

The apostles were not speaking in that ecstatic utterance known as glosso-
lalia, but in words that made sense to visitors from different lands. They were
actually communicating so that people could listen and understand. And they
spoke about "God's deeds of power," the very basis upon which new and rec-
onciled lives could be built.

In short, Acts 2 gives us a foretaste of that day when the reign of God is
fully manifested among us and the curse of Babel will be no more. As a preview of a "peaceable kingdom," it points to the same age at which the prophets

pointed when they foresaw a day when destructive alienation between people and with the natural order would cease, when "They will not hurt or destroy on all my holy mountain" (Isa. 11:9), and when "nation shall not lift up sword against nation, neither shall they learn war any more" (Micah 4:3).

But Acts 2 is not the end of the biblical story; it is only the story of the birthday of the church. For the eschatological vision of the full manifestation of the reign of God on earth, we have to go to Revelation 21:22–26:

> I saw no temple in the city, for its temple is the Lord God the Almighty and the Lamb. And the city has no need of sun or moon to shine on it, for the glory of God is its light, and its lamp is the Lamb. The nations will walk by its light, and the kings of the earth will bring their glory into it. Its gates will never be shut by day—and there will be no night there. People will bring into it the glory and the honor of the nations.

The foreign nations are free to walk into the New Jerusalem envisioned here, led by the "kings of the earth," who elsewhere in the New Testament are the enemies of the gospel (see, for example, Acts 4:26; Rev. 6:15; 17:2; 19:19). The fact that "its gates will never be shut by day" is all the more dramatic when one reads the full context of this passage in Revelation 20–21, for nothing has survived the judgment of God except the New Jerusalem with its saints, and the lake of fire. People coming out of the lake of fire with the smell of judgment still clinging to them bring into the kingdom of God all their glory and lay it before the Lamb. This is a magnificent vision of the very opposite of Babel! All the alienation and dispersion that flowed from the human grab for unshakable solidarity are now undone. Now even hell gives up its diverse, scattered peoples and all harmoniously and gladly gather before the throne of God. They bring their special gifts; they remain diverse and variously gifted. But they are alienated no more. The Bible culminates in a vision of the putting right in end times of all that went wrong in the earliest times of human existence. "Primeval history is recapitulated in end time" (see commentary on 1:1–2:4a).

If all peoples find peace around the throne of the Lamb in the end, then it is not the name we make for ourselves that makes possible our true solidarity and security, but rather the gracious welcome of God. The protective dome over us is God's gift; that is what counts. For Americans living at the beginning of a new millennium, that faith has practical application to questions of technology, national defense, and peace.

Technology as tower. For many years, Americans had the sense that we were isolated from the troubles of the rest of the world. We were like innocent children living in our own new garden of Eden, free to pursue our destiny on our own without being touched by the corrupting influences of various old worlds. Then all of a sudden we catapulted into the nuclear age. The vast seas and skies that once kept us innocent and free no longer mattered. We found ourselves on the front line along with all the rest of the world's struggling, angry, alienated peoples.

Along came a proposal to put an antimissile defense dome overhead that would shut out the threat and restore the safety of our continent and the innocence of our Eden. Once again we could live in safety, without having to mess with the masses and their grief and anger and hatred of us. Many embraced this effort to "make a name for ourselves [lest we] be scattered" and dead. But there was a fatal flaw in this peace shield. What if just one got through?

This is not to say that good technology cannot provide sóme of the means necessary to control the dangers of bad technology. But by our own machines can we assure our own invulnerability? Is a Patriot missile the only answer to a Scud missile? The lesson of Babel and the direction of the Bible story should be clear: True human security lies in doing the will of God, in seeking the good of all the peoples, in establishing justice and making peace. Apart from these things there is no abiding security in missiles and antimissile missiles. Of course, we cannot permanently secure justice and peace this side of the day when God completes the work of blessing in the world and the New Jerusalem is built on the earth by God's own hand. But we can try! We can give foretastes of the new age. We can put our hands in the hand of the founder and caregiver of the world and, trusting in God and not in our own tower and name, launch out into human adventures in reconciliation.

9. From Human Family to One Family
Genesis 11:10–32

The end of Genesis 11 falls into two distinct parts. Verses 10–26 comprise a linear genealogy sharply focused in its forward movement from Shem, the son of Noah and survivor of the Flood, to Terah, the father of Abram, and to Abram himself. This linear list comprises ten generations exactly as did the list of pre-Flood patriarchs from Adam to Noah. It is devoid of engaging narrative detail. In contrast, verses 27–32 are a branched genealogy of Terah's immediate family, which comprises only portions of three generations but lists three children of Terah, the spouses of two, and the son of the third. This brief text has narrative aspects, for it introduces a major problem that will affect all the texts that are to follow—the barrenness of Sarai (v. 30).

Is Genesis 11:10–32 the conclusion of the primeval history that has gone before? Is it intended to illustrate the way in which God's purpose works out even after the calamity of the Tower of Babel that dispersed the human family into warring and alienated factions? Or does this text come as an introduction to the next great segment of the book of Genesis, which will disclose God's plan to make one person the focus of blessing and the medium of salvation for all the rest? Perhaps this unit is the narrow passageway from one saga to the other. In such an hourglass model, all of humanity narrows down to one person, Abram, whose name is now mentioned for the first time. Then, beginning in chapter 12, it broadens out again into the twelve-branched clan of Israel, which will play a key role in the plan of God for all humanity.

Yet another option would be to link the two parts of Genesis 11:10–32 with the material that precedes it and follow it, respectively. We could then understand vv. 11:10–26 as the necessary bridge combining the Flood and the temporally unlocated Tower of Babel with the beginnings of Israel in the person of the Aramean foreigner, Abram. Verses 27–32 would then be the prologue to the second half of Genesis, the story of the mothers and the fathers—Sarai and Abram, Rebekah and Isaac, Rachel and Jacob.

The current scholarly trend seems to hold that the primeval history concludes with the story of the tower and that the entire genealogy that follows is the necessary introduction to the story of the fathers and the mothers. Naomi Steinberg makes a case for this division in her book *Kinship and Marriage in Genesis*. She begins with the three cycles of family stories in Genesis: Sarai-Hagar, Rebekah, and Rachel-Leah. She shows that each cycle contains three elements: (a) a genealogical superscription or prologue to a segment of the saga of the elect family (e.g., Shem, 11:10–26; Ishmael, 25:12–18; and Esau, 36:1–43), (b) an ensuing genealogy of the descendants of Terah, Isaac, or Jacob (Terah, 11:27–32; Isaac, 25:19–26; and Jacob, 37:2), and (c) a lengthy narrative resolution of the challenges to the continuation of the chosen line. By this analysis, then, the genealogy descending from Shem is a necessary prelude to the branched genealogy of Terah and is parallel to similar linear genealogies associated with the other two great patriarchal names. For her, then, part 2 of this commentary should start with Genesis 11:10.

This strong argument notwithstanding, I stay in this book with the more traditional division of Genesis. Accordingly, part 1 of this commentary deals with primeval history, culminating in the last names on the list of ten post-Flood patriarchs. Part 2 deals with the saga of Abram's family, beginning at Genesis 12:1. The formal similarity of Genesis 11:10–32 with the list of the pre-Flood patriarchs (5:1–32), including the ten-name structure of each, suggests that this passage is intended to be the conclusion of the primeval history. Yet it obviously points forward as well as backward. It sets the stage for the introduction of the chosen family in the second half of Genesis. No master of modern narrative art could offer a segue more expectant of what is to follow than that offered by this author in the simple but daunting sentence of verse 30: "Now Sarai was barren; she had no child."

[11:10–26] Something funny happened on the way to history after the Tower of Babel. The tower was not the special sin of the descendants of Shem. In fact, the chronological place of the tower story in relation to the Flood is impossible to determine. It happened somewhere along the line of ten generations after the Flood. The descendants of Shem were affected just the way others were—they were scattered across the face of the earth. Of course, that scattering was already underway in chapter 10, even before the story of the tower. So we have to conclude that the story of the tower is inserted into the text in a narratively awkward place.

As we compare the built-in chronology of the linear genealogy of verses 10–26 with the similar genealogy in chapter 5, we note not only the similarity of the ten-generation scheme, but also some marked differences. Life spans are now shorter. The total number of years from the birth of Shem to the death of the tenth generation, Abraham, is a mere 565. In chapter 5, in contrast, 2006 years had elapsed from the birth of Adam to the death of Noah. Furthermore, life spans differ markedly. The first ten patriarchs lived an average of 858.4 years, compared to only 317.1 years after the Flood down through the death of Abraham. Even within the table of Genesis 11:10–26 a shift takes place. The first five generations, Shem through Peleg, overlap the table of the nations in 10:21–25. Four of these lives exceed four hundred years, but beginning with Peleg, life spans drop off by another fifty percent. Furthermore, the ages of the fathers at the conception of their eldest sons become much lower. The exceptions are Shem, the last of the old-style patriarchs, who becomes a first-time father at 100, and Terah, the last parent in the list. His seventy years prior to the birth of Abram prefigure the challenge of childlessness that is continually to confront the emerging family of Israel. Other worthies on the list become fathers in their twenties and thirties, ages deemed normal even by our standards. In short, this list is a transition toward predictable human expectation. The Old Testament does not consistently report normal birth and conception dates and life spans until after the death of Moses at 120 and Joshua at 110. However, the movement away from legend toward family saga and eventually the history-like record of the judges and the kings of Israel and Judah is underway. Shortening life spans give us evidence of the changing character of the literature. This text is an early part of the transition.

Several of the names in the list of twelve post-Flood patriarchs are known better to us as places. Serug probably reflects the ancient city of Sarugi, not far north of Haran. Similarly, Nahor is known in the eighteenth-century B.C. cuneiform texts of Mari both as a personal name and as a city. Even the name Terah sounds like a place located by later Assyrian sources near Haran and Nahor in the upper Balikh valley in the northwest quadrant of Mesopotamia.

[27–30] From the information contained in verse 26, we can determine that Terah was born in 1876 *anno mundi* and died in 2081, and that he bore three sons apparently simultaneously! In the branched genealogy of the single family that follows in verses 27–30, much fascinating narrative information is offered. For example, we learn that Haran died before his father did, a circumstance that was always considered tragic in biblical times, and that also produced a potential heir for Abram in the person of his nephew Lot. We learn that the second brother, Nahor, married his niece Milcah, another child of Haran. About a third child, another daughter, Iscah, no further information is ever given. The narrator does not tell us all about the characters that are mentioned, but in a beautiful literary manner withholds much information that will prove fascinating later in the story. The names of the children of Nahor and Milcah are part of that withheld information (see 22:20–24).

We learn also that Abram took a wife. From whence we do not learn here (though we find out in 20:12 that she is Abram's half-sister by Terah and a wife other than Abram's mother). But we do learn that Sarai is barren (v. 30). By this simple sentence, the narrator sets up one of the great challenges to the emergence of Israel in history. Who will be the heir? If Sarai is really barren, what strategy for finding an appropriate heir will be followed? Will Lot be adopted as primary heir (a strategy often followed in kinship systems where the nephew is a prime adoptive son)? Will Abram produce an heir through a secondary wife or concubine, thus incurring difficulties with the primary line through Sarai? None of this is hinted at here, but only the challenge: "Now Sarai was barren; she had no child." In Genesis 12:1–3, the great themes of blessing and faithfulness are introduced through Abram, but the narrator has anticipated those great themes with an earlier and perhaps even greater one: How will the true line of Israel emerge?

[31–32] Terah and his family emigrate from Chaldea, the land of Terah's birth, to Haran. Again, the narrator does not tell us all we might want to know. Terah takes with him only Abram, Sarai, and Lot, leaving Nahor behind in Ur. Why does Nahor stay at home? That question too will prove important when Abraham, having at last gotten an heir, finds a daughter-in-law back in the old country among the prolific descendants of Nahor and Milcah (chap. 24).

The location of Ur of the Chaldeans poses something of a problem for the text. The great city-state of Ur in lower Mesopotamia is well located and well excavated. Its greatest period was its third dynasty, about 2060–1950 B.C. This was an Indo-European Sumerian dynasty, not a Semitic one. The Chaldeans, a Semitic people related to Arameans, do not appear in lower Mesopotamia until the eleventh century B.C.—too late for a hypothetical mid-second-millennium B.C. date for Abram. An upper Mesopotamian Ur would fit in much better with the other places alluded to in these verses: Haran, Nahor, and Terah.

The principal god of Ur was Sin, the moon god. Milcah could be a variant of Melcah, "queen," which was a title of the goddess Ishtar, daughter of Sin. These coincidences, coupled with the name Terah itself—which may have some connection with Yareah, "moon"—all point to a memory of the pagan ancestry of the founding family of Israel. The memory corresponds well with the primitive memory of Israel reflected in Joshua's speech in Joshua 24:2: "Thus says the LORD, the

God of Israel: Long ago your ancestors—Terah and his sons Abraham and Nahor—lived beyond the Euphrates and served other gods." The memory of a prior pagan ancestry further underscores the drama of Israel's discovery of Yahweh and its covenant with the one God of Israel, whose name they first learned, according to the Elohist, at Mount Sinai (Ex. 3:14).

The big theological question left with the readers of Genesis 11:10–32 is this: How can God restore the human community to the harmony it enjoyed before the folly of the tower? The challenges presented here are two. First, Terah, Abram, Sarai, and Lot are idolaters, living in a land where the moon god Sin holds sway. Second, Sarai, the primary wife of Terah's son, Abram, who is to be elected the founder of the chosen people of God, is barren. With consummate skill, the narrators of the great family saga of Genesis 12–50 will gradually disclose to us God's solution to these challenges. For now, though, we are left to conjure with this starkly realistic theological truth: Even in this period of prehistory, the Bible presents God's work within the human community as a work woven into the fabric of human frailty and finitude. God's work and God's word are always incarnate. They never simply displace the human condition, nor are they mediated through any form other than human families, female wombs, cultural constraints, or the levels of understanding reached by a particular generation. This is the wonder of the mysterious interweaving of God's will with human freedom. It is an interweaving that preserves human dignity even while it advances God's purpose.

Part 2: The Fathers and Mothers

An Overview of the Saga
of the Fathers and the Mothers

One of the many good reasons for talking to your grandparents before they die is to collect family stories to pass on to your children. Sometimes the children are not very interested at first; sometimes they never are. However, a well-told family history is always a dramatic narrative and usually involves elements of courage and hope, tragedy and stupidity, marriage and family, children and barrenness, old age and death. If one assembles the genealogical books and traces one's family further back through the American saga, be it through the records of an immigrant-carrying ship, or through links to the slave trade and to family roots in Africa, or through the majestic and mournful story of the Native American past, almost without exception every family has a story to recite that runs the full gamut of human experience.

The book of Genesis contains the family saga of Israel. Whether the stories of the fathers and the mothers—Abraham and Sarah, Isaac and Rebekah, Jacob and Rachel, Joseph and Asenath—began as a single family saga, or were connected secondarily in such a way that they came to be viewed as a single saga is a matter of scholarly debate and discussion. Many scholars believe that individual patriarchs and matriarchs originated at local sanctuaries in Canaan and were revered as founders of such places as Bethel, Beer-sheba, and Hebron. Others contend that the stories of the patriarchs and the matriarchs were originally tribal legends designed to explain how Israel came to be organized into a confederation of twelve tribes. For some scholars, it was the theological genius of the earliest Pentateuchal writers, the Yahwist and Elohist (see the introduction), that took these materials and worked them into the single coherent family saga that is recounted in Genesis 12–50. However it came about, what we are given in the bulk of the book of Genesis is the tragicomic, heroic story of the origin and the descent of the family of Israel.

When you try telling your own family saga to your children, you may find yourself searching for the incandescent idea that illuminates it. "See, children, we were a family of courage!" "We were a family of opportunity!" "We dared to go west!" "We were survivors!" "We had a lot of bizarre but truly interesting fruits on our family tree!" The saga of Israel's family origins, too, has an incandescent idea that discloses the meaning of it all. The stories of Israel's progenitors are history-like stories "worked by the Word of God" (von Rad's phrase).

As we make our way through the individual units of the patriarchal/ matriarchal narrative, it will become increasingly clear what the incandescent idea, or word of God, is that permeates all of these stories. Why not let the cat out of the bag right here at the beginning? Then you can check this assertion against the evidence as it emerges.

Simply put, the idea that runs through all of these stories is the fulfillment of the promise of blessing. At one level, this blessing is seen in very material, visible ways: offspring, land, crops, and national identity. At a more sophisticated level, blessing is understood as a God-given source of vitality that flows from a specific source on the earth. From this source all the peoples of the earth can draw strength and so find full and free lives. That source of blessing at the center point on the earth is Israel, the people who spring from the loins of Abraham.

The motif of promise ("You will be a blessing") winds its way through various interim fulfillments in the family saga of Genesis 12–50 and then on out into the broad sweeps of later history. Of course, the fulfillments usually fall short and revert back to promise again. The journey along the rocky path that runs between the promise and the reality that Israel should be a blessing to all the peoples of the earth has to be resumed again and again through the ages. The fulfillment is yet fully to be manifest, but the promise remains: "You shall be for me a priestly kingdom and a holy nation" (Ex. 19:6). In the New Covenant, you are summoned to be the body of Christ, through whom all the peoples of the earth shall find a blessing.

The intention of this family saga, then, is to tell the readers who they are, where they came from, and what incandescent idea guides their destiny. In the service of this saga, and in the movement from the promise to Abraham to the beginnings of the fulfillment in the multiplication of the people of Israel in Egypt, every type of human personality, every shade of joy and sorrow, every sin, every triumph, is pressed into service. Think what profound risks God has taken to disclose the divine will and purpose for us through the medium of human experience! Yet, think what strengths our faith can draw from the discovery that the word of God is always an incarnate word, not only in the Christ event, but in the Old Testament too. It is not "virtual," it is not mystical, it is not a voice that comes from heaven; it is a word that enlists in its service all that we really are in actual human experience.

Were there ever really any patriarchs? Did they belong to the age of the Mesopotamian kingdom of Mari in the eighteenth century B.C., or perhaps to the Hurrian people of Nuzi in the fourteenth century B.C.? Some recent scholars even argue that the patriarchal legends originated only in the sixth century B.C. Does it really matter? In these pages, we will regard the patriarchs as deeply human and very strong personalities. Whether those personalities belonged to real people of deep antiquity or whether they evolved through the work of the storytellers and tradition-ers of ancient Israel will not matter that much. The point will be that the incandescent idea—movement of the promise to the fulfillment of bless-ing through this one family—is what these narratives are now intended to demonstrate. God's interactions with the patriarchs, reported in these stories, will have profound significance for the career of the ancient people of Israel as well as for their living spiritual children, the Jews and the Christians, and even their cousins, the Muslims.

The stage is set at the outset in Genesis 12:1–4a, where the incandes-cent idea is already indicated: "In you all the families of the earth shall be blessed." No sooner is that word spoken into the ears of Abram as a kind of programmatic statement for the whole patriarchal saga than that grand ideal has to squeeze through a very tight place. Abram and Sarai, acting without any divine instruction, enlist Sarai's beauty in their cause (12:10–20). Sarai is "beautiful," but even more: the passage makes clear that she is really desirable! Her beauty is going to be used to counter a threat to Abram's pursuit of the promise of progeny and of land, namely, the threat of his destitute condition. He had left the land of the Chaldeans without anything except Sarai, Lot, and a lot of sheep. Now he needs to begin to build the kind of wealth and power that will put feet under the blessing. Not by God's gift but with Sarai's help, he sets about to do it on his own. Sex is the bait. In exchange for Sarai in the house of Pharaoh, he is now richly rewarded. "For her sake [Pharaoh] dealt well with Abram; and he had sheep, oxen, male donkeys, male and female slaves, female donkeys, and camels" (12:16). For all we know, Pharaoh acts in good faith; after all, Abram has instructed Sarai to pass herself off as his sister. And yet, Yahweh punishes the king with grievous plagues (12:17). Is that fair? Is it moral? Is the whole story moral? The saga is not interested in answering these questions or in casing out the family closet. The main point is that Abram gets his stake in the new land. Now he has donkeys and camels. The first sign of blessing, and therefore the possi-bility of fulfillment, appears. Furthermore, Sarai has no child by Pharaoh, so the line of destiny is protected.

From this rocky start, the saga writer proceeds toward the promise through the still very narrow path of the separation from Lot in chapter 13. Why did Abram separate from Lot? It is difficult to determine. In our own family sagas we hear of northern branches and southern branches and those who went to Canada and those who returned to the old country. Perhaps they simply felt a call to do these things. Perhaps money was involved. Scholars who want to understand the patriarchal traditions from the side of the social conditions of ancient culture argue that economic factors come into play here. For example, the Israeli scholar S. Yeivin urges that the patriarchs were neither pastoralists nor merchants but "haulage contractors" and that the migration from Ur is to be explained by the fact that the demand for caravans of donkeys to transport merchandise was declining at Ur (cited in McKane, 9). In Haran in Mesopotamia, the sons of Terah, the father of Abram, came into conflict with other groups that had a vested interest in hiring donkeys. It was this situation that led to further migration of the Abrahamites while the Nahorites remained in Haran.

The reason the patriarchs are represented in the book of Genesis as stockbreeders and not caravaneers is that the business of hiring donkeys had declined and they had been forced to seek another means of livelihood. The high roads of commerce were becoming more and more hazardous. International trade was being reduced to a mere trickle. Economic emphasis had to be shifted more and more into stockbreeding, and that meant conflict over pasture land and ultimately the division of tribes into different areas. Out of this new means of livelihood, stockbreeding and grazing, came the conflict that accounts for the split between Abram and Lot, according to this view.

In the end, an economic explanation of the division between Lot and Abram may be no more convincing than a simple literary observation like this: "The story teaches us that we come from Abraham. However, it also tells us about another line that heads off in another direction. This explains the existence of a related but also different people on our horizon. They may be distant cousins, but they are not our group. That line had to be lopped off so that the incandescent idea could be channeled through our family, the family that matters most!" Even as the promise is being channeled away from Lot, however, the narrative of Genesis 13 stresses the amicability and fairness of Abram in his dealings with him. Those human qualities too are enlisted in the service of the great saga of promise to fulfillment.

In the story of Hagar and Ishmael in chapter 16, the beautiful Sarai shows her shadow side. The idea of blessing flickers under the impact of her jealousy and her cruel decision to send the helpless handmaid and her baby into the wilderness. The narrators deemed this action necessary, though, so that Israel's line might be clear, and so that those who heard might know where they stood and what role they played in the fulfillment of God's promise.

In chapter 17, the rich tapestry of human passions and decisions is not depleted but enhanced by the Priestly writers, who added a layer of narrative hundreds of years after the Yahwistic writer. In this Priestly account of the covenant of circumcision, Abram (at this auspicious moment in the story now renamed Abraham) is presented as an obedient patriarch. Through his obedience, promise moves toward fulfillment. Another threat to that inexorable flow appears, however. Although Abraham is obedient, he is obedient, you might say, with his fingers crossed. When told by God that Sarai (now renamed Sarah) will give birth to a son, he doesn't just chuckle, he falls on his face and laughs! (17:17) He laughs at the promise of God. Believe that my old wife and my old body can still team up to produce a child? No way!

Can the incandescent idea shine through disbelief? Is a doubtful patriarch a broken lens for such a light? Paul faced these questions too as he contemplated the story of Abraham.

> Hoping against hope, he believed that he would become "the father of many nations," according to what was said, "So numerous shall your descendants be." He did not weaken in faith when he considered his own body, which was already as good as dead (for he was about a hundred years old), or when he considered the barrenness of Sarah's womb. No distrust made him waver concerning the promise of God, but he grew strong in his faith as he gave glory to God, being fully convinced that God was able to do what he had promised. Therefore his faith "was reckoned to him as righteousness." (Rom 4:18–22)

Paul recognized how unlikely the fulfillment of the promise was, but even he could not quite match Abraham's own incredulity. Ignoring Abraham's raucous laughter, Paul says of him, "He did not weaken in faith. . . . He was fully convinced that God could do what he promised." In the end, of course, Abraham's temporary laughter pales in the face of God's manifest trustworthiness. Paul's answer to doubt is resounding: Faith is manifested precisely when it makes the counterintuitive affirmation that God keeps promises.

In the episode recounted in chapter 20, which, according to the source critics, comes from the hand of the Elohist, we have a later retelling of the Yahwist's story about Sarai and Pharaoh. Note the changes in this version. Not to Pharaoh, but to Abimelech, a lesser king, Abraham says of Sarah, "She is my sister." Beauty is not enlisted in the cause; at least nothing is made of Sarah's stunning looks. Furthermore, Abimelech does not touch Sarah (20:6). Nor does Abraham lie in this version of the story; indeed, Sarah is in fact his half-sister (v. 12). So the king is exonerated, Abraham is exonerated, Sarah is exonerated, and Abraham still gets his money (v. 16). In short, the later Elohistic transformation of the older scripture has smoothed out and "improved" the older version. It does not advance the incandescent idea. If anything, it shows that another generation was less daring in its acknowledgment that God enlists all human dimensions into the cause of driving forward the promise.

In chapter 21, the movement toward the promise opens up into a broad highway. The thing that was thought to be impossible, the thing that made Abraham laugh, takes place after all. Isaac is born! The threat of barrenness with which the family saga had to deal is eliminated when, in her old age, Sarah sprouts a new branch of the family. The path narrows to the extreme in the very next chapter, however, when it leads up the side of Mount Moriah. The hand that is raised with the knife of sacrifice in Genesis 22 will cut the line off altogether and end any possibility of the fulfillment of the promise of blessing through the descendants of the one man Abraham. Here the writer enlists human piety in the cause. The piety that took up the knife in response to the command of God also puts it down when it recognizes that a substitute is available. In obedience Abraham backs away from human sacrifice.

Chapter 23, the story of the death of Sarah, is a kind of interlude in this ongoing family saga. It will be discussed more fully as we look at that chapter in detail. All deaths, of course, are threats to the promise, and yet the death of the patriarchs and their wives, one by one, is inevitable. The promise itself moves on. In chapter 24, the way between the promise and fulfillment reaches one of its broadest and most joyous moments in the story of the enlistment of Rebekah for marriage to Isaac. Drawn into the picture in this stage in the movement from promise to fulfillment are all the emotions of tenderness, beauty, love, mutual respect, and tough-mindedness. A young woman who is asked to leave her parental family, go to a foreign land and marry someone she has never met says right off, "I will go!" (24:58). She goes into the unknown future, to the foreign land of Canaan.

By chapter 27, however, the honorable and tender Rebekah becomes the double-dealing Rebekah who sees to it that Jacob and not Esau receives the birthright. Yet history honors her for it as history honors the continental women who hid the church's silver from the British redcoats and the Yankee women who hid the runaway slaves and the Confederate women who smoothly eased the federal raiders on down the road. Her deceit is enlisted in the cause. The line of promise has to run through Jacob, not through Esau. Like Sarai with Pharaoh, like the barren Sarah with child, it is the woman who is the hero as she gets her son Jacob out of town and on his way to Paddan-aram.

Through the device of a dream, in Genesis 28 God enlists the human propensities toward gratitude and awe to bring about a reaffirmation of that which must exist if the promise is to move on to fulfillment. At Bethel, for the first time Jacob affirms his trust in God and expresses absolute loyalty to God's leadership. The dream as such is not as important as its consequences, although Christian preaching and hymnody have always represented it as the prototypical pious dream. Its reaffirmation of faith and trust is the matter of first importance.

Genesis 29 is yet another idyll involving tenderness and deception. Rachel meets Jacob at the well. Seven years later, when the morning light falls on the wedding bed to reveal not the ravishing Rachel, for whom Jacob had worked, but the "weak-eyed" Leah, another human emotion—hatred—is enlisted in the cause. (On the current state of Leah's eyes, see the commentary.) Hatred of Rachel drives Leah back time and again into Jacob's bed to conceive sons and thus to outperform her sister/rival. From these sons of Leah's rivalry with Rachel descend half of the tribes of Israel. They will be essential to the fulfillment of the promise of blessing.

We could continue in this vein throughout the patriarchal saga, but by now the point is clear: every human emotion, behavior, and aspiration is brought in to advance the promise. The trickery and embezzlement of chapter 31 are only the sequels to all that has gone before. In the long Joseph story (chaps. 37–50) that follows the story of Jacob, arrogance, fratricide, seduction, wisdom, tenderness, and great maturity all add further human dimensions to the saga.

The sum of this overview, then, is this: The line of promise makes its way through the vicissitudes of family saga, drawn down through the generations toward the fulfillment. The narrators and theologians do not just tell us that the way is rocky and the threats are many. They render its stresses and pains for us by walking with us down that path. They do not just tell us that the route to blessing is fraught with adventures, close calls, and cries to God. They evoke the faithfulness of God and make the responding gasps of faithfulness by the fathers and the mothers credible by enlisting all the propensities of the patriarchs in the service of this grand account. Deception, fraud, penitence, piety, racism, sexism, love, tenderness, jealousy—these are the warp into which the woof of theology is woven. Out of it all comes a tapestry emblazoned with towering, memorable figures.

The fathers and the mothers are successful at evoking the response of generations to follow too. Yes, we say, these are our fathers and mothers in faith. We recognize in them our own passions and our own needs for forgiveness and direction. Yes, we too participate in their destiny to move toward the fulfillment of the promise, that through their descendants in the faith, all the peoples of the earth can find a blessing. In the end we can testify to our profound gratitude that God chose to disclose to us where we came from and where we are going in the saga of a family. That is the incarnate form of the word of God, and it is as authentic and powerful as the sagas of our own immediate families. It is, in fact, a faith saga into which our own sagas are woven.

10. The Saga of Abraham and Sarah
Genesis 12:1–23:20

THE ELECTION OF ABRAM
Genesis 12:1–4a

12:1 **Now the Lord said to Abram, "Go from your country and your kindred and your father's house to the land that I will show you. ²I will make of you a great nation, and I will bless you, and make your name great, so that you will be a blessing. ³I will bless those who bless you, and the one who curses you I will curse; and in you all the families of the earth shall be blessed."**

⁴**So Abram went, as the Lord had told him; and Lot went with him.**

This passage is probably not a call narrative in the strict sense. Other texts, including Exodus 3:1–12 (Moses), Judges 6:11–27 (Gideon), Isaiah 6:1–13, and Jeremiah 1:1–10, reveal the sequence of divine appearance, commission, human objection, and divine reassurance that call narratives more typically follow. This short narrative reports a unilateral promise and donation made by God to a favored individual. In the ears of Christian faith, however, the sound of God's voice calling or summoning an individual to do a specific task is first heard here at the very beginning of the history of ancient Israel. Abram is called to go—and he goes! In all the years since, others have heard that voice and have done likewise.

[12:1] Out of the blue, Yahweh, whom the forerunners of Israel have yet to know by name, issues to a seventy-five-year-old Mesopotamian of Ur, Abram, a stunning imperative, "Go!" The imperative is given further valences that we mobile masses of modernity can scarcely grasp. The command penetrates through concentric circles to the very heart of a primitive tribal person's identity: "Go from your country"—from the fatherland, that piece of earth that your people claim and their neighbors recognize, the territory that offers the safety of defined limits and the lifegiving routine of seedtime and harvest. "Go from your kindred"—

from the clan, that vast network of blood relationships that defines tribal loyalty. "Go from your father's house"—from that nuclear unit of human relationships, wherein the lonely individual finds the guidance of the elders, the loyal support of siblings, the helping hand in moments of crisis. Leave all that, this unknown Yahweh says. The echo of that imperative rings down through the millennia.

A contemporary Israeli political historian even says that the deep origins of the modern state of Israel are disclosed in the Lord's words, "Go . . . to the land that I will show you." Walter Brueggemann agrees:

> In 12:1–9, Abraham is presented as the perfectly faithful man. He is called and he goes. He relies only on the name (12:8) and the word (12:1–4a) of this god who has suddenly inverted his life. The call of God has been fully embraced. *That is where the history of Israel begins.* (Brueggemann, 125, emphasis added)

Israel's history is a history of migration, of pilgrimage. To be sure, there are phases in that history in which the pilgrim people occupy the specific territory that God will now show Abram (centered around Shechem in Gen. 12:7, but enlarged in later reiterations of the promise of land; see 13:14–18 and 15:18–21). However, pilgrimage, exile, and faithfulness in diaspora seem to be the abiding truths of the life of Israel.

[2] Yahweh justifies the stunning command "Go!" with a series of statements of purpose. The Hebrew syntax of the verse strongly suggests that it be read as follows: "[Go] . . . so that I may make of you a great nation, so that I may bless you and make your name great, so that you will be a blessing." The Lord proposes to accomplish a great thing for all peoples by blessing one person.

Does the future of the human race hang on the obedience of one person? Is it within Abram's power to thwart God's intention to overcome with reconciliation the curse of Babel? The issue deserves the further discussion it will receive in the commentary on verse 4. The point of Yahweh's speech, however, is not to showcase Abram's obedience, but rather to disclose God's daring plan to spread blessing throughout the world beginning at one tiny, specific human starting point. However the verbs of verse 2 are to be construed, they culminate in that clear statement of purpose: "Go . . . so that you will be a blessing." The promise is also the announcement of a divine program, which God will certainly pursue with or without Abram's obedience.

The Lord promises Abram to "make your name great." Excitement rises! Juxtaposed to chapter 11, this emerges as a direct answer to the foolish builders of the Tower of Babel who said, "Let us make a name for ourselves; otherwise we shall be scattered abroad upon the face of the whole earth" (11:4). The purest expression of human autonomy is to try to create a destiny so grand and dazzling that not even heaven can threaten it. They tried it and their great self-made name vanished. Now, however, God unilaterally and freely offers to one humble Aramaean of Mesopotamia a name whose true greatness will be manifested in the blessing that it brings to others. This is the act of grace by which God answers the fourth and most terrible "fall," that of the tower. Through this act, God will ultimately heal the curse of confusion and alienation that the tower provoked. (On the four "falls" of Genesis 3–11, see "Reflections on Human Alienation" in chapter 8.)

[3] The series of clauses building up the purpose of universal blessing is set aside momentarily to acknowledge the possibility of some bad news. A lot of blessing will result from God's choice of Abram and his descendants, but the odd curse may also fall upon despisers of the man. Readers often overlook the fact that the future blessing and the cursing projected by God for the future are not equal, but that the good news for "*those* who bless you" far outweighs the bad news for "*the one* who curses you."

The last clause of verse 3 is surely the climax of the election of Abram. In fact, this clause may well be a programmatic statement for the entire Yahwistic narrative of the fathers and mothers and an orientation of the reader toward a proper understanding of the entire destiny of the people Israel, who are their ultimate descendants. The promissory statements of verses 2–3a (statements of intention rather than predictions of fact) now culminate in what in the Hebrew is clearly a result clause. The end result of the election and the blessing of Abram will be this certain outcome: "[Thus] in you all the families of the earth shall be blessed."

The Hebrew form of the verb that the NRSV translates "shall be blessed" has three possible readings: passive (NRSV text; see also Acts 3:25 and Gal. 3:6–8); reflexive, "shall bless themselves" (NRSV note); or "middle," "shall find a blessing" (Wolff). None of the modern English versions of the Old Testament employs the latter option, but in some ways it is most satisfying, for it gives the most sensible answer to the question, How do the gentile nations lay hold of this blessing that is being offered by God to them through the intermediation of Abraham/Israel? It is neither through passive waiting and inaction ("be blessed") nor through the muttering of formulas or formalized approaches and petitions to Israel ("bless themselves"). Instead, it is through a mature discovery of what God intends to do for humankind through the life and teachings of Abraham/Israel and all their sons and daughters that leads the families of the earth to say, "We see in the faith of Israel the possibility of overcoming the curse of Babel, the possibility

of reconciliation, for which we have been seeking. We experience blessing from Israel and we find our own blessing there."

Read this way, the unilateral, extraordinary promise of God to Abram
is an open-ended, abiding announcement of potentiality: The blessing
that you nations seek can always be found here if you will take action to
find it. For their part, Abram and his descendants (especially the tenth-
century community that first received the Yahwist's version of the
Pentateuch) are challenged by this promise always to be active in specific,
concrete acts of intercession, peacemaking, and economic aid (see Wolff,
59). I will note points at which Abram acts in just these ways.

To sum up this discussion of verses 1–3, we can analyze this story of
the election of Abram as follows:

v. 1 The Lord's Command: "Go!"
vv. 2–3a Purpose: Spread of blessing
v. 3b Result: Universal blessing

If this analysis is correct, the climax or punch line of the text seems to
be verse 3b. A sermon preached or a lesson taught on the election of
Abram should really focus on this main point: God has an audacious plan
to bless all human communities quite apart from their worthiness or obedience. God will use one little Mesopotamian and his progeny as the
instruments of this blessing, and through them will reunite the nations in
reconciliation and peace.

In his Genesis commentary, Gerhard von Rad argues that this little
passage was composed ad hoc by J, the Yahwist, the earliest of the four
Pentateuchal writers. J created this intimate election scene (to which no
eyewitnesses attest) and put this speech in Yahweh's mouth in order to set
forth a program for the family saga of the origins of Israel. Through
vicissitudes viscous and thin, the story of Israel is going to be a story of
the reintroduction of blessing into a world left accursed after the four
great falls of primeval times. The plot of the story of humankind is the
slow discovery by the nations of the world of the yellow brick road that
leads back to the garden of peace and happiness.

[4a] "So Abram went. . . ." Up to this point we have heard only from the
Lord, who surprisingly elects and calls a hitherto unremarkable
Mesopotamian, a worshiper of strange gods (Josh. 24:2). When the spotlight shifts to Abram, we see him make a free decision to obey God's command. Because of his instant obedience, many Jews and Christians have
understood this to be above all a story of Abram's exemplary faith. Stephen
begins his fatal sermon to the council with a simple recital of Abraham's
obedience (Acts 7:1–4). In Hebrews 11 it becomes a major component in
the great essay on faith and obedience (see especially Heb. 11:8).

However, Abram's response is brought forth by the Lord's prior gracious offer of blessing to all of humankind through the mediation of Abram's family. We must conclude, then, that the story has not one but two heroes. Abram is one of these. He deserves to be taken as a prototype of the obedient person, a great hero of the faith. Happy was Abram that he accepted the challenge to be God's pioneer! The issues here are also relevant to the New Testament conviction that human response to the message of the gospel is a vital part of the story of salvation. Happy are those who can enlist in God's cause!

The other hero of this little narrative is God. Before we chose God, God chose us. God's decision in our favor, manifested not only in the election of Abram but also in the incarnation, crucifixion, and resurrection of Jesus Christ, calls forth from our forefather in faith, as it can and does from us, the answering response of faithful obedience.

Brueggemann sums up the juxtaposition of elements in Genesis 12:1–4a in these words:

> [God's unilateral] promise of 12:1–2 dominates our pericope. It stands between the immobilized family of 11:30 and the responsive family of 12:4ff. Things are changed from the one to the other by this promise. Yet, though the text is fully focused on the promise in God's speech of verses 1–3, it is verse 4 that announces the motif that characterizes all of chapters 12:1–25:18. God's call to Abraham is accepted and embraced. Abraham went (v. 4)! . . . Abraham stands as the prototype for all disciples who forsake everything and follow (Mark 10:28). The remainder of the drama of Abraham and Sarah is to probe that embrace, to find out if it can be honored, and to assess the cost of such a decision. (Brueggemann, 121)

COVENANT AND ELECTION

Today when we use the term "covenant" in such contexts as property transfers and marriages, we think of a bilateral agreement. The relevant documents have places for two or more signatures. Can a unilateral act like this one be a covenant? Or is the language of "election" more appropriate here?

God's plan is clear and it is God's own: God intends to cure the cancerous alienation of Babel by inserting a glowing, radioactive capsule of blessing into the mass. God's success is not contingent on what anyone else does, although a person and a people will be caught up in the implementation of the plan. It is as if the Lord said, "The human community tried to make their own name great and it didn't work. Now I'm going to do something! No matter what you do, I am going to lay the groundwork for your salvation."

At the conclusion of the Sinai covenant ceremony, "all the people answered with one voice, and said, 'All the words that the LORD has spoken we will do'" (Ex. 24:3), and their promise is sealed with the spilling of the blood of the covenant. In Joshua 24:26–27, the people's promise to serve only the Lord is sealed by the erection of a memorial stone upon which is inscribed a record of the covenant provisions. On the other hand, Abram's obedient departure following the announcement of God's promise has more the character of a grateful and appropriate response than the binding ratification of a legal relationship. He does not act to seize a dangled carrot—"If you do this you will receive the reward of my blessing." There is no "if" here at all; the blessing is already committed.

For these reasons this commentary has joined with others to describe the transaction of Genesis 12:1–4a not as a covenant at all, but as an election announcement, coupled with a gift or grant. It has the character of an offer by one free agent to another, as in the case of Jesus' free offer of discipleship to the twelve. Their decisions, though momentous, were free responses. The community of the church looks at them much the way Israel looks at Abraham—with gratitude that they acted in loving acceptance, not because they had to but because they could. As noted earlier, some have said that the story of Israel, if not its actual history, begins right here. Perhaps we should state more broadly that the beginning of the hope of humankind is to be found right here, and the beginning of our long quest for peace and right relationships.

One hears Beethoven's overture to *Fidelio* far more frequently than one hears or sees the whole of *Fidelio*, the only opera that Beethoven ever wrote. This suggests that an overture can stand on its own feet. The book of Genesis, clearly an overture to the whole of the Bible, stands on its own feet. Yet, as Thomas W. Mann remarks, "Genesis leaves the reader at a moment of temporal tension, not only at the end but also at the beginning of an adventure" (352). When Genesis ends, the promise is riding on some seventy persons who are not even in their land but in Egypt. Something more has to happen. Genesis is not only an introduction; it is a prefiguration of things to come, and it is a very open-ended one at that. Open-endedness is part of the model for God's work in the world that Genesis gives us. We have yet to see the day in which the universal blessing promised to Abram is manifested. The great opera of history is still playing. What are we expecting in this universal blessing? Ezekiel 34 paints a picture of what we are expecting that includes no more wild beasts in the land, showers of blessing, and the end of violence and oppression. For Christians, the word and work of Jesus and the proclamation of the gospel of reconciliation throughout the world are part and parcel of this future.

The story of Abram claims that concentric circles will flow out from one small starting point until they encompass all people. This promise itself is not contingent, but the need for response is universal.

THE LORD'S FIRST PROMISE TO ABRAM
Genesis 12:4b–9

This interlude, except for verse 4b the work of the Yahwist, traces the route of the foreign forefather Abram and all of his retinue from Haran in Mesopotamia to specified localities in the land of Canaan.

[12:4b] This chronological notice introduces a general framework that the Priestly writers use to sketch out the remainder of Abram's life cycle: in Canaan at seventy-five, circumcised and renamed at ninety-nine (17:1), proud father of Isaac at one hundred (21:5), dead at 175, exactly a century after his emigration (25:7).

[5–6] Only three members of the party of immigrants are mentioned by name, but the entire retinue of servants, herders, Lot's family, and friends was probably quite large. The intention to go more than five hundred miles southwest from Haran to Canaan, already announced in Genesis 11:31, but apparently long deferred, now comes to fruition. The long haul immediately becomes a series of short movements for the nomadic Abramite group. The first stop is at a special spot ("the place") at Shechem, an ancient city located between Mount Ebal and Mount Gerizim about thirty-eight miles north of Jerusalem, and one and a half miles east of the modern West Bank city of Nablus. The "oak of Moreh" made the place special, even sacred. It might have been a talking or oracle-giving tree. (*Moreh* means "teacher" or "oracle giver." Shechem seems to have had a number of noteworthy trees: see Gen. 35:4, Josh. 24:26, Judg. 9:6.) Abram's route goes from one existing sanctuary to a second—both of which belong to the "Canaanites [who] were in the land."

[7] Abram creates a shrine of his own at the sacred tree, however, to commemorate the theophany that now occurs. If Abram sees God, nothing is made of that experience. All that counts is what he hears. Shechem will play a prominent role in the religious imagination of ancient Israel forever after, for it is here that the Lord gives to Abram's descendants "this land" (v. 7a). How specific did Yahweh mean to be? Does "this land" mean Shechem and its environs, or does it mean all the land of Canaan? (In later usage, "the land" often means the land of Israel.) Whichever it is, this promise provides a patrimony of property that the promise of blessing in 12:3 did not.

[8–9] Though Bethel later gets its name and its sacred pillar from Jacob (28:10–22), Abram had already planted a cultic installation here. The preexistence of a Canaanite sanctuary and even a Canaanite name, "house of El" (the high god of the Canaanite pantheon) both seem likely. No theophany occurs here, but Abram makes it his own anyway. This site, about thirteen miles north of Jerusalem, was a mere stopping point on Abram's continuing journey southward. Later, however, it became the central sanctuary of the secessionist northern kingdom of Israel (1 Kings 12:25–33; Amos 7:10–13).

THE UNGAINLY STORY OF ABRAM AND SARAI IN EGYPT
Genesis 12:10–20

12:10 Now there was a famine in the land. So Abram went down to Egypt to reside there as an alien, for the famine was severe in the land. [11] When he was about to enter Egypt, he said to his wife Sarai, "I know well that you are a woman beautiful in appearance; [12] and when the Egyptians see you, they will say, 'This is his wife'; then they will kill me, but they will let you live. [13] Say you are my sister, so that it may go well with me because of you, and that my life may be spared on your account." [14] When Abram entered Egypt the Egyptians saw that the woman was very beautiful. [15] When the officials of Pharaoh saw her, they praised her to Pharaoh. And the woman was taken into Pharaoh's house. [16] And for her sake he dealt well with Abram; and he had sheep, oxen, male donkeys, male and female slaves, female donkeys, and camels.

[17] But the LORD afflicted Pharaoh and his house with great plagues because of Sarai, Abram's wife. [18] So Pharaoh called Abram, and said, "What is this you have done to me? Why did you not tell me that she was your wife? [19] Why did you say, 'She is my sister,' so that I took her for my wife? Now then, here is your wife, take her, and be gone." [20] And Pharaoh gave his men orders concerning him; and they sent him on the way, with his wife and all that he had.

[10–15] The second incident in the story of the elect man and his family is just awful. It was not the famine that was awful, although, like that which afflicted Jacob and his sons, it drove his family down to the fertile lands in Egypt. In verses 12–13, Abram makes the fateful proposal that Sarai pass herself off to the Egyptians as his sister rather than his wife, to the end that his life be spared. Her sacrifice will secure his life; indeed, it may foreshadow the big leg up for the future that Abram seeks ("that it may go well with me").

In the cultural setting of this text, marriage bound all parties to respect the exclusive rights of the husband. A sister, on the other hand, was at the brother's disposal.

[16] Now we learn that Abram has gotten his stake. He has come from a great distance as a refugee from famine with almost nothing—no child, no money, no donkeys. The only asset that he has, his beautiful wife, he has successfully parlayed into the economic basis necessary to begin implementing the promise of verses 1–3. Is this a fair and just way to do it? The narrator is not concerned with that. The narrator evidently cares only to trace the winding path that leads from promise to fulfillment. Abram may have been a big tribal chief when he and Lot and all their possessions arrived in Canaan (12:5). But now he is even bigger in camels and slaves, thanks to the intrinsic value of the beautiful Sarai.

Brueggemann thinks this is a non-Israelite story that was taken over and used three times in Genesis (see also 20:1–18 and 26:6–11). Maybe that reduces the scandal of it just a tad: Hey, everyone was doing this; it is a well-known Middle Eastern transaction. He even supports the theory that she actually was his sister as well as his wife, either biologically or through some kind of ceremonial adoption.

[17] Through no fault of his own, aside from the standard lust that men of power feel for vulnerable women, Pharaoh and all his house are afflicted by God with grievous plagues. Is this the way God operates, or did the Yahwist make the Lord over into our own image here? Sodom and Gomorrah; David's enemy, the foolish Nabal; Ananias and Sapphira—all of these stories picture God smiting people and getting them out of the way. Is this legitimate Jewish or Christian theology, or is it primitive anthropomorphism?

The word "primitive" is not pejorative here, but refers to the level of sophistication of the story. In this case we can judge that relativity quite accurately, because the story is told twice more, but with the harshest features of the story as it is told here softened. In this sense, the version of the story in Genesis 12:10–20 is the most primitive recounting of the tradition.

The punch line or climax of this story is disclosed by an outline of it. The story is bracketed by an introduction (v. 10) and a conclusion (v. 20). Sandwiched between these are two speeches, one by Abram (vv. 11–13) and one by Pharaoh (vv. 17–19). That leaves an unmatched scene in the middle (vv. 14–16) in which Abram gets his camels. That may have been the climax at some earlier stage of the story. Now, however, that big point seems to have been subverted by verse 17, in which the narrator assures us that the Lord answers wrongdoing with appropriate penalties.

Did Sarai and Pharaoh have sexual relations? The story neither confirms nor denies the matter, but there is no reason to think that they did not, since she had been taken to his harem (v. 15). She did not become pregnant, of course, because she was barren (11:30). But in this version of the story, no effort is made to protect Sarai's chastity. In contrast, in the version in 20:1–18 (thought to be from the hand of the Elohist), the villain of the piece is no longer Pharaoh but Abimelech, king of Gerar. As before, the king gives Abraham his gold and silver, but only as a severance gift. God closes all the wombs in Abimelech's house (v. 18) as part of the punitive plague. Presumably Sarah's womb alone was not closed, but it did not matter, because the king never approached her (v. 4). Finally it turns out that Sarah is indeed Abraham's half-sister (v. 12). In short, there has been a theological "improvement" of the story over the century or so between the two tellings, in which some of its roughest features have been eliminated.

In the third version, Genesis 26:6–11, the protagonists are Isaac and Rebekah. Isaac is afraid that the men of Gerar might kill him to acquire Rebekah. The Philistine king Abimelech never even gets control of Rebekah, though, because he sees Isaac "fondling" her. He warns everyone to stay clear, and scolds Isaac for his lie. The process of domesticating the story seems to have continued, for all the characters have become more correct. The need to have God "smite" someone is removed. (All this assumes, of course, that this is not a sequential history of the modern sort, and that we are not dealing here with three actual separate historical events.)

Here are four different angles on this interesting but theologically bizarre text. Perhaps something can be drawn from each one for the purposes of interpretation in synagogue and church.

Psychoanalytic. The story is more fantasy than reality. A man fantasizes he is part of a love triangle, and he is sharing his wife with another man.

Normative. This is only one piece of the larger saga about Abram/Abraham. In this introduction to the full story, the hero has just received the wonderful promise of 12:1–3, has acted in verse 4a with exemplary faith and obedience, and then has turned right around and committed this shoddy act. A norm is disclosed: like other human beings, biblical heroes are often flawed.

Contextual. Scripture is its own best interpreter. In this case, the story has to be told three times until the storytellers get it right. After the theologians who gave us the book of Genesis thought the story through at more length, they decided to tell it another way. Sarai, Sarah, and Rebekah become less and less like pawns who are moved around by men. Victimization of them decreases, although even by the third telling the woman's situation is still not one of dignity and independence.

Theological. In all three of its versions, the story is not really about sex but about power and the misuse of one person by another. At the same time, in every case God acts to protect the woman, even when the hero himself places her in harm's way.

In the full context of the canon, this ancient story about an ancestor who is abusively acted upon should be placed alongside other biblical stories in which a woman acts on her own behalf and exhibits remarkable strength and independence (e.g., Eve in the garden [3:1–7]; Rebekah's decisiveness [24:58]; Hagar's survival [21:8–21]; Ruth; Esther; Mary).

THE LORD'S SECOND PROMISE TO ABRAM
Genesis 13:1–18

This chapter, thought to be largely from the Yahwist, could equally well be called, with the NRSV, "Abram and Lot Separate." The space given to the account of their separation (vv. 8–13) slightly exceeds that given to the promise (vv. 14–18). However, the significance of the land promise in later scripture and Jewish history down to the present day makes it the weightier burden of this passage.

[13:1–7] The parallel between the sojourn in Egypt of the Abramites and that of the later Israelites is plain to see. They both get rich there (see Ex. 12:36), especially in livestock but also in gold and silver, and they both are turned out of Egypt (Gen. 12:20). In Abram's case, however, it is a friendly expulsion and nobody pursues him. His problem arises within his own group. Any ancient hearer or reader would have known that the Negeb—the steppe and desert region between Egypt and Canaan through which the nomadic Abram moved—would have provided meager forage for flocks. Even after the party reaches the rocky hill country around Bethel from which they had come (12:8), the range is inadequate. With little forage and no barbed wire, sheep wars break out between the communities of Abram and Lot. No doubt the indigenous "Canaanites and the Perizzites" who lived around Bethel want their share of the fodder as well! (The Perizzites are mentioned twenty-three times in the Old Testament—paired four times with the Canaanites—and still no one knows for sure who they were.)

[8–13] After the shady episode with Sarai in Egypt, Abram gets back on track as an amicable peacemaker. His manner illustrates how he and his descendants, the Israelites of the United Monarchy (the audience being addressed by the Yahwist), might be a blessing among the peoples (the thematic motif sounded first in 12:3b; see the commentary on that verse). Abram moves to resolve the tension between the two clans by generously giving Lot first choice of the lands in which they might settle.

Lot decides to head eastward, down into the well-watered and fertile Rift Valley, or the "plain of the Jordan." Zoar, Sodom, and Gomorrah are listed among the cities of the plain. By settling in the already established precincts of that sinful city of Sodom, Lot—himself an innocent—gets linked in the tradition with crime and punishment (18:16–19:29). One can hardly blame him for choosing the plain of Jordan, though. With exquisite brevity and suggestiveness, the narrator identifies that plain with fruitful gardens of the fabled past and future: "[It was] well watered everywhere like the garden of the LORD [that is, Eden], like the land of Egypt" (v. 10).

[14–17] In the first election account in Genesis 12:1–3, the Lord promised Abram progeny, a great name, and above all, blessedness. In the second, Genesis 12:7, the Lord promised to give to Abram's offspring "this land"—either the land in the vicinity of Bethel or perhaps the whole of Canaan (see commentary). In this third promissory speech, a true land grant takes place. God gives Abram all the land that he can see in every direction, including, presumably, that which Lot has taken. (The Dead Sea scroll *Genesis Apocryphon* 21:8–10 suggests that at this moment Abram was standing at the highest spot [3291 feet] in the central hill country, some five miles northeast of Bethel. From this spot one can see from the Mediterranean on the west to the highlands of Gilead across the Jordan on the east.) Furthermore, he gives it to him *and* his countless (v. 16) offspring *forever* (v. 15). As if to give legal validity to the grant, the Lord instructs Abram to walk around its boundaries (v. 17). This act seems to mirror the periodic ceremonial traverse of their lands by kings and other landholders known in Egyptian, Hittite, and even Roman property law (see Sarna, 100). In fact, in Britain some churches still "beat the bounds" on Ascension Day. Crucifer, priests, and choristers march around the perimeter of parish, borough, or at least the cathedral close, striking certain boundary points with willow wands.

Readers will recognize the significance of these land-promise texts for Judaism through the ages. The concluding cry of the Passover seder, "Next year in Jerusalem!" represents a genuine longing in the hearts of an exiled ethnic community to return to its ancestral land. Many Jews argue that the Jewish people can best fulfill their destiny to be the community in whom the "families of the earth" can find a blessing by continuing to live all over the earth as citizens of many nations. However, millions now seek their security and their future in the rebuilt Jewish state, and among those are significant numbers who base their claim on the promise of the land that God made here and elsewhere in Genesis. Scripture continues to give shape to the narratives contemporary people tell about their own lives! (See the commentary on 15:17–21 and "Reflections on Biblical Interpretation," which follows it.)

[18] For the third time, Abram consecrates to Yahweh what was probably a preexisting Canaanite shrine by building an altar and worshiping there. In 12:7 it was at the "oak of Moreh" near Shechem. In 12:8 it was at Bethel. Now it is at "the oaks of Mamre," near Hebron. The meaning of *Mamre* is unknown, though in Genesis 23:19 a gloss (a parenthetical remark by the narrator) simply equates it with Hebron. Hebron, of course, is as well known now as it was in antiquity. Situated on the slopes of a ridge about nineteen miles south of Jerusalem on the road to Beersheba and the Negeb, the city was a Canaanite royal center long before

it became Israelite. (Numbers 13:22 thinks it was built about 1737 B.C., a calculation based on what is known about the foundation of the Egyptian city of Zoan [Tanis].) Archaeological evidence shows Early Bronze Age occupation (third millennium B.C.). The reference to Hebron here establishes the beginning of the long and deep tradition that associates Hebron with Abram/Abraham (see commentary on chap. 23).

ABRAM AND THE KINGS
Genesis 14:1–24

Even the source critics decline to offer a literary history for this strange chapter. Typically they assign it neither to J, E, D, nor P, but simply regard it as an old tradition that came into our book of Genesis without a lot of theological retouching.

This narrative of the encounters of Abram with the kings around him takes place in two scenes:

14:1–17 Four foreign kings invade the Rift Valley
    a. They defeat the local kings around Sodom
    b. They capture Lot
    c. Abram and 318 of his men rescue Lot
14:18–24 Abram's greatness and magnanimity
    a. He is blessed by Melchizedek, king of Salem
    b. He refuses to enrich himself with spoil

[14:1–12] On the face of it, a tradition like this appears to be of historical value, even if its theological interest is slight. The four invading kings and their countries are named and dates are given. The five subjugated kings native to the "Valley of Siddim" (which the narrator or a later glossator assures us is the Dead Sea or Great Rift Valley) rule cities familiar in the tradition: Sodom, Gomorrah, Admah, Zeboiim (Canaanites all, according to 10:19; see also Hos. 11:8), and Bela (=Zoar; already identified with Lot in 13:10, it becomes his place of refuge in 19:20–23). The problem is that archaeological exploration has been unable to identify any of these cities of the Valley of Siddim with any extant site. The names of their five kings are not attested in extrabiblical sources, nor are those of the four foreign kings. (Three late Babylonian tablets published in 1897 tell of four foreign kings who sack Babylon and then meet tragic ends. The names of three of the kings mentioned in these "Chedorlaomer Texts" are somewhat similar to three mentioned in Genesis 14, suggesting that Babylonian tradition may lie behind this

narrative.) Two of their countries, Elam and perhaps Shinar, can be identified; two cannot. (The Old Testament generally identifies Shinar with
Babylon; see Gen. 10:10; 11:1–9; Dan. 1:2.) Furthermore, the enemies
that they subdue as they return to the valley to put down the revolt of the
five native vassal kings include legendary giants such as the Rephaim and
Emim (v. 5). Even the name of the valley, Siddim, is used only in this
chapter, though the tar pits (v. 10) seem to fit with the region of the Dead
Sea (*Mare asphaltitis* to Josephus; *Bahr Lut*, "Sea of Lot," to the Arabs).

In short, the account of the war with the four kings is so enriched with
legend that any core of historical event is probably unrecoverable.

[13–16] This judgment helps explain why the still relatively lowly
nomad of Genesis 13, Abram, suddenly appears here as a significant war-
lord. In fact, he is called a "Hebrew" in 14:13. This is the first use of the
term in the Hebrew Bible; later it will be used to describe Joseph (see
39:14 and commentary). It is not intended to identify Abram ethnically
with the Jews of later years nor as a speaker of the Hebrew language;
instead, "Hebrew" may identify him with the *habiru/hapiru*, "transients,
fugitives, outlaws," an element in the population of Palestine mentioned
in Akkadian texts of the Middle Bronze Age (about 2100–1500 B.C.) and
the Late Bronze Age (about 1500–1200 B.C., the period into which the
patriarchs seem to fit best). Now he is allied with three Amorite brothers—Mamre (who now makes a cameo appearance as the owner of the
oaks by which Abram was camped in 13:18), Eshcol ("grape cluster"; see
Num. 13:23–24), and Aner. The *habiru* chief, the 318 men "born in his
house," and the local allies are able to muster the force necessary to drive
the four foreign kings clear beyond Damascus and to rescue Lot "with his
goods, and the women and the people." Surely an element of folklore is
present in this account.

[17] The king of Sodom, whose goods and provisions were presumably
also rescued, suddenly issues forth to meet the victorious Hebrew. Why
had he not assisted in the pursuit? Where is the Valley of Shaveh? (Even
early readers did not know, so the glossator gives them a not-very-helpful
hand. In 2 Sam. 18:18, the "King's Valley" is associated with Absalom's
Monument, which tradition, in turn, associates with the Valley of Kidron
east of Jerusalem.) One senses that the story had been told in several different ways, and that layers of that literary history can still be detected.

[18–24] Also rich with the flavor of folklore is the ensuing independent
narrative of the blessing of Abram by Melchizedek, king of Salem. This
king, whose name means "My king is righteousness," is also a priest of El
Elyon, the Most High God.

Melchizedek appears from nowhere. His title links him with Salem
(*shalem*), a place mentioned elsewhere in the Hebrew Bible only in Psalm

76:3, where it is paralleled with "Zion." Although ancient Near Eastern texts never refer to Jerusalem as "Salem," the history of Jewish and Christian interpretation of this passage always makes the connection. Furthermore, as a priest, shouldn't this man officiate at a temple in a holy city? It all fits, except that the temple would have to be a Canaanite (or more accurately, a Jebusite) one. Jerusalem, which Abram has not visited and which is mentioned for the first time by that name only in Joshua 10, did not come into Israelite hands until David's men shinnied up the water shaft and captured it about 980 B.C. (2 Sam. 5:6–8).

All of this suggests that in the story of the blessing of Abram by Melchizedek we may see syncretism at work. Scholars have long held that *El Elyon* was a title of the Canaanite high God, and that Israel identified this indigenous deity, together with El's sanctuaries, liturgical texts, and even priesthoods, with its own maturing tradition. For the Israelites, El Elyon may have begun as their neighbors' god, but in time they found that god to be but a manifestation of their own Elohim (the Hebrew generic word for "God," which is the plural form of the noun *El*). Abram makes this identification explicit in verse 22. The priest of Salem, too, may have represented to Israel the acknowledgment by the neighboring peoples of the centrality and power of the Abramic nation. Abram, the one in whom all the nations would find a blessing, is himself blessed by the nations in this reciprocal act of Melchizedek. The blessing is quickly acknowledged by Abram by the tithe of his booty to the priest-king and his magnanimous refusal to keep anything that the king of Sodom might regard as his own (vv. 21–24). Through Abram these persons experience economic recovery of the most blessed kind.

The sudden appearance of Melchizedek and his mysterious persona invited the imaginative construals of his significance that later interpreters offer. In the royal Psalm 110:4, the Lord merges secular and sacred authority in the person of the king: "You are a priest forever according to the order of Melchizedek." In the writings of the first century B.C. Jewish philosopher Philo of Alexandria, Melchizedek takes on more dignity and becomes the very cosmic word of God (*logos*). For the writer of Hebrews, the identification of the scion of the house of David, Jesus, with the superpriesthood of Melchizedek was the next logical step (Heb. 7:1–28). Jesus' unique preeminence is underscored in this analogy: like Melchizedek he is not descended from the priestly caste of Levi, yet his priesthood is superior (Heb. 7:7). Years of speculation and midrash (homiletical commentary) lie behind the characterization of Melchizedek in Hebrews 7:3: "Without father, without mother, without genealogy, having neither beginning of days nor end of life, but resembling the Son of God, he remains a priest forever." Such a construal makes the preexistent and risen Christ the most perfect antitype to the Melchizedek prototype. Small wonder, then, that in about 1625 the Renaissance painter Peter Paul Rubens presented Melchizedek as an aged yet illustrious potentate whose meeting with Abram took place under a canopy supported by cherubim.

THE LORD'S THIRD PROMISE TO ABRAM
Genesis 15:1–21

Genesis 15 consists of two parts, both of which contain further unilateral promises by the Lord to Abram. The first of these, verses 1–6, is presented in the form of a vision within which the first recorded dialogue between Yahweh and Abram takes place. The Lord makes a promise, Abram objects, the Lord reassures him in word and act. The promise is like that of Genesis 13:16—Abram will have progeny. The second of the two parts, verses 7–21, is presented, in part at least, in the form of a dream. The dialogue that takes place is structured the same way: Yahweh's promise, Abram's objection, Yahweh's reassurance in word and act. The promise this time is like that of Genesis 13:14–15—Abram's descendants are given a land to dwell in. Neither of these speeches by Yahweh returns to the theme of the first promise, blessing (12:3b), which overarches the entire saga of the fathers and mothers. Viewed from the perspective of the divine plan, progeny and land can be understood as strategies designed to achieve the goal of establishing Israel as the source of blessing in the midst of the nations.

Source analysts discern in this chapter the first traces of the Elohistic or E source, often thought to have emanated from the northern kingdom of Israel in the ninth century B.C., a century or more after the Yahwist first wrote down the ancient oral traditions in Jerusalem (see introduction). The earliest prophets—Elijah, Elisha, Micaiah ben Imlah (1 Kings 22)—were already at work in Israel by that time. A certain prophetic impulse seems to be at work in this chapter, particularly in the small unit assigned to E, verses 13–16. The subject matter of this section is futuristic, as befits a prophetic word. Furthermore, it is irrelevant to the question at hand ("How am I to know that I shall possess [this land]?"), and can be lifted out of its context without disturbing the account of Yahweh's promise of the land. That is what one might expect of a supplement to an older story.

15:1 **After these things the word of the LORD came to Abram in a vision, "Do not be afraid, Abram, I am your shield; your reward shall be very** great." 2 But Abram said, "O Lord GOD, what will you give me, for I continue childless, and the heir of my house is Eliezer of Damascus?"

3 And Abram said, "You have given me no offspring, and so a slave born in my house is to be my heir." 4 But the word of the LORD came to him, "This man shall not be your heir; no one but your very own issue shall be your heir." 5 He brought him outside and said, "Look toward heaven and count the stars, if you are able to count them." Then he said to him, "So shall your descendants be." 6 And he believed the LORD; and the LORD reckoned it to him as righteousness.

[15:1] In this first vision, Yahweh appears as Abram's "shield" (see Ps. 18:2, 30, 35) and makes the announcement, "Your reward shall be very great." The form of this sentence brings to mind other theophanies (divine appearances). By way of self-introduction at the burning bush, the Lord says to Moses, "I am the God of your father." To Gideon at the threshing floor, God says, "The LORD is with you, you mighty warrior" (Judg. 6:12). To Mary at the annunciation, the angel says, "Greetings, favored one. The Lord is with you" (Luke 1:28). To the whole of Israel at Mount Sinai, God says through Moses, "I am the LORD your God, who brought you out of the land of Egypt" (Ex. 20:2). Because an encounter with God lies at the root of the call of the prophets, they too sometimes have a vision, followed by an announcement of election and commission (see, for example, 1 Sam. 3:1–14 and Jer. 1:4–5). So the form of Abram's vision compares to what a person might experience in any encounter with the holy and, by extension, to the prophets' experiences of their calls.

The reward that the Lord promises Abram here will more than compensate for the losses he voluntarily accepted in the previous chapter by tithing to Melchizedek and by refusing to take the goods that belonged to the king of Sodom. Thus do the writers of this chapter weave that rather different one into the ongoing narrative flow.

[2–3] Like the prophets and others in scripture who encounter the holy, Abram raises an objection to Yahweh's wonderful promise. Whoever "Eliezer of Damascus" might be, apparently he is about to be "adopted" by Abram as a surrogate son and heir since Abram has no biological descendant to name as his beneficiary.

[4–5] The Lord's reaffirmation of the promise of a legitimate heir is followed by a fresh confirming demonstration. The two protagonists go outside to get from the stars a hint of how numerous the descendants of Abram will be. Are stars more numerous than the particles of dust on the earth? (13:16) Now we know that they might just be! This act of assurance follows the divine appearance and objection, and nicely parallels assurances offered to Moses, Gideon, Jeremiah, and even Mary. In other words, in this three-part sequence we are looking at a stereotyped literary pattern that we can name *call*. As noted above, it has particular affinities with the prophetic tradition.

Was Abram a prophet then? Or is his calling, like Mary's, to procreate a significant, elect child?

[6] Perhaps this famous verse applies to both of the promises of this chapter and serves as a kind of pivot on which the chapter turns. In any case, this verse establishes for posterity Abram/Abraham as the prototype of a person of faith.

ABRAHAM AND HIS FAITH IN THE NEW TESTAMENT

Based largely upon Genesis 15:6, the New Testament selects Abraham's faith as that facet of his character most to be admired and emulated. Like makers of paper silhouettes, Paul and the writer of Hebrews use scissors and paste to shape the contours of biblical Abraham in this way. In other words, in the process of re-presenting him in new narratives they transform him. This process of re-presentation goes on all the time within the Bible (as it continues to go on in preaching even today), and it leaves the believer with a dilemma: Which version is normative for our faith? Is it possible that all of the portraits of a hero are given to us for our edification, even if they differ from one another?

The ancestor of Israel and the worshiper of Yahweh is invoked many times in the New Testament. These include the stories of Lazarus and the rich man (Luke 16:22–30), the controversy with the leaders of the Jews in which Jesus says, "Before Abraham was, I am" (John 8:31–59), Stephen's sermon (Acts 7:2–8), Abraham's glorification of the high priest Melchizedek (Heb. 7:1–9), and even the contention in the epistle of James that Abraham's faith was justified by his "works," that is, his willingness to sacrifice Isaac (James 2:21–23). Most of these references are not made in order to further explicate Abraham, however, but rather to explicate Jesus. Abraham himself is re-presented in significant ways three times: Romans 4:1–25, Galatians 3:6–18, and Hebrews 11:8–17.

Paul enlists the example of Abraham in Romans 4 to prove his claim that "a person is justified by faith apart from works prescribed by the law" (Rom. 3:28). He bases the argument on the verse before us, Genesis 15:6. Abraham did not work for his justification, but it was given to him because he had faith. Paul takes seriously the literary context of the Genesis quotation when he points out that Abraham was reckoned righteous *before* he was circumcised. Therefore, circumcision was for him "a seal of the righteousness that he had by faith while he was still uncircumcised" (Rom. 4:11). Paul also stresses that "the promise that he would inherit the world" was a gift, and not something that Abraham earned by obeying the law. Paul then circles back to the motif "faith was reckoned to him as righteousness" through a commentary on the promise of a child. At this point, Paul does some silhouette snipping on the

Genesis portrait: "No distrust made him waver" (v. 20). (What about the laughter, Paul?) At the same time, he offers a moving assessment of Abraham when he says that he was "fully convinced that God was able to do what he had promised" (v. 21).

At the end of his argument, Paul teaches that the same justification by faith is available to all who believe in the God who raised Jesus from the dead, for, as Paul says elsewhere, "If you belong to Christ, then you are Abraham's off-spring, heirs according to the promise" (Gal. 3:29).

Paul's argument in Galatians 3:6–18 also begins by quoting Genesis 15:6. Now the aim is to show that the gentiles can share in the righteousness that is attributed to Abraham as well as the promises made to him. How can this be? Paul recalls that God "declared the gospel beforehand to Abraham, say-ing, 'All the gentiles shall be blessed in you' " (Gal. 3:8, quoting Gen. 12:3b). Paul argues that the promise made to Abraham and his offspring (singular)—that is to say, Christ—continues in force apart from the later Sinai covenant. Now the re-presentation of Abraham has made him the father of all believers.

By now it should be clear that, like all narratives, the Abraham story in Genesis is open-ended. The theological interpreter is able to derive new meanings from it at many points. That is particularly evident in the retelling of the Abraham story in Hebrews 11:8–19. In the context of this great chap-ter on the faith of the heroes of old, the writer says that "By faith he stayed for a time in the land he had been promised. . . . [H]e looked forward to the city that has foundations, whose architect and builder is God" (11:9–10). The writer of Hebrews subverts Abraham's relationship to the land by this state-ment. His Abraham only camps in the land that was given him; his eyes are on the ideal Jerusalem (see Ps. 87:1), even the heavenly one (Heb. 11:16).

Furthermore, in Hebrews 11:17–19, the recollection of the sacrifice of Isaac (Genesis 22) leads to a hint of the resurrection of Isaac from the dead. There is nothing in that chapter of Genesis that suggests Abraham thought he could raise Isaac from the dead after the incident on Mount Moriah (though see the commentary on 22:19). If Abraham did think that way, he was the only Old Testament figure except for Elijah and Elisha to do so until the very end of the Hebrew canon, because until then there was no concept of life after death.

Here then is the situation. We have the Old Testament story. We have the New Testament retellings of the story. We are aware that changes have been made. The question for Christian readers of scripture is this: Can we admit that Paul and Hebrews tell the story of Abraham's faith in a way that is dif-ferent from the way it is told in the Old Testament itself, and that we have somehow to live with both versions of the story?

Traditional commentators such as Calvin and Luther wanted where possi-ble to read the Old Testament story through the New Testament lens. The New Testament was the authoritative interpretation, the standard by which the Old Testament story was to be interpreted. When one reads modern commentaries, the difference is apparent. Of course Christian interpreters take the New Testament account seriously as scripture; indeed, we regard the incarnation as the centerpoint of all scripture. But we want to read the Old Testament story on its own terms. Of course, Christian interpreters of the Old Testament bring Christian understandings with them, and to deny that predisposition is to fail to admit the context within which interpretation takes place. Our goal as historical-critical interpreters, however, is to try to set as much of that aside until we are convinced we have heard the text on its own terms.

One might say that the Abraham who is the archetypal man of faith in Hebrews 11 is really a different character than the one who appears in the Yahwistic account in Genesis and that one is not bound to link the two. To say that, however, would be to fly in the face of the plain intention of the writer of Hebrews 11 to integrate the heroes of the Old Testament into the great cloud of witnesses that lead up "to Jesus, the pioneer and perfecter of our faith" (Heb. 12:1–2). A better metaphor might be that the rope that tied Abraham to the pier of patriarchal saga had, by the time of the New Testament, come loose, and that Abraham had floated free from his narrative moorings to become available to serve as the archetype of faith.

By way of concluding this reflection, let us consider two principles. First, as much as we may be bothered at times by the New Testament's uses of the Old Testament, we are not free to ignore them. Second, we are not free to do the same thing with the Old Testament that the New Testament does. Allegory and reading our own beliefs into the text are now considered unfair; we have to struggle with the Old Testament until we arrive at its plain meaning. However, though we cannot use the methods of the New Testament writers, we have to live with their results. In the end, we are given a binocular view of Old Testament figures like Abraham. That is all right. Binoculars bring important things up close!

[7–11] The second part of the Lord's third promise to Abram is about land. It too is accompanied by an objection by the now very vocal promisee. Perhaps Abram is frustrated after years of wandering from Haran to Shechem to Bethel to Hebron to Egypt, then back to Bethel and Hebron again. Now, in this unidentified time and place, the Lord directs Abram to slaughter three beasts and two birds. This offering will be the locus of the act that will reconfirm the promise.

Abram has been building altars all along the way, but to this point we have not heard that he has made any offering. Here he prepares to do so but without any fire or altar. This is only the second offering of flesh to God of which Genesis has spoken. The first was Noah's offering after the Flood (8:20). The food gifts of Cain and Abel were not burned on an altar, as was the sacrificial custom, but were apparently simply presented to the Lord. Even here, the lack of altar and fire keep this incident from reaching the technical status of a sacrifice. Full-fledged cultic regulation of sacrifice was apparently developed only after the temple was in place in fact, the biblical record of it is largely confined to the Priestly source (especially in Leviticus), the exilic or postexilic stratum of the Pentateuch.

The practice of animal sacrifice, however, goes back to antiquity. It served many social purposes, but a simple psychological motivation seems to underlie the custom everywhere. That motivation is easy to see in the custom of the scapegoat (Lev. 16:8, 10, 26). On the Day of Atonement, the contamination and guilt of the people were transferred to the animal by the laying on of hands, and, according to later rabbinic sources, the goat was led to a cliff in the wilderness and pushed over.

In short, in animal sacrifice, the suppliant seeks to transfer to the victim guilt for past or even future transgressions; the victim then receives the punishment that the suppliant deserves.

[12] The "deep sleep" that falls on Abram is the same kind of anesthesia that the Lord sent on Adam for the rib surgery (see commentary on 2:21). Though the "deep sleep" was perhaps originally intended to prepare Abram to see Yahweh's surrogate, the "flaming torch" (v. 17), and to hear the promise of the land, it now also enables him to receive the prophecy concerning the time that will be required to make good on the land promise.

[13–16] The assignment of this passage to the Elohist is based on two considerations: (a) its awkwardness in its present narrative context suggests that it once led a separate existence or, at the least, has an agenda different from that of the surrounding story; and (b) the term "Amorites" in verse 16 is the preferred term in the E source for the Canaanites who inhabited the land before Israel.

The preview of the destiny of his descendants that *elohim* now gives to Abram anticipates a four-hundred-year sojourn in Egyptian bondage (v. 13; this differs slightly from the four-hundred-thirty-year figure given in Ex. 12:40 and greatly from the same figure given in Gal. 3:13 for the entire time between the land promise to Abram and the Sinai event). It also foresees the despoiling of the Egyptians and the exodus, Abram's own peaceful and timely death, and the conquest under Joshua. Clearly the writer knew the full Pentateuchal tradition very well. The prophecy was after the fact! Not surprisingly, since it requires a flash forward, this is the only reference to the story of the exodus in the entire book of Genesis.

Israel's occupancy of this promised land cannot occur until the iniquity of the Amorites is "complete" (v. 16). Think about that! Salvation history takes account of the behavior not only of the elect people, but also of the nonelect nations. The election of Abram is not to be understood so ethnocentrically that the other nations are, at the same moment, stamped "rejected." If repentance and loyalty to Yahweh should enter into the hearts of the Amorites, could they too find favor in God's eyes? From the Yahwist's vantage point the question is purely speculative; he already knows that they lost their hegemony over the land. Within the larger context of the canon, though, the question remains open. After all, the original promise to Abram is that the gentile nations would find a blessing in his people (12:3b). Blessing for the Amorites and the other nations is God's big objective. The New Testament moves even more emphatically away from ethnocentrism; the gospel of Jesus is to be preached to all nations.

[17–18] The conclusion of the dream flows smoothly from verse 12. The offering Abram had prepared and protected from the vultures before he was put to sleep is acceptable to the Lord. The Lord enters into binding covenant by sweeping between the cut pieces in the guise of "smoking fire pot and . . . flaming torch." So essential was animal slaughter to the ritual of covenant making, both between God and human beings and between people themselves, that the very phrase translated in English versions as "make a covenant" in Hebrew is "cut a covenant." (Similar phrases and practices occur elsewhere in the ancient world as well.) For example, the full-fledged, bilateral national covenant made between Yahweh and Israel at Mount Sinai culminates in the ritual slaughter of oxen and the splashing of blood on people and altar (Ex. 24:1–8). The more private covenant or treaty cut between Laban and Jacob also involves slaughter (Gen. 31:44, 54). As in the case of the scapegoat, a sympathetic relationship between people and animals seems to underly this custom. The human parties to the covenant do to the animals what they agree would properly be done to them should they break their covenant obligations. This becomes explicit in Jeremiah 34:17–20, when Yahweh, speaking through the prophet, threatens to make covenant breakers "like the calf when they cut it in two and passed between its parts."

Except for the covenant of the rainbow with Noah (in connection with which the verb "cut" is never used), the term "covenant" (*berit*) has not been used hitherto to characterize the promises, elections, and gifts that the Lord has bestowed upon humankind. Yet any notion that a covenant must be bilateral (as in our modern English usage) is dispelled here. Yahweh unilaterally promises land to the descendants of Abram. No strings are attached.

The boundaries of the land promised to Abram's descendants now reach their greatest extent. In Genesis 12:7 it was the land around Shechem; in 13:14–17 it was all of Canaan visible to and traversable by Abram. Now it is everything from "the river of Egypt to . . . the river

Euphrates." Given the valence that this text has in contemporary political discussions, it is not surprising that a good deal of ink has been spilled on the question of what is meant by "the river (*nahar*) of Egypt" (a term used nowhere but here). Commentators agree that this is not the Nile (called simply *ye'or* in biblical Hebrew). It may be another term for the usual southwestern boundary of Canaan, "the Wadi (*nahal*) of Egypt" (Josh. 15:4), modern Wadi el-Arish, about fifty miles southwest of Gaza. The Euphrates is clearly the river that rises in eastern Turkey, flows to a point about 325 air miles northeast of Jerusalem, and then waters the Fertile Crescent in Iraq before emptying into the Persian Gulf. According to 1 Kings 4:21 and 27, during the United Monarchy of David and Solomon (about 1000-922 B.C., the time during which the Yahwist put this tradition into writing, we believe) Israel did in fact briefly exercise suzerainty over conquered peoples and territory "from the Euphrates . . . to the border of Egypt." That was the largest political expansion of ancient Israel; the usual limits of the ancient patrimony were "from Dan to Beer-sheba" (1 Kings 4:25).

[19–21] The geographical limits of the promised land are supplemented with a list of ten pre-Israelite ethnic groups that inhabited the land of Canaan (i.e., the land from Dan to Beer-sheba). Some of these peoples (Hittites, Amorites, Jebusites, and especially Canaanites) are known from other texts in and outside of the Hebrew Bible. Others are either otherwise unknown or are clearly legendary (Rephaim—see commentary on 14:5). Efforts to pin each one down to a district, a period of time, or a place of origin have yet to become definitive. In a general way, Israel understands them all to be Canaanites, that is, descendants of Canaan (see Gen. 10:16 = 1 Chron. 1:14). The list is best understood as a way of saying that every indigenous group in the land will come under sovereignty of Abram's descendants.

This list of peoples who must yield the stage to Israel becomes a stereotyped cliche. Though never again ten in number, the seven- and six-nation forms of it occur eighteen times in the canonical books of the Old Testament and twice in the Apocrypha. Some names never appear again; the four best known plus the Perizzites always appear. Another people, the Hivites, appears in all but this and one other canonical version of it. One can follow the drama of Israel's establishment in the land by looking up all the places in which the list is used. The promise that the lands of these peoples would become the patrimony of Israel is repeated in Exodus. In Deuteronomy 7:1 and 20:16–18, the question of how their lands would become Israel's land is answered: They are to be exterminated. In Joshua 3:10 they are to be driven out. Later in Joshua we hear about the battles between this coalition and the band of Israelites with

Joshua until, in Joshua 24:11, they are defeated at Jericho. Yet, in the so-called negative conquest tradition in Judges, we hear that Israel continued to live among these same peoples, intermarried with them, and even worshiped their gods (Judg. 3:5). Later generations condemned this synergy (Ezra 9:1). The last we hear of these peoples is that Solomon enslaved the remnants of them (1 Kings 9:20–21 = 2 Chron. 8:7–8).

Diana Lipton discerns in the entire account of Abram's dream-vision in Genesis 15:1–21 a pattern that is repeated in four other patriarchal dreams: those of Abimelech (20:1–18), Jacob at Bethel (28:10–22), Jacob with the flocks (31:10–13), and Laban (31:24). In every case the dream (a) is received during a period of anxiety or danger, (b) concerns descendants, (c) signals a change in status, (d) highlights divine involvement in human affairs, (e) concerns the relationship between Israelites and non-Israelites, and (f) deals with absence from the land. In the dream-vision of the "covenant of the parts," the last two themes are developed to assure exilic Israel of its legitimate succession from the founder, its liberation from oppression, and its delayed but eventual inheritance of the promised land (Lipton, 217–18).

REFLECTIONS ON BIBLICAL INTERPRETATION

Anyone who thinks that the Bible is irrelevant to modern life had better look at this passage. Like many others in Genesis, it addresses issues that are current among us. Here is what Nahum Sarna says about the Lord's covenant with Abram:

> For the first time in the history of religions, God becomes the contracting party, promising a national territory to a people yet unborn. This pledge constitutes the main historic title of the Jewish people to its land, a title that is unconditional and irrevocable, secured by a divine covenant whose validity transcends space and time. (Sarna, 115)

Conversely, anyone who thinks that modern Christians and Jews have no hermeneutical problem with the Hebrew Bible (see the introduction) had better look at this passage. If it is not irrelevant and meaningless, should the passage be taken literally? Metaphorically? Prototypically? In other words, exactly how does this promise broach our experience today? What intermediate interpretive steps have to be taken to link what it meant then to what it means now? Are Jews and Christians meant to read it the same way? Is this promise good for all time or is it specific to the Kenites, Kenizzites, etc.? Does this lay the groundwork for warfare, expulsion (now renamed "ethnic cleansing"), and even extermination? Can other peoples who have a sense of destiny appeal to this promise to dispossess less powerful groups who might stand in their way (for example, the European settlers with regard to the Native

Americans)? Does this colloquy between the Lord and Abram provide an adequate basis to make political and economic decisions in the Middle East of the twenty-first century? In short, what message does God send us through Genesis 15:7–21 for our guidance today?

Adequate answers to these questions require careful reading of the text so that no meaning is attributed to it that is not there. That is the historical-critical method; that is the task of exegesis. Observable factors will need to be taken into account. Though the first thing promised to Abraham is that his descendants will be a source of blessing, the promise of land is also integral to the Abraham saga: the boundaries given here are not given elsewhere; the list of peoples is stereotyped, suggesting that it is a longhand way of speaking of all the indigenous peoples; the expulsion apparently never happened and the writer knew it (see Judg. 3:5). Beyond these realities, the form and function of the narrative should be taken into account. This is a faith narrative, not a piece of history writing. The distinction can be sharpened this way: History says, "The Lord gave Abraham the land." Faith says, "The Lord gives Abraham the land." The latter perspective suggests that the promise of the land is part of the Lord's ancient and continuing empowerment of the people who are elected to be a locus of blessing in the midst of the nations. God has provided for them and will continue to do so. If and when God elects other people to do blessing-work in the world, God will provide for them too. The gift of land can be seen even by us who are far off in time and ethnicity as a prototype of the providential care and empowerment offered by God.

In the end, the question of to whom various parts of the ancient region of Canaan properly belong in our time will be decided pragmatically, through politically negotiated agreements, we hope. However, all the parties are taught by Genesis that God's providence provides the things that permit continued life in the world—land, sustenance, wealth, and progeny—to the end that God's elect people(s) can get on with their work of being a blessing to their neighbors and to the whole world.

THE REJECTED MOTHER AND SON: HAGAR AND ISHMAEL
Genesis 16:1–16

16:1 Now Sarai, Abram's wife, bore him no children. She had an Egyptian slave-girl whose name was Hagar, 2 and Sarai said to Abram, "You see that the LORD has prevented me from bearing children; go in to my slave-girl; it may be that I shall obtain children by her." And Abram listened to the voice of Sarai. 3 So, after Abram had lived ten years in the land of Canaan, Sarai, Abram's wife, took Hagar the Egyptian, her slave-girl, and gave her to her husband Abram as a wife. 4 He went in to Hagar, and she conceived; and when she saw that she had conceived, she looked with contempt on her mistress. 5 Then Sarai said to Abram, "May the wrong done to me be on you! I gave my slave-girl to your embrace, and when she saw that she had conceived, she looked on me with contempt. May the LORD judge between you and me!" 6 But Abram said to Sarai, "Your slave-girl is in your power; do to her as you please." Then Sarai dealt harshly with her, and she ran away from her.

7 The angel of the LORD found her by a spring of water in the wilderness, the spring on the way to Shur. 8 And he said, "Hagar, slave-girl of Sarai, where have you come from and where are you going?" She said, "I am running away from my mistress Sarai." 9 The angel of the LORD said to her, "Return to your mistress, and submit to her." 10 The angel of the LORD also said to her, "I will so greatly multiply your offspring that they cannot be counted for multitude." 11 And the angel of the LORD said to her,

"Now you have conceived and shall bear a son;
        you shall call him Ishmael,
        for the LORD has given heed to your affliction.
12 He shall be a wild ass of a man,
        with his hand against everyone,
        and everyone's hand against him;
        and he shall live at odds with all his kin."

13 So she named the LORD who spoke to her, "You are El-roi"; for she said, "Have I really seen God and remained alive after seeing him?"

14 Therefore the well was called Beer-lahai-roi; it lies between Kadesh and Bered.

15 Hagar bore Abram a son; and Abram named his son, whom Hagar bore, Ishmael. 16 Abram was eighty-six years old when Hagar bore him Ishmael.

In this chapter, the Yahwist artfully tells a story about Abram's domestic life. All the marks of good storytelling are here. Tension rises as Sarai plots and then changes her mind (vv. 1–6). After a scene change, the climax of the story is reached in Hagar's colloquy with the Lord (vv. 7–12). The tension falls again in the resolution and summation (vv. 13–16). The characters are skillfully developed in surprising ways: We end up admiring the slave-girl more than the master and his lady, and we love the Lord's tender solicitude. Teachers, preachers, and commentators should treat this story holistically because it is a satisfying whole. Even source critics find little reason to dissect this narrative, other than perhaps to assign verses 3 and 15–16 to the Priestly source on account of their chronological interest.

At the same time, readers should also be aware that this story is part of a larger narrative about Abram's eldest son, Ishmael. That story line carries him through his circumcision (17:18–27), his expulsion as a teenager along with his mother (21:8–21), his reunion with his brother at their father's funeral (25:9), and word of his success at founding a twelve-tribe dynasty (25:12–18). For that larger subsaga of Ishmael, this chapter is only the rising action.

To this already rich literary function has also to be added the relationship of this Hagar and Ishmael story to the big theme of the overarching saga of Genesis 12–50: the Lord's choice of a single family to be the mediators of blessing in the world. Even before the saga really got underway, the narrators shared with us information that challenged that choice before the Lord ever made it: "Now Sarai was barren; she had no child" (11:30).

This story is rich with themes of importance to biblical thought as well as to our own: the status of women, slavery, polygamy, barrenness, surrogate motherhood, an older versus a younger brother, chosenness versus alien status, and justice. Quite understandably it is a text that has attracted the attention of feminist and liberationist interpreters, not only because the issues are great and the protagonists are women, but also because the disadvantaged foreign woman is presented so sympathetically by the Yahwist. Through the ages, Hagar and Ishmael have been lifted up and interpreted by Hellenists (Philo, Paul), the ancient rabbis, the Qur'an and Islam, Christian interpreters, and the artists of the Western world.

[16:1–6] The barren Sarai owns an Egyptian slave-girl. The rabbis of the first two centuries A.D. naturally assumed Sarai acquired her when she and Abram were in Egypt (12:10–20). In fact, they supposed that Pharaoh offered her any slave she wanted and she chose Hagar. Perhaps they had had a close and affectionate relationship. The Sarai of Egypt was beautiful and sexually desirable; her husband "sold" her there as his sister in order to get his stake in life. Now she prepares to "sell" her Egyptian slave in order to get her stake in destiny. The alienness and ethnic incorrectness of Hagar seems to be no problem. All that matters is that she act as Sarai's surrogate, conceiving by Sarai's husband a child whom Sarai can call her own. (We are not told how old Sarai is at this time, but Abram is eighty-six when Hagar's child is born [16:16]. Extrapolation from Genesis 17:17, when she is ninety, suggests she was about seventy-five year old. Since she and Abram had left Haran only ten years previously [16:3] and had been to Egypt since then, her ability at her age to attract the attention of Pharaoh was extraordinary to say the least! And she has another escapade yet to go [20:1–18].)

Examples of surrogate motherhood can be drawn from the ancient Near East, but we can find another one closer to this passage. That is the story of Rachel, desperate for a child, thrusting her maid Bilhah upon her passive husband with the words, "Go in to her, that she may bear upon my knees and that I too may have children through her" (30:3). Everything about childlessness was bad for an ancient woman. She became the butt of scorn (16:4), and she became convinced that God showed her displeasure by preventing her pregnancy (16:2). In Sarai's case, no child meant the failure of God's promise of progeny and an elect line.

Abram the Hebrew chieftan acted with fierce independence when he fought the four kings before Sodom, but in the matter of procreation he—like his grandson Jacob—just does what he is told. He makes Hagar a cowife with Sarai. The experiment fails, however. The woman who was Sarai's property becomes her equal, and this cowife becomes sassy to boot!

This sort of thing happened in Babylon too. The Code of Hammurabi has a rule for it: A concubine who claims equality with her mistress because she bears children gets busted back to slave status. Now the same human behavior confronts a Hebrew wife. Angrily, she blames Abram for the contemptuous behavior of Hagar and even pronounces a kind of imprecation on Abram (v. 5). He blandly turns Hagar over to Sarai who "oppresses" her (see Ex. 1:11–12, where the same verb is used to describe Pharaoh's treatment of the Israelites).

Did Abram sin in turning Hagar back to her angry mistress? Did Sarai sin in treating her so, after having proposed the alliance in the first place? Jewish and Christian commentators alike have thought so. Clearly the Yahwist's sympathies are with this disenfranchised foreigner, and that is why we readers incline toward her as well.

[7–12] It immediately appears that the Lord, too, inclines toward Hagar, showing toward her that preferential option for the poor with which liberation theology credits God. The runaway slave girl stops at a spring (the same Hebrew word means "eye") "on the way to Shur." (References to Shur in Gen. 25:18 and 1 Sam. 15:7 place it northeast of Egypt; however, its significance here may be its similarity to a Hebrew verb *shur*, meaning "to see.").There she has her own theophany! Yes, the "angel" of the Lord *is* the Lord, as Hagar recognizes (v. 13). Angels become distinct entities with names like Michael and Gabriel only late in the Old Testament canon. As early stories like Moses at the burning bush show, a meeting with that manifestation of divinity called "messenger" or "angel" quickly resolves itself into a face-to-face encounter with Yahweh (see Ex. 3:2, 4). In this early story, Hagar talks with God at least fifteen years before Sarai does—if we can even call Genesis 18:15 a conversation!

The scene that follows prefigures in interesting ways the annunciation to Mary in the Gospel of Luke. Both women are poor and in ambiguous marital situations. Mary is told that she will conceive and bear a son. Hagar is told that the child she already knows she has conceived will be a son. Both are told to give their sons names that indicate their meaningful present and future relationships with God. The "angel" tells Hagar to make the hard choice of submitting herself once again to her angry mistress (v. 9). From the Lord's side she receives two assurances, not as rewards for her obedience but simply as announcements of the Lord's plans for her: (a) her progeny will be, like Abram's, innumerable (v. 10; compare 13:16; 15:5); and (b) the son she will bear—Abram's eldest—will grow into a "wild ass of a man." The latter promise is not said mockingly, but descriptively: He will be a tough, combative guy! The angel/Lord tells Hagar to give the child the name Ishmael ("God hears"), for God heard her "affliction." (We are not told that Hagar prayed to Yahweh; after all, she is an Egyptian, whose high god might have been Amon-Re. What the Lord "hears" is the voiced or unvoiced cry of woe that arises from oppression.)

[13–16] As the story slants down to its conclusion, it is tagged with names, places, and dates. Hagar tells the deity who met her by the well, "You are El-roi" ("Seeing God"). This personal title for the God perhaps hitherto unknown to her both underscores the visual nature of her experience (after all, she was at the "spring" or "eye" of "Shur" or "seeing") and explains the meaning of a place name also mentioned in the Isaac cycle (24:62; 25:11). If the Kadesh mentioned in verse 14 is Kadesh-Barnea in the Negeb, Hagar's experience occurred about seventy-five air miles south of Hebron, where Abram was living (13:18).

Hagar returns to the household of Abram as she is told to do. There the child is born and is named Ishmael by his father. He does not have a separate revelation of the name. It is simpler to assume that Hagar told him about hers. We can be proud of both of them for communicating about important things! By naming the boy, the eighty-six-year-old father recognizes him as his own.

We will hear more about Hagar, Ishmael, and the tribes that spring from this mixed cultural liaison. For now, let it simply be noted that the Yahweh of this narrative is not ethnocentric. Even though another line yet unborn from the loins of Abram is the one elected to carry forward the promise of blessing, God loves this line too. God has an important future in store for Hagar's descendants. The Ishmaelites will not live outside the sphere of God's providential care. As for Hagar herself, her courage and her willingness to follow God's direction encouraged African-American pastor Eugene Rivers to say this: "I'm going to embrace a vision of myself that says I am more than the sum total of the brutal acts committed against me. I am more than all the attempts to denigrate my being and to suggest that I am anything less than a child of God" (quoted in Moyers, 208).

COVENANT, NEW NAMES, PROMISE OF A SON
Genesis 17:1–18:15

At the heart of these two very different chapters is the same event. Both chapters deal with a divine "annunciation" of a God-favored child, such as also occurs in Genesis 16. In this case, Abram/Abraham and Sarai/Sarah are once again promised a son and heir in the elect line. Imbedded in this twice-told tale is also the acknowledgment that the human protagonists doubt that God is really able to fulfill the promise.

The two chapters enlarge on this common story line in very different ways, however. Chapter 17, from the hands of the Priestly writers, deals at length with the institution of circumcision, a practice they regard as a hallmark of Israel and about which they teach a number of times. It uses the formula "everlasting covenant" three times (out of a total of thirteen uses of the word "covenant"), reports name changes, emphasizes chronology, and calls God *El Shaddai* ("God Almighty"). All of these features typify the Priestly source.

In contrast, Genesis 18:1–15 makes no mention of covenant, consistently uses the proper divine name Yahweh, and, in the humanistic spirit so typical of the Yahwist, focuses on the tent, the food, the etiquette, and frailties of the human couple.

The main point of these two chapters is stated right at the beginning: "I will make my covenant . . . and will make you exceedingly numerous." God is going to do an impossible thing, bringing a child out of their old bodies. The flawed hero and heroine cannot help but chortle. That disbelief is part of the tension that arises and needs resolution in these narratives. The other tension is this: Unlike the election and grant narrative in Genesis 12:1–3 or any of the other promises that have gone before, this covenant with Abraham will be bilateral—a true covenant in our usual understanding of that term. Although the covenant will be grounded upon the Lord's prior gracious decision for the elect one, this promise carries with it a stipulation of circumcision without which it cannot be implemented. If the individual does not respond appropriately, the covenant is canceled as far as that individual is concerned. If a community does not follow the law of circumcision, it too is no participant in the covenant. Simply put, the narrative tension is this: Will they or won't they?

[17:1–2] The Lord "appears" to Abram and once more announces the election of Abram and his tribe. The experience is not new. The same formula, "the Lord appeared," was used in Genesis 12:7 and will be used again in 18:1. Abram's dream of 15:1 also counts as theophany, as does Hagar's encounter in 16:7–12. Theophany typically happens at a sanctuary. (Isaiah, for example, was in the temple when he saw the Lord [Isa. 6:1].) If this text is from the hand of the sixth-century B.C. Priestly writers, living in Babylonian exile or in the devastated homeland, it comes from a community that no longer had such a reliable place in which to encounter God. Perhaps they believed that the story itself was set implicitly at a sanctuary. After all, Abram had built an altar at the "oaks of Mamre" (13:18; 18:1) where he lives.

The Lord appears to Abram as a stranger called *El Shaddai*, "God Almighty." (Later, the Lord makes clear to Moses that this is not a name but a title; see Ex. 6:3.) Commentators have paid much attention to this title. More than thirty times in the Book of Job, God is called simply *Shaddai*, "the Almighty." Five of the seven uses of the full Hebrew title occur in Genesis, always in connection with one of the patriarchs. In three of these it is used as the Lord's formula of self-introduction in place of the more usual "I am Yahweh" (15:7; 23:13; see also Ex. 21:1, etc.). Every name or title of God used in the narratives of the fathers and the mothers is significant; with each one, something more is disclosed about the writer's view of God. As noted earlier, this title for the Lord is a signature of the Priestly source, so the speeches the Lord gives in chapter 17 should have a Priestly flavor.

A historical argument for the special relationship of *El Shaddai* with the patriarchs would go something like this. As Israel came slowly into existence as a twelve-tribe league in the land of Canaan, it incorporated many existing Canaanite groups, each of which brought its own gods into the Israelite mix. Israel's way of handling these local deities was simply to identify them all with Yahweh. *El Shaddai*, according to this theory, would once have been an epithet of one of these local numens, perhaps even the one venerated at the Canaanite sanctuary at Hebron. (Cross, 60, is led by the extrabiblical evidence to suggest that *El Shaddai* was an epithet of the Amorite high god, El, that came to be applied to the Canaanite El.) The heavy use of this ancient title in Genesis by the latest source fits with an archaizing tendency in the Priestly writers: they wanted to recover, restore, and record "the old-time religion."

Since Abraham was the local hero of that sanctuary, he and *El Shaddai* might have come into the unified Israelite tradition as a pair rooted in the Hebron tradition. The Isaac cycle, in contrast, seems to be more closely identified with Beer-sheba and with the divine epithet "the Fear of Isaac." Jacob, in turn, was venerated as the founder of the sanctuary at Bethel and identified with the local divine title, "the Mighty One of Jacob." (See the commentary on 49:24–25, where it is noted that *El Shaddai* also is used by Jacob, several times in connection with Bethel.) The Yahweh speech of Exodus 6:3 seems to remember that an identification of the pre-Mosaic El Shaddai with the post-burning-bush Israelite Yahweh had taken place.

Before we leave 17:1, a question remains. Is the "appearance" and face-to-face conversation of God in any way normative for our own notion of revelation? The very literary form of the verse can help answer the question. The fact that verse 1 employs a theophany *formula* suggests that the visionary experience had already been pressed into a standard mold in ancient Israel. When a formula is used, a hearer or reader knows what is about to happen in the story; in contrast, real-life experiences do not happen in formulas. A believer then or now may well have a sense of having received a divine call, but it will probably have come to her in a unique, special way. Only when the individual seeks to turn her call into a paying position within a religious community does that community invoke the right to test and validate her individual experience. Even then, it will probably no longer use the formula "the Lord appeared . . . and said" as the test.

[3–8] English translations such as the RSV have rendered the sentence, "You shall be the ancestor of a multitude of nations" (v. 4) as "You shall be the father . . ." The Hebrew word *ab*, "father," does not have to be taken in the literal sense of the biological male progenitor. It can also mean patron, founder, master. The English term "ancestor" certainly points to a biological role for Abraham, but preserves some of the fuller sense of "founder" of a confederation of clans that descend from a common source. The word *ab* is now combined with a different Hebrew word than before. Instead of *ab* ("father") + *ram* ("exalted"), it is now *ab* + *raham* ("multitude"). Thus does another etymological etiology (see commentary on 2:23) explain what is in a name! Beyond the meaning of the specific name, the very fact that God can change a person's name bespeaks God's superiority and authority over that person. (Note that no comparable significance is attributed to Sarai's name change in v. 15. Furthermore, she learns of the change from her husband rather than from God.)

In verse 7 God promises Abraham, "I will establish my covenant between me and you, and your offspring after you throughout their generations, for an everlasting covenant." The Hebrew word translated "offspring" or "seed" is singular in number. The writer of Galatians 3:16 took the singularity literally when he understood "seed" to be a reference forward to Christ: "It does not say your offsprings, but your offspring, that is one person, who is Christ." The presence of the term "in their generations," however, makes clear that the word "seed" in Hebrew is really a collective term like "progeny," and that this promise, like the others before it, is directed not to a single future descendant of Abraham but rather to the entire people of Israel.

The phrase "for an everlasting covenant" is also significant. As noted above, it is a signature of the Priestly source. The addition of the element of timelessness here seems to inform the reader that the stories of the fathers and mothers in Genesis are an overture to the rest of history. One can read all the way through the Hebrew Bible and even to the end of the book of Revelation and the "everlasting" covenant will still be in force, open-ended and available to help God's people make sense of their abiding relationship with God. This point is all the more interesting when one remembers that the Priestly writers probably were operating during or shortly after the time of the Babylonian exile, a period during which the certainty that the covenant was really everlasting must have been profoundly shaken.

The news of this everlasting covenant is not simply an assurance to the perishing that, "Hey, in spite of everything, God loves you!" It is an announcement that God is always ready to enter into relationship with individuals and the community of God's people. Such people may have suffered mightily and may even have understood the events of history as heavy-handed divine retribution for their sins. Such people may in fact be in exile. If the covenant is an everlasting one, the fact of exile itself should not be taken as evidence of the removal of God's favor and a cancellation of this covenant. Within an everlasting covenant, the possibility of entering into right relationship with God remains open always.

Now all of Canaan is the land being promised (v. 8). The territorial scope is narrowed considerably from its maximum extent in Genesis 15:17–21, and is more in line with the promise of 13:14–15. Another similarity links these two versions as well. In the earlier J text, the land is given "forever"; here Canaan is to be a "perpetual holding." "Perpetual" is a long time, and the promise continues to have political implications to this very day (see commentary on 15:17–21 and the ensuing "Reflections on Biblical Interpretation"). It should be noted here that the primary promise is that Abraham's progeny will be "exceedingly numerous"; in fact, they will be "a multitude of nations"—rather more than could crowd into the land of Canaan, it would seem.

The fact that this is the Priestly version of the land-promise tradition, and comes, therefore, from circles that had actually lost the land, puts a special valence on this text. These theologians are linking the well-being of Israel, for which progeny and the means of sustenance (land) are necessary conditions, to a bigger reality. That reality can exist, or it can fail, equally well in Canaan or in exile. That reality is the people's obedience to God's command.

[9–14] Unlike Genesis 12:1–3a, this covenant is reciprocal. Even though the covenant that God establishes is open-ended and eternal, the community must insure that every male takes action in order to enjoy this right relationship. The covenant condition imposed here on Abraham and every male descendant or slave is not the general "blamelessness" of verse 1. That verse does not read, "If you are blameless (Hebrew: "perfect") I will keep covenant with you." Even if the term "blameless" is construed as more akin to integrity than perfection, God is not saying, "My covenant with you is contingent upon your prior qualification of extreme integrity." Hebrew syntax would permit the beginning of verse 2 to be translated as a purpose clause: "so that I may make my covenant." Fortunately, the further explanation of "covenant" given in verse 10 renders such a theologically difficult reading unlikely. Of course, the degree to which Abraham can walk "blamelessly" will be a factor in the way in which the covenant is made effective in his life and in the life of his descendants. But that narrative also shows that if the condition of the covenant is perfection, Abraham's own behavior in texts such as chapter 16 already renders him ineligible.

The initially qualifying rite of entrance for males into this covenant community is circumcision. Bits of priestly legislation about the practice are included in verses 10–14: circumcision is a universal requirement for males (v. 10, but no genital mutilation for females, contrary to what is still practiced in some neighboring cultures); it should be done on the eighth day of an infant's life (v. 12); native-born and purchased slaves also must be circumcised (vv. 12–13); any noncompliant male must be "cut off," that is, shunned or excommunicated (v. 14). Surprisingly little legislation about the practice is preserved elsewhere in the Hebrew Bible; Mishnah and Talmud are the repositories of the details for Jewish practice. (The rite is not even mentioned in the Qur'an, but it is widely practiced among Muslims.) We know that Egyptians and many of the peoples of the ancient Near East (but not the Philistines!) practiced circumcision, so it was not unique to the Israelites. Except for a passing comment in another Priestly text (Lev. 12:3), all of the other Old Testament references deal with the circumcision of older males: thirteen-year-old Ishmael, as well as Abraham himself and all his household (Gen. 17:23–27); Moses, under mysterious circumstances (Ex. 4:24-26, where the "flint knife" is mentioned for the first time); and an entire generation of Israelites before the conquest of Canaan (Josh. 5:2–9). All of this suggests that the custom of circumcising baby boys was a later priestly development.

Once again the exilic setting of the Priestly source comes into play here, for it was in exile that the circumcision of all males became a hallmark of the Israelite community, along with Sabbath keeping and certain conventions of prayer (perhaps even the synagogue). In this text we see the Priestly writers projecting back into deep antiquity the origins of an institution that had become important in their own time. Furthermore, the provision in this text for the circumcision of foreigners suggests some individuals from the majority culture of Babylon identified with the people of Israel and even converted to their religion.

Verse 13 introduces an interesting relationship between the broader concept of covenant and the rule of circumcision. Followers of other covenants such as the Ten Commandments manifest their loyalty in obedient behavior. Even the covenant with Noah, incumbent upon all humankind, expects that people will not eat blood, will not murder, and will propagate. The covenant of circumcision also requires obedience; however, adherence to it is manifested in a physical mark. Christian baptism, too, involves a physical act of water on the human body, but after an hour no one sees wetness anymore; circumcision marks the human body forever. The physicality of this covenant is brought out if we introduce the second clause of verse 13 with the subordinating conjunction "so that": "Both the slave born in your house and the one bought with your money must be circumcised, *so that* my covenant can be in your flesh an everlasting covenant."

Calvin was impressed with this syntactical relationship. In his comment on verse 13, he remarks, "As formerly, covenants were not only committed to public records, but were also wont to be engraved in brass, or sculptured on stones, in order that the memory of them might be more fully recorded, and more highly celebrated; so in the present instance, God inscribes his covenant in the flesh of Abraham" (Calvin, *Genesis*, 451). When a covenant is engraved on the body, each person becomes a walking testimony to it.

Already in the preexilic prophets, circumcision of the flesh was becoming a metaphor for submission to the will of God: "Circumcise yourselves to the LORD, remove the foreskin of your hearts" (Jer. 4:4; see also Jer. 9:25–26). Paul goes even further. "Real circumcision," says he, "is a matter of the heart—it is spiritual and not literal" (Rom. 2:29). He does not reject the Jewish practice or advocate the surgical removal of the marks of circumcision, as some others in the early church evidently were doing, but he puts the weight on sincere obedience: "Circumcision is nothing, and uncircumcision is nothing; but obeying the commandments of God is everything" (1 Cor. 7:19). Each in its own way, ancient Israel and early Christianity underscored the cost and the abiding marks of discipleship. To incarnate a covenant relationship with God is never a matter of cheap grace.

Brueggemann's liberationist treatment of the covenant of circumcision flows from his conviction that scripture and its teachings are able to subvert the power of the established political order on behalf of the marginal and the oppressed. Taking seriously the exilic context of the writing of the Priestly source and its great emphasis on circumcision, he remarks that circumcision "marks the faith of the outsiders in Babylon" (Brueggemann, 155). This marginal people who are captives in a strange land have a way of creating a group identity that can resist any efforts by the regime to eradicate it. Three centuries after the Priestly writers issued the final edition of the Pentateuch with this chapter included, the Hellenistic tyrant of Antioch in Syria, Antiochus IV Epiphanes (175–163 B.C.) launched history's first large-scale pogrom of the Jews. He zeroed right in on Torah, temple, and circumcision: "According to [his] decree, they put to death the women who had their children circumcised, and their families and those who circumcised them; and they hung the infants from their mothers' necks" (1 Macc. 1:60–61).

Those mothers and their families kept right on circumcising. Even Auschwitz could not stop this subversive act. Circumcision is one of the reasons that the Jewish community exists today.

[15–21] The third section of the Priestly "annunciation" story of Genesis 17 now focuses on the woman who will bear the child of destiny. God promises that nations and kings will spring from this ninety-year-old woman, and, as a sign of her important new role, gives her (via Abraham) a new name. (Unlike Abraham's new name, "Sarah" is assigned no special meaning. Only the fact of the change itself matters.)

Not only does Abraham doubt the likelihood of this pregnancy; he "fell on his face and laughed" (v. 17). Out loud, he reverts to appeals on behalf of his only and eldest son, Ishmael. God takes no offense at the change of subject, but goes on to make a distinction. God will "bless" Ishmael and will make him the father of a great nation and twelve princes (v. 20). But with the child of Sarah, who is to be named Isaac ("he laughed"), God will *covenant*. In fact, like the covenant with Abraham (v.7), it is to be an "everlasting covenant." The covenant of circumcision, too, is an everlasting one (v. 13), and that one includes Ishmael. However, the "everlasting covenant" with Isaac (v. 19) will not include Ishmael, suggesting that the same phrase has different content depending on who the parties to the covenant are. What is the surplus beyond circumcision in the everlasting covenant with Isaac? Verse 7 probably gives us the clue: It will be a bond of mutual loyalty between God and God's elect people. It will include the land of Canaan. Even the Sinai covenant yet to come may be in mind, for that covenant, too, is a distinction between Isaac and Ishmael different from circumcision. Ishmaelites and their descendants, traditionally held to be the Arab tribes, were known to Priestly circles as circumcisers, and were apparently respected for it. They are not, however, the recipients of the promises and the burdens of the elect.

[22] At the end of the theophany, "God went up from Abraham." The early rabbis and the transmitters of the tradition of the Hebrew Bible were very nervous about stories in which someone meets God face to face. In fact, in some instances they even altered the received Hebrew text, so that the hero would come and stand before God rather than vice versa. This Priestly account of a personal conversation between God (not Yahweh, except in v. 1) is not squeamish about this. Nor does it alter the spatial location of God. God's abode is heaven above, as usual. (Remember that the Lord "came down" in Gen. 11:5 to get a closer look at the mighty tower.) Perhaps the writers intended to speak more figuratively: "'to go up' means the termination of divine communication" (Sarna, 127). Perhaps. Note, however, that even in the twenty-first century, many of us Jews and Christians who no longer think of God as having any particular location still look up when we ask God for help or simply want to render praise.

[23–27] The scene of this first "annunciation" story closes with the implementation of the covenant of circumcision on every male in the entire clan of Abraham, including the founder himself. Because the narrative sets out to pinpoint the origin of the practice among Israelites and to explain to later generations why it has to be respected, the Priestly rule that circumcision should occur eight days after birth cannot be applied to this very first case. Abraham is circumcised at age ninety-nine, and Ishmael at age thirteen—chronological hooks that will be important in the ensuing narrative as well as in the reflection by later writers upon the obedience of Abraham.

[18:1–15] The Yahwistic account of the "annunciation" to Sarah is both delightful and self-explanatory. It is constructed on the same themes that underlie the previous panel: Sarah will bear a child of destiny in her old age, and even to think about it makes her laugh.

The panel opens with exactly the same formula as in Genesis 17:1, "the LORD appeared to Abraham" (v. 1). Abraham is at his camp "by the oaks of Mamre," which we suspect is also a sanctuary. The scene is homey in a patriarchal sort of way: the man is sitting, the woman is inside thinking about lunch. Readers judge the identity of the "three men" who approach Abraham from the headline, "the LORD appeared to Abraham." We assume that they are divine beings, and that the Lord is one of them. (Traditional Christian preachers and commentators discovered the Holy Trinity in this visit.)

Abraham does not know who they are at first. While entertaining angels unawares, Abraham extends to the visitors the normal hospitality that a bedouin sheik would owe to strangers. They get a washup, a rest, and the best food Abraham and Sarah can provide. The bread is choice, the calf is an expensive main course, and the milk and yogurt are delicacies. (Josephus and rabbinical commentators worried about angels actually eating, so they assumed that the three men only appeared to eat!)

Once the preliminaries are out of the way, one of the three strangers announces, "I will surely return to you in due season, and your wife Sarah will have a son" (v. 10). In the delightful humanistic narrative style of the Yahwistic source, postmenopausal Sarah is caught eavesdropping when she laughs at the thought of sexual "pleasure." (The rare Hebrew word may have something to do with "moisture"—the very antithesis of the "withered" condition of the old woman.) The panel ends with the Lord's reminder to everyone that nothing is beyond God's competency. The Lord does not chastise Sarah for her laughter, but she is reminded of it—and the reader anticipates the coming of "Isaac."

The entire panel is wonderful in its simplicity. The reader wishes to know many more details, such as the real identity of the "three men." Like Abraham and Sarah in the story, the reader too wishes to know how pregnancy could happen with people so old. (Embryo implants were not yet done in Mamre!) We wonder what the Lord means by the sentence, "At the set time I will return to you, in due season, and Sarah shall have a son" (v. 14). Is there a hint of divine intervention here? The narrator does not say. The story hurries on toward the fulfillment of the promise of blessing.

THE REJECTION OF SODOM AND GOMORRAH
Genesis 18:16–19:29

Second only to the Flood, the ensuing story is the longest sustained narrative in Genesis up to this point. Attributed entirely to the Yahwist, the story is made up of three large units. All of these have miniplots of their own, but each contributes to the overall plot of the narrative as well and throws further light on the characters of Abraham's clan. In verses 16–33, Abraham learns of the Lord's intention to wipe out the foul blot on humanity made by sinful Sodom and its sister city, Gomorrah. This segment gives Abraham a chance to conduct his work of blessing as he intercedes for the doomed cities. The next unit, 19:1–11, serves to reintroduce Lot, who was last seen taking up residence near sinful Sodom (13:12–13) and then being taken into the captivity of the four kings who sacked the region of the Dead Sea (chap. 14). This unit also underscores the depravity of the place; indeed, it is from these verses that the English terms of law *sodomy* and *sodomize*, are derived. Finally, 19:12–29 tells of the actual destruction of the wicked cities. From these verses, Sodom and

Gomorrah become bywords for the wrath of God, and Lot's wife becomes the archetype of fatal ambivalence.

[16–21] Verse 16 makes a transition between the visit at Abraham's tent and the overview of the fate of Sodom. Courteously accompanied by Abraham, the three men set out from Mamre to the southeast toward Sodom. The narrator treats us to a glimpse of the Lord's thought process, who reflects inwardly about how much information to trust to Abraham, his chosen agent (vv. 17–19). Finally the Lord speaks out, saying, "I must go down and see" (v. 21).

[22–32] Two of the three "men" depart (19:1) and the Lord remains. The NRSV note to verse 22 points out that it contains one of the so-called corrections of the scribes. As early as the third century A.D., the scribal transmitters of the received consonantal Hebrew text felt constrained to "correct" it up to five times in Genesis. (Rabbinical sources preserve lists of between seven and eighteen of such emendations made throughout the Old Testament.) In this verse, their problem seems to have been a flagrant anthropomorphism. The text that once said "while the LORD remained standing before Abraham" is now reversed to say, "while Abraham remained standing before the LORD." It just did not do to have the Lord standing hat in hand before a human being, unless, as one rabbinic source suggests, the Lord's pastoral call occurred while Abraham was still recovering from the effects of his circumcision!

In the spirited colloquy between the Lord and Abraham that follows, the patriarch bargains tenaciously for the lives of the innocent people of Sodom. He raises the possibility that fifty righteous persons might become "collateral damage" when God blitzes the city. He even hints that the Lord would be unjust. The tone, if not the literal text, of verse 25 says "Shame on you!"

After the Lord agrees to forgive the whole city for the sake of fifty, the masterful and compassionate haggler, Abraham, after an appropriate abasement of himself as "dust and ashes" (v. 27), suggests a limit of forty-five. The expression "dust and ashes" occurs only here and in Job 30:19 and 42:6. In that latter occurrence, Job's position is like Abraham's in that he is preparing to intercede with God for people who are threatened with divine punishment. Perhaps this story about Abraham throws light on how to understand the end of the book of Job. Though dust and ashes compared to their Creator, they are authorized by God to speak up for justice even to God's own face. So then, by extension, are we!

Abraham and the Lord finally agree in verse 32 that the Lord will spare all of Sodom for the sake of a mere ten righteous citizens. Has God changed the divine mind? So it seems. This belongs among those passages that are important for modern faith because they present God as engaged with the human community, one who changes direction in the light of new developments, a God who is on the way rather than rooted in place. This picture makes God a participant in human dilemmas rather than a stern judge meting out penalties from high up on the bench. This picture imagines God over here with us, an immanent God, rather than over there in the lonely company of the transcendent attributes of omnipotence and omniscience. This image of God's justice being worked out in the crunch of real life rather than in pure abstraction prefigures the gospel of the eternal Logos made incarnate in the flux and tragedy of human existence.

[33] The Yahwist's ability deftly to describe the Lord's ease in moving around the world of people and places is unmatched in scripture. "The LORD went his way" is reminiscent of Yahweh's walk in the garden in the cool of the evening (3:8), or of Yahweh smelling the pleasing odor of Noah's sacrifice (8:21). This comfortable God of here *below* has an awesome side, though. The Yahwist often locates that side *above*, from where the Lord will soon rain sulfur and fire on Sodom and Gomorrah (19:24).

[19:1–11] Now it is Lot's turn to receive the two mysterious visitors, who are identified as "angels." Like Abraham he shows hospitality. He is not a nomad with a tent but a city-dweller in a house with a door, provisions for supper, and a place for the guests to spend the night. The similarities of the two visits end at verse 4, however. At this point a notably understated but terrifying scene takes place. We learn now how rotten Sodom really was. All the men and boys of Sodom gather around the house and demand that Lot turn the visitors out so that they might "know" (read: rape) them. Lot, still scornfully regarded as a foreigner (v. 9), has the courage to place himself between the crowd and his door and to implore them to desist. His nobility tarnishes before our latter-day eyes, though, when he offers to let women pay the price that will preserve the integrity of the honored guests. He offers to let the crowd rape his two virgin daughters (v. 8). (Later, particularly in the days of the judges, we hear stories of women who were shamefully used to protect the honor or provide for the sexual needs of men. Think of Jephthah's daughter [Judg. 11], the four hundred virgins of Jabesh-gilead and the abducted daughters of Shiloh [Judg. 21:8–25].) The daughters are virgins, but they are betrothed (see v. 14). The code of Deuteronomy makes sexual assault on a betrothed virgin a capital crime (Deut. 22:22–27). That code does not speak to the case of a father who offers his betrothed, virgin daughters to a rapist. Either such a thing never happened, or, appalling as it might seem to us, ancient patriarchal society might have considered that it fell within the rights of a father with his children.

Just as it appears that Lot will be overcome by the angry crowd, the angels drag Lot back into the house and strike the men with blindness (v. 11). The word "dazzled" might be a better translation of the underlying Hebrew word than "struck with blindness." The term is used elsewhere only in 2 Kings 6:18, where the Lord strikes invading Arameans with this kind of retinal fatigue.

The entire episode serves to underscore how corrupt the Sodomite culture was. The fact that we have no secure extrabiblical evidence that there ever were a Sodom and a Gomorrah need not deflect us from taking the point of the story. Evil corrupts and destroys everything around it, and the Lord will not tolerate it forever.

[12–29] The drama of escape reaches a fevered pitch in these verses. The angel visitors have to prod and pull to get Lot and his family to evacuate. The prospective sons-in-law do not take the approaching crisis seriously (v. 14). In the end, only Lot, his wife, and two daughters escape. The nuclear family of four falls well below the minimum of ten righteous persons necessary to spare the city. "Flee for your life; do not look back," they are told (v. 17). At the very last minute Lot drags his feet, not wanting to go to the hills overlooking the Great Rift Valley (v. 19). For some reason he thinks refuge in the hamlet of Zoar (its very name means "little") would be safer. The request is granted; for the sake of the four Lotites, Zoar is spared, the sun rises, and wow! A rain of sulfur and fire overthrows the entire Plain of the Jordan and all that grows there (vv. 24–25). Then Lot's wife—she of imperfect righteousness, she who will have no future role in the history of salvation—looks back (v. 26). This is the climax of the story. Afterward the tension drops rapidly into quiet summation by the narrator.

The association of Sodom and Gomorrah with the Great Rift Valley and the Dead Sea led the Israelis to give the name Sedom to the locality around their Dead Sea mineral extraction plants on the southwest shore of the sea. Visitors to this modern Sedom are shown a salt pillar called "Lot's Wife." The Sodom of this story cannot really be located anymore, though if anything at all grew there, as Genesis 19:25 suggests it did (remember also 13:10), it must have been somewhere else than the modern Sedom. Perhaps the storytellers thought of it as having stood north of the Dead Sea near the well-watered oasis of Jericho.

Zoar is the one place mentioned in connection with Sodom and Gomorrah whose existence is witnessed to by such later extrabiblical sources as Josephus, the Mishnah, and the early church historian Eusebius. The Byzantine church mosaic floor map at Medeba in Jordan locates it on the southeast shore of the Dead Sea. That is the general area on the Jordanian side of the Dead Sea that has yielded archaeological evidence of a number of settlements of the Early Bronze Age (3000–2000

B.C.)—too early for Abraham perhaps, but never too early to leave traditions behind.

Sodom is a place of legend and so is its fall. It is not a Pompeii East. All efforts to historicize the sulfur and fire as a volcanic eruption must fail before the simple faith claim of the story that the Lord did it. Once that faith claim is accepted, the importance of the historicity of the story recedes and the real substance of it emerges: God cannot tolerate human corruption forever. Someone has called the Judeo-Christian tradition theologically monistic and ethically dualistic. God is one, and is good; human beings are torn between their good and evil sides. The moral of this story fits with that teaching. Uncontrolled human lust and violence produce a harsh destiny that is not itself evil, since it is bestowed or at least permitted by the good God, but destroys the perpetrators of such evil. Paul said, "The wages of sin is death" (Rom. 6:23), and both scripture and everyday experience demonstrate the inexorable force of this principle.

INCEST BLOTS THE FAMILY TREE
Genesis 19:30–38

The denouement of the Lot story is inglorious, to say the least. At the end we feel that Sodom had no righteous citizens whatever! The Yahwist uses the departure of Lot and his daughters from the stage as an occasion to besmirch the origins of two of the peoples whose territories bordered the kingdom of David and Solomon on the east. As in the case of Ham, the father of Canaan (9:20–27), drunkenness and illicit sex are the media of contempt. After this tale, Lot and his daughters play no further role in the history of salvation.

Ironies abound in this story. Lot's two daughters, apparently unworthy even to be introduced by name, are worried that they will never find a suitable man and never bear children. So they do unto their father that which he was prepared to have them do with strangers (see 19:8). They rape their father on two successive nights, and they both become pregnant. Intercourse with an old man knocked unconscious by alcohol and not on Viagra may seem unlikely, but the narrator is unconcerned with such details and hurries on to the point of the story. As he tells it, at least, the point is to explain the origins of the neighboring clans. This will answer the question, Why are our neighbors so much like us and yet so obnoxious?

The son of the first daughter is named Moab (v. 37), a play on the Hebrew phrase *me-ab*, "from [my] father." From the time of the appear-

ance of the people Israel in Canaan (ca. 1220 B.C.) until the beginning of
the Babylonian Exile (587 B.C.), the indigenous, Semitic-speaking kingdom of Moab bordered Israel on the southeast. It lay beyond the Dead
Sea in what is now the west-central section of the Hashemite kingdom of
Jordan. Many hostile interactions between Israel and Moab are recorded
in texts from both sides. For example, on the famous Moabite Stone,
King Mesha records his success in gaining independence in about
849 B.C. from his overlord, Joram, the king of Israel. Other stories make
the relationship sound more friendly. Ruth the Moabite is welcomed into
the household of the Bethlehemite Boaz, and she is recorded as the
ancestor of David and of Jesus. Moab's political independence and culture seem to have been snuffed out in the sixth century B.C., probably by
the Babylonians.

The other child was named Ben-ammi (v. 38), which means something
like "son of my uncle" or "paternal kinsman." (The Septuagint adds the
phrase, "son of my family.") Like the name Moab, this name both echoes
the name of the neighboring people of Ammon and has meaning appropriate to the incestuous origins of that clan. The indigenous, Semitic-
speaking Ammonite kingdom, too, interacted with Israel and Judah until
it disappeared from history at about the same time—and probably for the
same reason—that Moab did. It lay east of the Jordan, north of Moab, in
what is now north-central Jordan. Its name is retained in the modern
capital of that country, Amman. Allusions to both Moabites and
Ammonites continue to be made in literature down to Christian times.
Eventually they are swallowed up into Arab culture, though no doubt
their descendants still walk the streets of the cities and villages of Jordan.

THE UNGAINLY STORY TWICE TOLD
Genesis 20:1–18

This independent and fully formed story is usually attributed to the
Elohist. (Note that except for verse 18, the deity is always called "God,"
or in the mouth of Abimelech in v. 4, "Lord"—the actual word, and not
the euphemism for Yahweh.) It is a doublet or second version of the wife-
sister narrative about Abram and Sarai in the house of Pharaoh
(12:10–20). Though the plot is the same, significant differences in the
telling can also be found. Perhaps cultural changes in the century
between the Yahwist and the Elohist, or even the Elohist's own keener
sense of discretion, cause this story to be less bold and bawdy than the
previous version. Now the details tend to burnish the images of Abraham
and Sarah.

Let us enumerate significant points at which Genesis 20:1–18 differs from 12:10–20.

1. This wife-sister narrative is laid in the part of the Negeb that borders Egypt, rather than in Egypt itself (v. 1). Though we do not know where Gerar was, Shur was the place on the way to Egypt to which Hagar fled in Genesis 16:7.

2. While staying "as an alien" in Gerar, Abraham encounters not Pharaoh but Abimelech, the king of that city. In Genesis 21:32 the king is described as a Philistine, but that designation is not of historical value since we know from secular sources that the Philistines arrived in Canaan only in the thirteenth century B.C. at the same time the Israelites did. Nothing we read in Genesis is history-writing as we now understand and practice that art. The book of Genesis gives us theology in narrative form; it renders for us a portrait of God bringing the elect people from the promise of blessing to its visible flowering.

3. In the house of Pharaoh, Sarai became a full-fledged member of the harem. She escaped becoming pregnant presumably only because she was barren. In this more seemly version of the story, the king never touches Sarah because he is warned by God in a dream that she is a married woman. (On the function of dreams in the patriarchal stories, see the commentary on 15:12–16.)

4. Like Abraham in the negotiation over Sodom and Gomorrah, Abimelech chides God for nearly perpetrating an injustice (v. 4), and protests his innocence. He even seems to be a worshiper of Yahweh. In the earlier version, Pharaoh never speaks directly to the Lord or seems even to be aware of God's role in the matter.

5. In the course of their colloquy, God tells the king that Abraham is "a prophet," that is to say, a man of intercessory prayer (v. 7). It is as if God, having experienced Abraham's hard bargaining on behalf of Sodom, has come to view him as an effective and credible attorney for the defense. God already knows that the hero will save the king, though God claims some of the credit too, saying, "I did not let you touch her" (v. 6). This situation gives Abraham another chance to extend blessing to one of the other families of the earth (see 12:3b), the very role to which he was called.

6. In the ensuing confrontation with Abraham, the reader's sympathies lie with the foreign king. His reasoning is fair and his cause is just. In his response, Abraham gives us information that was not brought out in Genesis 12:10–20 or anywhere else: "She is indeed my sister, the daughter of my father but not the daughter of my mother" (v. 12). This burnishes the image of Abraham if not Sarah. At least he is not a liar.

7. As in the case of the version set in Egypt, Abraham and Sarah become richer because of their adventure. They gain more livestock,

slaves, land, and silver. The addition here is the complete public exoneration of Sarah by the king (v. 16).

8. Only at the end of this story do we learn that God "had closed fast all the wombs" of the women in Abimelech's household. God tailored the retribution for a likely sexual misdemeanor to disable fecundity for everyone. Death had threatened, but infertility was already in process until Abraham offers his intercessory prayer (v. 17). Then, as in the case of Sodom before and Job later (Job 42:7–9), God relents and changes course.

This version of the story subverts the meaning of the earlier version. There the story functions to show how the impoverished immigrant got his financial stake; here it displays his positive role in political relations with other peoples and his ability to effect blessing for them through intercession.

ISAAC COMES, ISHMAEL GOES
Genesis 21:1–21

Chapter 21 functions as a conclusion to matters left pending and a bridge to the latter years of Abraham and Sarah. In the category of bridge to the future combined with fulfillment of a past promise is the birth to Abraham of a son by Sarah (vv. 1–8). The melancholy end of the story of the first son, Ishmael (vv. 9–21), and the little noted account of the treaty with Abimelech (vv. 22–34) tidy up other matters that had been left unresolved.

[21:1–7] The announcement of Isaac's birth exhibits Priestly concerns. The baby is circumcised at eight days as the Priestly legislation in Genesis 17:12 required. Abraham's age is given as one hundred years. Further play on the name of Isaac and the theme of laughter goes on (v. 6). It all happens according to promises and commands imbedded in the preceding narrative, the text of which lay before the Priestly writers as they worked.

[8] Perhaps three years later a traditional weaning feast is held. Even today in some traditional cultures weaning is delayed to three to five years of age, so that the child can receive milk and so that, as they believe, the lactating mother will not menstruate. If Isaac was weaned at three years of age, Ishmael would have been eighteen at the time, for he was thirteen when Abraham was ninety-nine (see 17:24–25).

21:9 **But Sarah saw the son of Hagar the Egyptian, whom she had borne to Abraham, playing with her son Isaac.** [10] **So she said to Abraham, "Cast out** this slave woman with her son; for the son of this slave woman shall not inherit along with my son Isaac." ¹¹ The matter was very distressing to Abraham on account of his son. ¹² But God said to Abraham, "Do not be distressed because of the boy and because of your slave woman; whatever Sarah says to you, do as she tells you, for it is through Isaac that offspring shall be named for you. ¹³ As for the son of the slave woman, I will make a nation of him also, because he is your offspring." ¹⁴ So Abraham rose early in the morning, and took bread and a skin of water, and gave it to Hagar, putting it on her shoulder, along with the child, and sent her away. And she departed, and wandered about in the wilderness of Beer-sheba.

¹⁵ When the water in the skin was gone, she cast the child under one of the bushes. ¹⁶ Then she went and sat down opposite him a good way off, about the distance of a bowshot; for she said, "Do not let me look on the death of the child." And as she sat opposite him, she lifted up her voice and wept. ¹⁷ And God heard the voice of the boy; and the angel of God called to Hagar from heaven, and said to her, "What troubles you, Hagar? Do not be afraid; for God has heard the voice of the boy where he is. ¹⁸ Come, lift up the boy and hold him fast with your hand, for I will make a great nation of him." ¹⁹ Then God opened her eyes and she saw a well of water. She went, and filled the skin with water, and gave the boy a drink.

²⁰ God was with the boy, and he grew up; he lived in the wilderness, and became an expert with the bow. ²¹ He lived in the wilderness of Paran; and his mother got a wife for him from the land of Egypt.

[21:9] This Elohistic narrative opens with a troubled Sarah watching Ishmael "playing." (The same verbal stem also gives us the name "Isaac," so chances are a pun is afoot here.) The Hebrew text lacks any predicate for the verb "playing." We do not know from the Hebrew whether Ishmael was playing checkers, volleyball, or perhaps even with Abraham. The Septuagint, either working from a different Hebrew original or simply solving a problem as it so often does, clarifies that Ishmael was playing with Isaac (see the NRSV footnote). Most parents would be happy to see big brother playing nicely with little brother. Not Sarah. It made her blood boil. Maybe the rabbinic commentators were right in thinking that Ishmael was teasing the baby or even persecuting him (an idea known to Paul; see Gal. 4:29).

[10–13] The real issue in Sarah's mind only now emerges. She is concerned lest Ishmael inherit along with Isaac. Given the overarching promise-fulfillment scheme of Genesis, money may not have been her primary worry, but rather Isaac's eligibility to inherit the promise made to Abraham's heirs—the promise of progeny, land, and the greatness of an elect destiny. There is a subtext here, perhaps arising out of the corrupted form of Yahwism found (as we know from the prophets) in the time and place of the Elohist—the northern kingdom of Israel in the ninth century B.C. That subtext is this: The religion of Canaan will pollute the religion of Israel if the lines between them are not kept clear. Although he is Abraham's son, Ishmael represents through his mother the culture and religion of Canaan and of Egypt. He is the Other, beloved to be sure, but alien just the same. Mixed in with this subtext is the obvious claim that Ishmael might have as the eldest son. Sarah need not have worried about primogeniture; cultural norms notwithstanding, eldest sons do not fare very well in the Genesis narrative. God confirms to Abraham that the line of promise will run through Isaac, even as God tells him that Ishmael is to be gifted with his own rich destiny (see 16:10).

[14–21] Abraham displays the milk of human kindness toward his second wife Hagar and his son Ishmael—sort of. He packs them a lunch before sending them out into the wilderness. God, who had cleared the way for the divorce (v. 12), displays divine kindness toward the despairing Hagar as she and Ishmael are about to die in a wilderness that routinely dehydrates its victims. In verses 15–17 the adolescent Ishmael seems to become a baby again when his mother hides him under a bush. They both cry, but God hears the boy. The life-giving spring (v. 19) and the words of encouragement renew their strength. We get a glimpse of the future: a rugged Ishmael makes the wilderness his home. His mother sends to the old country for a wife for him and, as we learn in Genesis 25:12–18, Ishmael becomes the father of twelve sons.

THEOLOGICAL REFLECTIONS ON HAGAR AND ISHMAEL

Abraham is not a brute toward his own progeny. Both Ishmael and Isaac are his children, and he feels a responsibility toward both of them. He values both deeply. Yet their relationships toward their father differ. Brueggemann discusses the difference in this way. Ishmael is the child of reason, planning, and a human effort to ensure the continuation of the patrimony and the promise. Isaac, in contrast, is a surprise, an act of grace, and it is through the gift and not the plan that the promise is to be conveyed and furthered. By setting the story up this way, Brueggemann discovers a general validation of Paul's treatment of these two figures in Galatians 4:21–31 (Brueggemann, 184). Readers often feel that Paul's allegorical rendition of Hagar as Mount Sinai in Arabia who languishes in the bonds of law, and Sarah as the Jerusalem that is above and who is our mother, takes the two figures too far from their originals. But let us take another look. The contrast between coercion and necessity on the one hand and freedom and spirit on the other is present already in the Genesis saga itself, and Paul merely draws it out. Ishmael was conceived in response to the cry, "Let us do it alone! Let us get ourselves an heir!" When you have to do it on your own, that is slavery, and Paul has it right in that respect. Only when you cut loose and put yourself in the realm of the freedom that God offers do you escape that slavery. (Guided by Paul, various patristic writers and later reformers—Origen, Chrysostom, Augustine, and Luther—in many ways made Hagar the prototype of nature/flesh/slavery and Sarah the prototype of spirituality/promise/freedom.)

Savina Teubal is one of several recent feminist interpreters who have taken special interest in Hagar. She argues that God is presented by the patriarchal theologians of ancient Israel as a powerful male figure who oppressively pushes women around. Teubal believes that an original matriarchal stage in Israelite religion was later overridden and suppressed by a patriarchal stage. Near the end of her book on Hagar, Teubal (drawing also on her earlier work on Sarah), remarks,

> [These stories] are not about banal wives or concubines. They are, in part, stories of oracular priestesses and visionaries, who acknowledged the female deities of the land and were empowered to prophesy and envision the future through divine inspiration. Furthermore, these matriarchs were empowered—or empowered themselves—to change the social order. (Teubal, 199)

The theory advanced by Teubal and a number of other scholars that the religious tradition of ancient Israel began with a matriarchal orientation and with goddess veneration has been severely challenged as standing more on inferences than on solid internal evidence. However, the concern it addresses is certainly legitimate. Stories such as Lot's daughters in Genesis 19:1–11 and Hagar in Genesis 16 and 21 picture women being oppressed by men. Men decide their fate, not they themselves.

Indeed, men have been known to seize upon stories like these as warrant to continue the oppression of women, particularly vulnerable women like slaves. Hagar was in fact treated that way in the Civil War period. Sermons claimed that because Hagar was a slave, her rights were not equivalent to those of a full-fledged wife and mother, and she could be sent away at the will of the master. Robert L. Dabney, sometime personal chaplain to Stonewall Jackson, whose 1867 book defending slavery from the Bible must surely stand as one of the most poorly timed publications in history, treats Hagar in this way. Speaking of the angel's instruction to her to return to Sarai, Dabney argues,

> Had her subjection to Sarai been, as the Abolitionists say slavery is, a condition of unjust persecution, the Saviour's instructions to her would doubtless have been: "Now that you have escaped the injustice of her that wronged you, flee to another city." His remanding her to Sarai shows that the subjection was lawful and right. (Dabney, 113)

Can we find a positive place in Christian preaching and theology for the story of Abraham's treatment of Hagar? Considering that Hagar represents a rival ethnic group and that her son is revered by the Arabs as their ancestor, she is treated remarkably tenderly in this story. In the end, after all, God rescues her and assures her that she will be the mother of many nations and that she and Ishmael have a place in God's plans too. Ishmael's line is not the line that God has elected to do the work of the spreading of blessing in the world, but he is valued nonetheless. This approach also shows how people who have a sense of being chosen for a special role in God's plan for the world can still relate to other peoples around them with respect and support. The election of Abraham in Genesis 12:1–3a was not without its cost: When God elects one people, other peoples feel unelected. Even with the problems that Genesis 21:9–21 poses, it lays the groundwork for a remarkably beneficent and accepting attitude toward those other peoples.

ISHMAEL IN JUDAISM AND ISLAM

Ishmael appears both early and late in the Pentateuchal sources J, E, and P, which means he is well-rooted in the tradition. In J he is called a wild ass of a man (16:12). E adds that he became an expert with the bow (21:20). P supplies the details typical of that source: Abraham was eighty-six years old when Ishmael was born (16:16); he circumcised Ishmael when the boy was thirteen years old (17:25); Ishmael lived to be 137 years old (25:17).

The descendants of Ishmael from their ancestor crop up from time to time in texts such as Genesis 37:25–28, where they buy the slave Joseph, or Judges 8:24, where they wear golden earrings, or Psalm 83:6, where they conspire with Edom, Moab, Ammon, and "the Hagrite," among others, against Israel. The confusion between the Ishmaelites and the Midianites evident in the account of the enslavement of Joseph leads scholars to suggest that the Ishmaelites were not so much a tribe as such, but more like the generic class of nomadic traders.

The originating circumstances of the Ishmaelites are a useful corrective to subsequent assessments of the group because interpreters have played somewhat fast and loose with Ishmael through the centuries. Rabbinic interpreters, for example, play on the name Ishmael ("God hears"), saying that this name indicates that God hears whenever Israel suffers at the hands of Ishmael. In general, in rabbinic literature, Ishmael is not a friendly character. He is a threat to Isaac and, as Sarah may have feared (see 21:10), he asks for two-thirds of the inheritance. One of the Jewish legends is that Sarah put the evil eye on Ishmael, and that is why Hagar had to carry him out into the wilderness even though he was a strapping teenager. Other rabbinic stories absolve Sarah in the case by saying that Ishmael shot an arrow into Isaac in the course of the "playing," and that he worshiped idols, lay with harlots, and generally misbehaved. Another legend pictures Ishmael's second wife as kind and attentive toward the aging Abraham.

In Islam, Ismail (Ishmael) is regarded as a true prophet. In the Islamic tradition, he is the prototype of faithfulness. He is a good hunter and an arrow maker. In his role as prophet, he converts many heathen to the worship of the true God. He is mentioned eight times in the Qur'an, mostly in lists of famous men. No story about his life is recorded there. He is not always regarded as the son of Ibrahim (Abraham). In Islamic literature after the Qur'an, it appears that Ismail and not Isaac is the one whom Abraham was prepared to sacrifice. According to the Islamic tradition, Ibrahim does not merely send Hagar and Ismail into the desert, but accompanies them as far as Mecca. During their pilgrimage to that sacred city, Muslims run or walk seven times between two hills, remembering Hagar's search for food and water for her child. They also drink from the sacred spring of Zamzam, believing it to be the very well that sprang up in the wilderness when the parched young Ismail scratched the ground.

The Western artistic tradition has given us many memorable treatments of this story. Paul's allegorical put-down of Hagar seems to have had no effect on the painters. Hagar is always sympathetically presented as a beautiful but tragic figure who has been unjustly used. Ishmael is often portrayed as a lad about eight years of age. The nineteenth-century realist painter Vernet shows the expulsion of Hagar and her son by a richly turbaned but stony-faced Abraham—no grief or tenderness there. Millet's impressionist treatment of the story has no angel and no bushes, but only the emaciated child, an empty water jar, and an agonized African-looking Hagar, sprawled half-naked on a hot orange desert floor, awaiting death.

Herman Melville's novel *Moby Dick* opens with the famous sentence, "Call me Ishmael." The narrator, Ishmael, a perennial wanderer, survives the sufferings of the crew of the ship that is relentlessly driven by Captain Ahab in his obsessive pursuit of the white whale. Ishmael's role in American and English literature, from Shakespeare to Byron to Melville to Willa Cather, seems to be the archetypal outcast and survivor.

In recent political discourse, much reference is made to Ishmael as forefather of the Arabs. Jimmy Carter's book *The Blood of Abraham* contains a brief study of the Ishmael saga. In the West at least, people have often projected violent themes onto this story, always to the disadvantage of Ishmael. Properly read, of course, the story presents God not as rejecting Ishmael, but treating him as a beloved son and father of many nations in his own right. The alleged fraternal relationship of Arabs and Israelis as children of Abraham has little historical value, but does it have symbolic and spiritual value that can assist in peacemaking? Jimmy Carter thinks it does, and he reports that former Egyptian president Anwar Sadat found the concept inspiring as well. Certainly a broad human relationship exists between any warring parties; in the case of Arabs and Israelis, however, there is more than that. No blood relationship is meaningful, there being no Jewish race and no Arab race, but just the Caucasian race that most of them share. However, linguistic and ethnic ties together with a kinship of religious tradition bind them together.

The legends about Ishmael in the Jewish and Christian tradition can lead us to say, "We acknowledge there are other people out here who are a lot like us and with whom we have some kind of fraternal relationship. Their self-understanding and their history are not the same as ours, but we have the shared experience of being spiritual children of Abraham who are bound by covenant allegiance to the same Lord." If this kind of confession about

Ishmael can provide a basis for making peace between Israelis and Arabs, between Jews, Muslims, and Christians, then good for Ishmael!

ABRAHAM MAKES PEACE WITH HIS NEIGHBORS
Genesis 21:22–34

One more loose end has to be tied up before the saga of the fathers and the mothers can move on. At last report (20:1), Abraham and Sarah were living as aliens in the domains of King Abimelech of Gerar. The near tragedy over the wife/sister deception has receded into the past. The time has come to make a lasting covenant of peace between the two men and their respective clans. Abimelech, with his general Phicol by his side, gets Abraham to swear an oath of loyalty to him, a "Philistine" king, in the name of Elohim, Abraham's ever-supportive God (vv. 22–24). The next scene (vv. 25–31) has all the marks of an elaborate explanation for the place name Beer-sheba. After a near conflict over a well—always potentially a subject of dispute between nomads operating in arid territories— Abraham engages in a rather elaborate procedure that will allow Abimelech to attest to Abraham's ownership of a new well. Even Abimelech has to ask what Abraham is doing with seven ewe lambs from his flock, so their use as a witness to the property agreement must have been unusual. The Hebrew reader senses that they might explain the name of the new well, Beer ("well") + sheba ("seven"). That same reader also realizes that a pun is involved here too, for the same words can mean Beer ("well") + sheba ("oath").

Only a well has been named here; the city will be named later (see 26:33). However, the city was surely in the writer's mind.

[21:32–34] Beer-sheba, about twenty-eight miles southwest of Hebron, has long been the chief city of the Negeb. In the Old Testament it is frequently mentioned as the southern boundary of the land of Israel, which went "from Dan to Beer-sheba" (Judg. 20:1, and many other references). In spite of verse 34, it was never considered part of Philistia; besides, the Philistines arrived in the land that came to be named for them, Palestine, only in the Early Iron Age (1200–900 B.C.). The movements of Aramean peoples of which the patriarchs are thought to have been a part occurred more than six centuries earlier, early in the Middle Bronze Age (2000–1500 B.C.).

Archaeology confirms Iron Age settlement at Beer-sheba and, in the surrounding basin, occupation as early as the fifth millennium B.C. Chances are good, therefore, that a pre-Israelite settlement and sanctuary existed there. As at Shechem, Bethel, and Mamre/Hebron, Abraham worships at Beer-sheba (v. 33), and calls Yahweh by yet another title, *El Olam*, "Everlasting God." Scholars are quick to suggest that that was the name of the high god associated with Beer-sheba, and that, as in the case of Melchizedek's El Elyon (see commentary on 14:17–24), the tradition here gives Abraham the honor of identifying that local deity with Yahweh.

ISAAC UNDER THE KNIFE
Genesis 22:1–19, 20–24

The story in Genesis 22:1–19 of God's command to Abraham to sacrifice his beloved son Isaac is the most powerful and memorable of all that is told us about the patriarch. Yet, if source analysis is correct, it is not part of the earliest stratum, but came into the saga in its re-presentation by the Elohist. (Except for the perhaps already extant place name in verse 14, the deity is mostly known by the generic designation *Elohim*. Furthermore, a favorite theme of the Elohist, "the fear of God" [see commentary on 50:19–21], lies close to the heart of this passage [v. 12].)

In Judaism, this chapter is known as the *Akedah*, "the binding," a noun derived from the verb in verse 9b. That designation highlights the horror of a drama in which a father binds his son and places him on an altar, prepared to slaughter him with a knife and then burn the corpse in obedience to God's command.

In fact, many interpreters have taken this story to be the Elohist's way of announcing the abolition of human sacrifice in Israel. Certainly other ancient peoples in both hemispheres practiced it (including the king of Moab [2 Kings 3:21–27]). It occasionally happened in Israel too, although the incidents recorded in scripture all come from later times (see the deposit of the bodies of two sacrificed sons under the walls of Jericho by Hiel of Bethel [1 Kings 16:34] and also the mention that two bad kings of Judah, Ahaz and Manasseh, made their sons "pass through the fire" [2 Kings 16:3; 21:6]). There was, of course, the ancient rule that the first thing that opened the womb of any female, whether woman or beast, belonged to God. This rule is introduced for the first time in the Old Testament in Exodus 13:2, where it is set opposite to the slaying of the firstborn of Egypt. However, as later elaborated in Deuteronomy 15:19–23 and Numbers 18:17–18, only the firstborn of the herd and flock were to be butchered, with their fat burned on the altar and their blood poured on the ground. In contrast, "The firstborn of human beings you shall redeem" (Num. 18:15). God would accept the priestly caste of Levites as substitutes for the firstborn children of Israel (Num. 3:11–13).

Admittedly, Deuteronomic and Priestly legislation developed after this story was already sacred scripture, but these texts underscore the likelihood that human sacrifice was never tolerated in Israel. Sarna rejects the notion that this story is a polemic against human sacrifice by pointing out that the accounts of previous sacrifices of Abel and Noah involved only animals (Sarna, 392–93). Finally, this particular story offers no reason why an angry God would need to be placated with the most precious offering available.

As it stands in the canonical saga of Abraham, this is the culminating event in his life. It is really the end of his biography; nothing about him that follows is comparable in significance. It is a bookend to match the beginning of the Abraham saga in Genesis 12:1–4. In both cases, Abraham is told to go into the unknown. In Hebrew, the expression "go" is more emphatic in 12:1 and 22:2 than the English suggests. It does not occur again in the Bible in exactly this form. In both cases, Abraham goes unquestioningly. Once again a comparison with Job comes to mind (see commentary on 18:27): Though severely tested, Abraham proves to be as steadfast as a friend of God should be. At both the beginning and the end of the saga, the spotlight is on Abraham, not on Sarah or even Isaac. He shares that focus with another character though, namely, God. The reader wants to know whether or not there will be justice and love on God's side of this intimate relationship. God, too, is tested and, like Abraham, passes with flying colors.

Genesis 22:1–19 can be outlined more or less in the shape of a mountain. The reader climbs from the beginning of the tension on the left (I) to its peak at (V) and then down again on the right.

V. Theophany and new orders, 11–12

IV. Preparations, 9–10   VI. New Preparations: the ram, 13

III. "God will provide," 7–8   VII. "The Lord will provide," 14

II. Rising action, 3–6   VIII. Falling action, 15–18

I. The test: sacrifice son 1–2   IX. Test completed, 19

Though the narrative climax is reached when the cry from heaven stops the man with the poised knife (vv. 11–12), the theological meat of the passage is to be found in the repeated sentence, "God will provide" (vv. 8, 14). Those words answer both of the burning questions that run throughout this structure: Will Abraham be faithful? Will God be faithful?

22:1 **After these things God tested Abraham. He said to him, "Abraham!" And he said, "Here I am." 2 He said, "Take your son, your only son Isaac,** whom you love, and go to the land of Moriah, and offer him there as a burnt offering on one of the mountains that I shall show you." ³ So Abraham rose early in the morning, saddled his donkey, and took two of his young men with him, and his son Isaac; he cut the wood for the burnt offering, and set out and went to the place in the distance that God had shown him. ⁴ On the third day Abraham looked up and saw the place far away. ⁵ Then Abraham said to his young men, "Stay here with the donkey; the boy and I will go over there; we will worship, and then we will come back to you." ⁶ Abraham took the wood of the burnt offering and laid it on his son Isaac, and he himself carried the fire and the knife. So the two of them walked on together. ⁷ Isaac said to his father Abraham, "Father!" And he said, "Here I am, my son." He said, "The fire and the wood are here, but where is the lamb for a burnt offering?" ⁸ Abraham said, "God himself will provide the lamb for a burnt offering, my son." So the two of them walked on together.

⁹ When they came to the place that God had shown him, Abraham built an altar there and laid the wood in order. He bound his son Isaac, and laid him on the altar, on top of the wood. ¹⁰ Then Abraham reached out his hand and took the knife to kill his son. ¹¹ But the angel of the LORD called to him from heaven, and said, "Abraham, Abraham!" And he said, "Here I am." ¹² He said, "Do not lay your hand on the boy or do anything to him; for now I know that you fear God, since you have not withheld your son, your only son, from me." ¹³ And Abraham looked up and saw a ram, caught in a thicket by its horns. Abraham went and took the ram and offered it up as a burnt offering instead of his son. ¹⁴ So Abraham called that place "The LORD will provide"; as it is said to this day, "On the mount of the LORD it shall be provided."

[22:1] Right from the outset the reader learns that the events that follow are only a "test." The same word is used about the manna; it too will test or prove whether an utterly dependent Israel, wandering in the wilderness, will obey God's ban on gathering on the Sabbath, or not (Ex. 16:4). Israel flunks that test in week one, but the Lord never fails. God provides! The reader hopes that Abraham will not fail, and trusts that God will not.

[2] The awfulness of the command to sacrifice Isaac is underscored by the phrase, "whom you love." Questions such as "What kind of God would order such a thing?" have always abounded. Remembering that this is not factual history but theology in story form helps some, but even to tell a story in which God puts a beloved servant to this kind of test seems to make God cruel. It is essential that the key sentence of the story, "God will provide," be borne in mind at all times.

The only other mention of "Moriah" in scripture is in 2 Chronicles 3:1: "Solomon began to build the house of the LORD in Jerusalem on Mount Moriah." In the five centuries that elapsed between the Elohist and the work of the Chronicler, the identification of Mount Moriah with the Temple Mount evidently had become complete. That confirmed to readers that the massive stone outcropping preserved in the temple precincts as the place of the sacrifice of Isaac was authentic. Muhammad's even more elaborate vision of a night journey from this rock to the Seventh Heaven provided the Omayyad Caliph Abd al-Malik of Damascus the warrant necessary to cover that rock in A.D. 687–691 with the earliest and one of the most beautiful Islamic shrines in the world, the Dome of the Rock.

By itself, Genesis 22 can hardly sustain all of this development. We are told that Moriah lay three days travel by donkey from Beer-sheba, but we are not told in which direction it lay. (Modern Jerusalem is fifty-three road miles from modern Beer-sheba, or about eighteen hours of steady walking.) Nor do we know what the name means. It could be derived from any of the following verbal roots: *ra'ah*, "see," *yare'*, "fear," or *yarah*, "teach" (which also gives us the similar sounding noun, *moreh*, "teacher"). Because each of these could be related to the content of this story, an elaborate play on words may be involved. The fact that in the Hebrew "Moriah" has an article ("the Moriah") makes a wordplay seem even more likely.

[3–6] In this section of rising action, time-specific details of preparation for a sacrifice are offered. Two motivations are implied for Abraham's request that his two young servants stay behind with the donkey. Either the mountain is too holy to be trod upon by those not called to do so (rather like Sinai in Ex. 19:23) or Abraham does not want them to witness a murder.

[7–8] In this little colloquy the son now speaks for the first time. Apparently he is no infant. The last time we saw him, he had just been weaned (21:8), perhaps at three to five years of age. Now he is big enough to walk three days and at the end to carry a load of wood up the mountainside. The artistic portrayals of him as about ten years old might be right. His demeanor throughout is more trusting and unprotesting than a teenager's would be, if twenty-first-century teenagers can be used as evidence!

Isaac's question about the lack of an actual sacrificial animal sounds a note of deep pathos, matched only by the pathos of his father's reassurance, "God himself will provide" (v. 8). We readers do not know whether or not Abraham believed his own assurance, though we expect that what he says will prove to be true because we have known all along that this is a test. The Latin words that underlie the English "provide," *pro* ("forward") + *videre* ("see"), point to the related English adjective, "provident" ("using foresight"), and the theological noun "providence" ("divine guidance and care"). Whether he wholeheartedly believed it at that terrible moment or not, Abraham's message is that God sustains the world and especially those who love and obey God.

[9–10] No one speaks as the grim preparations are made. In the Hebrew text, the word "altar" has an article, suggesting that Abraham reassembles a little used but already sacred place of sacrifice. Moriah is no elaborate pyramid like Chichén-Itzá or Uxmal in Mexico, with a smooth and well-drained stone table for the taking of human hearts, but at this moment its dramatic function is the same.

[11–12] The crisis is averted! The narrator keeps it spare, telling only what is necessary and leaving it up to Isaac and the reader to exhale deeply. In the voice of the divine alter ego, "the angel of the LORD," God issues new orders. Abraham passes the test; he fears God—a favorite theme of the Elohist. This means that he holds God in profound respect and awe. In some forms, the Hebrew word for "fear" looks and sounds very much like the word for "see, appear." A play on these words runs through the entire chapter (see comments on "Moriah" above, and on v. 14 below).

[13] Unlike sacrificial animals generally, this ram gives up its life not for Abraham's sins but for Isaac's life. It is not a ransom for many, but a substitute for one.

[14] The name given the holy place by Abraham echoes the faith he expressed in verse 8. Holy places and their names endure longer than the explanations people give for how they came about. Perhaps an altar or shrine named *YHWH yireh* ("The LORD will provide," a slogan sometimes inscribed on the Communion table or reredos of a church) existed before it was associated with Abraham. Be that as it may, the name aptly sums up the moral of this story. As is so often the case with biblical names, the meaning assigned it in the story is only one of several possible interpretations. The same words also mean "Yahweh sees." The popular or editorial explanation of the name that follows can also mean "On the mountain Yahweh is seen," or "there is vision." Puns abound!

Was Abraham justified before God by his faith or by his works? The epistle of James combines Genesis 15:6 with this account to argue that his faith was brought to completion by his work of offering his son (James 2:18–24). Perhaps so. However, the resounding echo, "The LORD will provide" puts the emphasis on God's providential care. That care is real whether we trust it or not. Happy are those, like Abraham, who both trust God and experience divine providence.

[15–18] In the declining action after the test is finished, the "angel of the LORD" reiterates the earlier promise of progeny (see 12:7; 13:16; 15:5; 17:6). He wraps that promise in the great overarching banner of blessing by restating Genesis 12:3b using a clearly reflexive form of the verb: "all the nations of the earth gain blessing for themselves."

[19] Commentators ancient and modern have puzzled over why Abraham alone rejoins his servants and returns to Beer-sheba. In some earlier version of the story, did the father sacrifice the son after all? In that tradition was Isaac later resurrected from the dead? Some midrashim toyed with these ideas, though nothing in scripture supports this approach except perhaps the enigmatic words of Hebrews 11:19: "[Abraham] considered the fact that God is able even to raise someone from the dead—and figuratively speaking, he did receive him back."

[20–24] Obviously this brief family history about the children of Abraham's brother Nahor (11:29) is not part of the Akedah. It confirms a kinship relationship with Aram (the Arameans or Syrians, another ethnic group so close to Israel that children were taught to say, "A wandering Aramean was my ancestor." [Deut. 26:5]). More important for the family saga of Israel, it establishes the pedigree of Rebekah, through whom, after her marriage to Isaac, her first cousin once removed, the line of promise will run.

This most powerful of all the patriarchal narratives is rich with theological issues. Above all, it demonstrates the precariousness of the promise of blessing through Abraham's people. That promise of Genesis 12:3b has already been challenged by poverty, perfidy, barrenness, the false start with Ishmael. Now it hangs to its fulfillment by a mere thread as the knife flashes over Abraham's head. What great risks God took in choosing to guide the world to reunion and blessing through a human family and an elect people! As early as the time of the fathers and the mothers, God works from within the human story, in an incarnate way. People stumble along in following God's call, but God provides. God's loving providence reaches under and around us even in our agony.

With Hagar, Abraham and Sarah took matters into their own hands; together they got a son for Abraham by scheming. That son Abraham lost to the alien world. After Ishmael, Sarah and Abraham did not take matters into their own hands; laughing, they got a son by hope and miracle. That son Abraham almost lost too, but God provided. Such a precedent is difficult for all who follow. Most of us would consider it irresponsible to launch out into the blue this radically. Certainly God wants us to use our brains. But providence stands beside us in the daily round and in the extreme crisis.

Christians have always seen this story as a prefiguration of the passion of Jesus. The passion of Isaac is also the passion of his father, and from that prototype we discern that the passion of Jesus is also the passion of his Father as well. In both accounts, obedience requires the son to remain steadfast to the end. Abraham and Isaac make no protest, though little Isaac wonders about the absence of a lamb. Jesus knows he is the lamb. He says, "My Father, if it is possible, let this cup pass from me; yet not what I want but what you want" (Matt. 26:39). God's silence is the answer. Yet God provides, and the slender cord linking the promise of blessing to all peoples and its future fulfillment is never severed.

THE AKEDAH IN THE ARTS

The dramatic story of vicarious sacrifice became a theme of Jewish and Christian art very early on. As early as A.D. 519, the charmingly naive mosaic floor of the Hellenistic synagogue at Beth Alpha in Israel set forth the essential features of most renditions of the story. The scene is captured at the moment of greatest tension. The fire is already burning on the altar, Abraham holds the boy with his left hand and raises the knife with his right, a ram struggles in a bush, and a hand reaches down from heaven to symbolize the voice of the angel of the Lord. The same elements are present in the medieval illuminated manuscripts and are powerfully represented on Ghiberti's bronze doors of the baptistery in Florence (1401–1402). The angel grows bigger and more beautiful in the sixteenth-century paintings of Titian and Caravaggio. But perhaps no treatment by the masters captures the pathos of the story more than Rembrandt's version of 1635. The old but purposeful father covers his son's face with a powerful grip, as if forcing him back onto the wood of the altar. A rather urgent but strong-looking angel has actually seized Abraham's right hand, causing the ornate knife to fall. Etchings and Bible illustrations sometimes emblazon the scene with the words of providence, "*YHWH yireh.*"

The understanding of the relationship of this story to the passion of Jesus is often revealed in the way this scene is juxtaposed to the rest of the Bible story. The sacrifice of Isaac is a major artistic motif in the National Cathedral in Washington, D.C. Not only does one of the huge stained glass windows of the nave depict an elongated Abraham writhing in agony like unto that of God at the crucifixion of the Son, but the motif reappears in a stone carving at the base of an archway in one of the side aisles. There the sacrifice takes place over the head of the Danish theologian Kierkegaard, who reflected deeply on this story in his great book *Fear and Trembling*. Another sprightly young Isaac leads a donkey loaded with firewood in a wrought iron grill over a window in the front door. Many interpretations can be offered for why the story is told this way or that way in art. By nature such depictions are open-ended; the viewer's response is part of the meaning of the picture or the sculpture. Thus is the scope of the the original story extended, and its essential message is proclaimed: "God will provide."

Writers too have reflected time and again on this story, beginning with the expository commentaries (midrashim) of the early rabbis, and the writings of the church fathers. The latter always read the story as a type of the crucifixion and a foreshadowing of the Eucharist. Medieval morality plays took it the same way, though they tended to make Isaac the hero and to focus on how he must have felt as he took his place on the altar. Of the countless treatments of and references to the story, a modern one stands out for its pathos as it dares to imagine what would happen—indeed, did happen—if the father refused to substitute the ram. It is the poem of World War I soldier Wilfred Owen, entitled "The Parable of the Old Man and the Young."

> So Abram rose, and clave the wood, and went
> And took the fire with him, and a knife.
> And as they sojourned both of them together,
> Isaac the first-born spake and said, My Father,
> Behold the preparations, fire and iron,
> But where the lamb for this burnt offering?
> Then Abram bound the youth with belts and straps,
> And builded parapets and trenches there,
> And stretched forth the knife to slay his son.
> When lo! an angel called him out of heaven.
> Saying, Lay not thy hand upon the lad,
> Neither do anything to him. Behold,
> A ram, caught in a thicket by its horns;
> Offer the Ram of Pride instead of him.
> But the old man would not so, but slew his son,
> And half the seed of Europe, one by one.

SARAH'S DEATH AND BURIAL AT HEBRON
Genesis 23:1–20

In due course Sarah dies, having had a good life of 127 years. The story about her burial is a delightful one, rich in detail and local color. If humor is to be found anywhere in the Bible, it is found here. Little commentary is needed, especially for readers who have lived in traditional societies where bargaining and barter are the approved ways of doing business.

Like a place name, a burial site can endure for a time, and often traditions about the person buried there cluster around the tomb or shrine or pyramid that marks the spot. So it may have been with Sarah. This entire legend may have grown up around a tomb venerated as hers that stood near the sanctuary at Mamre, of which she and Abraham were considered founders. In due course, she is joined there by her husband (25:9–10), her son Isaac and his wife Rebekah, Jacob and his wife Leah (49:31; 50:13)— a regular necropolis for the family of destiny. To this day one of the strangest and most dramatic shrines in the Holy Land is the Haram el-Khalil at Hebron. This mosque, which stands on a magnificent Herodian platform, is a Crusader building dating to about A.D. 1115. It incorporates Byzantine and Mameluke elements as well as two minarets added by Saladin. Since 1967, part of the building has also served as a synagogue. Visitors peer through grills at cenotaphs (memorials) honoring the fathers and mothers, whose actual graves are said to be in the caves of Machpelah far below.

In the saga, Abraham and Sarah become associated with Hebron when they pitch their tent by the oaks of Mamre (Gen. 13:18). Abraham seems to have had his eye on the cave of Machpelah as a possible burying place. It belonged to one Ephron son of Zohar, one of "the Hittites, the people of the land" (v. 7). For a long time this ethnic designation has vexed scholars. The Hittites were an Indo-European people of Anatolia, whose empire, destroyed about 1200 B.C., never reached south of the Orontes River in northwest Syria. Yet here they are settled in Hebron, bearing good Hebrew names. Later Assyrian and Babylonian records vaguely refer to all the land between the Euphrates and Egypt as "Hittite." Probably we should take verse 7 as a clue that the narrator is using "Hittite" as an umbrella term for the indigenous people and considering them as a branch of the Canaanites (see 10:16, where Heth, the ancestor of the Hittites, is listed as a son of Canaan).

The negotiation itself is what is fun about this chapter. In verse 4, Abraham, the longtime resident but still not one of the old families (sound familiar?), states his intention to buy a burial place. The "Hittites" reply that they would withhold no options from so mighty a prince (v. 6). Abraham plays his first card: He wants the cave of Machpelah and he is prepared to pay the full price, yet unsettled (vv. 8–9).

Now Ephron plays a card: "I give you the field, and . . . the cave" (v. 11). Probably no one intended actually to give it to the man, nor did Abraham want it as a gift. He wanted the clear title that only public attestation of a purchase could give him.

Abraham plays his next card: "No, I want to pay."

Ephron plays his trump card, managing to mention a fairly steep price of 400 shekels of silver (at about 8.26 grams per shekel, that would equal 3.304 kilograms of silver worth about $585 in the year A.D. 2000). The offhand mention of the price is accompanied by further protestations from Ephron—"What is that between you and me?"

Abraham pays up without a further word. All the people attest to the sale (v. 18).

Thus ends the story of how the tomb of Sarah and all the patriarchs came to be located in Hebron.

11. The Saga of Isaac and Rebekah
Genesis 24:1–28:9

Compared with the twelve chapters that Genesis devotes to the story of Abraham, the thirteen it gives to Joseph, or even the seven that tell about Jacob and his family, the four chapters that Genesis partially gives to Isaac and his family seem rather paltry. Even though the beloved formula of later years—"your fathers, Abraham, Isaac, and Jacob"—puts the three founders on a par, some scholars doubt that there is a separate Isaac cycle within the saga of the fathers and the mothers. In spite of that, this commentary will treat Genesis 24–27 as a minicycle, even while acknowledging that the data on Isaac himself is thin and that much of the material has to do with his wife, sons and other figures.

One could almost speak of this section as the Rebekah cycle, for she is the hero of chapter 24, the young mother in 25:19–26, and is a major player in the wife/sister episode in 26:1–11 and in the scam of chapter 27. Even as a beautiful young virgin at her father's house in the homeland in Mesopotamia, she manages to convey a sense of dignity, virtue, and courage without seeming to be a mere pawn in the hands of her brother, father, and suitor. When asked, "Will you go with this man?" (24:58) her response is masterful in its simplicity: "I will go." The sense of destiny that enabled her to marry a stranger in a strange land and thus to become the next in the line of the great women who bore the ancestors of Israel has made her the prototypical fiancée. Many American homes treasure as an heirloom an ornately framed copy of a late nineteenth-century polychrome wedding certificate inscribed with the names of ancestors and illustrated with a picture of Rebekah arriving on her camel before the eyes of her future husband. The hallowed words of the wedding service, "For better, for worse, for richer, for poorer, in sickness and in health, to love and to cherish, till death do us part" seem perfectly appropriate to the story of Rebekah and Isaac.

In chapter 24 the transition from Abraham to Isaac takes place slowly.

Abraham sends his servant to find a wife for his son from among the
Arameans from whence he came rather than from among the local
Canaanites or "Hittites." One can say that the promise of blessing
through Abraham's descendants hangs on the thin cord of this anonymous servant during the course of this longest chapter of the book of
Genesis. The completion of this servant's work and the successful transition of the saga to the next generation is signaled when he who was the
oldest of all of Abraham's staff is identified at the end as Isaac's servant
(24:56, 65). That transition is underscored by the repetition of the obedient journey that Abraham took from Haran to Hebron in the obedient
journey that Rebekah now takes. The blessing pronounced upon
Rebekah by her family in verse 60 echoes the blessing that the Lord pronounces upon Abraham after he passes the test on Mount Moriah
(22:17). Furthermore, though the Lord does not speak in this idyll, the
invisible hand of providence is at work, assuring that the promise of
blessing that was made by God to Abraham in Genesis 12:1–3 will pass
down through the chosen line of Isaac. Indeed, providence continues to
bend events in the direction of success and away from disaster throughout the Isaac story.

ROMANCING REBEKAH AT THE WELL
Genesis 24:1–67

[24:1–9] The Abraham cycle ends and the Isaac narrative opens with a
colloquy between an old Abraham and an old and trusted servant. Even
the younger son Isaac is far from youthful. According to Genesis 25:20,
he married at age forty. (Since Abraham was a hundred years old when
Isaac was born, he might be about 139 in this story. However, he still has
thirty-six years and another marriage and family to go [see 25:1–11]).
Clearly the time has come to arrange for the succession of the promise of
blessing.

We can be grateful that oath taking no longer involves putting one's
hand under the other's testes. Symbolic gestures still accompany oath
taking, of course, such as placing one hand on the Bible and raising the
other. However, such gestures place no emphasis on sexuality and procreation. This touching of the "thigh" (actually understood to be a
euphemism for the penis in this case) may have been unusual even in
ancient Israel; the Bible mentions it again only once, when the dying
Jacob exacts a promise from his sons (47:29). Perhaps the symbol was
intended to place a violator under the sanction of infertility.

Abraham administers the oath: The servant must find a wife for

Isaac from among the cousins still living in Mesopotamia. In verse 7 the patriarch refers to his own migration from that place and quotes the simple version of the land promise from Genesis 12:7. Why that promise requires that offspring be born of a wife taken from the same family is not made clear. Perhaps the Yahwist had a sense that the election of the family of Abraham to the special role and burden of land and blessing required reinforcement from both sides. Indeed, the wives of Abraham, Isaac, and Jacob are all related by blood to their husbands.

The oath binds the servant to complete the mission. He can be released from it only if the chosen woman refuses to come with him back to Canaan (v. 8). That provision sets up a tension in the plot of the story that will be released only at its climax in verse 58.

[10–27] The alert reader may recall that Terah was the father of Abram, Nahor, and Haran (11:27). After Haran died in Ur of the Chaldeans, Terah took his son Abram and Haran's son Lot to the city of Haran in what today is northern Syria, over six hundred miles northwest from Ur. To this point in the story we have not heard that Nahor made this migration, though we do know that he had a family, including a granddaughter, Rebekah (22:23). Now, however, when Abraham's servant goes to look for a wife for Isaac, he goes to "the city of Nahor" (24:10), which must either be Haran or its near neighbor. We can deduce that in two ways from the name "Aram-naharaim": (1) The name itself means something like "Aram of the Two Rivers" or "Aram beside the River"; and (2) one of the two other references in the Bible to this place, the superscription to Psalm 60, links it with Aram-Zobah, where, according to 2 Samuel 8:3–8, David had a great victory while on his way to the Euphrates. This association of Aram-naharaim with the region of the Great Bend of the Euphrates, with Haran in its midst, is further confirmed by the name of that very region in extrabiblical Near Eastern sources as *Naharaim*.

In short, the servant takes Abraham's ten camels and his many gifts, and returns to the source of Abraham himself and to his kinfolk there.

The earliest mention in ancient Near Eastern texts of the camel as a domesticated animal can be dated to 1069 B.C. Archaeological evidence suggests that camel domestication had spread from eastern Iran and the Indus Valley into southern Arabia by 1500 B.C., the beginning of the chronological horizon of the patriarchal saga. Whether or not domesticated camels were known in northern Syria and Canaan that early is open to serious question. Certainly by the time of the Yahwist six centuries later, they were a familiar sight throughout the Near East. However, Abraham's ten camels of verse 10 may well be a bit anachronistic.

In a prayer to Yahweh, the servant proposes a kind of ordeal or test. (The reader can decide whether it is a test of Yahweh or of the servant!) Whatever girl comes to the well and shows the courtesy of offering water both to the servant and to the camels will be the one whom the Lord has selected for Isaac.

Rebekah, the woman of destiny, is presented in verse 15 as the granddaughter of Milcah, the wife of Nahor (see also 11:29; 22:23; 24:24). It is somewhat unusual to identify a person by mentioning her grandmother's name when frequently even the mother goes unmentioned. Perhaps Milcah was a woman of legendary virtue.

Rebekah is a "very fair . . . virgin" (v. 16). The question of how the narrator came by all of this information is eased somewhat by the observation that the Hebrew word *betulah* means more than the English word "virgin," with its stress on physical condition. Joel 1:8 illustrates the point: "Lament like a virgin dressed in sackcloth for the husband of her youth." In other words, a *betulah* is a marriageable young woman. The narrator does underscore the chastity of Rebekah, however, by adding the same qualification that Lot had used about his daughters (19:8): "whom no man had known."

Rebekah's beauty and innocence were not criteria stated in the test of the bride-to-be, but they can only add to her eligibility to become the woman of destiny. Her behavior matches the test perfectly. Her courtesy even exceeds what was stipulated: she calls the servant "My lord" (v. 18), perhaps dignifying him beyond his usual rank.

Satisfied at the success of his errand, the servant presents a gift of gold jewelry to Rebekah. Bracelets and a nose ring weighing 10.5 shekels in gold would equal 3.85 troy ounces (1 shekel = 11.41 grams). At today's price of gold, that would be worth $1,117. Adjusted for inflation since the Late Bronze Age (since ca. 1500 B.C.), this is a serious gift! It is probably the bride-price, given separately from the ordinary wedding gifts presented in verse 53 (see commentary on 34:12).

After Rebekah identifies herself as the granddaughter of Milcah and Nahor (making her all the more eligible, as Isaac's first cousin once removed), and increases her hospitality by agreeing to put the servant, his camels, and retinue up for the night, the servant concludes this panel of the story with a prayer of benediction shaped by oral transmission into classic form (v. 27): formula ("Blessed be the Lord") + epithet ("the God of my master Abraham") + the attribution to the Lord of *hesed*, "steadfast love" + specific thanks for the boon that the Lord has granted.

[28–49] The panel that follows begins with a report home by Rebekah, followed by an offer of hospitality to the servant by Laban, Rebekah's brother, who now appears for the first time. The servant then gives an elaborate account of all that has transpired, no doubt designed to persuade his hearers that the Lord's hand is in it all. He tells of Abraham's charge to him to find Ms. Right for Isaac, of the self-imposed test, and of Rebekah's identification by means of the test. (Incidentally, the angel whom the Lord promised to send along with the servant [vv. 7, 40] never makes an appearance. Perhaps it is the providence of Yahweh that goes before him.) The servant concludes his side of the conversation with a charge to the brother and father to tell him Yes or No.

[50–61] Brother Laban and father Bethuel are persuaded. They recognize that the Lord has picked a husband for their sister. They tell the servant to "take her and go" (v. 51).

However, the departure is not immediate. The servant produces more presents of jewelry and clothing from his camel saddlebags, including gifts for Laban and Rebekah's unnamed mother. The next morning the servant is ready to go, but the mother and brother plead for ten more days with their daughter. When the servant resists the delay, they show a famously uncommon solicitude for the desire of their daughter. In the climactic moment of the narrative, they summon Rebekah and say to her, "Will you go with this man?" Rebekah replies, "I will" (v. 57). Off she goes, then, accompanied by her "nurse" (v. 59). (This is hardly a wet nurse, as the Hebrew word usually indicates, but is someone whom Rebekah loves. We get that impression when we hear later of the death and burial of this nurse, whose name was Deborah [35:8].) Rebekah is also accompanied by a blessing pronounced over her by her family, in which they express the hope that her "offspring" (singular) will possess "the gates of their (plural) foes" (v. 60). From this formulation it is clear that "offspring" is a collective noun, and that traditional readings of it as singular in Genesis 3:15, 13:16, and elsewhere are not convincing.

[62–67] The action of the story slowly declines now as the camera swings from Rebekah to Isaac. He is in the Negeb now, perhaps in the Beer-sheba area with which he is identified (26:33). Otherwise he may be in Beer-lahai-roi (see NRSV footnote), Hagar's old place of theophany, where Isaac is soon to "settle" (25:11). He sees her coming on the camels, she sees him coming on foot, she determines from the servant that it is his "master" and therefore her future husband, and she veils herself as a sign not of her modesty but of her betrothal. Isaac knows who she is. He brings her to Sarah's tent (v. 67), in effect installing her as his mother's successor in the line of the matriarchs of Israel.

THE END OF ABRAHAM AND THE DESTINY OF ISHMAEL
Genesis 25:1–18

[25:1–6] Sometime between the death of Sarah, when he was 137 years old, and his own death at 175, Abraham took Keturah as a wife (v. 1) or concubine (v. 6; see also 1 Chron. 1:32–33). Scripture tells us about neither her origin nor her fate. However, her sons, listed in the same order in the 1 Chronicles passage (though without mention of the sons of Dedan), are the ancestors of nomadic peoples known to ancient Israel. Midian figures most prominently among them. The Midianites are interchangeable with Ishmaelites in the tale of the sale of Joseph into Egyptian bondage (37:25, 28). One of them, Zipporah, is given in marriage to Moses by her father, Reuel, a.k.a. Jethro, priest of Midian (Ex. 2:18). Gideon's greatest triumph was his victory over the forces of Midian (Judg. 7).

The narrator sweeps these kindred but nonelect peoples off the stage of the saga of blessing with the dismissive comment that Abraham gave them gifts and sent them eastward (which would be, of course, into trans-Jordan and the northern reaches of the Arabian desert). In contrast, "Abraham gave all he had to Isaac" (v. 5).

[7–11] The miscellany of chapter 25 continues with a Priestly notice of Abraham's death, complete with the usual chronological and geographical details. The surprise is that Ishmael reappears as a peer of Isaac. They act together to bury Abraham in the cave of Machpelah, the necropolis of the fathers and mothers (chap. 23). Ishmael, whose mother learned of his destiny at Beer-lahai-roi and gave it its meaningful name (16:13–14), is no longer identified with it. His half-brother Isaac has displaced him from that place (v. 11), which is said to have been located in the neighborhood of Kadesh-barnea (16:14) on the southern border of ancient Israel. That would place it on the eastern side of the Sinai peninsula, about fifty miles southwest of Beer-sheba.

[12–18] The reappearance of Ishmael gives the Priestly editor of Genesis a chance to tidy up the record on this eldest son of Abraham. His marriage to the unnamed Egyptian wife whom his mother picked for him (21:21) has been fruitful. The twelve tribes promised by God to his father (17:10) now can be listed. The names fit with various biblical and extrabiblical references to tribes and villages, largely to the south and east of historical Israel. Shur (v. 18) is probably the border area between the Sinai peninsula of Egypt and Israel (see commentary on 16:7). The name "Assyria" (Ashshur) in this case may just be a variant of Shur.

SIBLING RIVALRY BETWEEN THE TWINS ESAU AND JACOB
Genesis 25:19–34

25:19 These are the descendants of Isaac, Abraham's son: Abraham was the father of Isaac, ²⁰ and Isaac was forty years old when he married Rebekah, daughter of Bethuel the Aramean of Paddan-aram, sister of Laban the Aramean. ²¹ Isaac prayed to the LORD for his wife, because she was barren; and the LORD granted his prayer, and his wife Rebekah conceived. ²² The children struggled together within her; and she said, "If it is to be this way, why do I live?" So she went to inquire of the LORD. ²³ And the LORD said to her,

"Two nations are in your womb,
   and two peoples born of you shall be divided;
the one shall be stronger than the other,
   the elder shall serve the younger."

²⁴ When her time to give birth was at hand, there were twins in her womb. ²⁵ The first came out red, all his body like a hairy mantle; so they named him Esau. ²⁶ Afterward his brother came out, with his hand gripping Esau's heel; so he was named Jacob. Isaac was sixty years old when she bore them.

²⁷ When the boys grew up, Esau was a skillful hunter, a man of the field, while Jacob was a quiet man, living in tents. ²⁸ Isaac loved Esau, because he was fond of game; but Rebekah loved Jacob.

²⁹ Once when Jacob was cooking a stew, Esau came in from the field, and he was famished. ³⁰ Esau said to Jacob, "Let me eat some of that red stuff, for I am famished!" (Therefore he was called Edom.) ³¹ Jacob said, "First sell me your birthright." ³² Esau said, "I am about to die; of what use is a birthright to me?" ³³ Jacob said, "Swear to me first." So he swore to him, and sold his birthright to Jacob. ³⁴ Then Jacob gave Esau bread and lentil stew, and he ate and drank, and rose and went his way. Thus Esau despised his birthright.

[25:19–20] By now the reader will recognize these two verses as part of the Priestly narrative framework of Genesis, for they supply the dates, names, and places that give the entire work its sequential structure. The only new information is the name of Bethuel's hometown, Paddan-aram. The "aram" element refers to the Aramean cultural environment out of which Abraham and his family come. (For our purposes we can equate it roughly with modern Syria.) Paddan-aram, a place mentioned only in the patriarchal stories in Genesis, is evidently equal to or located in the region around Haran called Aram-naharaim in Genesis 24:10 (see commentary).

[21] The story of the birth of Rebekah's twins is transmitted in the usual earthy, vivid style of the Yahwist. The old bugaboo of barrenness that

threatens the chosen line from beginning to end makes an appearance here too. Indeed, with verses 20a and 26b as our narrative guides, the couple was childless for twenty years. In the end the trouble is averted by Isaac's prayer. One wonders where and how Isaac offers the prayer, and why Rebekah does not take part. The Hebrew narrator offers no clue, but hurries on.

[22–26] The vigorous movements of the twin fetuses in the uterus evidently manifest to the narrator's mind their future animosity. (The motif is not uncommon in folklore elsewhere.) In frustration and perhaps not even knowing she is carrying twins, Rebekah goes somewhere to pray to Yahweh, her husband's God whom she has apparently embraced, though her brother Laban remained an idolater (31:19). Practices familiar to the tenth-century-B.C. Yahwist rather than the pre-Israelite sixteenth-century matriarch may underlie the scene.

Compare Rebekah's actions with those of another barren woman, Hannah. In 1 Samuel 1, Hannah prays fervently at the sanctuary at Shiloh, the Lord hears her prayer, she conceives a special child who will be dedicated to the Lord's service, and she gives him the significant name Samuel, "God hears." Most of these elements are present in Rebekah's prayer and its sequel. She is handy to the very sanctuary at Beer-lahai-roi at which Hagar received God's message about her child (16:7–14). The unique element in this tale is the question that the woman asks the Lord. She asks why she has to suffer with the struggle going on within her. The answer: The two babies are two peoples who will always struggle with each other; furthermore, normal expectations will be reversed, for the older and stronger boy/people will be subordinate to the younger and weaker (v. 23).

When the twins are born, the one who should have enjoyed preference, the one with the red hair who emerged first, is named Esau. Plays on words are involved: *admoni*, "red," sounds like Edom (the land of the red Nubian sandstone dramatically visible around Petra in Jordan), Esau's other name (v. 30); *sear* sounds like Seir, another name for Edom (32:3). The narrator ties the significance of the name of the second-born, Jacob, to the similar sounding word for "heel" (*aqeb*). Jacob seemed to be trying to hold back his brother's birth in order to supplant him.

Now the etiological significance of this story becomes clear: The Lord's oracle and the strange birth explain the relative status of Israel and Edom in later times. In the Yahwist's own time, Edom was subject to Israel, having been defeated by David (2 Sam. 8:13–14). Furthermore, the story shows that Jacob's enrollment in the line of blessing is God's own choice made before his birth and not the result of Jacob's later trickery and deceit. The Lord's choice of the younger son is consistent with God's freedom. In the Lord's dispensation, the first may be last and the last may be first! Is it just? Is it fair? Does it square with what later Israel observed to be the case? The narrator does not linger over matters such as these, but hurries on.

[27–28] Occupation, location, and disposition are all rolled into the sibling rivalry (and national destinies) that exists between the twins. Esau/Edom is a hunter-gatherer of the steppe; Jacob/Israel is a more sedentary dweller of the sown land (the same relationship that existed between the doomed Abel and the survivor Cain). The parents are not wise but play favorites. Rebekah casts her lot with the elect one.

[29–34] The election of Jacob, already announced by the Lord in the oracle of verse 23, now becomes a legal fact. To make it so, Jacob pulls a con job as successful as his father's wife/sister scam (26:6–11). So flagrant is this act that the very sentence, "He sold his birthright for a mess of pottage," has become proverbial among us. It implies terminal shortsightedness!

Though Esau is the hunter, as befits a man of the field, Jacob is the cook, as befits a man who dwells in tents. On this occasion Esau is so hungry that he is willing to trade off his entire stake in the future for a meal of reddish-looking lentil stew. The word *adom*, "red," sounds like *edom*, thus allowing the narrator to make explicit the Esau/Edom connection already hinted at in verse 25. It also sounds like *dam*, "blood," suggesting that Esau may have thought the pot contained something more meaty than mere lentils.

The Hebrew word for "birthright" (*bekorah*) sounds something like the word for "blessing" (*berakah*). The birthright—the double portion, two-thirds of the estate, or even, in the case of the king's eldest, kingship itself—belongs to the eldest son, no matter how much the father may prefer another (Deut. 21:15–17). The very existence of the Deuteronomic legislation on the matter implies that people were not always honoring the absolute priority of the eldest son, and of course biblical narratives from Isaac and Jacob, Joseph and Ephraim (Gen. 48:17–19), through David and Solomon bear that out. None of them was an eldest son!

THE UNGAINLY STORY THRICE TOLD
AND OTHER MISCELLANIES
Genesis 26:1–35

The slightly modified repetition in this chapter of several earlier narratives suggests that the Isaac tradition was not very deeply rooted. Isaac's story seems to be derived from the saga of his father; he seems to be a transitional figure between that greater patriarch and his own greater son. The Yahwist tells the tales.

[26:1–5] Isaac and his clan suffer from a famine just like Abraham did (12:10). The Lord "appears" to him (without the usual accouterments of theophany) and directs him to the "Philistine" king of Gerar, Abimelech. (See the commentary on Gen. 20:1–18 on why "Philistine" has to be set off in quotation marks.) Abraham had dwelt in Gerar with an Abimelech too, in Genesis 20–21; perhaps a son or grandson is envisioned here. The Lord reiterates the promises of countless progeny and lands made to Abraham and, most important of all, sounds the overarching theme of the entire saga of the fathers and the mothers in its reflexive form: "All the nations of the earth shall gain blessing for themselves through your off-spring" (v. 4; the language of the promise and its underlying blessing closely follows the words spoken by God to Abraham at the end of the "test" on Mount Moriah [22:17–18]).

[6–11] The third wife/sister episode is the least scandalous of the lot (compare 12:10–20 [J] and 20:1–18 [E]). An Abimelech is still involved, but the principals are now Isaac and Rebekah, not Abraham and Sarah. As in the other versions, the presenting problem is the status of the Hebrew aliens and the vulnerability of the beautiful woman. Now, how-ever, no one lays a hand on Rebekah except Isaac (*yitshaq*), who is seen "fondling" or "playing with" (verbal root: *tsahaq*) her. (This "playing" is the same that upset Sarah when she saw Ishmael doing it in 21:9.) In this second but attenuated Yahwistic version, the host king comes off as more realistic than Isaac and more righteous than Pharaoh. The Lord does not intervene with him, for he knows what is right. He has no need to apol-ogize or to pay anyone off. He merely declares the foreign couple off lim-its (v. 11).

[12–25] Although in this version there is no causal connection, the sequel to Isaac's wife/sister deception is the same as it was in Abraham's first deception in Genesis 12:10–20: He gets rich, not only as a herder but also as a farmer. A second sequel parallels that of the Abraham-Abimelech encounter in Genesis 20–21: The two clans quarrel over water rights. In fact, Abimelech kicks Isaac out of Gerar (location unknown) on the grounds that "you have become too powerful for us" (26:16; this was Pharaoh's worry too [Ex. 1:9]).

Isaac does not go very far away, apparently, but only to the "valley of Gerar," perhaps arable lands outside the recognized urban limits of Gerar. Isaac's clan is able to reopen old wells dug by Abraham's clan years earlier and later refilled by the "Philistines." The names of wells or desert oases familiar to later generations are explained on the basis of this his-toric animosity (vv. 21–23). Finally, Isaac goes to Beer-sheba, where he has the cultic experience of theophany. For the first time the Lord takes the identifying title, "the God of your father Abraham"; for the first time the Lord says that the promise of progeny will be fulfilled "for my servant Abraham's sake." The merit of that patriarch is sufficient to bring blessing to his successors. Rabbinic Judaism develops this concept of the merits of the fathers, visualizing a treasury from which the surplus merit deposited by the ancestors can be drawn down by later generations.

As befits a place of theophany, Isaac builds an altar for Beer-sheba (v. 25). Abraham's prayer and tamarisk tree had already suggested that the site was a sanctuary (21:33). Isaac's servants also dig a well there, as befits a place whose name means "Well of Seven."

[26–33] Or does it? The meeting between Isaac and Abimelech, Ahuzzath and Phicol is largely a duplicate of the peace parley in 21:22–34. However, the name of the *city* (not just the oasis) of Beer-sheba is explained in a way different from what was said there. Now the play is on the verb *shaba*, "swear [an oath]," from which could be derived a noun, *Shibah*, "oath." In this recension, then, the etiology of the name Beer-sheba, "Well of the Oath," ties back to the peace that Isaac and Abimelech forged there (see commentary on 21:22–34).

[34–35] From the point of view of the Israelite narrators of the saga of the fathers and mothers, spouses taken from outside the clan of Terah are usually problematical. (Exceptions are Judah's Canaanite wife Shua [38:2] and Joseph's Egyptian wife, Asenath [41:45].) That was true of Lot's prospective sons-in-law (19:14), Hagar, and now, in this Priestly notice, it is true of the "Hittite" wives with the Hebrew names whom Esau marries without prior authorization from anyone. (In these stories "Hittite" means local Canaanite; see commentary on 23:1–20.) The vexation they cause Isaac and Rebekah motivates the parents to send Jacob back to the old country for a wife (28:1–5); it also motivates Esau to take another, more acceptable one (28:6–9). We hear no more about Judith, but Basemath, renamed Adah, figures in the Priestly lists of the Edomite tribes descended from Esau (36:1–14; in 36:2 Adah is called both a Canaanite and a Hittite).

ISAAC'S LEGACY
Genesis 27:1–40

The Isaac minicycle closes with the famous conspiracy of the beautiful Rebekah and her favored son, Jacob, to steal the father's blessing from the eldest son. Once again, the noble drama of promise and fulfillment that underlies the plot of Genesis 12–50 has to contend with the shortcomings

of the frail human characters that people the drama. God's choice of the
line of Abraham, Isaac, and Jacob to be the bearers of blessing to the peoples of the earth (12:3b) is not defeated. God can use even the foibles of
the elect to move the plan ahead. The players in the drama are all the
more credible precisely because they are not plastic saints but recog-
nizable sinners.

Readers should also remember that at the time her twins were born,
Rebekah received an oracle from the Lord promising that the suzerainty
would go to Jacob (25:23). Now she feels she has to take steps on her own
to make God's promise come to pass. Is it a fault to hold God to the
promise? All in all, this tale "reveals a deep divine vulnerability, for it
links God with people whose reputations are not stellar and opens God's
ways in the world to sharp criticism" (Fretheim, 538).

Chapter 27 is beautifully told and largely self-interpreting. Yet the
reader should bear in mind that the burden of Israel's election to its special role in the world takes a step forward in this chapter when a man
called Laughter accidentally conveys chosenness to the man called
Supplanter. The church too, which sees itself as composed of children
whom God has raised up to Abraham, looks to this election of its spiritual ancestor as a key to understanding its own existence. Both Israel and
the church are elected not to enjoy privilege and riches, but in order that
through them the nations of the world might find a blessing.

[27:1-4] Old Isaac can no longer see. This disability not only sets up
the plot of the story, but it hints at the spiritual situation as well. The
father who cannot tell Jacob from Esau is also blind to the true destinies
of the two men. Unlike Rebekah, he cannot see where the elect line runs.
Isaac likes to eat meat, and meat is what the he-man Esau brings to him
from the steppe. Now he sends his oldest son out to the hunt so that a
feast may be prepared to accompany a planned ritual of blessing.

Isaac is deprived of the sense of sight, but not of the other senses. The
narrator makes rich use of them all in this sensuous story: taste, smell,
sound (and our sight, at least) will all be kept in full play to delight us and
draw us in.

[5-17] The readers share with Rebekah knowledge that will create a
dramatic irony in this story. We know that the Lord has already given her
an oracle that sets the destiny of the younger twin ahead of that of the
older (25:23). So her preference for Jacob also conforms to God's purpose. Is deceit in service of the future of her people a sin?

One could argue that Rebekah is the strong person in this story. She
actualizes in real life God's election of the next in line. Perhaps she takes
account of the personalities of her two sons and makes her own decision
about which one is most likely to move God's purpose of blessing toward

its fulfillment. Will it be the hunter, the military man, the virile one who has already displeased her by marrying two "Hittite" women without permission? Or will it be the more reflective, indoor boy whom she knows better? Can she engineer the demotion of the eldest from the place guaranteed him by law and custom?

The deception that she perpetrates on the blind man looks too crude to Jacob. He worries that he will be found out (v. 12). Strong Rebekah says, "Let your curse be on me, my son" (v. 13). In a patriarchal world, how else could she effect her purpose (and God's)? Out-and-out negotiation with her husband (called "her lord" or "her master" in Hebrew) might not have worked. She is willing to take the risk and the rap.

After her strong self-imprecation, Jacob makes no further protest. He just does what he is told. He puts on his brother's clothes with the distinctive scent about them and attaches to his hands the lambskins that will make him as hairy as Esau. With or without full knowledge, Jacob conspires with his mother to transmit the covenant of blessing through the line that God has chosen.

[18–29] The narrator hints that Isaac suspects a ruse. He recognizes the voice as Jacob's (v. 22), but the hands confuse him (The Old Masters invariably capture this story in their paintings at the moment the old, blind, bedridden father gently touches the back of a hand of the conniving son, while the coconspiring mother looks on encouragingly.) Nevertheless, "He blessed him" (v. 23). Isn't that what Jacob is after?

Verses 24–27 suggest that the words of blessing can be qualified or even taken back. The old man decides he wants more evidence, so now the tests of taste and smell are applied. If Isaac knows all along that he is being deceived, as some have suggested, he has to be careful. The situation is dangerous. Preference could lead to fratricide, as it did in the story of Cain and Abel. The reader's suspicion that he might subtly be cooperating in the demotion of the firstborn is enhanced by the speed and ease with which he knowingly blesses Jacob as the rightful heir in Genesis 28:3–4.

Once Jacob passes the tests of taste and smell, the blessing that he receives reiterates familiar themes. His father wishes that God will give his son "the dew of heaven" (v. 28). During the dry months of summer, dewfall is a prime source of moisture for the coastal area of the eastern Mediterranean. In the Jewish liturgical tradition, a prayer for dew is part of the Additional Service for the first day of Passover. The Ninth Benediction of the daily Amidah (or Standing) Prayer of the synagogue also asks for dew (see Sarna, 192–93).

Isaac also wishes for his son plenty of the fruits of the earth and hegemony over other peoples, including the tribes of his own brothers. (This formulation comes as a surprise, because we know of only one brother.

Perhaps Esau's children are also included; as we will learn in chapter 36, they will be numerous.) The blessing concludes in verse 29b with the only echo we hear in all of Genesis of Genesis 12:3a. There, in the Lord's original blessing of Abram, we heard of many blessers and only one curser of Abram. Here, in contrast, the two groups are at parity.

As this prayer clearly demonstrates, blessing in ancient Israel was not some vague and wordy spiritual concept. It revolved around the very practical notion of material welfare—the sort of thing people have in mind today when they say, "We have been blessed." However, the mere fact that a parent touches and kisses a child and pronounces words of positive hope over the child adds a true spiritual dimension to even such a material blessing. Naomi Rosenblatt captures this abiding sense of blessing: "By internalizing the blessing of our parents' love, we acquire self-esteem, self-confidence, and a deep sense of security. Their blessing tells us we matter, that we are valued. All his life Jacob yearns for the genuine blessing he never got from his father Isaac" (quoted in Moyers, 265). One might quarrel with that last sentence, in the light of the blessing without any deceit involved that is later given by Isaac to Jacob (28:3–4). But we can certainly affirm that blessing is intended to give physical and emotional empowerment.

We can agree with all that is said here about the dynamic concept of blessing without indulging in discussion of its alleged magical power. Scholars have long claimed that in the minds of ancient peoples generally and also in ancient Israel, language was thought to be dynamistic. Once a word was said, it did its work independently from the blesser and even of God. A blessing or a curse, once released, could not be retracted or even changed.

This passage throws a different light on the blessing. It appears here less like a magical formula and more like an oath or bond between the speaker and the recipient. Isaac acknowledges that in verse 37. It can, however, be modified or qualified. The additional blessing that Isaac gives to Esau later in the chapter reveals that. The blessing is not automatically effective either. It may express the intention and direction of the blesser, but it has to be nourished and further decisions have to be made on the basis of its promise. The entire story of Genesis 12–50 recounts the slow, winding, and constantly reinforced implementation of the Lord's original blessing to Abram. No rabbit was pulled out of the hat when God said, "I will bless you."

So now Jacob has gotten by deceit what he, his mother, and Yahweh want. Is it a hollow victory? Maybe so. Jacob is dogged by deceit throughout his career. His own deceit sets the stage, but Laban also deceives him in the matter of Rachel and Leah. His own sons deceive him in the matter of the supposed death of his second-youngest and favorite son, Joseph. Jacob's victory is certainly not a safe one, for he immediately has to run away from Esau, whom he has swindled. The rest of Jacob's career is taken up with his struggles to actualize his blessing. The blessing obtained by deceit is greatly strengthened by the apparently genuine and open-hearted blessing that Isaac gives him in Genesis 28:3–4. Another twenty years have to pass, however, before a more mature Jacob receives a blessing from the "man" at Peniel (32:22–32) and receives the name Israel that will bind him to the rest of history.

[30–40] When Isaac recognizes Esau and discovers that Esau has been cheated, he "trembled violently" (v. 33). It is the first "trembling" to occur in Genesis, and it is the only evidence offered by the narrator that Isaac feels any emotion. The rest of the story seems to imply that he accepts what has happened without question. Esau does all the emoting. After his fears that the blessing has already been given are confirmed, Esau cries, "Bless me, me also, father!" (v. 34). For the first time he mentions publicly that he had lost the birthright to his brother (v. 36). Does this foolish, impulsive act disqualify him from receiving the blessing?

The difference between the birthright (*bekorah*) and a blessing (*berakah*) may simply be a legal one. As has been noted (see commentary on 25:29–34), Deuteronomy 21:15–17 specifically states that the eldest son is entitled to a double portion. That is the birthright guaranteed by law. The father's blessing, on the other hand, is not reserved for the eldest son, nor is that of the mother or a priest or even God. These powerful figures can bless whomever they choose to bless. The problem for Esau, as Isaac spells it out, is that the word he has given to Jacob already "supplants" most of what he could have offered to the older brother.

Once again the narrator shows literary mastery by swinging the sympathy of the reader toward the rough and hitherto unattractive Esau. Who can help but feel for him as he lifts up his voice and weeps. Is he pitiable? Certainly he has been rejected by brother and mother and now even father; certainly he seems to be vulnerable and perhaps even gullible. However, as the saga unfolds, he is the one who can forgive his brother and embrace him (33:4). Pitiable? Only temporarily. Tragic? Not by the end of the tale. Unjustly used? Absolutely.

At the end of the dialogue between Isaac and Esau, the old blind man pronounces a restrained but powerful word over Esau. He is to live in the steppe, far from the "fatness" and "dew" of the fertile coastal plain (27:39). (The description is fairly apt for Edom.) Furthermore, he is to live by the sword, sometimes but not always subject to his brother (v. 40). (The description fits the Edom-Israel relationship throughout the biblical period.) Beyond the literal terms of this "blessing," it becomes clear that

Esau too has a covenant with God, mediated through his father's words. The Yahwist and the other narrators of Genesis have a wonderful ability to include within their account the perspective of the excluded and the marginalized. Momentarily, at least, readers can see things through their eyes and can recognize that God's care and sovereignty extend even to these nonelect peoples. The losers are treated with generosity, and the winners' betrayals are not covered over. Esau is not the first marginal person to be blessed. Ishmael too has his blessing and has his own salvation history with God. Although great animosity existed over the centuries between Israel and its neighbors, scripture suggests that "the interests of the people of promise are not served well by finding ways of speaking negatively about those outside [their] community, or seeking to limit the blessing activity of God among them" (Fretheim, 539).

JACOB'S FLIGHT AND ESAU'S MARRIAGE
Genesis 27:41–28:9

[27:41–46] The ever watchful Rebekah learns of Esau's desire to get revenge on his brother by killing him. She implores her younger son to flee to the safety of the old country, to his uncle Laban in Haran in Mesopotamia, until Esau's anger blows over. The killer of a brother would have to be executed by the community, of course. Then she who is mother of both would lose both sons in one day, an exponential increase in tragedy (v. 45). She approaches Isaac about the matter obliquely, however. She shrewdly reverts to the offense that Esau gave to both of them when he married the two "Hittite" women without his parents' consent (see commentary on 26:34–35).

[28:1–5] Isaac takes the hint. Rather than send a servant to find a wife for his son as his own father Abraham did, Isaac proposes to send Jacob himself. The terminus of the trip is to be Paddan-aram, which, judging from Genesis 25:20, is identical with the Aram-naharaim of 24:10. The Aramean kinfolk are still there, and among the daughters of Laban— Jacob's first cousins—he will find a wife. Now the father blesses the tricky son directly, though still in a somewhat standoffish way—May El Shaddai (see commentary on 17:1) give you the blessing and the land of Abraham (vv. 3–4). In fact, the last recorded word of Isaac is just that: "Abraham." Perhaps it is appropriate that a character as underdeveloped and transitional as he would close his career by speaking his mighty father's name to his mighty son. The blessing of offspring and land that the Lord gave Abraham many times is bestowed on Jacob soon after (28:13–15).

[6–9] The Isaac minisaga closes with a parting look at Esau's efforts to ingratiate himself with his parents. He finally understands that the Canaanite/Hittite women whom he married without leave (26:34–35) and who were not very good daughters-in-law to Rebekah (27:46) do not help his standing with Isaac. So he marries a third wife, still from a marginal clan but closer to the elect line. She is the previously unmentioned daughter of Ishmael, Mahalath, renamed Basemath in the genealogy of the Esau clans in Genesis 36.

12. The Saga of Jacob and Rachel
Genesis 28:10–36:43

The cycle of stories about Jacob in these chapters has inspired countless sermons, hymns, works of art, and pious reflections. Odd, isn't it, that a trickster and his dysfunctional family should excite such a strong and positive response. Jacob's gradual reinvention as a dignified patriarch and the founder of God's elect people begins at Bethel and concludes at Bethel years later. So it is not surprising that Bethel figures prominently in this hymnic representation of the Jacob story.

> Though like the wanderer,
> The sun gone down,
> Darkness be over me,
> My rest a stone;
> Yet in my dreams I'll be
> Nearer, my God, to Thee,
> Nearer, my God, to Thee,
> Nearer to Thee!
>
> There let the way appear
> Steps unto heaven:
> All that Thou sendest me
> In mercy given:
> Angels to beckon me
> Nearer, my God, to Thee. . . .
>
> Then, with my waking thoughts
> Bright with Thy praise,
> Out of my stony griefs
> Bethel I'll raise;
> So by my woes to be
> Nearer, my God, to Thee. . . .

Some people sing "Nearer, My God, to Thee" for years without realizing that it is a commentary on Genesis 28:10–22, the story of Jacob's dream at Bethel. Since the 1998 film "Titanic," they are at least more familiar with the story (affirmed by survivor Charlotte Collyer in 1912) that this was the tune the band was playing as the great ship went to the bottom. We can only hope that, in their minds at least, they had reached verse 5 before they became nearer to God:

> Or if on joyful wing
> Cleaving the sky,
> Sun, moon, and stars forgot,
> Upward I fly,
> Still all my song shall be
> Nearer, my God, to Thee,
> Nearer, my God, to Thee,
> Nearer to Thee!

Sarah Adams, the composer of this hymn, understood the story of Jacob at Bethel in the terms of nineteenth-century evangelical piety. She turned it into a story of the migration of the soul to heaven. In terms of what we know about Old Testament faith, such a way of using the story of the angels ascending and descending the ladder has no validity. Until very late in the Old Testament period there were no doctrines of life after death or the separability of the soul from the body. However, when Jacob names the place Bethel, "House of God," he adds "this is the gate of heaven" (28:17). Once one expands the older Old Testament notion of heaven as the place where God and the heavenly host reside (together with a few especially chosen individuals like Enoch and Elijah) into the place where all the righteous dead go, then this understanding of Bethel makes sense. The idea is echoed is a less well-known ninth-century Latin hymn, "Only-Begotten Word of God Eternal":

> Hallowed this dwelling where our Lord abideth;
> This is none other than the gate of heaven;
> Strangers and pilgrims seeking homes eternal
> Pass through its portals.

In his hymn "Thy Mansion Is the Christian's Heart" (1779), William Cowper focuses on Jacob's worship at Bethel, both during and after his dream:

> Prayer makes the darkened cloud withdraw;
> prayer climbs the ladder Jacob saw,
> gives exercise to faith and love,
> brings every blessing from above.

A hymn by Philip Doddridge, "O God of Bethel," develops an element of the text that is closer to the Old Testament intention than the idea of dying and going to heaven, namely, the theme of pilgrimage. "O God of Bethel, by whose hand thy people still are fed, who through this weary pilgrimage hast all Thy people led . . ." The story in Genesis 28:10–22 is not exactly about a pilgrimage, but let's face it, Jacob is on the lam! He is scared and he is moving. At the beginning of his exile, he receives the wonderful promise that God intends to be with him in this pilgrimage. The line between pilgrim and refugee is a fine one, and it probably exists as much in the mind as it does in the political reality. From a neutral observer's point of view, the Israelites wandering forty years in the wilderness must have looked like miserable refugees. In the tradition of scripture, however, that period was construed almost as a golden age of pilgrimage from the land of bondage to the land of freedom. Perhaps what makes flight into pilgrimage is intentional movement toward some God-given objective. A landless and oppressed person might put that kind of construction upon his or her situation, thereby turning the misery of flight into the promise of attaining a lofty goal.

Several hymns pick up other parts of the Jacob story as well. To tie the well-known words of "God Be with You Till We Meet Again" to the so-called "Mizpah Benediction" (31:49) seems far-fetched, given that Jacob's words there are a sanction, almost a curse, on Laban. But Charles Wesley's hymn "Come, O Thou Traveler Unknown" (1739) is an explicit exposition of the second dramatic nighttime episode in Jacob's life, the wrestling match at Peniel (32:22–32). Wesley's transformation of the angel into a Christ figure is deft; his understanding of Jacob as the prototype of every believer guarantees that their combat will be both desperate and redemptive.

> Come, O thou traveler unknown
> Whom still I hold but cannot see;
> My company before is gone,
> And I am left alone with thee;
> With thee all night I mean to stay
> And wrestle till the break of day. . . .
>
> Yield to me now, for I am weak
> But confident in self-despair;
> Speak to my heart, in blessings speak;
> Be conquered by my instant prayer;
> Speak or thou never hence shall move,
> And tell me if thy name is love. . . .

'Tis love! 'tis love, thou diedst for me;
I hear thy whisper in my heart;
The morning breaks, the shadows flee,
Pure universal love thou art!
To me, to all, thy mercies move;
Thy nature and thy name is love. . . .

Who is Jacob anyway? Various terms apply. He is, of course, son of Isaac, son of "laughter." He is a mama's boy, a trickster who got the paternal blessing away from Esau with the connivance of his mother, Rebekah. Overall, he comes through as a rather unattractive personality. This story of the theophany at Bethel is the first time we hear Jacob acknowledge any personal connection with God. It is as though until this moment he has not known about God or encountered God. We might assume that Abraham and Isaac would have passed the word on to their grandson and son about their great encounters with Yahweh. Yet as it stands at the beginning of his saga, we have no evidence that he has any training in the faith at all.

Jacob is on the run because of his hairy-handed dirty tricks. The purchase of Esau's birthright for a mess of pottage was fair and square, although shoddy in the extreme. But the trickery with the old man was a plain scam. Even the slow-witted Esau quickly figured out that he had been had. His dangerous anger is the real reason that Jacob is on the move.

From beginning to end, the Jacob cycle is assigned to the Yahwistic source, with a few Elohistic strands woven into the story of Jacob's dream at Bethel (28:10–22), the covenant with Laban (especially 31:4–16), and elsewhere. The storyteller's language is vivid and earthy; the story displays the humanistic affection for its characters typical of the Yahwist. With the exception of the intrusive tale of the rape of Dinah (chap. 34), the entire cycle, from Genesis 28:10 through chapter 35, reads like a coherent short story rather than a collection of short texts secondarily joined together. The commentary in the pages that follow will try to reflect the continuation and coherence of the story through chapter after chapter.

JACOB RETURNS TO THE SOURCE, VIA BETHEL
Genesis 28:10–22

28:10 Jacob left Beer-sheba and went toward Haran. 11 He came to a certain place and stayed there for the night, because the sun had set. Taking one of the stones of the place, he put it under his head and lay down in that place. 12 And he dreamed that there was a ladder set up on the earth, the top

of it reaching to heaven; and the angels of God were ascending and descending on it. ¹³ And the LORD stood beside him and said, "I am the LORD, the God of Abraham your father and the God of Isaac; the land on which you lie I will give to you and to your offspring; ¹⁴ and your offspring shall be like the dust of the earth, and you shall spread abroad to the west and to the east and to the north and to the south; and all the families of the earth shall be blessed in you and in your offspring. ¹⁵ Know that I am with you and will keep you wherever you go, and will bring you back to this land; for I will not leave you until I have done what I have promised you." ¹⁶ Then Jacob woke from his sleep and said, "Surely the LORD is in this place—and I did not know it!" ¹⁷ And he was afraid, and said, "How awesome is this place! This is none other than the house of God, and this is the gate of heaven."

¹⁸ So Jacob rose early in the morning, and he took the stone that he had put under his head and set it up for a pillar and poured oil on the top of it. ¹⁹ He called that place Bethel; but the name of the city was Luz at the first. ²⁰ Then Jacob made a vow, saying, "If God will be with me, and will keep me in this way that I go, and will give me bread to eat and clothing to wear, ²¹ so that I come again to my father's house in peace, then the LORD shall be my God, ²² and this stone, which I have set up for a pillar, shall be God's house; and of all that you give me I will surely give one tenth to you."

[28:10–17] Obedient to his father's command (and his mother's earlier entreaty), Jacob heads east to Haran. Verse 11 says that Jacob uses a stone as a pillow for his head. If the idea underlying this act is the erection of a stele, an obelisk, or some other memorial more suitable to a holy site than a pile of rocks, questions still remain: How could he have wrestled such a monolith into place? How could it have served as a pillow? Furthermore, Jacob erects his stone at "a certain place," apparently an already known site. Is it a sanctuary in its own right, that is now being reconsecrated by Jacob to the worship of Yahweh? Remember, Abram had pitched his tent east of Bethel, built an altar, and worshiped there (12:8).

In the Hellenistic synagogue of Dura-Europos in Syria (A.D. 246), beautiful wall paintings depict scenes from the Bible. Several of these scenes, including this scene of Jacob at Bethel, are introduced in the Bible with the term "the place." From later Jewish sources we know that a synagogue could be referred to as "the place." Does this suggest that the painters of the synagogue at Dura-Europos understood that the place where Jacob worshiped at Bethel was a prototype of their own synagogue? Certainly both his place and theirs were set apart for the worship of God. In any case, the phrase "a certain place" seems to indicate that this spot is filled with significance that will be known to the reader in due course.

Was this "certain place" haunted? Was it peculiarly fraught with the presence of deity, a kind of Sedona, Arizona of old? Near the end of the story, Jacob says, "Surely the LORD is in this place—and I did not know it!" (v. 16). His own experience now confirms that Bethel was a place at which heaven and earth met and at which God could be encountered.

Sometimes "a certain place" or sanctuary had topographic significance, that is, it was a high place or a particularly dramatic, scary one. Certainly it would have been a traditional holy spot with an accompanying legend. As has been noted earlier, it seems that many of the early Israelite sanctuaries had already been holy places in earlier Canaanite culture. The transfer of holy sites from one culture to another is a well-known phenomenon. One thinks of the cathedral in Mexico City standing on top of the ruined foundation of the Great Pyramid of Montezuma, or Hagia Sofia in Istanbul, refitted from Byzantine church to majestic mosque. When the Israelites conquered the Canaanites, similar transfers took place. Scholars agree, for example, that Jerusalem was a holy city of the Jebusites with a temple and a priesthood before Israel ever captured it.

It seems that all of the patriarchal stories cycle around old Canaanite sanctuaries that existed prior to the emergence of the Habiru band from across the Jordan. It also seems that Jacob was the local hero honored at the sanctuary at Bethel. Bethel and Jacob together became part of the united patriarchal saga as the people of that place identified themselves with the emerging twelve-tribe league of Israel. It is not hard to imagine then that all Israel would eventually accept the idea that Jacob was their forefather and that he got his calling during a dream at Bethel.

In the ancient Near East the sanctuary was always the place to go to meet God. A fortunate visitor might receive a waking theophany there or meet God in a dream. (In fact, the incubation dream that a person could intentionally induce by sleeping at a sanctuary was a well-known medium of revelation.) Jacob was one such fortunate visitor. In verse 12, we see the visual content of Jacob's dream. It is of a ladder with its base on the earth and its top in the heavens, and angels ascending and descending. This is the third of the five dream revelations recounted in the saga of the fathers and the mothers. Abram received a message and had a vision while he was in a deep sleep (15:12–16), and Yahweh vouchsafed a revelatory dream to Abimelech, the king of the Philistines. He was warned by God in a dream not to touch Sarah (20:3–7). Like those, Jacob's dream is structured by the conventions of ancient sanctuary behavior and the approved mode of receiving divine revelation in a culture that accepted the possibility of God speaking in dreams. The angels that descend the ladder are part of God's heavenly court, God's army, the "host" of which God is the Lord. These spiritual beings are the pale remnants of pre-Israelite polytheistic religion, now reduced to being the courtiers who surround the Lord (see commentary on 1:26). They play no part in the transaction of the dream, nor does the ladder (or ramp or stairway) give Jacob access to heaven, as similar ladders did for the dead in the Egyptian mythological tradition. (The other two patriarchal dreams are Jacob's with the flocks in 31:10–13 and Laban's in 31:24. Their common features are discussed in the commentary on 15:12–16.)

The Lord finally appears in verse 13. The story seems to imply that God assumes an intimate face-to-face position with Jacob, not standing up on top of the ladder as the iconographic tradition would have it.

The Lord uses the formula of self-introduction that, with modifications, is standard for theophanies (compare Gen. 15:7 and Ex. 3:6). Then comes the eighth reiteration of the divine promise of the land to a patriarch and the seventh direct or indirect repetition of the promise of numerous progeny (vv. 13–14). The Lord also makes the fifth and final statement of the overarching theme of blessing to the nations (see commentary on 12:3). The NRSV translates this "bless" in the passive voice: "All the families of the earth shall be blessed in you and your offspring." (Other passive iterations of the theme are 12:3b and 18:18; in 22:18 and 26:4 the NRSV translates reflexively.)

All of this is the "blessing of Abraham" that Isaac had wished for his son in verse 4. Now Jacob receives it as his own, together with the Lord's promise never to leave him until all is accomplished. No wonder Jacob awakens in awe and pronounces the place "the house of God, . . . the gate of heaven" (v. 17).

[18–22] It is also no wonder that Jacob formally converts his pillow into a pillar, dedicates it with oil, and renames the place Bethel ("house of God"). He then imposes a vow upon himself, making what was a unilateral donation by God into a bilateral covenant in the "if . . . then" pattern. If all goes well, he will name Yahweh as his God, formally recognize the pillar as "God's house" (i.e., a sanctuary of the Yahweh cult), and give God a tithe of all his possessions. This tithe appears to be a one-time offering, not the annual obligation that it later became (see Deut. 14:22–29). The peculiar thing about this vow by Jacob is that it exacts no obligation from the Lord. Yahweh has already promised to bestow the blessings.

ROMANCING RACHEL AT THE WELL
Genesis 29:1–30

This story is similar to Genesis 24:1–67, in which Isaac's servant meets Rebekah at a well. The petitioner from Canaan in the west arrives at a well in the east. A kinswoman comes to the well and is recognized as the beloved. A wedding is arranged, and the woman becomes one of the mothers of Israel. There are differences, to be sure. Jacob's stay in the east is greatly extended, for example, and the scene with Rebekah at the well and with her family is more opulently told, with camels and a real house and lavish gifts. Essentially, however, the event is the same, and, as in the case of the three wife/sister narratives, the possibility that one version is derived from the other has to be considered

Frederick Buechner captures the visual, audial, and even olfactory sensations of this story in his retelling of the Jacob story in his novel *Son of Laughter.* For those of us whose imaginations are more challenged, a good way of visualizing the setting of a biblical story is to invoke a modern technique by imagining that we are making a videotape of the scene. After all, biblical study is not just a matter of the left brain extrapolating theology from a written and fixed text, but it is also a matter of the right brain imagining its way into insights that are incipient within the text. Aside from stimulating the vividness of imagination, trying to videotape a biblical story can also quickly detect where barriers to understanding lurk within the text. We have to ask: How would it be staged? What would the backdrop look like? What would the characters look like? We may sense that the lighting is wrong, or that the landscape or personality of a character do not clearly emerge out of the text. If one cannot get any picture at all, then the text poses a big barrier to understanding, and serious interpretive work has to be done.

[29:1–3] Let us imagine the scene that now confronts us in this way. The camcorder at Jacob's side sweeps over a flat arid steppe. A well, marked by hardly anything except tracks leading to it, is surrounded by flocks of sheep. A stone at the mouth of the well serves as a plug. The very presence of this stone raises the question of the historical and geographical setting of the story. Jacob's journey has taken him back to his mother's homeland, "the land of the people of the east," known variously as Paddan-aram (28:5), Aram-naharaim (24:10), and Haran (11:31; 29:4). What kind of stones are lying around in the arid landscape of north-central Syria that would be suitable to cover such a well? Bear in mind that the storytellers themselves are in Israel, not in Syria or Mesopotamia, and that the abundant stones that they see lying around them are of a different character. They are not boulders worn smooth by glaciation or water, but limestone blocks or outcroppings. Their stone could indeed be worked into a cover to fit a well flush to the ground. If Haran was in the alluvial flood plain between the Tigris and the Euphrates, it would have had few rocks of any kind. On the other hand, if Haran lay in the foothills of the Taurus Mountains in the north of Syria, almost in present-day Kurdistan, it might have had plenty of rocks, but too many of them would have been unworkably hard. In other words, the stone that stopped up the well poses a small barrier to understanding and therefore a challenge to the video project. What color is it? What shape is it? Why does it take so many shepherds to move it? Is it there simply to keep people and animals from falling into the well, or does it establish riparian rights for Laban's shepherds and warn other tribes to stay away from this well?

[4–8] The next scene focuses on the reception that Jacob receives at the well. We see shepherds out in a dry wilderness miles from anywhere patiently waiting to water their flocks. The camera, now on their side, pans across the horizon where figures have appeared. The leader is riding up on a donkey. (Camels figure in the Jacob story in 30:43 and 31:34, but they probably should not; see commentary on 24:1–9.) One imagines that the shepherds feel anxious. The stranger arrives and suddenly language proves no barrier. The storyteller has all the parties speaking Hebrew, of course, but if we put it in its ostensible setting, they might have been able to communicate in Aramaic. That northwest Semitic language, cognate to Hebrew, was spoken by the Aramean peoples of Syria out of which the patriarchs are thought to have emerged early in the Late Bronze Age.

The stranger looks rough to the shepherds. (Who wouldn't, after riding hundreds of miles on a donkey!) The shepherds too must present an unkempt, unshaven, rangy, and probably odoriferous picture to the newly arrived Jacob. This makes the salutation that is exchanged between Jacob and the shepherds very important. Jacob may not be unwelcome in a thinly populated community—another body, even if it is that of a stranger, can be another helping hand. Yet he, like every alien, is vulnerable.

The name dropping included within the salutation is carefully and ritualistically stated. In Hebrew, Jacob's inquiry about Laban is literally, "How is his shalom?" (v. 6). The sentence is more than a mere pleasantry. It is a serious inquiry, not just into health, but into all of the life-circumstances of the other person. The question is not designed just to give Jacob an opening, but rather to feel out the situation: Is Laban's life in order? Is he in a set of right relationships? Can I expect from him a wholesome and normal reception, or is he angry and violent?

In the Old Testament, the normal state of affairs is not enmity, violence, and warfare, but shalom. Anything that is not shalom is out of order; it is broken and needs to be fixed. God created the world in a state of shalom, so anyone who wants to get with the program that God has laid out needs to be in a set of right relationships. Jacob comes in peace on an errand having to do with family relationships, but there will be no shalom unless Laban and his family are also in order. All the great theological concepts of the Old Testament are relational: justice, righteousness, shalom. It takes at least two to demonstrate any of them. Reciprocity is the essence of shalom.

So the inquiry, "How is his shalom?" though it is routine and normal, is also serious. Jacob's greeting is more than just "Hi!" or "How is Laban?" It is a fundamental attempt to establish that Laban's relationships are sound and wholesome. A paraphrase might run like this: "I am friendly/healthy/whole, and I hope he is too." The NRSV rendition is both sensitive to these nuances and closer to the Hebrew: "Is it well with him?" (v. 6).

At verse 6, Rachel appears on the scene with her father's sheep. Jacob tries to get rid of the shepherds (v. 7), but they are rigid about their schedule for opening the well. Verses 4–8 stress the tentativeness of all parties.

[9–14] In contrast to verses 4–8, verses 9–14 exhibit the boldness of Jacob and Rachel. Over the protests of the shepherds, and with one eye on the approaching Rachel (and perhaps on her father's sheep as well, if the schemer is true to form), an inspired Jacob single-handedly rolls or twists the stone away and waters her sheep. More is at play here than the fast-beating heart of a young man who wants to show off for a young, desirable woman. Jacob and the reader share knowledge that Rachel does not yet have. We all know, for example, that Jacob is her first cousin and that his father has sent him here to get a wife from the family of Rachel's father, Laban (see 28:2). From the kiss and the tears in verse 11 we suspect that he knows he has found his wife-to-be. Rachel had no advance warning, but her reaction when she hears that this man is her long-lost cousin suggests that she realizes how important this visit is (v. 12). The kiss and the tears signal the recognition necessary to move the story from tentativeness and fear to the joy of family reunion. A family bonding reading would also explain Laban's kiss in verse 13 and his exclamation, "Surely you are my bone and my flesh!" (v. 14), almost the exact words that inaugurated the first family, uttered by the first husband when he met the first wife in the garden (2:23).

29:15 Then Laban said to Jacob, "Because you are my kinsman, should you therefore serve me for nothing? Tell me, what shall your wages be?" 16 Now Laban had two daughters; the name of the elder was Leah, and the name of the younger was Rachel. 17 Leah's eyes were lovely, and Rachel was graceful and beautiful. 18 Jacob loved Rachel; so he said, "I will serve you seven years for your younger daughter Rachel." 19 Laban said, "It is better that I give her to you than that I should give her to any other man; stay with me." 20 So Jacob served seven years for Rachel, and they seemed to him but a few days because of the love he had for her.

²¹ Then Jacob said to Laban, "Give me my wife that I may go in to her, for my time is completed." ²² So Laban gathered together all the people of the place, and made a feast. ²³ But in the evening he took his daughter Leah and brought her to Jacob; and he went in to her. ²⁴ (Laban gave his maid Zilpah to his daughter Leah to be her maid.) ²⁵ When morning came, it was Leah! And Jacob said to Laban, "What is this you have done to me? Did I not serve with you for Rachel? Why then have you deceived me?" ²⁶ Laban said, "This is not done in our country—giving the younger before the first-born. ²⁷ Complete the week of this one, and we will give you the other also in return for serving me another seven years." ²⁸ Jacob did so, and completed her week; then Laban gave him his daughter Rachel as a wife. ²⁹ (Laban gave his maid Bilhah to his daughter Rachel to be her maid.) ³⁰ So Jacob went in to Rachel also, and he loved Rachel more than Leah. He served Laban for another seven years.

[29:15–30] We now move forward a month to a very different scene. The mood is no longer established by shepherds and their smelly sheep. Human relations set the mood: "Now Laban had two daughters: the name of the elder was Leah, and the name of the younger was Rachel" (v. 16). This sounds as though we are being reintroduced to Rachel. Certainly new information is now brought to bear on the romance at the well, namely, the presence and eligibility of her sister. This new information raises a question natural to a traditional society: What is wrong with the older daughter that her hand is not being asked for, when in a normal course of events she would be the first to wed? Was it her bad eyes?

We have always thought that Jacob found Leah ugly because of her "weak" eyes. Now that the NRSV has given Leah "lovely" eyes, we are deprived of that explanation. At issue is a single word in verse 17. The Hebrew adjective *rak* can mean "soft," "tender," or "delicate." Nowhere else in the Old Testament is it applied to "eyes." The issue with Leah's eyes is encompassed within the English word, "tender." Tender means both soft and sore. Perhaps Leah's eyes were defective in the sense of having an infection or being supersensitive to the sun—or perhaps they were lovely and soft.

Rachel, in contrast, was "graceful and beautiful" (v. 17). (The conjunction following the word "lovely" [v. 17], translated "and" in the NRSV, could just as well be translated with the adversative conjunction "but," because the same Hebrew particle works for both English conjunctions. That translation would pit the two women against each other even more sharply.) The Hebrew underlying these English words suggests "shapely and beautiful." It seems that Jacob or the narrator was struck with Leah's eyes but took in all of Rachel. Leah's name may mean "cow" (Rachel means "ewe"). We all know that cows have big, beautiful brown eyes, though maybe a little too droopy for some tastes. The judgment of tradition that Leah was defective on account of weak eyes may reflect as much an effort to justify Jacob's behavior as it does an accurate reading of the Hebrew text. In any event, the NRSV has opened the door to a reconsideration of Leah, perhaps encouraging readers to regard Jacob as fortunate to have wound up with two wives instead of just one, and both of them desirable women. The eyes themselves play no further role in the story.

Jacob offers seven years of service to Laban as an in-kind payment of the bride-price (the money paid by the groom to the family of a bride for the loss of her services to the family). Deuteronomy 22:28–29 sets the bride-price for a virgin who has been raped at fifty shekels of silver; this might suggest that Jacob's offer of seven years' indentured servitude is generous. Laban's answer (v. 19) is a model of ambiguity, but Jacob takes it to be affirmative. The deal is struck.

[21–24] The action now shifts forward seven years to a wedding feast, called in Hebrew a *mishteh*, a drinking party. Time is terribly truncated at this feast; no words are even said. Then the bride is brought to Jacob and the marriage is consummated. This reflects a practice still observed to this day in traditional Middle Eastern communities. During a wedding celebration the bride and groom retire to private chambers while the feast goes on. Perhaps one of the roles of the attendant Zilpah is to display the bloody sheets that are the tokens of virginity to the crowd. They would respond enthusiastically; after all, the community's interests are at stake in what happens under the bridal canopy and in the marriage bed. In marginal societies, especially in antiquity, the community is always threatened with extinction. Successful marital bonding leads to pregnancy and progeny, and children are a prime manifestation of blessing (see commentary on 6:1–4).

[29:25] Jacob worked out his full stint
To win Rachel, with never a hint
That ought was awry—
Then Laban so sly
said, "Now, *bubbie*, read the small print."
(Benson)

The confusion by morning light might be understandable, if (a) the party truly was a drinking party and Jacob was drunk, or (b) the consummation took place in pitch darkness, or (c) Leah and Rachel were both veiled. A more puzzling question for us modern readers is why the women went along with Laban's scheme? Were they brutalized into accepting the swap of mates, or had they never been told by Laban which one was being promised to Jacob? In any case, the women are totally under their father's command. The behavior of Leah and Rachel in this narrative contrasts unfavorably with Rebekah and her family in the parallel story in chapter 24. When asked her opinion about the marriage to Isaac, she said crisply, "I will go" (24:58).

A literary dynamic is at work in this moment of deception. Jacob has tricked his way from his blind father's house to this place; now it is his turn to be tricked in the dark. A theological dynamic is at work as well: God can bring good even out of betrayals, as God will do with Joseph and his brothers (see 50:20). From the unhappy but prolific union of Leah and Jacob will come six of the twelve tribes of Israel, including the father of the royal line, Judah, and the father of the priestly line, Levi. However, the reason Laban immediately gives for his deception is a cultural one (that he had never brought up before): "This is not done in our country— giving the younger before the firstborn" (v. 26). What would the neighbors say? Laban's solution is to offer a twofer. For another seven years of indentured service he will give Rachel to Jacob as well. The second marriage can occur as soon as the weeklong festivities of the first are finished (v. 27). (Marriage to the sister of one's wife during the wife's lifetime was later banned as a form of incest; see Lev. 18:18.) So everything is settled: Jacob ends up with a total indenture of fourteen years, two wives, and their two maidservants, Zilpah and Bilhah. As we soon learn, all four of these women become Jacob's sexual partners and all bear him sons.

Returning for a moment to the question of how Leah could have been mistaken for Rachel, it is useful to look at Roland de Vaux's study of the sociology of ancient Israel. In his section on marriage ceremonies, de Vaux opts for the veil as the solution to the problem. Bearing in mind that a marriage ceremony was really a matter of contractual agreement, an exchange of money or perhaps even the signing of documents, rather than a religious rite,

> the chief ceremony was the entry of the bride into the bridegroom's house. The bridegroom, wearing a diadem (Ct 3:11; Is 61:10) and accompanied by his friends with tambourines and a band . . . proceeded to the bride's house. She was richly dressed and adorned with jewels . . . but she wore a veil (Ct 4:1, 3; 6:7) that she took off only in the bridal chamber. This explains why Rebecca veiled herself upon seeing Isaac, her fiancé (Gn 24:65), and how Laban was able to substitute Leah for Rachel at Jacob's first marriage (Gn 29:23–25). . . . The blood-stained linen of this nuptial night was preserved; it proved the bride's virginity and would be evidence if she were slandered by her husband (Dt 22:13–21). (de Vaux, 33–34)

In short, cultural context seems vital to making sense of the story of Jacob, Leah, and Rachel. Our wedding customs are different from those in this story, and the interpretive gap looms very large. We can hardly expect to use these stories as handbooks for wedding etiquette in the twenty-first century, nor do they provide all the help we need to make our marriages work today. Even though the stories of Isaac and Rebekah and of Jacob and Rachel are stories of love affairs and marriages, they will not help us much in counseling situations, simply because they are so fraught with the cultural baggage of the ancient community in which they originated. They do not fully display our values of mutual dignity, respect, and close listening. However, they do emphasize one value of importance in our lives today. These parallel stories say to the spouse, "Don't give up on your vision! You have every right to pursue your own destiny and that of your children yet unborn."

A fear running through these stories is the threat of childlessness. How does that confront us today? In ancient times, barrenness threatened the very existence of the community. Now, in contrast, the very opposite threatens the existence of the community. Projections suggest that the turn-of-the-millennium world population of six billion souls will double by 2050. In such a context, limitless reproduction is irresponsible. Childlessness is still a personal sorrow for many couples, of course, but synagogue and church should do nothing on the basis of these texts to suggest that childlessness, whether through biology or through choice, condemns families to less than a full human existence. We need to affirm that there can be a blessing in childlessness too, even though the Old Testament implies that it is a curse. To be childless is to be free to serve God and community in other ways.

RACHEL AND LEAH,
THE MOTHERS OF ALL ISRAEL
Genesis 29:31–30:24

[29:31–35] Yahweh tries to improve Jacob's unloving attitude toward Leah by "opening her womb" four times in a row, while Rachel remains childless. Are we then to affirm that God has a direct hand in childbirth? Let us realize that the ancient people took every blessing to be from God and understood every child to be a blessing. The corollary: childlessness is, if not a curse, a negative message from God. For our part, we need not attribute childbirth so directly to divine intervention but can understand it to be one of the human capacities that God placed within the sphere of our responsibility (a truth that the Priestly writers apparently understood; see 1:28).

Leah gives a significant name to each of her first four sons. According to the popular etymologies placed in her mouth, Reuben is a play on the Hebrew words for "see" and "son" (*raah* + *ben*), and Simeon is related to *shama* ("hear"). Seeing and hearing have been themes running throughout the patriarchal saga. Although this text makes no allusion to the histories of the tribes of Israel whose names are taken from Jacob's sons, it is worth noting that the tribes founded by these two eldest sons play no real historical role after the conquest narrative in Joshua. Levi ("joined") and Judah ("praise"), on the other hand, become the priestly and royal families of historical Israel.

[30:1–13] The generation of the twelve sons/tribes of Israel continues apace. An early recorded version of a marital argument that is repeated even to this day breaks out between Rachel and Jacob. When she blames him for their failure to get pregnant, he passes the buck to God. Providence is the business of God, not of God's human agents. (Joseph makes the very same affirmation in 50:19.) To these people, or at least to the Yahwist, procreation falls under the heading of providence.

Rachel's proposed solution to the problem of their childlessness is surrogate motherhood, effected more directly than we practice it today, but aimed at the same goal: children for Rachel. Her fertile servant Bilhah will do for Jacob what Hagar did for Abraham, but unlike Sarah, Rachel will claim the offspring as her own: Bilhah will "bear [them] upon [Rachel's] knees" (v. 3). Scholars are generally agreed that with this gesture, mentioned again in Genesis 48:12 and 50:23 and in Job 3:12, a person accepts responsibility for a biological or adopted child. In Akkadian, the language of Assyria, "knee" could be a euphemism for sexual parts; thus the phrase "one who has no knees" means an impotent man. However, the Hebrew verbal stem *barak*, "kneel," from which the noun for "knee," *berek*, is derived, also means "bless." Perhaps, therefore, bouncing a baby on the knees was just a way of blessing the child. That seems to be the case in Genesis 48:12. Then again, the knees of an assistant may simply have been a standard and necessary part of the birthing procedure. That could be the case here and in Job 3:12.

In any event, Bilhah gives birth to two more sons. They are Rachel's too, so she gets to give them their significant and down-to-earth names tied by popular etymologies to Hebrew verbs: Dan ("judged") and Naphtali ("wrestled").

Not to be outdone, Leah, wrongly thinking herself beyond the childbearing age (v. 9), gives her maid to Jacob for the same purpose of surrogate motherhood. So Zilpah produces Gad ("fortune") and Asher ("happy").

[14–24] The rivalry between the sisters continues until all twelve of the namesakes of the twelve tribes are born, plus their sister, Dinah. In these verses, however, Rachel, still childless and therefore not esteemed in the world of women and families, wants mandrakes, a small, fragrant fruit widely believed in the ancient world to be an aphrodisiac (see S. of Sol. 7:13). Maybe they will help her pregnancy project. Leah has mandrakes, thanks to her helpful son Reuben. Perhaps she is using them in her project to win Jacob's love. The sisters strike a deal: The beloved one will give up her man for a night to the rejected one in exchange for mandrakes (v. 15). Jacob, apparently unconcerned with who his partner might be, follows orders without a murmur (v. 16). The result is Issachar (sounds like Hebrew for "hire"). Another son, Zebulun (related to "honor"), and a daughter, Dinah, follow. (No folk etymology is offered for her name, but it seems to be a feminine form of *dan*, "judge.") Dinah is mentioned even though other daughters are not because she will figure importantly in the crisis of Genesis 34.

Only after ten sons are born to Jacob, including six by Leah, does Rachel finally bear him a son, Joseph. She attributes her eventual success neither to her schemes nor to Jacob's attentiveness nor to the mandrakes, but to God (v. 22). The narrator agrees. Providence alone can account for the miracle of birth. The name she gives him is derived from the verb *asaf*, "add." Not only is the child an add-on to the already large family, but his name is designed to have a dynamic effect on the future. As Rachel says, "May the LORD add to me another son!" It is ironic that this long-awaited and beloved son of the beloved wife is the only son who will not bestow his name upon a tribe of Israel.

RIVALRY BETWEEN JACOB AND LABAN
Genesis 30:25–32:2

The story of Jacob's deteriorating relationship with Laban and his final return to Canaan is a coherent whole. This commentary will run alongside this largely self-interpreting story. Throughout the narrative, we see the deceit and cunning of the chief characters, including Rachel.

The account begins with Jacob's request of Laban to return home as had always been his intention. Laban announces that he has learned "by divination" that all his success is the work of Yahweh acting on Jacob's behalf (v. 27). This is the first time divination has been mentioned by anyone in Genesis. It is a practice that Joseph later pretends to have mastered (44:15) and that the Deuteronomic code strictly forbids as an abhorrent, foreign practice (Deut. 18:9–14). Laban is neither an Israelite nor a worshiper of Yahweh, of course, so his reference to divination excites no editorial criticism. It is also possible that the Hebrew word in question does not mean "divination" at all, in spite of the NRSV. Jacob agrees that Laban's success is indeed the work of the Lord (v. 30). Readers will remember that the great overarching theme of the patriarchal saga is the spread of blessing from Abraham and his descendants at the center of the peoples of the earth. Here it seems to have happened!

In verse 28 Laban rather cannily asks Jacob to name his price for his twenty years of service (see 31:38). Now Jacob comes up with a rather straightforward proposal for reimbursement. Jacob has had responsibility for Laban's flocks, so he is presumably well aware of the makeup and condition of these assets. He offers to take as his payment any goat or sheep that is spotted, speckled, mottled, black, or otherwise naturally branded. This would presumably leave Laban with only solid-colored livestock, black goats perhaps, and sheep the color of *laban*, "white." Laban agrees, but then secretly drives off such "defective" sheep and goats and puts them in the charge of his sons.

Perhaps Jacob discovered Laban's latest perfidy, or perhaps he had his own scheme already in mind. In any case, he outwits Laban by trading on the primitive presupposition that an offspring of any species will mirror something of whatever its mother was looking at while mating. By putting mottled sticks before the best ewes of Laban's flock, or by causing them to look at black sheep as they were breeding, he creates for himself a flock of speckled but otherwise healthy animals. Thus by trickery does Jacob get his fiscal stake in the future, just as his grandfather had done in the wife/sister scam with Pharaoh (12:10–20). Thus through such motley servants does the Lord advance the chosen line toward the fulfillment of the promise of blessing.

Jacob is aware that Laban is looking with disfavor on him, so he calls his wives Leah and Rachel to a meeting in a field (31:4). The consultation is remarkably amicable. He accuses their father of cheating him and of changing his wages ten times (v. 7). The cheating we have been aware of, but this is the first we have had the wage information. (Part of the story-telling style of the Yahwist is to release new information only when necessary and never to fill in all the gaps.) Jacob tells a barefaced lie when he piously attributes his good fortune in acquiring striped and speckled flock to direct divine intervention (v. 8); the reader knows that he was doing it all himself. In a more general way, he brings the invisible hand of providence out for all to see when he says "God did not permit [Laban] to harm me" (v. 7). Jacob then tells Leah and Rachel that he had a dream in which an angel related his success in Paddan-aram to the vow that he took at Bethel (28:20–22) and then ordered him to go back to Canaan at once.

Jacob's candor and rhetoric fan the passions of the two women. For th first time they express anger at their father not only for selling them (essentially true), but also for keeping the proceeds of the sale. (If a groom had money, he would deposit the bridal-price with the bride's father to provide an endowment for her security later on. In Jacob's case, his years of slave labor should have been converted by Laban into cash as an endowment for Jacob's wives.)

The new spirit of defiance bears fruit immediately (vv. 17–21). Jacob flees west across the Euphrates with all of his property and his family. In the stealthy excitement of this exodus, Rachel steals the god-figurines of Laban's household (v. 19), a foreshadowing of the despoiling of the Egyptians by the fleeing Israelites (Ex. 12:36). These "household gods" (*terafim* in Hebrew; the word may be related to the verb *taraf*, "rot" and another noun, *terefah*, "carrion") are listed in 2 Kings 23:24 among the pagan abominations attacked by the good King Josiah. These statuettes or amulets were probably small (Rachel successfully hides them by sitting on them later in the story) and made of clay or metal. We are given no hint why Rachel wanted them. Perhaps they were made of valuable gold or silver and would provide her with her missing endowment. Perhaps she still worshiped them (see 35:2). In any case, they must have played an important role as guardian deities and good-luck pieces in the religious life of Laban's household, for their disappearance angers him more than anything else.

Laban pursues Jacob and his party and overtakes them in seven days in Gilead (v. 23). They must have had express camels and donkeys, for they covered over three hundred miles as the crow flies, or about forty-three miles per day. The Lord sent Laban, the Aramean polytheist, a revelatory dream that warned him to back off of Jacob (v. 24; on patriarchal dreams see commentary on 15:12–21). Even so, the meeting starts in an atmosphere of hostility, with Laban feigning offense at having been deprived of the opportunity to say good-bye. In verse 30, he reveals the main thing that rankles him—the theft of the household gods. Not knowing Rachel has them, Jacob puts her life in jeopardy by vowing to execute anyone who has them in his or her possession (v. 32). All turns out well, however; Laban cannot find the gods because Rachel, who has them in her camel's saddle and is sitting on them, will not stand up for her father because she is menstruating (vv. 34–35). Israelite readers would realize that she effectively has desecrated the idols, for bodily discharges render ritually unclean a person and all that he or she touches (see Lev. 15:19–24 for later Priestly legislation about the menstruating woman).

Now it is Jacob's turn to get angry. He tells of the twenty years of injustice he has suffered at Laban's hand. In fact, he would now be empty-handed, had "the God of my father, the God of Abraham and the Fear of

Isaac, not been on my side" (v. 42). Note that God's title is becoming more elaborate as the generations pass. Twice in this chapter (but nowhere else) God is given the epithet "the Fear of Isaac." Some have argued that this was a pre-Israelite name of a deity from around Beersheba that came into the united Israelite tradition with the Isaac stories. No strong evidence supports that theory, however. Certainly God is sometimes presented as a fearful and awesome force (in Isa. 2:10, 19, 21, for example, the phrase "the terror of the LORD" is used). However, except for Genesis 22, the Lord has not appeared as fearful to the fathers and mothers. Based on a cognate word in Arabic, some scholars now say the term may mean, "the Protection of Isaac" (Westermann, *Genesis 12–36*, 497). That epithet would fit very well with the general theme of God's providential care that Jacob has been emphasizing.

With the quarrel dropped, Laban proposes a covenant (v. 44). In the best tradition of covenant-making, a stele (inscribed memorial stone) is set up next to a cairn of stones, and the place is called, both in Laban's Aramaic and in Jacob's Hebrew, "the Heap of Witness" (v. 47). What amounts to a mutual imprecation is pronounced by Laban. This well-known "Mizpah Benediction" is often misunderstood in the church as a happy farewell, largely because v. 49 is read without v. 50. The second sentence makes clear that this is a sanction that is being imposed against Jacob. Laban makes clear that he and his people will not pass the stele and the heap of stones en route "for harm" to Jacob (v. 52); Galeed/Mizpah is to be the border between them. He concludes with a rather surprising benediction: "'May the God of Abraham and the God of Nahor'—the God of their father—'judge between us'" (v. 53). This new information that Nahor also was a devotee of Yahweh is highlighted by a scribe who has interrupted the narrative with a gloss (a marginal note) that speaks of the ancestors in the third person.

After the mandatory covenant feast and Laban's kisses, the story ends with a vision of angels by Jacob (32:1). Exactly why that moves him to name the place "Twin camps" (*mahanaim*) is not clear. Perhaps he saw the angels ascending and descending as at Bethel. Or perhaps "Two camps" provides a segue to the long-delayed but now imminent confrontation with his twin brother, Esau.

PRELIMINARIES FOR PEACE WITH ESAU
Genesis 32:3–21

With his uncle Laban on his way east, Jacob's attention now turns to the confrontation with his brother. In these verses the narrator gradually increases the readers' anxiety by keeping us alongside Jacob in his camp

Neither he nor we know whether Esau's mood will have changed over the twenty years that have separated the twins. We empathize with Jacob's worry, for we know as he knows that he did his brother wrong.

The preparations are carefully done. A messenger is sent to Edom, Esau's base, with word of the arrival of the Jacob clan and mention of Jacob's riches (vv. 4–5). The messenger returns with word that Esau is coming with his militia of four hundred men. Jacob takes the precaution of dividing his forces, not for combat but to facilitate escape (vv. 6–8). He takes his anxiety to the Lord in prayer, appealing to God's *hesed*, "steadfast love," and asking God to make good on the election of Jacob's line and the promise of countless progeny (vv. 9–12). He then camps for the night after having organized the next day's march in such a way that Esau will see the riches in livestock that Jacob means to give him as a token of peace before he sees his brother's own "face" (*panim*, a word that will recur in the place names Peniel and Penuel later in the chapter).

JACOB WRESTLES WITH "A MAN"
Genesis 32:22–32

> 32:22 The same night he got up and took his two wives, his two maids, and his eleven children, and crossed the ford of the Jabbok. 23 He took them and sent them across the stream, and likewise everything that he had. 24 Jacob was left alone; and a man wrestled with him until daybreak. 25 When the man saw that he did not prevail against Jacob, he struck him on the hip socket; and Jacob's hip was put out of joint as he wrestled with him. 26 Then he said, "Let me go, for the day is breaking." But Jacob said, "I will not let you go, unless you bless me." 27 So he said to him, "What is your name?" And he said, "Jacob." 28 Then the man said, "You shall no longer be called Jacob, but Israel, for you have striven with God and with humans, and have prevailed." 29 Then Jacob asked him, "Please tell me your name." But he said, "Why is it that you ask my name?" And there he blessed him. 30 So Jacob called the place Peniel, saying, "For I have seen God face to face, and yet my life is preserved." 31 The sun rose upon him as he passed Penuel, limping because of his hip. 32 Therefore to this day the Israelites do not eat the thigh muscle that is on the hip socket, because he struck Jacob on the hip socket at the thigh muscle.

Strange things can happen to a person who is wallowing in anxiety. Few of us have experienced anything as strange as Jacob does, though, on the night before his meeting with Esau. The party has been camped in the trans-Jordanian hill country of Gilead, which is bisected by the River Jabbok. (The Jabbok empties into the River Jordan from the east, about halfway between the Sea of Galilee and the Dead Sea.) If Jacob sends his family and flocks across the Jabbok for protection from Esau, he must send them from the south side to the north because Esau is coming from Seir (Edom), south of the Dead Sea.

The story of the wrestling match with the "man" that lasted until dawn serves to explain the meaning of Jacob's new name, "Israel"—"let God (*el*) struggle or contend (*yisrah*)." Indeed, the name may have preceded the story and given rise to it. The "man" is, of course, God. Some commentators, perhaps because they cannot see why God would behave like this, deny that the "man" is God or even God's angel (= God). Westermann, for example, says it is a powerful and hostile river demon (*Genesis 12–36*, 519). The narrator makes God the most likely suspect, however, by having Jacob name the spot Peniel ("Face of God").

This strange narrative leaves us with many questions. Why would God want to wrestle with a chosen mortal all night? How could that mortal prevail in the match unless God allowed him to do so? Why will the "man" not give his name? The entire experience must have been some kind of ordeal or test of Jacob, comparable in that sense to the test of Abraham on Mount Moriah in Genesis 22. Jacob's courage and tenacity in the struggle cause the divinity not only to award him a meaningful new name (Abram and Sarai got theirs in the course of a direct encounter with God as well), but also to give him the coveted blessing. That blessing will enable Jacob to cope with Esau in their struggle yet to come. It will also strengthen Jacob's place in the succession of those founders whom God elected to bring blessing to all the peoples of the earth (12:3b).

Jacob sees God face to face and survives (v. 30)! The folk of ancient Israel believed that to look upon God was to die (a fear expressed by Manoah and his wife, the parents of Samson [Judg. 13:22]; see also Ex. 19:21). There were always many exceptions, however. All of the great figures of primeval history held personal colloquies with God, as did Abraham, Sarah, Hagar, Isaac, and Rachel. In later times Moses and the elders see God (Ex. 24:10), the prophets Micaiah ben Imlah (see 1 Kings 22:19), Isaiah, Ezekiel, and Amos all have theophanies, and Job hopes to see God (Job 19:26). Now, to his amazement Jacob too sees God and lives. He sustains an injury, though, when the "man" cripples him with a blow to the "hip socket at the thigh muscle" (v. 32). Some later glossator remarks that "to this day" Israelites do not eat the thigh muscle (v. 32) of an animal. The Old Testament makes no further mention of this prohibition, and a ban on eating the sciatic nerve or whatever else is in mind here no longer plays a significant role in Jewish dietary law.

JACOB AND ESAU ARE RECONCILED
Genesis 33:1–20

No doubt tired but spiritually renewed by his night of wrestling with God, Jacob is now ready to meet Esau. As the two clans draw near each other, Jacob arranges his family so that Esau will meet concubines, wives, and children in order of their status, with Rachel and Joseph in the place of honor. The rising tension that readers have been sharing with Jacob culminates in verse 3 when the patriarch steps out ahead of the entire company to make repeated obeisance to his brother.

The climax of the narrative about Jacob's reunion with Esau is reached in verse 4, and all is well. Esau, the founding father of the usually hostile neighboring people, the Edomites, and not a member of the elect line whom God chose to spread blessing in the world, proves to be a *mensch*! Whatever hatred he may have harbored toward his twin brother has dissipated, and Esau bestows on Jacob the now familiar hugs, kisses, and tears of familial bonding (see 29:11–13). Evidently Esau had not had word about Jacob for twenty years, so the wives, the children, and the riches come to him as total surprises. The humane and now rather likable Esau asks about the flocks that he met en route to this meeting with his brother. Jacob is up-front about his strategy. Using a common Hebrew idiom, he answers that he has displayed his wealth "to find favor with my lord" (v. 8). The little negotiation that follows is reminiscent of the stately waltz over the purchase of the Cave of Machpelah in which Abraham and the "Hittites" engaged (chap. 23) in that the outcome is going to include an acceptance of a purchase or a gift, and a happy ending (v. 11). Yet there is an earnest sincerity in Jacob's entreaty to his brother to accept his gift in order that he "find favor" in his brother's eyes. Furthermore, the flocks that Jacob means to give Esau are more than Jacob even needs, so graciously has God dealt with him (v. 11).

His relief at finding Esau so kindly disposed toward him makes his brother's face appear to him "like the face of God" (v. 10). "The face of God" picks up the theme of the previous night, in which Jacob saw the face of God, received God's blessing, and named the site of the theophany Peniel, "the Face of God." Furthermore, it echoes the hope expressed by Jacob in Genesis 32:20 that the dreaded face-to-face encounter with Esau would result in the acceptance that has now materialized. To encounter another person's face is to be close and intimate, as our English idiom "face-to-face" suggests. Such close encounters can be dangerous or joyous, depending upon the attitude of the parties. The face is the naked part of the human anatomy that betrays the passions that will color the close encounter. Esau's face smiles on Jacob, and all is well.

The encounter leads the Jacob clan to make a lengthy stay with the Esau clan. Although Esau offers to accompany Jacob on his trip westward, Jacob demurs, pleading a need to go slowly because of the children and the nursing flocks (v. 13). He says he will follow Esau all the way to Seir, that is, Edom. If he actually ever intended to do this, we do not know; in any case, he does not do so. Is this yet another lie to his brother? No onus seems to be attached to his no-show in Seir.

Instead, Jacob goes to Succoth ("Booths"), a nearby place in transJordanian Gilead mentioned in Joshua 13:27, Judges 8:5–9, and elsewhere. He calls it "Booths" because he builds temporary cattle shelters there. His journey finally ends when he reaches Shechem on the west side of the Jordan in Canaan. It is noteworthy that Shechem was the first place Abram camped when he came to Canaan from Haran in Syria (12:6). Indeed, it was there that Yahweh first promised the land of Canaan to him. As was his wont, Abram built an altar and worshiped the Lord there on the site of his theophany. Jacob also builds an altar in Shechem, not because he had a revelation there, but probably because he wishes to reassert his claim and that of Yahweh in the land of the Canaanites. He calls the holy spot, "God, the God of Israel" (El-Elohe-Israel, v. 20), perhaps an indigenous Shechemite or even a peculiarly Jacobite designation for the God (El) who has also been called God Most High (El Elyon), God Almighty (El Shaddai), and Everlasting God (El Olam). Here we hear for the first time of the family of Hamor the Canaanite, one of whose sons, Shechem, is apparently the founding father of that city. Hamor means "he-ass" in Hebrew, so a note of contempt is sounded as soon as these Canaanite characters are introduced.

RAPE AND REVENGE AT SHECHEM
Genesis 34:1–31

Fast forward now a decade or more to another event in the saga of Jacob and his family. This event poses yet another challenge to the integrity of the elect line of Jacob as well as to their safety in the land that God has promised to give them. The promised land, the Land of Canaan, was not a land with no people for a people with no land. It had an indigenous population, who had, no doubt, mixed feelings about the settlement of this band of Arameans in their midst. If they are to survive the years between the promise of universal blessing through the descendants of Abraham and the fulfillment of that promise, the Israelites will have to find a way to live with the Canaanites and their indigenous kinfolk that takes a middle path between assimilation and extermination. The story of Genesis 34 sets a frightening precedent in the early days of that long relationship.

[34:1–4] Dinah, born of Leah (see 30:21), is the only daughter of the wives and concubines of Jacob who is ever mentioned. (A granddaughter, Serah, child of Asher, is listed among the sixty-six descendants who go with Jacob to the land of Egypt [46:17]. Strangely enough, though Dinah is mentioned by name in that same connection [46:15], she is apparently not one of the sixty-six; see commentary on 46:8–27.) She is not the founder of a tribe, because she never has children. Ancient readers would have understood that the violation she now suffers rendered her forever ineligible for marriage.

Dinah is a good neighbor, for she pays a visit to the local Canaanite women of Shechem. She is rewarded for her pains by being raped by Shechem ben Hamor, now called a Hivite. (The post-Flood table of nations lists the Hivites among the descendants of Ham and Canaan [see 10:17]. Nothing is known about this group but it is remembered as part of the pluralistic community of Shechem.) The arrogant fellow acts first, then speaks "tenderly" afterward and even takes steps to marry this foreign woman (v. 4).

A terrible precedent is set for the future relations of newcomers and natives. It is set by the locals, and it is a precedent of betrayal, oppression of the woman, violence against her person, and, from a later Israelite point of view, miscegenation. It contrasts sharply with the peaceful precedent established by Abraham in his purchase of the cave from the "Hittites." But then no living woman was at issue there, only a dead one.

[5–12] In spite of their anger, Jacob and his sons bide their time when they hear about the outrage. In traditional societies a rapist can expect to be pursued and lynched by the male relatives of the violated woman, even though reaction that severe may not be justified before the law (see, for example, Deut. 22:22–30, where the penalty for raping a nonbetrothed virgin is a fine of fifty shekels of silver, payable to the father of the woman, and marriage with the virgin with no possibility of divorce). If the violation occurs within a family, a degree of incest is added to the crime of rape (see forbidden sexual relationships listed in Lev. 18:6–23); in Levitical legislation the penalty is expulsion from the community. These legal formulations suggest that Absalom broke the law by murdering his brother Amnon as punishment for raping their sister, Tamar (2 Sam. 13:7–29). Amnon might have expected it would happen, however, whether inside or outside the law, for the honor of a woman of the family was at stake.

It is difficult to decide whether the "he-ass," Hamor, comes on with such a friendly manner because he fears the retaliation that might lie ahead, or because he thinks his son is covered under rules like those of Deuteronomy 22:22–30 mentioned above. Perhaps the Israelite reader would simply recognize in his deportment the loose, unholy behavior with which the Canaanites were stigmatized in the Israelite consciousness, behavior that leads the Priestly writers to say, "You shall not do as they do in the land of Canaan, to which I am bringing you" (Lev. 18:3). For whatever reason, Hamor proposes a nonviolent resolution to this foolish affront by his son. He asks for Dinah's hand in marriage to Shechem; he offers widespread intermarriage between the clans, and the sale of property. Shechem himself uses the familiar idiom, "Let me find favor with you," and offers to pay whatever bride-price and give whatever bridal presents are asked (v. 12). (The distinction between the bride-price and later wedding gifts from the groom to the bride and her family is drawn sharply here; both played their parts in the courtship of Rebekah, however; see 24:22 and 53.)

[13–24] Perhaps because they are outnumbered, or perhaps because it is simply their modus operandi, the sons of Jacob (but not, apparently, their father) decide on trickery as their way to get revenge. "Yes," they say in effect, "we will agree to everything, but only if you will accept circumcision. After all, it is well known that we cannot abide sex with the uncircumcised." On the face of it, their proposal is a far cry from the call for total separation from and rejection of the indigenous people of the land sounded by the very old legislation in the Covenant Code of Israel (see Ex. 23:23–33).

Young Shechem, crazy in love with Dinah (v. 19), takes the lead in selling the plan to the Shechemites. He sweetens the offer by suggesting that they will end up not only with the daughters of Israel but also with their livestock (v. 23).

[25–31] Three days after the mass circumcision the men are all still in pain. Moments later they are put out of their misery by the slashing swords of the sons of Jacob. It is these men and not the Shechemites who end up with the women and children, the flocks, and the real estate. Only father Jacob plays the part of Cassandra, looking ahead to years of enmity and danger from the Canaanites. After all, a second precedent has now been set: One way to deal with the uncircumcised non-Yahwistic indigenous people of the land is to swindle them, rob them, and kill them. The road from the promise of blessing to the nations through Israel to its fulfillment is made all the more perilous and rocky by an event like this (v. 30). An appeal to honor (v. 31) will not change that fact.

RACHEL DIES, AND AN ERA ENDS
Genesis 35:1–29

This final chapter of the Jacob cycle has the flavor of a miscellany. Because of its use of *Elohim* as the name of God, much of it is attributed to the Elohistic source. However, the repetition of the promise theophany in verses 9–13 is given to the Priestly source, as is the so-called archival ending of the entire Jacob saga (vv. 22b–29).

[35:1–4] God tells Jacob to move on to Bethel now. It is the place with which he is particularly associated because of his dream of the ladder and the altar he built there in chapter 28. A little secret is now revealed. It appears that in the baggage of the entourage that came from Paddan-aram are more than just the household gods that Rachel stole. Other people have their charms, amulets, and statuettes, as well as gold earrings that may have some pagan significance. Now Jacob collects them all and buries them under the oak that was near Shechem. That must be the sacred oak of Moreh near which Abram camped (12:6). That tree or its successor was still standing at the sanctuary at Shechem when Joshua led the people in a great postconquest covenant renewal ceremony (Josh. 24:26).

[5–8] Whether because of the way the sons of Jacob handled the rape scandal at Shechem or because of a spiritual "terror" sent on them by God directly, the Canaanite cities through which they pass make no resistance. They make it safely to Luz/Bethel (28:19). Now Jacob names the altar that he establishes after the God he encountered there. The name is another of the Canaanite-style *El* compounds, *El-Bethel*. (Remember that the high god of Canaan was also called *El*; his descendant among the Arabs today is still called *Allah* ["The El"]. For other names of this type, see commentary on 33:18–20.)

Rebekah's old nurse Deborah also dies and is buried at Bethel, perhaps inaugurating an Israelite necropolis at that sanctuary (v. 8). That holy place too has an oak. Readers will already have noted the association of trees with sacred places at Shechem and Hebron. The phenomenon was known throughout the ancient world and in traditional societies even to our own time. A stately tree was a thing of beauty and life, and an evident shelter for spirits. Centuries later the Hebrew prophets cried out against sacred groves and the fertility rites practiced in and around them (see Hosea 4:12–14, for example).

[9–13] This Priestly pastiche of various promises made by God to the patriarchs seems to have been collated from earlier stories. The divine renaming of Jacob/Israel, to which the Yahwist gave a narrative setting in Genesis 32:22–32, is given here without any narrative attached. Without attempting to argue that the wrestling narrative grew up to explain the name change, verse 10 at least shows that the renaming by God circulated without the story attached. In the theophany, God uses the self-identification *El Shaddai*, "God Almighty." That title occurs first with Abram in the Priestly covenant of circumcision (17:1). It occurs a second time in another Priestly context—Isaac's farewell to Jacob, who is about to set out in search of a wife (28:3). In other words, it is a title of God in the Priestly tradition.

The ninth repetition in the saga of the fathers and mothers of the promise of many descendants occurs in verse 11, coupled with the ninth reiteration of the land promise (v. 12). These themes are held in common by all the Pentateuchal sources, but the particular way in which the promise of progeny is expressed here—"a company of nations shall come from you"—occurs only once before, in Genesis 17:5, a Priestly narrative.

At the end of this new theophany at Bethel, "God went up from him" (v. 13). That is the very phrase found in the Priestly story of God's renaming of Abraham (17:22). All of these features—the renaming, the use of "God Almighty," and God "going up"—tie God's promise to Jacob in Genesis 35:10–13 to the Priestly source in general and to the promise to Abraham in particular.

[14–15] The consecration of the pillar and sanctuary at Bethel, on the other hand, is a reprise of the Elohistic conclusion to the earlier story of Jacob at Bethel in Genesis 28:18–22.

[16–21] The Jacob party moves southward toward Hebron. Near Bethlehem, Rachel dies in childbirth. The name the dying mother gives her second son does not stick. In a rare case of naming by a father, the boy is known in history by the name Benjamin, "son of the right hand." The story of Rachel's burial, not in Hebron with the rest of the clan but along the way, provides an explanation for a site known centuries later in the time of the Elohist. The writer says as much in an aside to the reader: it "is there to this day" (v. 20). In his final life review, Jacob explains to Joseph why he had to bury his beloved wife elsewhere than in the family tomb (see 48:7).

[22a] Included in this miscellany is the strange notice that Jacob's eldest son Reuben had sexual relations with his father's concubine Bilhah and apparently received no reprimand for it. The event seems inconsequential. Deuteronomic law forbids a man from marrying his father's wife (Deut. 22:30) but makes no mention of a concubine. Violating one's father's concubine seems to have been an expression of rejection of the authority of the father. That was certainly the operative motivation when, after usurping the throne, Absalom had sexual relations with David's ten

concubines on the roof of the palace in Jerusalem in order to make himself odious to his father (2 Sam. 16:20–23). Later Priestly legislation is specific that a man who lies with his father's wife should be put to death, together with the wife (Lev. 20:11). Apparently in this early period, lying with a father's concubine bore no severe onus, though on his deathbed Jacob finally condemns Reuben for this act (49:4).

[22b–29] The Priestly conclusion to the Jacob cycle sums up and tidies up. First, the standard list of the twelve sons of Jacob is given, broken down by mothers. This list reflects the widespread tradition of later years that the people of Israel existed in twelve tribes. Lists found elsewhere in the Old Testament differ both in number and in names: Deborah sings of only ten tribes (Judg. 5:14–23), whereas at the division of the United Monarchy into two kingdoms we hear of eleven tribes (1 Kings 11:31–32). In some lists, Levi and Joseph are omitted and are replaced by Ephraim and Manasseh, the sons of Joseph, to maintain the twelve-tribe scheme. In all, the Old Testament records more than twenty variations of the list of the twelve tribes (see commentary on 49:1–28).

The Jacob cycle of stories ends not with Jacob's death, but with that of his aged father, Isaac, who has been living in Mamre/Kiriath-arba/Hebron all this time (see 26:33). As was the case at Abraham's funeral (25:9), both the elect and the nonelect sons come to bury their father. This text does not say so, but Genesis 49:31 places Isaac's burial place in the family mausoleum, the cave of Machpelah, in Hebron.

THE DESCENDANTS OF ESAU
Genesis 36:1–43

Students of biblical ethnology take delight in chapters like this excellent example of a Priestly table of descent; so do those who wish to understand the attitude toward surrounding peoples revealed in the Pentateuch's last recension In the genealogy of Esau's descendants one can discern the names of some tribes and cities that will prove to be important adversaries to historical Israel. Nevertheless, the list is given with sober neutrality.

Deuteronomy 23:7–8 forbids an Israelite from abhorring an Edomite, "for they are your kin." However, as Obadiah 1–14 shows, such tolerance had limits at various times in history. In 129 B.C., the Edomite/Arab territory of Idumea was conquered by the Jewish Hasmonean king John Hyrcanus I, and all its non-Jewish males were forcibly circumcised. In that quasi-Jewish homeland Herod the Great was born half a century later.

For our purposes, no detailed study of these matters is necessary. Readers who are interested in pursuing some of these names further are urged to examine Westermann's commentary on Genesis 12–36, Sarna's commentary, or the article on "Edom" in volume 2 of *The Anchor Bible Dictionary*.

[36:1–8] After an editor or glossator firmly ties the knot linking Esau to Edom, the chapter begins with an elaboration of the information about Esau's marriages already given in Genesis 26:34–35 and 28:9. The two unacceptable "Hittite" wives of chapter 26 mutate a bit. Generically they are now "Canaanites"; specifically, Judith is now Oholibamah, a Hivite, and Basemath is now Adah, a Hittite. Intermarriage with them began the assimilation of the Esau line into the ranks of nations that encircled historical Israel. The third wife, more acceptable because she is Ishmael's daughter (28:9), is no longer Mahalath but has become Basemath. These three wives bore to Esau a total of five sons (and a number of daughters) before Esau migrated to Seir ("shaggy").

Seir is the high plateau and mountain region that runs north and south along the east side of the Great Rift Valley from a point just beyond the southern end of the Dead Sea, the great canyon of the Brook Zered (Wadi el-Hesa), to the Gulf of Aqaba. (In ancient times Seir was forested ["shaggy"]; the last of those woodlands was cut down by the Ottoman Turks before and during World War I to provide ties and fuel for the Hejaz Railway.) Seir defined the north-south boundaries of the ancient land of Edom and became synonymous with it. Though arid, the high Seir enjoys enough rain and snow to provide forage for flocks. Esau's reason for migrating southeast to less crowded pastures makes sense (v. 7). Furthermore, it follows the pattern of nomadic movement to less crowded (if not greener) pastures established by another nonelect branch of the family of Terah, Lot (13:8–13).

[9–14] The genealogy moves one generation forward with a list of the twelve legitimate grandsons of Esau, plus Amalek, the child of the concubine Timna (v. 12). The names seem intended to establish links with towns, regions, and tribes located south and east of Judah. Two of Eliphaz's sons figure elsewhere in the Old Testament. The first is Teman, also the name of a place thought to be adjacent to Petra, the most important ancient site in Edom. (One of Job's friends combines this father and this son in one name, Eliphaz the Temanite!) The second is Kenaz, founding father of the Kenizzites (15:19). This group is close enough to Israel to have produced one of its heroes, Caleb the son of Jephunneh the Kenizzite, who, with Joshua, was privileged to enter the Promised Land (Num. 32:12). Joshua 14:13 says that he received Hebron as his reward.

In contrast, Amalek, the son of Eliphaz by his concubine Timna

(v. 12), is the father one of the most hated enemies of Israel (see, for example, Ex. 17:8–16). Because his mother is a member of one of the Horite clans indigenous to Seir (vv. 20–22), she does not achieve the full status of wife on this list, nor does her son gain her any points in subsequent history.

[15–30] This section begins (vv. 15–19) with a slightly different list of the sons of Esau and their related "clans" of Edom. On this list Amalek moves up to full grandson status, and a second Korah makes an appearance as a son of Esau's first wife, Adah (see v. 16). It is followed by a genealogy of the Horites of Seir (vv. 20–30) with some of whom the Esau clan intermarried. (The Horites are already located in this area [14:6], in connection with the invasion of the kings of the East.) This genealogy begins with a name-giving ancestor, Seir himself. Although tradition has gathered around some of these names, with one exception the Bible teaches us nothing further about them. The exception is Uz (v. 28), said to be the name of Job's homeland (Job 1:1). This is another hint that the writers of Job intended to portray him as at least a quasi-Edomite.

[31–39] The notion that Edom had a native kingship tradition older than Israel's is not too far-fetched. The eight "kings" mentioned here might have been more like tribal chieftains, since there is no evidence of a sedentary population in Edom much prior to Saul's election to kingship in Israel in about 1020 B.C. (Rameses III of Egypt [1182–1151 B.C.] claims that he "razed the tents" of the people of Seir.) They are not yet a dynasty. Each one may have become "king" in his turn by some kind of election or public acclamation, rather like how the "judges" of Israel (and Saul) came to their leadership roles. Little or nothing is known from biblical or extrabiblical sources about any of these kings. Bela son of Beor (v. 32) is not the same as Balaam son of Beor, the seer whom the king of Moab recruited to curse the oncoming Israelites under Moses (Num. 22:5–6). Only the book of Job offers a minor exception. The Greek version of the book of Job includes a note that identifies Job with Jobab, son of Zerah of Bozrah (v. 33).

Once Israelite monarchy was established, first with Saul and then again with David, two Genesis promises are fulfilled: Kings spring from the line of Jacob (35:11), and Esau serves his brother (25:23; 27:40). The latter we deduce from accounts of the total victory by David over Edom (see 2 Sam. 8:13–14).

[40–43] The archive of Esau's descendants closes with a clan list that seems also to be a record of the localities occupied by the Edomites. Four of the eleven names recorded here have been mentioned earlier in the chapter. One of the new ones, Elah (probably Eilat on the Gulf of Aqaba) carries the reader to the southern border of Edom. Pinon may be the copper-mining settlement of Feinan, twenty miles southeast of the Dead Sea.

We leave Esau's genealogy with this question: How will the promise to Abram that his descendants will be a source of blessing for all the nations apply to Esau and Edom? The subsequent history of the relationship of these peoples is not exactly a peaceful and blessed one. It can be said, however, that the Pentateuchal writers took Esau seriously, sometimes portrayed him tenderly, and in the end, felt constrained to preserve a detailed account of the history of his family that would reserve him a permanent place on the margin of the elect line. Small comfort, perhaps, but better than silence.

13. The Story of Joseph and His Brothers
Genesis 37:1–50:26

We have now arrived at the last cycle of stories in the family saga of the fathers and the mothers. By now the likelihood that many of these traditions were originally separate from each other is no surprise. What is amazing is the skill with which several generations of storytellers wove them into one dramatic saga emblazoned with the towering figures of Abraham, Isaac, Jacob, Jacob's sons, and all of their remarkable wives. Right from the beginning this saga has been worked by an incandescent idea first stated in Genesis 12:3b: "I will bless those who bless you, and the one who curses you I will curse; and in you all the families of the earth shall be blessed."

Genesis 12–50 is the story of the spread of that blessing, told slowly and often dramatically. Before our very eyes the scarlet thread of promise moving toward its fulfillment has wound through the trickery of Abram and Sarai with Pharaoh, the threat of barrenness to Sarai, the danger of the knife to Isaac's throat, the treachery of Jacob and even his lovely wife, the fratricidal hate of Esau, and the peace between Jacob and Laban.

The Joseph story (chaps. 37–50) brings us to the end of the story of a single family, a clan of patriarchs now become a whole people, with whom God will work out the promise of blessing in the midst of history. The children of Israel will appear in the very first verses of the second book of the Pentateuch, living in Egypt where Joseph brought them, but about to set out in quest of their Promised Land.

The Joseph story is by far the longest single sustained narrative in the book of Genesis, and one of the longest in the entire Hebrew Bible to center around a single person. This fact, plus the rather elaborate plot line and the sustained development of the characters of Joseph and his brothers, suggest that from the beginning it may have been a written composition. This is not to insist that Joseph is a fictional character. He may have been remembered as a member of the twelve-tribe scheme in the oral tradition of the people. However, even if he were, his role is different from that of his predecessors or his peers. The formula, "The God of Abraham, Isaac and Jacob," excludes him from the first rank of the elect patriarchs. Although he earns a passing mention in the roster of men of faith in Hebrews 11 (and, in Wisdom 10:13–14, as one whom Lady Wisdom rescued), he is not listed among the great people of Israel's past in Sirach 44. Furthermore, no tribe of Israel bears his name. Joseph functions as a rather secular man; the Lord never speaks directly to him or appears to him in a theophany, and he never builds an altar or worships. In short, much about this novella (the genre often assigned to the Joseph story) distinguishes it from what has gone before and bears the marks of literary composition rather than a deeply rooted oral narrative of the people.

This idea of a coherent and complete written original runs into difficulties with source critics, who have discerned in the Joseph story the hands both of the Yahwist and of the Elohist. However, the postulation of two sources (with only slight touches from the Priestly source) could account for inconsistencies within the story. One of many such rough places appears right away in chapter 37: Were the traders who bought him and carried him to Egypt Ishmaelites (J; see v. 25) or Midianites (E; see v. 28)? This problem of disagreements in details within a very coherent larger novella could be handled by arguing that the Yahwist originally composed this story in its entirety and that the Elohist later supplemented it and introduced new theological themes and insights.

A structural analysis of the plot of the entire story suggests that at least one narrative source that preceded the work of the Yahwist may still be preserved within it.

Genesis 37:1–4	The problem (Joseph hated by his brothers)
37:5–36	Rising action (They sell Joseph into Egypt)
38	Sidebar: Judah and Tamar
39–41	Story within the story (Joseph in Egypt)
42–44	More rising action (Brothers come to Egypt)
45	Climax (Joseph revealed, reconciliation)
46–50	Falling action (Move to Egypt, Jacob dies)

The "story within the story" of chapters 39–41 explains how Joseph rose to power and came into a position to help his long-lost family in Canaan. However, these chapters also tell about events in Joseph's life quite unconnected to the main plot of family strife and peacemaking. Furthermore, two Egyptian tales that come down from antiquity seem particularly to reflect the culture of chapters 39–41. The "Tale of the Two Brothers" (known from one papyrus manuscript that can be dated to about 1210 B.C.) tells of a successful younger brother who is first seductively approached and then, upon his refusal, framed by the older brother's wife. The "Tale of Sinuhe" (about 1900 B.C.) pictures a young Egyptian official in exile who, by virtue of his discretion and etiquette, wins the esteem of his hosts abroad and, in the end, the court in Egypt. All of this suggests that the story of chapters 39–41 may have arisen separately from the rest of the novella, and was a source upon which the writer of the full narrative drew.

Whether descended from the oral tradition or written from the beginning, in its present context at the close of the saga of the fathers and the mothers, the Joseph novella serves several functions. First, it explains how Israel got down to Egypt. Without the movement of the Jacob clan in Joseph's time, there could not have been an exodus centuries later. By all accounts, the exodus and the Sinai event incorporated within it are the constitutive events in the theological account of the beginnings of Israel. Summarized in the "little historical credo" of Deuteronomy 26:5–9, that account has four elements: promise of land, slavery in Egypt, exodus, conquest (see also Deut. 6:21–23; Josh. 24:2–13). By explaining how Israel came to leave the land of promise and to sojourn in Egypt, this story sets up the exodus.

A second function of the Joseph story is to give the Yahwist (seconded by the Elohist) an opportunity to demonstrate what an ideal courtier and sage looks like. The Yahwist tells a story about courtly wisdom, about what a man of perception and discretion can accomplish as a servant of a king. These chapters put in story form the values and etiquette that are taught in the very different genre of wise precepts in the books of Proverbs and Ecclesiasticus (the Wisdom of ben Sira). Joseph is the kind of person that teachers at the court sought to train for the eight hundred years from David's time, through Solomon (who was himself a sage, the author of three thousand proverbs [1 Kings 4:32]), to ben Sira in about 200 B.C. If the Yahwist lived and worked at the court of the United Monarchy of David and Solomon, court wisdom would very likely have been valued and taught in that environment. In Joseph, the Yahwist gives that world a living example of the person formed by those values. Here is a courtier so wise, handsome, trustworthy with money, virtuous in the presence of seduction, and prudent in his advice that he can rise to the number two position in the superpower of Egypt (41:40).

Another Old Testament figure displays the gifts and competencies of a wise courtier on the model of Joseph, namely, Daniel. Indeed, Daniel is a veritable new Joseph, a young Israelite taken into captivity who, by dint of his wise counsel, his piety and unshaken integrity, and his ability to interpret dreams, rises to a very high position in the court of a foreign king. His story is elaborated even further than Joseph's, for not only can he interpret the king's dreams, but, with the help of God, he can also recover the memory of a dream that was forgotten (Dan. 2:27–30). The book of Daniel was written at the very end of the Old Testament period, long after the Joseph story had become scripture in ancient Israel. Nevertheless, like a mirror it shines back onto the Joseph story the skills and virtues expected of a graduate of an "academy of wisdom," and behold, they fit!

Finally, the Joseph novella serves a vital theological function for the book of Genesis as a whole. Here we see the way in which providence, God's invisible hand made visible to the reader, brings the promise of blessing many steps closer to fulfillment. The link with Exodus will lead directly to the re-entrance of the Israelites into the Promised Land. The promise of progeny is secured by the safe deliverance of the children of Jacob from the things that most threaten the elect line: famine, poverty, and, above all, fraternal strife. The growth of the family of the patriarchs into the people of Israel will be sanctified by the deathbed blessing of the last of the fathers, Jacob, and by the forgiveness of Joseph. One can even say that the promise of Genesis 12:3b that in Israel other nations will find a blessing—that great overarching motif of Genesis and of the Pentateuch as a whole—is brought closer to fulfillment in Joseph's fruitful relationship with the Egyptians and, because of that, in the assurance that Israel will survive. It is through Israel's survival, its subsequent nationhood, its kingship, its prophets, and its spiritual descendants, that God will in the end overcome the curse of Babel and bring us back to the garden. That is the full story of which Genesis is but the first chapter; the last chapters have yet to be written.

For all of its importance to the saga of the fathers and the mothers, few hymns if any respond directly to the story of Joseph. Clearly the temptation by Potiphar's wife is not something people want to sing about in church. However, the underlying theological theme of providence, which comes to its strongest expression in Genesis 45:8 and 50:20, is well represented in hymnody. The seventeenth-century hymn "O God, What You Ordain Is Right," by Samuel Rodigast, closes with a clause that resonates with the Elohistic theme of "the fear of God" (see 50:19; also 22:12). To fear God means not to try to overcome God's plans with human plans, but to trust that God will get it right.

> O God, what You ordain is right,
> Here shall my stand be taken.

Though sorrow, need, or death be mine,
Yet I am not forsaken.
Your watchful care is round me there;
You hold me that I shall not fall,
And so to you I leave it all.

Although few hymns interpret the Joseph story, a beloved operetta by Tim Rice and Andrew Lloyd Webber, "Joseph and the Amazing Technicolor Dreamcoat," puts a lively and loving spin on the account. Originally written in 1968 as a school play, the musical rightly senses the theatrical quality of the novella and the humor that results from the dramatic ironies shared by the readers, the narrator, and Joseph.

JOSEPH DREAMS OF GLORY AND PAYS FOR IT
Genesis 37:1-36

37:1 **Jacob settled in the land where his father had lived as an alien, the land of Canaan. 2 This is the story of the family of Jacob.**
   Joseph, being seventeen years old, was shepherding the flock with his brothers; he was a helper to the sons of Bilhah and Zilpah, his father's wives; and Joseph brought a bad report of them to their father. 3 Now Israel loved Joseph more than any other of his children, because he was the son of his old age; and he had made him a long robe with sleeves. 4 But when his brothers saw that their father loved him more than all his brothers, they hated him, and could not speak peaceably to him.

The problem that will drive the Joseph story is established in the first four verses. The seventeen-year-old son, eleventh born of the twelve sons of Jacob and one of the two children of his late but most beloved wife, Rachel, has the old man's ear when he comes home from the field and tattles on his brothers (v. 2). No sooner do we readers learn that Joseph is Jacob's favorite (v. 3) than images of sibling rivalry, family strife, and fratricide come into our minds. Matters are made worse by Jacob's gift to Joseph of a special, perhaps striped or long-sleeved, robe (a "coat of many colors" in the Greek Old Testament and in the tradition). No wonder the brothers could not speak to Joseph in shalom (v. 4). The theme of shalom will appear often in this story. In fact, eight of its eighteen occurrences in the book of Genesis are in the Joseph novella. (For more on the meaning of shalom, see the commentary on 29:4-8.)

37:5 **Once Joseph had a dream, and when he told it to his brothers, they hated him even more. 6 He said to them, "Listen to this dream that I** dreamed. ⁷ There we were, binding sheaves in the field. Suddenly my sheaf rose and stood upright; then your sheaves gathered around it, and bowed down to my sheaf." ⁸ His brothers said to him, "Are you indeed to reign over us? Are you indeed to have dominion over us?" So they hated him even more because of his dreams and his words.

9 He had another dream, and told it to his brothers, saying, "Look, I have had another dream: the sun, the moon, and eleven stars were bowing down to me." ¹⁰ But when he told it to his father and to his brothers, his father rebuked him, and said to him, "What kind of dream is this that you have had? Shall we indeed come, I and your mother and your brothers, and bow to the ground before you?" ¹¹ So his brothers were jealous of him, but his father kept the matter in mind.

No interpreter is needed to understand the meaning of young Joseph's two dreams. The imagery is drawn from nature, but the actions of sheaves and celestial bodies in bowing down is all mixed up in family dominance issues. Even Jacob takes some offense (v. 10). Of course, as the full novella unfolds, the dreams prove to be absolutely correct.

According to literary critic Robert Alter, the pivot on which the Joseph story turns is true versus false knowledge (Alter, 159). No character in the story, including Joseph, grasps the full meaning of the dream of the sheaves until much later in the story when Joseph's brothers prostrate themselves before him whom they did not know (42:6). Everyone is forced by events toward fuller external and internal knowledge.

37:12 Now his brothers went to pasture their father's flock near Shechem. ¹³ And Israel said to Joseph, "Are not your brothers pasturing the flock at Shechem? Come, I will send you to them." He answered, "Here I am." ¹⁴ So he said to him, "Go now, see if it is well with your brothers and with the flock; and bring word back to me." So he sent him from the valley of Hebron.

Jacob is apparently a very wealthy pastoralist, for his flocks can graze all the way from his current home base in Hebron (see also 35:27) to Shechem, a distance by today's roads of about sixty miles. Despite the distance, Joseph is willing to be the message bearer. His charge is to "see if it is well [shalom] with your brothers and with the flock" (v. 14). Are they in order, in balance, in right relationships?

37:14 He came to Shechem, ¹⁵ and a man found him wandering in the fields; the man asked him, "What are you seeking?" ¹⁶ "I am seeking my brothers," he said; "tell me, please, where they are pasturing the flock." ¹⁷ The man said, "They have gone away, for I heard them say, 'Let us go to Dothan.'" So Joseph went after his brothers, and found them at Dothan.

18 They saw him from a distance, and before he came near to them, they conspired to kill him. 19 They said to one another, "Here comes this dreamer. 20 Come now, let us kill him and throw him into one of the pits; then we shall say that a wild animal has devoured him, and we shall see what will become of his dreams." 21 But when Reuben heard it, he delivered him out of their hands, saying, "Let us not take his life." 22 Reuben said to them, "Shed no blood; throw him into this pit here in the wilderness, but lay no hand on him"—that he might rescue him out of their hand and restore him to his father. 23 So when Joseph came to his brothers, they stripped him of his robe, the long robe with sleeves that he wore; 24 and they took him and threw him into a pit. The pit was empty; there was no water in it.

When Joseph finally finds his ten older brothers (and perhaps Benjamin as well—we are not told) in the grazing lands near Dothan, some thirteen miles northwest of Shechem, they set upon him. Though he had done his share of fanning up the flames of envy by rudely reporting his dreams of glory (37:5–11), a brother does not deserve such brutal treatment from his siblings. Actually, they "conspired to kill him" (v. 18), and he escapes with his life, if not his cloak, only because Reuben argues against bloodshed (and earns everlasting credit for secretly planning to rescue Joseph when the coast is clear from the dry cistern into which they throw him [v. 22]). Clearly Joseph is victimized by the evil intention of his brothers. Does God intend it for good? (See 50:20.)

37:25 Then they sat down to eat; and looking up they saw a caravan of Ishmaelites coming from Gilead, with their camels carrying gum, balm, and resin, on their way to carry it down to Egypt. 26 Then Judah said to his brothers, "What profit is it if we kill our brother and conceal his blood? 27 Come, let us sell him to the Ishmaelites, and not lay our hands on him, for he is our brother, our own flesh." And his brothers agreed. 28 When some Midianite traders passed by, they drew Joseph up, lifting him out of the pit, and sold him to the Ishmaelites for twenty pieces of silver. And they took Joseph to Egypt.

Were the passing caravaneers Ishmaelites (v. 25) or Midianites (v. 28)? (Comments on the sources of the Joseph story may be found above in the introduction to these chapters.) Is there a difference? Theoretically, yes. The Ishmaelites descend from Isaac's half-brother by Hagar, whereas the Midianites descend from a different half-brother by Abraham's last wife, Keturah (see 25:2). Later tradition knows of a definite if variously located "land of Midian" populated by its own ethnic group (see Ex. 2:15 and Judg. 6:1–6). The less frequently used term "Ishmaelites," in contrast, seems to be not an ethnic designation at all but a generic term for nomadic traders. (On the anachronism of the camels see the commentary on 24:10–14.) Furthermore, there is no "land of Ishmael" in scripture. Perhaps this story is simply using the generic and the proper names for the same people. Does it matter? Probably not. All parties are kin to one another as far as Genesis is concerned, and so the sleaziness of the sale into slavery of one of their own to remote cousins is compounded.

Judah now earns a star in his crown for the same reason that Reuben did: He argues against shedding their brother's blood. God makes no appearance in the event, but we will learn in due course that divine providence is at work here, seizing upon yet another occasion of human sin to advance the cause of God.

If the twenty pieces of silver were shekels (v. 28), the brothers got a good average price for Joseph. In Leviticus 27:5, twenty shekels is the monetary equivalent of a male aged 5–20 years to be used when paying off a vow. By modern silver prices, this sale would have netted the brothers $130–$150—and who can say what purchasing power that amount of money had in the Late Bronze Age! The resale to the Egyptians no doubt was profitable to the traders. Egyptian documents of the second millennium B.C. reveal that at that time a brisk trade in slaves went on between Egypt and "Asia," that is, Syria and Canaan.

37:29 **When Reuben returned to the pit and saw that Joseph was not in the pit, he tore his clothes.** [30] **He returned to his brothers, and said, "The boy is gone; and I, where can I turn?"** [31] **Then they took Joseph's robe, slaughtered a goat, and dipped the robe in the blood.** [32] **They had the long robe with sleeves taken to their father, and they said, "This we have found; see now whether it is your son's robe or not."** [33] **He recognized it, and said, "It is my son's robe! A wild animal has devoured him; Joseph is without doubt torn to pieces."** [34] **Then Jacob tore his garments, and put sackcloth on his loins, and mourned for his son many days.** [35] **All his sons and all his daughters sought to comfort him; but he refused to be comforted, and said, "No, I shall go down to Sheol to my son, mourning." Thus his father bewailed him.** [36] **Meanwhile the Midianites had sold him in Egypt to Potiphar, one of Pharaoh's officials, the captain of the guard.**

Apparently Reuben had missed the picnic lunch and the sale of Joseph into slavery. When he discovers that the boy is gone, he engages in a demonstration of grief that is mentioned over twenty times in the Old Testament: He tears his clothes (v. 29). Soon Jacob will tear his for the same reason (v. 34). Before long all of the brothers will tear their clothes when they believe that Benjamin will be enslaved in Egypt like his brother before him (see 44:13). (The custom of *keriah*, "rending," continues even today to be a mourning practice in some Jewish circles.

The rip in a mourner's lapel should be at least four inches in length [Sarna, 261].)

The grief does not last long, however. The brothers decide to carry on the family tradition of deception and mistaken identity. The goat's blood with which they now stain Joseph's "coat of many colors" (v. 31) obviates any need to lie. Old Jacob draws his own conclusion, tears his own garments, and remains inconsolable for a long time. In fact, he says he will still be mourning his son when, at his own death, he goes down to Sheol (v. 35). This is the first of some sixty-five references in the Old Testament to this underworld to which all the dead, without exception, had to go. It was neither a place of punishment nor a place of reward. The dead who went there could do nothing (Eccl. 9:10), but merely continued to have a shadowy existence. No one who went there could ever return (Job 16:22), though on one occasion the medium of Endor was able to bring a protesting Samuel "up" to meet with Saul (1 Sam. 28:8–14). Similar concepts can be found in the religious literature of Canaan and Mesopotamia, though Egypt took a radically different view. Sheol provided no basis upon which a cult of the dead could be founded, and, unlike Egypt, none existed in Israel. Only at the very end of the Old Testament period did it become possible to be resurrected from death to new life in heaven or hell (see Dan. 12:1–3 and Isa. 26:19).

The Potiphar to whom the Midianites sell Joseph is not the Potiphera, priest of On, who will one day be Joseph's father-in-law (41:45). This man is identified as an "official" or "courtier" of Pharaoh (37:36), though the Hebrew term *saris* also means "eunuch." In some parts of the ancient Near East, certain royal courtiers, especially those who had contact with the harem, were castrated. That was true neither in Egypt nor in Israel, but the Hebrew term *saris* continued to serve for both meanings. In any case, the word is too ambiguous to use as an explanation for the subsequent behavior of Potiphar's wife!

A DIGRESSION: JUDAH AND TAMAR
Genesis 38:1–30

Before we reach the account of the interaction of Potiphar's wife and Joseph in Genesis 39, we hear in Genesis 38 another story from the Yahwist about a woman and a man. Similarities exist between the two narratives. In both of them the issue is honorable sexual behavior, in both the woman is the assertive one, and in both the patriarch of Israel is justified in the end. The biggest difference between the two is that one of the women—the one who gets pregnant and bears twins—goes down in history as more righteous than the man. In the rather sordid story of Judah and Tamar, only Tamar ("palm tree"), the probably Canaanite daughter-in-law of the founder of Israel's most dominant tribe, emerges with her honor intact. In fact, she has the honor of becoming the ancestor of King David and King Jesus through one of the sons of her liaison, Perez (see Matt. 1:3).

Readers of the Joseph novella have always wondered why the story of Judah and Tamar is placed here, where it so clearly interrupts the flow of the Joseph drama. No answer is definitive, but certain observations can be made. First, the story underscores Judah's rise to prominence among the twelve brothers. Along with Reuben, he saved Joseph from death in chapter 37. In succeeding chapters, he speaks for the brothers to their father (43:3–5, 8–10) and becomes head negotiator with Joseph on behalf of Benjamin (44:18–34). As Joseph rises, Judah rises. In the later history of Israel, Judah and Joseph (as the northern kingdom is called in Amos 6:6 and Zech. 10:6) are the two kingdoms that spring from the loins of Jacob (as promised in Gen. 35:11). Second, the story renews the theme of deception that has accompanied the family of Jacob all along and will continue to do so through the Joseph story. Third, that deception will feature two women in adjoining chapters, as has been noted.

[38:1–11] The story locates Judah neither in Hebron with his father nor anywhere near his brothers. He "went down" from the mountainous spine of eastern Canaan to Adullam, a place about sixteen miles southwest of Jerusalem, near the boundary between the later territories of Judah and the Philistines. (Like much else about Judah, his place of residence has associations with his descendant, David. See 1 Sam. 22:1–2 and 2 Sam. 23:13–14.) The fact that Judah is not criticized for marrying a Canaanite woman suggests that this story is very old. Certainly no narrator who had heard the preaching of the prophets or the injunctions of the Deuteronomist against intermarriage with the local population would tell this story this way.

Judah's unnamed Canaanite wife bears him three sons, Er, Onan, and Shelah. Enter Tamar, the wife whom Judah handpicked for Er (v. 6). The plot thickens around her when she becomes a widow. The passing comment that "the LORD put [Er] to death" because he was wicked (v. 7) is one of those little bombshells that explodes in the faces of some readers. They go away deploring the arbitrariness and violence of the God of the Old Testament. Their reaction is understandable, but the argument can be advanced that the narrator is not setting out to teach about God here, but about human duty and honor. Er has to be gotten out of the way to make the story work. God's hand was seen everywhere by the original audience, so they would have accepted this reason for his demise. Later readers are free to treat this as simply a narrative detail and to base their understanding of the nature of God on texts that intend to explore that subject (e.g., Isa. 40:1–11; Hos. 11:8–9; Ps. 121).

Israel had a provision for the care of widows called "levirate marriage." (The word has nothing to do with the priestly caste of Levites; it comes from the Latin term *levir*, "husband's brother.") We find the regulation in an Old Testament text later than the Yahwist, namely, in Deuteronomy 25:5–9. There is also a narrative illustration of it in Ruth 3–4. In the Deuteronomic version, the widow of a man should not be married to someone outside the family but should be married to her husband's brother (if the brothers resided together). The eldest son of that levirate marriage would "succeed to the name" of the dead brother, presumably including the estate of his uncle/"father." Through this curious form of surrogate paternity, the interests of the dead man would be secured by a legally recognized descendant, and the mother would have at least one child as her social security. The law in Deuteronomy also allows the brother-in-law to renounce the levirate duty, though to do so involves an element of public humiliation before the elders in the gate. The quittance is secured when the widow pulls off the brother-in-law's sandal and spits in his face.

The levirate marriage now forced by Judah upon Onan (38:8) is less nuanced than that provided for in Deuteronomy, in that Onan is given no opportunity to refuse. This may reflect an earlier form of the practice; the custom was widespread in Mesopotamia and Anatolia before the Pentateuch was written. Instead of impregnating Tamar, he practiced coitus interruptus (v. 9), precisely so that he would not father a child for Er, his dead brother. The Lord put him to death also, not, God forbid, for "spilling his semen on the ground," but because he violated his duty and dishonored himself and Tamar. (What weight these poor verses 9 and 10 have had to bear! "Onanism" has carried an onus ever since, though not even the super-straitlaced have thought of it as a capital crime.) It looks as though Tamar will have to wait for Judah's third son, Shelah, to have a chance at a child (v. 11).

[12–23] The plot moves quickly now. Judah himself has become a widower. Secure in the knowledge that Judah had erred in not giving her his third son in marriage, Tamar removes her mourning garb, hides her identity with a veil, and stations herself where Judah will find her as he makes his way past "the entrance to Enaim" (the Hebrew also means "the opening of the eyes") to shear his sheep. Veiling was not a usual practice by women in ancient Israel; both times it is mentioned in Genesis it is connected with a special moment in the erotic life of a woman (Rebekah's wedding veil in 24:65; Tamar's seduction veil here). Its most frequent mention in the Old Testament is in the sensual poetry of the Song of Solomon. Yet, if Assyrian law is any guide to early practice in Israel, for fear of corporal punishment a prostitute would never have veiled herself.

No surprise is expressed that Judah would make use of the services of a prostitute, and no blame is attached to him for it. The mistaken-identity ploy works for Tamar (v. 16). The arrangement seems routine, except that Tamar exacts not only payment but security that the payment will be sent, in this case the cylinder seal that Judah wore around his neck on a cord and with which he could stamp documents with his personal imprint. No one else would have one just like it. It was his credit card.

Of course, when Judah's Canaanite friend Hirah returns to the scene with the payment, there is no prostitute or "temple prostitute," as he rather more delicately puts it, allowing that she might have had some official function in the Canaanite fertility religion. Nor are Judah's personal effects to be found.

[24–26] The denouement begins when Tamar's pregnancy is disclosed to Judah. His power over her is absolute, greater even than her own father's, it appears. He condemns her to death by burning in the public place, as if he were the magistrate. Later Deuteronomic legislation prescribes death by stoning for a young woman who voluntarily engages in intercourse outside of marriage (Deut. 22:21, 24; see also John 8:5). Priestly legislation increases the penalty to death by burning for a man who has sexual relations with both his wife and his mother-in-law (Lev. 20:14), and for the daughter of a priest who prostitutes herself (Lev. 21:9). The talmudic tradition offers elaborate instruction on arrangements for the execution of persons guilty of capital crimes, including prohibited sexual relations, murder, blasphemy, idolatry, and sorcery. The methods used were hanging, burning, stoning, strangulation, and beheading. Criminals who were to be burned or strangled had to stand in dung up to their knees. In the light of this trend toward increasing severity, Judah's sentence of Tamar to death by burning seems prematurely harsh.

Tamar avoids recrimination, but merely presents Judah with incontrovertible evidence that he is the father of her child. He accepts post facto responsibility for the levirate duty that he prevented his son Shelah from performing, but he does not take Tamar as a wife with conjugal rights. Thus, in two respects his behavior does not agree with later rules: He impregnates his daughter-in-law (a capital crime for both parties, according to Lev. 20:12), and he does not marry the widow (as the *levir* is supposed to do, according to Deut. 25:5). He is not condemned for these shortcomings, however, perhaps because the story reflects an earlier stage or even a regional form of the practice. Tamar and Er get their heirs, and Tamar is praised in the verdict of history.

[27–30] As with Jacob and Esau, the exceptional birth turns out to be twin boys. Their meaningful names reflect not their respective destinies, but their unusual birth order. Their destinies are exceptional, though. Perez is the father of Hezron and Hamul (Gen. 46:12; 1 Chron. 2:5), the ancestor of Boaz, Jesse, David (Ruth 4:18–22), and, according to Matthew 1:2–16, of Jesus. The 468 descendants of Perez are listed among the Judahite leaders in the Jerusalem restored in Nehemiah's time (Neh. 11:4–6). Of Zerah we hear less, but he had five sons (1 Chron. 2:6). One of his descendants may have been Achan, the man who stole the things devoted to God and had to be put to death by stoning and burning (Josh. 7:25). Another was Pethahiah, a governor in Judah in the time of Nehemiah (Neh. 11:24).

Perhaps the best valedictory for Tamar and her strangely begotten son Perez was spoken by the people who were present when the kinsman with the levirate duty toward Ruth yielded the obligation to Boaz. They said to Boaz, "Through the children that the LORD will give you through this young woman, may your house be like the house of Perez, whom Tamar bore to Judah" (Ruth 4:12). Thus was the name of a woman of Canaan used in blessing a woman of Moab through whose offspring blessing would spread to the nations.

JOSEPH TURNS DOWN POTIPHAR'S WIFE AND PAYS FOR IT
Genesis 39:1–23

In a developmental sense, Joseph's history follows an expected course, something like this: He reaches adolescence, he leaves home and goes to "college" to seek his fortune, after some experimentation he finds a spouse and has children, and in the end he reconnects with his family in time to give them welcome help. This life cycle fits well with the literary structure of the novella. As noted above, the "story within the story" of Joseph on his own in Egypt found in chapters 39–41 may have had an earlier and separate existence from the full tale of Joseph and his brothers. However, the "rags to riches" change in Joseph's fortunes recounted in these chapters now serves as the turning point for the entire novella and makes possible the happy ending. Thus do the literary history and structure of the Joseph cycle match the normal life cycle of the man.

39:1 **Now Joseph was taken down to Egypt, and Potiphar, an officer of Pharaoh, the captain of the guard, an Egyptian, bought him from the Ishmaelites who had brought him down there. 2 The LORD was with Joseph,**

and he became a successful man; he was in the house of his Egyptian master. ³His master saw that the LORD was with him, and that the LORD caused
all that he did to prosper in his hands. ⁴So Joseph found favor in his sight
and attended him; he made him overseer of his house and put him in
charge of all that he had. ⁵From the time that he made him overseer in his
house and over all that he had, the LORD blessed the Egyptian's house for
Joseph's sake; the blessing of the LORD was on all that he had, in house and
field. ⁶So he left all that he had in Joseph's charge; and, with him there, he
had no concern for anything but the food that he ate.

We met Potiphar before we were distracted with the story of Judah and
Tamar in Genesis 38. He seems like a decent sort. The narrator even
makes him something of a Yahwist, for he, the narrator, shares with us
that Potiphar can see that Yahweh is bringing blessing to him through
this blessed servant. The Lord has been in the business of spreading
blessing through the descendants of Abraham ever since his initial gift to
the founder (12:3b). Now Joseph too nestles in under that overarching
scheme of blessing. So complete is Potiphar's trust in his slave that he
puts him in charge of everything except food preparation (v. 6a; this
exception anticipates Pharaoh's nearly complete trust in Joseph in 41:40).
This hands-off attitude of trust inadvertently sets the stage for the frame-
up and fall that follow.

39:66 Now Joseph was handsome and good-looking. ⁷And after a time his
master's wife cast her eyes on Joseph and said, "Lie with me." ⁸But he
refused and said to his master's wife, "Look, with me here, my master has
no concern about anything in the house, and he has put everything that he
has in my hand. ⁹He is not greater in this house than I am, nor has he kept
back anything from me except yourself, because you are his wife. How then
could I do this great wickedness, and sin against God?" ¹⁰And although she
spoke to Joseph day after day, he would not consent to lie beside her or to
be with her. ¹¹One day, however, when he went into the house to do his
work, and while no one else was in the house, ¹²she caught hold of his garment, saying, "Lie with me!" But he left his garment in her hand, and fled
and ran outside. ¹³When she saw that he had left his garment in her hand
and had fled outside, ¹⁴she called out to the members of her household and
said to them, "See, my husband has brought among us a Hebrew to insult
us! He came in to me to lie with me, and I cried out with a loud voice;
¹⁵and when he heard me raise my voice and cry out, he left his garment
beside me, and fled outside." ¹⁶Then she kept his garment by her until his
master came home, ¹⁷and she told him the same story, saying, "The
Hebrew servant, whom you have brought among us, came in to me to insult
me; ¹⁸but as soon as I raised my voice and cried out, he left his garment
beside me, and fled outside."

In verse 6b, Joseph is described in exactly the same Hebrew words that were used to describe his mother Rachel in Genesis 29:17, though the NRSV makes them sound more masculine: he is graceful and beautiful. Potiphar's wife (Zuleika by name, according to Jewish tradition) responds as directly to Joseph's charms (v. 7) as Judah did to the supposed prostitute (38:16), but Joseph refuses. In the stories (*midrashim*) that later rabbis told, Zuleika's friends feel her pain:

> She commanded her maidservants to prepare food for all the women, and she spread a banquet before them in her house. She placed knives upon the table to peel the oranges, and then ordered Joseph to appear, arrayed in costly garments, and wait upon her guests. When Joseph came in, the women could not take their eyes off him, and they all cut their hands with the knives, and the oranges in their hands were covered with blood, but they, not knowing what they were doing, continued to look upon the beauty of Joseph. . . . [Zuleika] then said: "This happened to you that looked upon him but a moment. . . . How, then can I control myself in whose house he abideth continually, who see him go in and out day after day?" (Ginzberg, 217–18)

In the ensuing exchange between mistress and servant, Joseph stresses the extent of the trust that the master has placed in him. The clause at the end of verse 9, "and sin against God" is an idiom in Hebrew that might also be translated as a kind of superlative, something like, "and sin to high heaven." (Even though the tale is told by the Yahwist, Joseph discretely uses the word *Elohim*, "God," rather than the proper name *Yahweh*, when speaking to the gentile woman.)

Potiphar's wife persists. We can assume that the two were in close physical proximity in verses 11–12 because she got hold of Joseph's outer cloak. (Had he been a poor person, he would have worn only one garment, but he was doing well in Potiphar's house.) The midrashim see this as the moment of near disaster for Joseph. They imagine that when Joseph came in to work,

> [Zuleika] stood before him suddenly in all her beauty of person and magnificence of raiment, and repeated the desire of her heart. It was the first and the last time that Joseph's steadfastness deserted him, but only for an instant. When he was on the point of complying with the wish of his mistress, the image of his mother Rachel appeared before him, and that of his aunt Leah, and the image of his father Jacob. . . . The vision of the dead, and especially the image of his father, brought Joseph to his senses. (Ginzberg, 219)

Potiphar's wife uses the word "Hebrew" pejoratively when she tells the servants, "See, my husband has brought among us a Hebrew to insult us!" (v. 14). One can imagine Potiphar's wife spitting out the word with considerable venom. This is only the second time the word has been used in the Bible to this point; the other use was when a great tribal chief was introduced as "Abram the Hebrew" (see commentary on 14:13). The majority of the subsequent uses of the term occur in the Joseph story and in Exodus 1–10, both of which are set in Egypt. Does this suggest that the word *Hebrew* has particular significance in the relationship between Israelites and Egyptians? We know that brigands and bandits called Habiru or Hapiru raided the Egyptian garrisons in Palestine in the fourteenth century B.C. during the reign of Amenhotep IV (Akh-en-aton). The texts of correspondence about this problem from Egyptian military commanders in Palestine are preserved in Akh-en-aton's library at Tell el-Amarna. The exact identity of these Habiru is not known, but the similarity of the term to the word *Hebrew* suggests that some of the tribal groups that, in the eyes of the Egyptians at least, later became Hebrews were already in Canaan prior to the exodus.

People who apply sociological models to ancient Near Eastern history and to the origins of Israel use the Habiru as evidence that Israel emerged onto the pages of history through the mechanism of rebellion by indigenous groups against their foreign imperialistic overlords. This account suggests that conditions in Canaan during the time covered by the Joseph story were already preparing the way for the emergence of a native kingdom able to overthrow Egyptian sovereignty in the area. How all of this links up with the story of Joseph's success in Egypt remains a puzzle, but it makes the willingness of Potiphar and eventually Pharaoh to place great trust in a Hebrew/Habiru even more remarkable.

Potiphar's wife plays the household servants off against her husband and establishes an alibi all at once (v. 14). By blaming her husband for importing into the household a Hebrew slave "to insult *us*," and to lie with her, she tries to enrage her staff against Joseph. Can't they see? They too are insulted! She also has his garment in her hand, and he has no chance to defend himself. The servants never speak; they are simply addressed as a silent audience. Perhaps we are to understand that they were on to her game from watching her in action day by day. Besides, they probably liked Joseph. Everyone in Egypt seems to have liked him.

When Potiphar arrives she phrases her accusation this way: "The Hebrew servant, whom you have brought among us, came in to me to insult me" (v. 17). Now the real offense is against her person only, and she aims to touch the possessive nerve of her lord and master. The servants seem to be absent when she tells her story to Potiphar. That might be no accident. Had they finally spoken up to set the record straight, she could not have made her accusation of Joseph stick.

39:19 When his master heard the words that his wife spoke to him, saying, "This is the way your servant treated me," he became enraged. 20 And Joseph's master took him and put him into the prison, the place where the king's prisoners were confined; he remained there in prison. 21 But the LORD was with Joseph and showed him steadfast love; he gave him favor in the sight of the chief jailer. 22 The chief jailer committed to Joseph's care all the prisoners who were in the prison, and whatever was done there, he was the one who did it. 23 The chief jailer paid no heed to anything that was in Joseph's care, because the LORD was with him; and whatever he did, the LORD made it prosper.

Potiphar's reaction to his wife's accusation is understandable. He becomes enraged and throws Joseph into the royal prison, from which position he will engage in new acts of wisdom and virtue in the ensuing chapters. The narrator helps us see providence at work; the Lord puts the power of blessing to work for and through Joseph (v. 23).

STRATEGIES FOR DISCERNING THE THEOLOGICAL VALUES IN GENESIS 39

The problem confronting the preacher, the teacher, or the reader of this story is how to explain it without piously moralizing on the role of woman as temptress. One strategy is to refuse to take the story in isolation, but to see it as part of the larger narrative about Joseph. This is the dramatic and humanistic means that the narrator uses to get Joseph into prison where he can reveal his real capability. God does not bring about the regrettable and destructive things that human beings do to one another, but God can weave them into the fabric of God's plan. The seduction story demonstrates once again that truth of this conviction, a conviction that is offered as a kind of general rule at the end of the Joseph story: "Even though you intended to do harm to me, God intended it for good" (50:20). This interpretive strategy points well beyond Genesis to Romans 8:28: "All things work together for good for those who love the Lord." This strategy embraces within it the evident intention of the story to teach discipline in the face of temptation. Moral restraint is good, but it is only one part of a larger narrative in which with the help of God Joseph makes his way through many pitfalls and tribulations to weave a life of blessing and to establish a bridge into the future for generations to come.

A second example of how the literary setting of the story can determine a strategy for its interpretation is in the sharp juxtaposition between Genesis 39:7–20 and the envelope of its immediate context, verses 1–6 plus 21–23. The beginning and the end of the chapter express confidence that all is well because the providential Lord who brings blessing even to the slave master for the sake of the slave (v. 5) is a God of steadfast love (*hesed*, v. 21). In between, in the drama of verses 7–20, we are shown that "*life must be lived at great risk*. Both [trust and risk] are true. Either taken by itself is false" (Brueggemann, 319).

If one stays simply with the story of Genesis 39 itself, can one discern a focus inherent within it? Of course the model of a hero who remains loyal to the loyal God even in the midst of great temptation is there and is intended for our edification. But the story also illustrates the wisdom ideal mentioned in the introduction to the Joseph novella. Here is the preeminent example of the ideal public servant: a truly wise man of discretion, the kind of man that every king would wish to have on his staff. Exhibiting virtues valued by wisdom circles in every age, perhaps even at the court of David and Solomon, this well-educated alumnus of Potiphar's academy of etiquette knows his limits, even though he has been put over everything in his master's house. Furthermore, he knows to avoid the seductions of Dame Folly and her Egyptian linens (see Prov. 7:16). Joseph is not portrayed as a naive denier of sexuality. Indeed, the rabbis thought it likely that this woman and this man felt attracted to each other. He is portrayed as a man who knows his boundaries.

In the end this is a story about right relationships. The steadfast love (*hesed*) that the Lord shows to Joseph in the jailhouse is not unrelated to the loyalty that Joseph shows toward Potiphar and, truth to tell, to his wife. Right relationships between God and God's human friends are manifested in right relationships at the human level. In time, even Joseph's brothers will experience this happy overflow from Joseph's newfound maturity in his loyalty to the Lord.

JOSEPH AND POTIPHAR'S WIFE IN ART

As the reader can well imagine, the painters of the Western world have been eager to interpret and often to refocus this story. The Master of the Joseph Legend (ca. A.D. 1500) shows prurient interest in it. In his picture, Joseph's slippers are on the floor and his right hand is on the woman's thigh, suggesting that impropriety was closer than the text would have us know. His Joseph is the one of rabbinic midrash, the one who has to combat his own desires very strongly. The Baroque painter Bartolomé Murillo (1617–1682) depicts Joseph as indecisive—his feet are pointed away from the woman's bed but his face is turned back and his eyes rest on her breasts. This picture juxtaposes jumbled textiles and draperies around the woman with a nice tidy carpet under Joseph's feet. It also juxtaposes darkness and light, much as Proverbs 7–8 contrasts Dame Folly and Dame Wisdom. The Joseph of Orazio gentileschi (ca. 1563–1639) is tidily put together, while Potiphar's wife is in great disarray as she holds the cloak that will serve as incriminating evidence. The red-curtained cubicle that hangs around the couch in this painting seems to raise the issue of the relation of public and private. Joseph is exiting back into the public from the private realm, little knowing that the activities of the private realm will soon deeply affect his public position. This painting also looks as though Joseph were leaving his coat with the wife as a souvenir. In this painting the light on Potiphar's wife and the point of focus on the cloak contrast with the relative obscurity of Joseph, suggesting that gentileschi was at least somewhat sympathetic with the woman.

In a 1634 etching by Rembrandt, the eye of the viewer enters the scene at a very strong bedpost on the right, then moves through the wife's body to Joseph's head on the left, which is the thematic center of the etching. Joseph is in an agony of ambiguity, hands in a rejecting position, posture awkward in the extreme. A door is only weakly hinted at; there seems to be no escape. The wife's upper body is twisted toward Joseph as she stretches to seize his cloak, but her naked lower body is oriented toward the viewer. Her lower body's fatness suggests that she might be pregnant. She seems to be exploited, jilted, made repulsive in her despair. Rembrandt gives the story a far different treatment in his famous painting "Joseph and Potiphar's Wife," on display at the National Gallery of Art in Washington, D.C. Of all the paintings surveyed, this is the only one that does not focus on verse 12. Instead, it illustrates a moment at about verse 19. Potiphar's only slightly rumpled wife is sitting on the bed gesturing at a youthful and innocent-looking Joseph standing at some distance. Potiphar himself is present and listening to her tale. The ambivalence in Potiphar's face leads the viewer to ask: Does he believe his wife? How severely is he going to crack down on Joseph?

JOSEPH INTERPRETS DREAMS AND GAINS BY IT
Genesis 40:1–41:57

We left Joseph in jail with the observation that the Lord put the power of blessing to work for and through Joseph. Because he could see this, the chief jailer leaves daily affairs in the hands of this extraordinary trusty (39:22–23). This leads in time to the appointment of Joseph to be a kind of warden over two government officials who are locked up with him in this white-collar prison (40:4). In three incremental steps, the story then chronicles Joseph's rise to power. The Lord makes no direct appearance along the way, but from time to time the narrator assures us readers that providence is at work.

What was the name of the Pharaoh who was Joseph's friend and patron? We do not know. The Joseph novella may contain a basic historical core, but as we have received it, it is a theological treatise about the emergence of the elect people through the providence of God to become a source of blessing in the midst of the world. It is not the careful record of secular events that we now expect historical documents to be (although most of ours still have axes to grind as well).

The stele of Pharaoh Merneptah (ca. 1220 B.C.), the first nonbiblical text to mention the existence of a people called Israel, provides a terminus for the (re)appearance of that people in Canaan. If we add to this the forty years for wilderness wandering and the 430 years of Egyptian sojourn given in Exodus 12:41 (an alternative is the 400-year figure given to Abram in his dream in Gen. 15:13), we arrive at 1700–1650 B.C. That period is known in Egyptian chronology as the Second Intermediate Period and in Palestinian archaeology as the Middle Bronze Age. It was a time of considerable instability for many pharaohs in Egypt and, in fact, a period during part of which foreign conquerors ruled the land (the Hyksos, possibly of Amorite or Canaanite origin). Many scholars suppose that the entry of Israel into Egypt happened in that period. Others think these dates are too high, and would bring the entry into Egypt down into the Late Bronze Age or, in Egyptian terms, New Kingdom times after 1550 B.C. Were that the case, one of the early pharaohs of the brilliant Eighteenth Dynasty (1552–1306 B.C.) might have sat for the portrait sketched in Genesis 41—Amenhotep I or Thutmosis I, perhaps. But remember, the Joseph novella is not history as we understand that term.

[40:1–23] Let us identify the time, place, and characters of these dream interpretation stories.

Time. These events take place "some time after this" (v. 1), that is, after Joseph's incarceration at the hands of Potiphar. Judging from his age when he enters Pharaoh's service (thirty years old; see 41:46), minus the two-year lapse reported in 41:1, we must think of him in his late twenties now, about ten years older (and wiser) that he was when he was sold into Egypt (see 37:2).

Place. This is puzzling. In Genesis 39:20, Joseph is taken to the royal prison by Potiphar. In 40:3, Joseph and the other VIP prisoners are being held in the prison "in the house of the captain of the guard"—Potiphar's title, according to 39:1. (Perhaps Potiphar lived over the store, so to speak.) That kind of minimum security prison sounds tolerable, except that Joseph later refers to the place as a "dungeon" (v. 15; the Hebrew word means "pit," and its use here recalls the "pit" where Joseph's adventures began in 37:20).

Characters. Before he displeased his master, the duties of Pharaoh's chief cupbearer would have been to vouch for the wine, stand near the king, keep his cup filled, and be prepared to offer information and advice. Egyptian documents confirm that this was a significant position in the Egyptian court. The chief baker's position was not so exalted, but he too had a sensitive role in preparing the king's food.

The two royal officers dream troubling dreams and lack any therapist to help them interpret the dreams (v. 8a). Joseph enunciates the principle that informs legitimate dream interpretation in Israel: "Do not interpretations belong to God?" (v. 8b; see also 41:16). This principle is demonstrated even more powerfully when God reveals both Nebuchadnezzar's dream and its interpretation to Daniel, and Daniel disclaims any personal role making this happen (see Dan. 2:17–45, esp. vv. 27–29; also Dan. 4:1–37, esp. v. 9). From many ancient Near Eastern sources we know that dream interpretation was a major "science," practiced by the sages, diviners, and soothsayers kept on the staffs of kings and sanctuaries. Indeed, "dream books," compilations of dreams and their meanings, survive from Mesopotamia and Egypt. Many rules for dreaming and dream interpretation were laid down. People went to their sanctuaries deliberately to sleep, perchance to dream (so-called incubation dreams).

Israel took a dim view of the machinations of professional dreamers and interpreters, as it did of magic in general. False prophecy was associated with dreams and fake interpretations (Deut. 13:1–5; see also Jer. 23:32 and Zech. 10:2). Yet, Israel shared with its neighbors the underlying conviction that God uses dreams to send messages to people. The dreams of foreigners could be revelatory to the intended recipient, as is the case with Gideon in Judges 7:13–15. Solomon has his own incubation dream at the sanctuary at Gibeon, during which he asks the Lord for wisdom (1 Kings 3:4–15; 2 Chron. 1:3–12). Simple, unencrypted dreams could be just as legitimate a mode of divine guidance as symbolic ones. Abimelech needed no interpreter to get the message about Sarah (Gen. 20:3–7) any more than Jacob did at Bethel (31:10–17). Joseph, who dreamed his own symbolic dreams in the past without fully understanding their meaning or that they were the messages from God that they would prove to be (37:5–11), now steps forward as a professional. He assures Pharaoh's officers—as he will assure Pharaoh himself—that the messages encoded in them are from God (called *Elohim* because the hearer is a gentile), and that he, Joseph, can make their meaning plain.

The dreams and their interpretations are simple enough. Neither archetypes nor phallic images are involved. Numbers equal time: Both officers dream about triads, which Joseph interprets as three days. The young Hebrew speaks honestly, conveying God's message as God intended it, whether the news is good or bad. In the end, everything turns out as he has said it would, to the joy of the chief cupbearer and the horror of the chief baker.

Joseph asks only one thing by way of reward for his service. He asks the man who stands just behind Pharaoh at every meal and whispers in his ear to put in a good word for Joseph, the innocent, kidnapped "Hebrew" (v. 14). Does the man do it? No. He forgets! (Another way of looking at it: In the slow working of providence, the time is not yet right. Pharaoh is going to have to need him first, just as Belshazzar has to have a desperate need for enlightenment before, on the advice of his queen,

Daniel can be brought out of obscurity to read the handwriting on the wall [Dan. 5:10–12].)

[41:1–36] Everything that transpired in the jailhouse with the servants of Pharaoh now happens at a more elaborate level with the king himself. Pharaoh is troubled with two dreams set in the only arable part of Egypt, the Nile Valley. Each dream features double heptads in which seven healthy, plump edibles (cows, ears of grain) are pitted against seven voracious, blighted ones.

In a departure from the simpler experience of chapter 40, Pharaoh sends for "all the magicians of Egypt and all of its wise men," who can of course make no sense of the dreams (41:8). Nebuchadnezzar and Belshazzar have the same experience in the book of Daniel (see Dan. 2:2; 4:7; 5:8). All their guilds of magicians, enchanters, sorcerers, and Chaldeans were phonies in the eyes of ancient Israel. "The fear of the Lord, that is wisdom" (Job 28:28). The wisdom that makes a person truly perceptive is founded on that deep respect for the Source. Only such a person can mediate the Word of God to the empire.

The forgetful cupbearer now remembers "the Hebrew" in the dungeon (v. 12). (This is the fifth of the six uses of the term in Genesis, all of which except 14:13 occur in the Joseph novella. The story more or less makes it the Egyptian term for the immigrants from Canaan. See the commentary on 39:14.) Joseph is brought out, then he changes and shaves (v. 14). Shaving the head or the face is often a punitive act in the Old Testament, but Egyptian tomb paintings and statues suggest that the smooth-shaven look was the norm in that hotter country. The Pharaohs often wore stylized goatees—even the female Pharaoh Hatshepsut sometimes did—as did their courtiers, but Joseph is not yet in that league.

We would like to know where Joseph got the new clothes, but the narrator does not tell. Joseph's clothes have been part of this story all along. Indeed, clothes almost unmade the man, beginning with his coat of many colors and including the garment that ended up in the hand of Potiphar's wife. Now the new clothes mean a fresh start.

Even before he hears about the dream from Pharaoh's own lips, Joseph disclaims his own role in the interpretation, and assures the king in advance that God's message to him will be favorable (v. 16). This is more prescient than Joseph's remark to the cupbearer and baker in Genesis 40:8. Was this just good political sense, or had Joseph already had intuition or information about the dream? The narrator hurries on without answering these questions. Pharaoh repeats the dreams to Joseph in accurate detail, adding that after the thin, ugly cows had eaten the fat ones, they looked no better than they had before (v. 21).

In his interpretation Joseph uses the same device as before: sets of numbers equal passage of time, but this time in years, not in days. All the dream episodes have involved two dreams dealing with the same subject matter; now Joseph says that this is God's way of underscoring the matter (v. 32). Seven lean years of drought and famine will wipe out the security gained by the seven plenteous ones, unless Pharaoh takes action. (Seven-year famines are a well-known literary convention, not only in Egypt, but also in the Gilgamesh Epic of Mesopotamia, the Canaanite Epic of Aqht, and even as a divine punishment of David in 2 Sam. 24:13.) Joseph recommends a food storage program based on a twenty percent reserve of grain, all under the direction of a "wise and discerning" central authority (v. 33). He is very discrete, and suggests nothing that would detract from Pharaoh's authority, but also phrases the recommendation in terms that fit himself better than anyone else. Joseph's suggestions make sense in a New Kingdom Egyptian context, for in that golden age the pharaonic bureaucracy was capable of mounting well-organized nationwide programs of taxation and public works. Drought and famine, too, fit with the Egyptian experience, as wall paintings and carvings show. The Egyptians maintained river gauges to give themselves advance warning of crop failure when the annual flood fell below normal.

[37–57] The turning point in this story within the story is now at hand. The young son who went off to "college" in Egypt has proved to be a fast learner and a man of good judgment. The kidnapped "Hebrew" now rises to a position of preeminence in his adopted land, and will soon be in a position to reconnect with his family and to succor them in their time of need. He will be providential toward them, repaying their evil with his good, just as the Lord's providential hand has been steady and sure in his own life. Yahweh's great promise of Genesis 12:3b is working its way toward its full fulfillment, one little fulfillment at a time. Now Joseph, representing all the descendants of Abraham, is beginning to pour out blessing—God's blessing—upon Pharaoh and all of his people.

Pharaoh recognizes that Joseph is the "discerning and wise" person he needs to oversee the preparation for the years of famine ahead. In one instant, he elevates the lowly Hebrew prisoner to the second officer of the land (v. 40). All the emblems of authority are put upon him. He receives Pharaoh's signet ring, his power-of-attorney as it were, so that he can issue documents in the king's name. He gets new clothes again, finer than before, a gold chain, and a place in the second chariot. These are all things that Egyptian texts mention in connection with the investiture of pharaohs. Now runners go before him crying, "*Abrek!*" (No one knows for sure what they were saying. Here is a sample of translations: Septuagint: "a herald made proclamation"; New English Bible, New International Version, and others: "Make way!"; Everett Fox: "*Avrekh!/*

Attention!"; King James and New Revised Standard Versions: "Bow the knee!" The decision by the Jewish Publication Society to leave the word untranslated in their version, assuming that it is an Egyptian cry of warning, may be the best solution.)

As part of the empowerment of Joseph, Pharaoh also gives him a new and presumably meaningful name. (It never caught on, for obvious reasons.) He also gives him a wife, Asenath, evidently the daughter of an important family. The only other thing we know about her from canonical literature is that she bore Joseph two sons (v. 50). Postcanonical Jewish and rabbinic literature retain or create much more information about her. Her father is "priest of On," a Hebrew transliteration of 'inw, the Egyptian name for Heliopolis. Now incorporated into the sprawl of modern Cairo, this was one of the major cult centers of ancient Egypt. Like his brother Judah, Joseph marries a foreigner. Like another "Hebrew" after him, Moses, Joseph marries into the family of a priest of another religion. Like both of them, the tradition holds him blameless.

The names of the two sons, Manasseh (from "to forget") and Ephraim (from "to be fruitful"), are accompanied by etiological sentences uttered by their father (vv. 51–52). The -aim ending of Ephraim indicates it was originally a place name, like Yerushalaim. In the eighth century B.C. Ephraim became an alternate term for the northern kingdom of Israel. Hosea uses it that way. These two sons displace Joseph from the standard roster of the twelve tribes (see commentary on 48:5).

The story within the story ends with the not unexpected announcement that everything turns out just as Joseph predicted. The fat years are fatter than anyone could have imagined (v. 40). The lean years are bad all over Egypt and over "all the world" (v. 57), but Egypt has grain to spare because of the discernment and wisdom of Joseph and the solid political backing of Pharaoh (v. 55).

JOSEPH DISCLOSES HIMSELF TO HIS BROTHERS
Genesis 42:1–45:28

If we can accept the reason he gave for naming his son Manasseh (41:51) Joseph had about succeeded in putting out of his mind the troubles of his youth. Then, just as the predicted seven-year famine gets well underway the parallel histories of the successful Joseph in Egypt and the failed family in Canaan suddenly intersect. So now we must leave the brilliantly told story of Joseph's life on his own in Egypt in order to rejoin the rising action of his rescuing role with his family. Thanks to all the vicissitudes that Joseph has endured and the victories he has won, he is now in a position of power that will enable him both to chasten his brothers and also to save them.

[42:1–25] The narrative of the reunion of the sons of Israel begins with the arrival in famine-stricken Canaan of news that grain is for sale in Egypt. Jacob sends all of his remaining sons except the youngest, Benjamin, to buy some (vv. 1–5).

The scene switches immediately to their arrival at their goal. Joseph is very much a hands-on administrator, for he is personally selling grain from the storehouses to customers from "all the world" (41:57). The plot thickens instantly. Joseph recognizes his brothers (42:7), though his identity remains hidden from them (v. 8). The omniscient narrator gets inside Joseph's mind to inform us that he now remembers the dream of Genesis 37:6–7, in which his brothers, symbolized by sheaves in the field, prostrate themselves to him. We are left to draw the conclusion that his dream was valid, and that the invisible hand of providence has been working all things around for the good. Now that Joseph knows the full meaning of this past event, his task is to bring his brothers to share that knowledge.

Mistaken identity is a beloved literary device (think of how often Shakespeare used it!), and the narrator has Joseph exploit it to the utmost. One feels for the brothers when Joseph accuses them of spying. They protest that they are "honest men" (v. 11), and one can believe that after all they have been through, by now they are.

They volunteer the information that they are ten of a formerly twelve-son family. "One is no more," they say (though they do not say why), and one is at home with their father (v. 13). Joseph gives them a three-day cooling-off period in jail. It keeps them stressed and guessing, for sure, but it also gives Joseph time further to develop a strategy based on his split-second decision to test the brothers while continuing to conceal his identity.

When the brothers are released, Joseph seems kinder and gentler. He tells them that he fears God (*Elohim*, their God [v. 18]). That might have seemed strange to them coming from a high Egyptian officer, though they may have understood him to mean that he recognized a transcendent moral order incumbent upon him and his nation that demanded justice and fair treatment of the disadvantaged. (The narrator would have us realize that the fear of God is indeed the source of Joseph's good name and discretion. When the strong man fears God, the vulnerable need not fear the strong man, as Joseph himself will assure his brothers in 50:19–21.) They cannot yet rest easy, however, for Joseph now has in mind for them further searing trials that may in time bring them to full knowledge.

Joseph frees the brothers to go home with their purchases on two conditions: (a) that they leave a hostage with him, and (b) that they return with their brother, Benjamin (vv. 19–20). By this he will know that they are indeed honest men, a knowledge that is essential to the restoration of right relationships (shalom) between them and him. The pressure toward full knowledge is working on everyone!

Maintaining his Egyptian persona, even to the extent of speaking to them through an interpreter, he can hide himself in their very presence. He can understand them as they talk among themselves in Hebrew about their regret and guilt over what they did to their brother Joseph. (In fact, we learn from them something the narrator never told us, namely, that Joseph pleaded with them not to do what they did [v. 21].) Joseph hears his oldest brother Reuben (the one who tried to save him [37:22]) chastise his brothers for the wrong they did him (v. 22). More knowledge comes to Joseph. He turns from them and weeps (v. 24), the first of three weepings that measure out his own maturation toward full understanding and acceptance (see also 43:30–31 and 45:1–2). He weeps at other times as well, but these moments mark particularly important turnings in the story.

The story moves on. Joseph picks his hostage, his second oldest brother, Simeon, and then sends them on their way with their sacks of grain and (without their knowledge) their money in their hands (vv. 24–25).

[26–38] A pack trip back to Canaan on donkeys is hard enough without the added burden of anxiety. When the brothers discover that at least one of them still has his grain money, they can only think that God the retributor is punishing them for the evil deeds of their past. Interesting, isn't it, how much our inner state shapes and colors the picture of God that we draw? The movement toward full knowledge and acceptance will carry them to a different view of God. In the end they will learn from the saving intervention of their wronged brother that the true color of God is providence. They recount the whole story to Jacob, discover that their culpability is worse than they thought (they all have their money) and break the bad news that Benjamin will have to return with them if things are ever to be put right and Simeon rescued. Reuben even offers his own two sons (out of an eventual four; see 46:9) as hostages in the hands of his father (v. 37). Jacob refuses to allow his youngest son to go, elaborating the slogan about going down in sorrow to Sheol (v. 38; see also 44:29, 31) that he first used in Genesis 37:35 (see commentary there).

[43:1–34] Everything remains up in the air in the household of Jacob except the famine. It keeps grinding grimly. Perhaps forgetting the terms under which they are to return, Jacob orders his sons to make another shopping trip to Egypt. This time Judah (like Reuben, one of the good guys of chapter 37) reviews the terms set down by "the man." On this retelling, Jacob criticizes the brothers for having told the vizier about the youngest brother back home (v. 6). Do they lie when they say, "The man questioned us carefully about ourselves and our kindred, saying, 'Is your father still alive? Have you another brother'" (v. 7)? Chapter 42 retains no record that Joseph asked those questions. However, in most respects Judah speaks accurately about the terms. In verse 11 Jacob reluctantly agrees and orders the sons to prepare a nice present of agricultural products of the kind that might still be available during a drought (nuts, ointments and gums, and "a little honey"—perhaps the latter is the syrup that is called *dibs* in the Levant, made of the sweet pulp of the carob pod). With double the money to underscore their honesty, they depart with Jacob's final blessing ringing in their ears. In praying for their safe return with Simeon and Benjamin. he invokes the patriarchal epithet for God, *El Shaddai* (see commentary on Gen. 17:1). Then, to cover the other eventuality, he says in effect, "Que será será" (v. 14b).

Somehow Joseph sees the brothers coming with Benjamin and he orders a very amicable reception to be prepared (v. 16). His steward receives the party and puts their minds at ease about the money that they had found in their sacks upon their previous return to Canaan by saying, "Rest assured [*shalom lakem*], do not be afraid" (v. 23a). As noted in the commentary on Genesis 29:6, shalom has to do with the spirit and health of the person to or about whom it is directed. To have shalom is to be in harmony, right relationships, and peace. Here, the steward urges the brothers to be tranquil, and even attributes the mysterious return of the money to divine providence. (The Egyptian idolater is able to represent God in this bright light, in contrast to the tendency of the brothers to view God as punitive, retributive, and gloomy—see 42:28.) We cannot tell if he is lying when he says, "I received your money" (v. 23b), or if some kind of quiet miracle has happened. Or perhaps Joseph's orders in Genesis 42:25 simply led him to write off the charges and close their account.

In any case, because they have not yet come to full knowledge, the brothers still have no idea that their own brother has engineered their return trip to Egypt and that he has done so in order to bless them and move the promise onward toward fulfillment.

The humble announcement of their reunion with Simeon has a tender quality; one can imagine what a relief it would be to find him alive and well. It would be a relief as well to clean up and feed the beasts, though the dreaded encounter with the vizier still lies ahead (vv. 23b–25).

The potentate turns out to be a pussycat. Twice in verse 27 he raises the question of their shalom (welfare, health) and that of their father, and they affirm Jacob's shalom (v. 28). Seeing Benjamin and invoking the providential (not the punitive) God over him, Joseph weeps for the second time (v. 30; see 41:24 and 45:1–2). Events have continued to drive his knowledge toward greater fullness. The banquet scene that follows is tender too, even though Joseph continues to conceal himself in Egyptian mores. Like any other Egyptian, he will not sit witḣ the foreigners. But he cultivates Benjamin with extra morsels from his own table, and they all drink, maybe rather copiously.

[44:1–17] Joseph draws his steward into a plan to put the brothers through yet another ordeal. Just before they leave on their donkeys for Canaan, he has his silver divining cup planted in Benjamin's sack. (From this we learn that Joseph practices divination, a skill of the wise man that is later forbidden in Israel [see Deut. 18:10].) The brothers are pursued and accused of theft. They hotly deny any guilt and rashly say that if one of them has the cup, he should die and the rest should be enslaved (v. 9). At the very end of the search the cup is found on Benjamin.

In his increasingly important role as leader of the eleven and counterpoise to Joseph, Judah speaks to the "offended" vizier on behalf of all the party. He attributes the disclosure to God, portrayed as the brothers are wont to do as the retributor (v. 16). All humbly submit to enslavement, though their vow of death to the offender is not mentioned. Joseph, however, backs away from his own threat and, using the trick as an excuse to keep Benjamin with him, orders the others to go on home in shalom (v. 17).

[18–34] Some shalom! Judah's passionate plea is summed up in his penultimate sentence: "How can I go back to my father if the boy is not with me?" (v. 34a). The sincere narrative about the special relationship between the old father and his youngest child culminates in the genuine fear that Jacob's gray hairs will be brought down to Sheol (vv. 29, 31; see also 42:38) if Benjamin does not return. In addition, Judah will personally bear the blame forever, for he has stood surety for the boy's safety (v. 32, referring back to 43:9–10).

The brothers still lack full knowledge, for they do not know that this "vizier" arranged Benjamin's "theft" of the silver cup. Because of Joseph's wise and skillful activity, they have been brought to a point of humble contrition for their past deeds. In his retelling of the story, Thomas Mann puts these words of total disclosure in Judah's mouth:

> Here before you, strange man, I take the frightful oath we brothers swore—with both hands I take that oath and break it in two across my knee. Our eleventh brother, the father's ewe lamb, first son of the true wife, him the beast did not rend; but we his brothers sold him into the world. (Thomas Mann, 453–54)

45:1 **Then Joseph could no longer control himself before all those who stood by him, and he cried out, "Send everyone away from me." So no one stayed with him when Joseph made himself known to his brothers. 2 And he wept so**

loudly that the Egyptians heard it, and the household of Pharaoh heard it. ³Joseph said to his brothers, "I am Joseph. Is my father still alive?" But his brothers could not answer him, so dismayed were they at his presence.

The brothers are now ready for the full disclosure, and at this point the story of Joseph and the brothers reaches its narrative climax. Little by little, the brothers, perhaps unwittingly, have begun to grasp the meaning of things. Under the pressure of the trials imposed on them by the "vizier," they take their first step toward self-knowledge when they admit their past guilt: "Alas, we are paying the penalty for what we did to our brother . . . That is why this anguish has come upon us" (42:21). Joseph concurrently gains more knowledge about them and about the fact that his brother Benjamin lives. Now he weeps for the third time (see also 42:24 and 43:30–31). His emotional growth now has reached the point where he can utter the long-awaited words, "I am Joseph. Is my father still alive?" (45:3). From this moment on, Joseph's knowledge and the brothers' knowledge are the same.

45:4 Then Joseph said to his brothers, "Come closer to me." And they came closer. He said, "I am your brother, Joseph, whom you sold into Egypt. ⁵ And now do not be distressed, or angry with yourselves, because you sold me here; for God sent me before you to preserve life. ⁶ For the famine has been in the land these two years; and there are five more years in which there will be neither plowing nor harvest. ⁷ God sent me before you to preserve for you a remnant on earth, and to keep alive for you many survivors. ⁸ So it was not you who sent me here, but God; he has made me a father to Pharaoh, and lord of all his house and ruler over all the land of Egypt. ⁹ Hurry and go up to my father and say to him, 'Thus says your son Joseph, God has made me lord of all Egypt; come down to me, do not delay. ¹⁰ You shall settle in the land of Goshen, and you shall be near me, you and your children and your children's children, as well as your flocks, your herds, and all that you have. ¹¹ I will provide for you there—since there are five more years of famine to come—so that you and your household, and all that you have, will not come to poverty.' ¹² And now your eyes and the eyes of my brother Benjamin see that it is my own mouth that speaks to you. ¹³ You must tell my father how greatly I am honored in Egypt, and all that you have seen. Hurry and bring my father down here." ¹⁴ Then he fell upon his brother Benjamin's neck and wept, while Benjamin wept upon his neck. ¹⁵ And he kissed all his brothers and wept upon them; and after that his brothers talked with him.

Shortly after the climax of the story, Joseph utters a theological truth claim both daring in its scope and difficult to comprehend: "God sent me before you to preserve for you a remnant on earth, and to keep alive for you many survivors. So it was not you who sent me here, but God" (45:7–8). In these words the theologian-narrator gives us the entire program of the novella. Joseph has feared God and not humans, has acknowledged God's authority, and has been obedient. Although the brothers failed him, Joseph has not failed them, nor has God. Because of Joseph's faithfulness and God's power, all of them will be saved.

The events that follow are the stuff of shalom-making. Peace breaks out between hostile brothers when one side admits its wrongdoing and the other forgives and embraces. When they can weep unashamedly on each other's necks and kiss and talk freely (vv. 14-15), it is clear that the strength and the wholeness of all have been renewed. This weeping no longer marks another stage in Joseph's maturation; this is just the normal expression of fraternal love.

Things happen fast as the story begins its descending action. Joseph promises to settle his old father and all his family in the land of Goshen (v. 9; see commentary on 46:28–34). When Pharaoh hears of the reunion, he thinks the same way Joseph does. He urges the family to accept from him "the best of the land of Egypt" that they may enjoy "the fat of the land" (v. 18). They need not even bring baggage—anything they want will be theirs (v. 20). On orders from Pharaoh, Joseph facilitates the move with genuine wagons for women and children, and ample provisions for the round trip (vv. 21–24).

When Jacob hears the news of Joseph's dignity and sees the evidence of his generosity, he casts away any reservations he may have had about moving into his new accommodations. He is not captivated by the prospect of nice new surroundings and three square meals a day, though, but by one thing only: "My son Joseph is still alive. I must go and see him before I die" (v. 28).

JACOB MOVES TO EGYPT
Genesis 46:1–47:28

Things begin to come full circle now as the story of Joseph and his brothers winds toward its conclusion. Our gaze turns toward Canaan to record Jacob's preparations for departure. His removal to Egypt will mark a literary transition as well. With this story, the saga of the fathers and mothers ends and a new story begins—the story of the emergence of the people of Israel, first out of one family and then out of their Egyptian bondage.

[46:1–27] The Elohist tells us that Jacob's first stop is Beer-sheba, the very place from which he set out at the beginning of his career to find a wife and a fortune (see 28:10). There he worships, presumably at the very sanctuary at which his father (26:25) and grandfather (21:33) had worshiped. God comes to Jacob "in visions of the night" (v. 2). Daniel's "visions of the night" include both audio and video (Dan. 7:7); in contrast, Jacob's is only an auditory experience and it is the last direct communication from God that he or any other character of the narrative receives until Moses gets his at the burning bush (Ex. 3:4). Joseph and the brothers carry on in their "secular" vein, but Jacob brings with him the I-Thou relationship with God that he has enjoyed ever since his dream at Bethel (28:10–22).

Like Moses and Samuel in later years, Jacob hears his name called twice. He responds, "the God" offers self-identification, tells Jacob not to fear (the word that has been on everyone's minds and lips), and then lays the groundwork for the beginning of the history of Israel during its Egyptian sojourn. God says, "I will make of you a great nation *there*" (v. 3). God promises to be more than a tribal and territorial deity, but to accompany Israel to Egypt, to be with them there, and to bring them out again (v. 4)—in other words, to break out of the frame of Israel's earlier picture of God.

The departure from Canaan is summed up in verses 5–7. In what is thought to be the beginning of the ensuing Priestly family table, verse 6 says that they did in fact take their goods and livestock, contrary to Pharaoh's specific instruction (see 45:20). The Priestly impulse to provide specific dates, names, and property estimates is manifested in what amounts to a general inventory in verses 6–7, followed by a roster in verses 8–27. The latter expands upon the short list of the family of Jacob given in Genesis 35:22b–26, and serves as a companion piece to the Esau genealogy of Genesis 36.

The roster serves both a genealogical function (through three and sometimes four generations) and a literary function. It fixes firmly the full complement of seventy persons (v. 27) who will inaugurate the next phase in the development of Israel into a full-fledged people. Their multiplication into a people will be handled in a single verse, Exodus 1:7. However, the movement of that people onward toward the fulfillment of God's promise to them will be the subject of the rest of the book of Exodus and of the Pentateuch as a whole. Suffice it to say, the list of the twelve brothers given here is fairly standard (see, for example, Ex. 1:2–5), though other versions drop Levi and Joseph in favor of Ephraim and Manasseh as fathers of tribes (see, for example, Num. 1:5–15). Most of the names of their sons and grandsons, plus Asher's daughter Serah (v. 17), recur in later recensions of this roster as well as elsewhere in the narrative. Poor Dinah (v. 15) drops out of sight after this list. Inveterate genealogists can review other versions of this family table in Numbers 26:5–62 and the highly elaborated version in 1 Chronicles 2–8. In the Numbers passage, the list of ancestral clans structures the census that Moses took in the wilderness. By that time, Israel is reported to have numbered 601,730 people twenty years of age and older, plus 23,000 male Levites of all ages. Not all the names are given, thank goodness.

The figures given for the descendants of each of Jacob's wives and concubines total seventy, including the dead sons of Judah, Er and Onan, and excluding Jacob and Dinah. The total number of immigrants "belonging to Jacob" is put at sixty-six, which includes Dinah but excludes Jacob himself, the dead Er and Onan, and the three who were already in Egypt—Joseph and his two sons. (Asenath is the only daughter-in-law of Jacob who is mentioned [v. 20], and she is neither an immigrant nor a descendant of Jacob.) Put Jacob and the three who were already in Egypt back in, and you arrive (with some ambiguity) at the seventy persons of verse 27.

[28–34] The "Goshen" to which Jacob arrives is not attested in Egyptian records. The name is Semitic. The clues we have about its location are those given right here in the Joseph novella. From the fact that Joseph "goes up" to meet Jacob (v. 29), we can infer that the narrator located Goshen north of the favored royal city of Memphis, which was south of modern Cairo. Perhaps he intercepted his father on the northeastern edge of the Nile Delta along the route between Egypt and Asia Minor. Twice Goshen is described as "the best of the land" (47:6, 11), and once it is placed "in the land of Rameses" (47:11). No Rameses had as yet ruled in Joseph's time, if his story implies a Second Intermediate Period or even Eighteenth Dynasty setting (see the discussion of date in the commentary on chapters 40–41). However, the narrator (J or E) might have known that Rameses II (1290–1224 B.C.) made Tanis (a.k.a. Avaris, Zoan, Rameses [?]) his capital. It was situated about where the land of Goshen seems to be.

A filmmaker would have a heyday with the scene that now follows (vv. 28–29). The dashing, lightly clad charioteer speeds up to the spot where the road-weary Hebrews from the land of Canaan have "circled their wagons" and made their camp. There is mutual and passionate crying on the neck for a father who had thought his son was dead and a son who had despaired of ever seeing his father again.

Joseph, the only person in the whole novella who understands the ways of two cultures, realizes that his father has violated Pharaoh's command in bringing his flocks of sheep with him. (No doubt these sheep are descendants of the spotted sheep that Jacob "liberated" from Laban long before.) So he rehearses how he will introduce these nomadic shepherds to the sedentary agriculturists in Pharaoh's court. We know from texts and tomb paintings that the ancient Egyptians maintained domestic animals, including cows and oxen, donkeys, pigs, goats, and sheep, so grazing as such was not unknown to them (though most animals must have been fed in feedlots rather than on open ranges). However, since the time of Cain and Abel, farmers and shepherds have never been comfortable with each other in Egypt or anywhere else; in this case, we are told, "all shepherds are abhorrent to the Egyptians" (v. 34).

The Joseph story leaves the general impression that the Egyptians of that time were rather xenophobic characters who found the habits and very presence of foreigners repulsive. They were not totally isolated from other peoples, however, because Egypt was an imperial power. Particularly in the Late Bronze Age it had extensive political, military, and commercial contacts with other ethnic groups and cultures, and imported slaves in large numbers. Perhaps that is the clue: Egyptians saw themselves as a class and breed apart from the common chattel, including the nomadic shepherds.

[47:1–12] The settling-in process continues with the curious episode of the presentation by Joseph of his brothers to Pharaoh. In the best style of the Yahwist, the event is both homey and humanistic. The king asks the brothers about their occupation. They follow the lines they have rehearsed: They tell him that they are shepherds "as our ancestors were" (v. 3)—a caveat that might resonate with the ruler of a land that honored ancestors and took pride in carrying on ancient traditions. When they ask for permission to settle and pasture their flocks, Pharaoh reiterates his earlier promise to Joseph to settle them in the land of Goshen (though he does not actually give them a quitclaim deed to the property) and even asks them to take charge of his own livestock.

The ensuing colloquy between the aged Jacob and Pharaoh is courtly, if a mite rustic, in manner. Twice the nomad blesses the mighty king, as though the king needed the benevolence of a refugee from a marginal culture. Evidently, though, Pharaoh shares the respect widespread in ancient cultures for the gray hair and the wisdom of old age. He even asks Jacob how old he is (v. 8). One cannot tell whether Jacob is being unduly modest or whether he really thinks 130 years is a short life (v. 9). It has indeed been a hard one, and relatively shorter than his grandfather's 175 years and his father's 180 years, but he still has seventeen years to go (v. 28)!

The settlement ends with the open hand of providence well and truly manifested through the generous hand of Pharaoh and his servant, Joseph (vv. 11–12).

[13–28] The panel closes with a final portrait of Joseph, the Egyptian public official—and it is not a very flattering one. In fact, the word ruthless springs to mind. In Genesis 41:46–57 we admired the man for his prudence and wisdom in implementing a policy of strategic reserves that would tide Egypt through the coming seven lean years. Now, loyal vizier that he is, he turns the general misfortune into Pharaoh's advantage. On Pharaoh's behalf and in exchange for grain, he corners all the cash in Egypt and Canaan alike (v. 14), then all the livestock (vv. 16–17), and then all the land (vv. 18–19). It is the economics of the Dust Bowl and Great Depression rolled into one. He goes even further than our lenders did in the dark days of the 1930s. He enslaves the people themselves, except for the priestly caste (v. 21). (As the NRSV footnote shows, the Hebrew text makes it sound as though he expelled the peasants from their now state-owned lands. But how could they support themselves in future years and pay their taxes if they had no land to farm? The NRSV emends the text, following the ancient versions.) Joseph maneuvers the people into thanking him for saving their lives by giving them seed (v. 25), even as he makes permanent the emergency twenty percent tax on all farm produce enacted at his suggestion ten or twelve years earlier (see 41:34). The situation of the Egyptian peasant was in fact not unlike the serfdom this verse describes. In theory all the land was controlled by Pharaoh and his priests, and the peasants lived, farmed, and paid their duties at the king's pleasure. Grain was heavily taxed throughout Egyptian history. Tomb paintings depict inspectors with measuring lines marking out the government's quota.

Only Israel in Goshen was spared these indignities (v. 27). Perhaps the narrator wishes to suggest that the ruthlessness that Egyptians of a later generation will show toward the enslaved Hebrews (Ex. 1:13) is payback for the serfdom to which the Egyptians are reduced by Joseph.

JACOB PREPARES TO DIE
Genesis 47:29–48:22

[47:29–31] The beginning of the end of the old order arrives as the last of the Big Three of the patriarchs prepares to die. Jacob resorts to the "hand under thigh" mode of oath-giving that we first encountered when the aged Abraham charged his servant to find a wife for Isaac (see commentary on 24:1–9). In this instance, the oath bound Joseph's very manhood to his father's wish to be buried with his grandparents, Abraham and Sarah, and his parents, Isaac and Rebekah, in the family tomb (the cave of Machpelah in Hebron; see 23:1–20; 25:9; 35:29; 49:29–32).

[48:1–7] With the exception of verses 3–6 (P), this chapter is attributed to the Elohist. That source is thought to have taken shape in the ninth century B.C. in the northern kingdom of Israel, sometimes alternately called Ephraim (see commentary on 41:51–52). Perhaps the adoption of the two centrally located tribes of Ephraim and Manasseh into the alternate list of the twelve and the preferential position given to Ephraim reflects the regional outlook of the Elohist.

Why does Joseph take his two sons born of the Egyptian mother to his father's deathbed? Does he simply want to introduce him to his grandsons? Does he have an interest in legitimating them in some way? Does he want his father to adopt them as his own? The narrator answers none of these questions, but hurries on.

Jacob's opening speech (vv. 3–6) comes from the Priestly writers. Invoking El Shaddai, "God Almighty," an epithet last used by Jacob himself in Genesis 43:14, Jacob harks back to his second theophany experience at Luz/Bethel (35:9–12). In that Priestly passage, God, self-identified as El Shaddai, reiterates to Jacob the promises made to Abraham and Isaac. Now Jacob recounts those promises to Joseph. In contrast to the temporary sanctuary that Pharaoh has given Israel in Egypt, God promised the land of Canaan to his offspring "for a perpetual holding" (v. 4). It is worth noting that of all the four ancestral males in Genesis 12–50, Joseph is the only one who never has a face-to-face encounter with God, and never receives the oft-repeated promise of descendants and land. This may be the result of the literary development of the Pentateuch, if the Joseph novella is not an original part of the patriarchal saga but a story written by the Yahwist and the Elohist to demonstrate wisdom ideals and to connect the saga of the fathers and mothers with the central event of the Pentateuch, the exodus. Be that as it may, the continuity of the promises of descendants and land skips a generation, as it were, when Jacob continues his speech with a "therefore": Therefore Ephraim and Manasseh are mine (v. 5). Thus are two of the traditional tribal groups within Israel given patriarchal justification for belonging in the list of twelve founding fathers and for receiving the promises given by God to the family of Abraham. It does not totally explain why their tribes should have been given allotments at the time of the conquest (see Josh. 13–19) rather than tribes named for their father Joseph or their priestly uncle Levi. It does put their claim at par with even the two eldest sons' (v. 5), though, for now in the eyes of the law they are Jacob's sons.

The rather obscure verse 6 seems to say that any other children of Joseph will be considered his, not his father's, but that they will not inherit in their own rights but as beneficiaries of Ephraim and Manasseh. This could explain why no tribe of Joseph arose secondarily, after the

removal of Ephraim and Manasseh from the Joseph lineage, except that
the whole matter is moot: Joseph had no further children.

One does sense that verse 7 belongs to a strand of tradition (E) different from that of verses 3–6 (P). The premature death of Rachel seems
irrelevant to the adoption of her grandchildren, unless Jacob is thinking
again about his second visit to Bethel and her death immediately afterward (35:16–21). Rabbinical commentators often took this remark to be
Jacob's rather lame excuse for not burying Rachel in the family crypt in
Hebron, pertinent now that he has sworn Joseph to go to the trouble of
carrying his body all the way there.

[8–22] One's instinct is to say that verses 8–11 introduce a new strand
of the tradition, for it suddenly appears that Jacob is meeting Joseph's
sons for the first time. True, since the beginning of chapter 48 Jacob has
been addressing Joseph alone, but we have had the impression that the
two boys were somewhere in the vicinity. If Ephraim and Manasseh had
been sitting on Jacob's knees (v. 12), that would, of course, have been hard
to ignore. They are big boys by now. They were born before the famine
began (see 41:50–52), Jacob came to Egypt well after the famine began,
and he has by now been there seventeen years (47:28); consequently, they
should be at least nineteen or twenty. It also seems odd that Jacob has
never seen his grandsons before, if that is the meaning of verse 11.

Traditional commentators have explained some of these anomalies by
pointing to verse 10: the old man was almost blind, and at most he has
seen dim shapes standing near his bed. Of course he has met his grandsons before; now he is simply expressing delight at seeing them in his
dying hours. As for the knees, perhaps he has immediately taken the
young men onto his lap in a traditional gesture of adoption, implementing the new relationship he has discussed in verse 5. We have heard of the
practice before, when Rachel expressed the hope that her maid Bilhah
would bear her children on Rachel's knees, "that I too may have children
through her" (30:3).

With the adoption completed, final blessing comes to the fore.
Parental and filial blessings punctuate dramatic turning points in the lives
of the fathers and the mothers throughout the saga. Rebekah is blessed
by her brother and family as she leaves her home forever (24:60). As he
lies old and blind, Isaac strongly blesses the disguised Jacob and weakly
blesses the disappointed Esau (chap. 27). Isaac blesses Jacob again as he
bids him farewell at his departure to find a wife in Paddan-aram (28:2–5).
Now it happens again at this turning point in the family saga; powerful
words that will shape future destinies are uttered by a dying ancestor.

The problem for the party gathered at the deathbed is that Jacob
switches hands and lays the more efficacious right hand on the head of the

younger boy, Ephraim (v. 14). This will create a new fact that will henceforth have to be incorporated into the history of Israel. Jacob's blessing is
directed at first to Joseph, though it is about Joseph's offspring. By way of
petition in benediction, he asks that "the God"/"the angel" who has providentially guided and protected the family since Abraham's days bless
them, preserving in them and in their numerous offspring the names of
the fathers of Israel (vv. 15–16). These verses perfectly capture the hope
for the future of a dying person in Old Testament times. That hope lay in
the perpetuation of the person's good name in memory and in the witness
of the living descendants. There was no other life after death.

Joseph, the man of great secular power in Egypt, objects to Jacob's
possibly befuddled decision to place his powerful right hand on the head
of the younger son, Ephraim, instead of the older Manasseh. However,
the old man knows what he is doing—he intends to put Ephraim ahead
of Manasseh, and he announces a different future for each clan (v. 19). At
the banquet with the returned brothers in Genesis 43:33, Joseph showed
a certain courtly etiquette in the matter of seniority, for he seated them
in birth order. Had he thought about the history of his family, however,
he need not have been surprised at this violation of that order by his
father toward his sons. After all, the younger brother had taken precedence over the older in the case of Isaac and Ishmael and in the case of
Jacob himself over Esau. There was even the strange case of Zerah and
Perez, the twin sons of Tamar by Judah. Zerah put his hand out, got his
crimson thread, retreated, and gave pride of place ever afterward to Perez
(38:27–30). God's election of persons to receive the promise and to convey it to later generations has been full of irregularities, and now another
surprise is happening before the eyes of Joseph. It is mediated through an
old grandfather giving his final blessing. His prediction that the younger
brother Ephraim shall be greater than the older, Manasseh (v. 19), may
reflect the northern orientation of the Elohistic writer, or it may grow
out of the fact that the greatest figures of the return to the Promised
Land, Joshua and Samuel, were Ephraimites.

The conclusion of the blessing sounds like a traditional, almost
proverbial benediction: "By you [masculine singular—is it Joseph or is it
Ephraim?] Israel will invoke blessings, saying, 'God make you [mascu-
line singular—it must be any addressee] like Ephraim and like
Manasseh" (v. 20).

One of Rembrandt's most moving works is his 1653 painting of Jacob's
blessing of Ephraim and Manasseh. They are little boys, apparently
about six and eight years of age. A richly turbaned Joseph stands behind
them and to his left stands a lovely dark-eyed Asenath. The old man's face
is deeply thoughtful—he knows exactly what he is doing with his crossed

hands. A fur pelt on his shoulders recalls the moment that his old and blind father was deceived into blessing him. The striking quality in this painting is its loving intimacy. The five people and a red blanket on the bed are all there is to be seen. Everything else has been eliminated. The family members lean toward each other in mutual devotion. The painting was done after Rembrandt had lost his own wife and three sons.

This section of private empowerment bestowed by Jacob on the favored family of Joseph closes with a final direct address to his son. He announces not as prophecy but as simple fact that in the end God will bring Joseph back to Canaan. This eventuality occurs centuries later after the conquest of Canaan is complete. Then the bones of Joseph that had been traveling with Israel since the night of the exodus from Egypt (Ex. 13:19) are finally buried at Shechem (see Josh. 24:32).

Shechem is on Jacob's mind too, it seems, for he may allude to it in a pun in verse 22. The Hebrew term translated by the NRSV as "portion" (*shekem*) is a homonym of the name of the city. Is Jacob giving Shechem to Joseph? He did buy a piece of property there from the local "Amorite" (= indigenous) ruler, Hamor (see 33:18–20). (According to Josh. 24:32, Joseph was buried on that plot.) But he did not take it from the "Amorites" by force. His sons did that, and he bawled them out for it (34:30). In short, it is not clear that it was his to give away. If Shechem is not meant, however, it is hard to say what "the portion" is.

JACOB'S LAST WORDS AND HIS DEATH
Genesis 49:1–33

The penultimate chapter of the book of Genesis is also the most difficult one to understand. It consists of a poetic ballad supported by brief prose bookends. The poem consists of sayings about the twelve sons of Israel, viewed as the name-giving ancestors of the twelve tribes of Israel. Its structure is simple. On his deathbed Jacob first addresses the six sons of Leah, beginning with Reuben, his eldest, and continuing mostly in birth order through Issachar (vv. 3–15). He then turns to the four sons of his concubines, namely, Dan (Bilhah), Gad and Asher (Zilpah), and Naphtali (Bilhah; vv. 16–21). Finally, he addresses the two sons of Rachel, Joseph and Benjamin (vv. 22–27).

Judah and Joseph merit five verses of poetry each. Birth order is not conclusive; more important is the preeminent role each has played in the preceding Joseph novella. The poem also reflects the relative ranks within the Israelite tribal structure of later times. Judah and Joseph (also represented by his sons Ephraim and Manasseh) came in time to dominate the twofold polity of Israel, a southern and a northern grouping respectively that were united under David and Solomon and existed independently thereafter. Some of the other sons/tribes, especially those descended from the concubines, rate as little attention from their father as they do in subsequent history.

The very form of this poem is difficult to pin down for several reasons. First, the prose introduction presents it as something akin to a prophetic oracle: "I [will] tell you what will happen to you in days to come" (v. 1). Indeed, tradition awards Jacob a kind of protoprophet status because of the prescience he shows in his various benedictions.

Second, we can rule out genealogy, for this poem branches through only the first generation after Jacob. It does cooperate well with the fully branched genealogy of Jacob in chapter 46, which performs the usual function of genealogies to disclose the kinship bonds within the clans of the nation. (See the discussion of types and functions of genealogies in the commentary on Genesis 4:17–26.)

Third, the fact that the poem systematically reviews the distinctive qualities and accomplishments of each of the twelve tribes puts it in a literary category we might call tribal ode. As such, it is comparable to a similar rendition of the tribes by Moses in Deuteronomy 33, and Deborah's rather more militaristic song about ten of the twelve in Judges 5.

Fourth, the other prose bookend, verse 28, understands the poem as a series of deathbed blessings. This fits poorly with the content of the passage, however, because, except for the verses devoted to Joseph (vv. 22–26), very few of the sentences really are blessings. Some of the verses almost amount to curses (especially v. 7); most of the rest are characterizations of the future destiny of the tribes.

Fifth, the poem's present location within the Joseph novella gives some weight to the designation "last will and testament." This view of the text runs up against the fact that Jacob does not bequeath anything to anyone, as he did with Joseph in the previous panel (48:22).

Sixth, perhaps the must accurate label for verses 3–27 is simply "farewell address" or "last words" (NRSV). Moses' speech in Deuteronomy 33 can be considered another example of the same genre.

The perspective of the sayings in the poem varies from reflections on events in the preceding novella to retrojections into Jacob's time of events and locations that belong to the period of the conquest and later. As a glance at the NRSV footnotes immediately suggests, many of the Hebrew idioms in the poem are obscure. These things hint that the poem is an old, orally transmitted ballad that the Pentateuchal editors incorporated into their story to serve as Jacob's last words but that is not as early as Jacob himself was.

Stunning contemporary artistic interpretations of Jacob's last words adorn the synagogue of the Hadassah Hospital in Jerusalem in the form of twelve stained glass windows by Marc Chagall that were installed there in 1962. The translucent warmth of these beautiful glass tapestries, one for each tribe, combines color with Chagall's iconography to underscore the real vividness of the agricultural and pastoral, bodily and political imagery of this poem. From time to time the effort will be made to add Chagall's artistic insights to the discussion that follows.

[49:1–15] The prescient prophet (v. 1) and dying father (v. 2) assembles his sons around his bed to receive his last words. The words will be neither blessings nor bequests but evocations of the sons' destinies.

In Reuben, the eldest son and first of the Leah group, Jacob discerns his own early sexual vigor (v. 3a). Birth order should put have him in the first rank (v. 3b), but Reuben's own sexuality has undone him. The fleetingly mentioned incident when Reuben lay with his father's concubine Bilhah (35:22) suggests he is "unstable as water" (v. 4). The recollection of this blot on Reuben's record explains why the firstborn is neither preferred by Jacob, nor receives the birthright (1 Chron. 5:1–2), nor plays an important role in subsequent history. In Moses' farewell address, Reuben, the first mentioned by order of seniority, gets only a single verse, and that stresses the marginality of the tribe: "May Reuben live, and not die out, even though his numbers are few" (Deut. 33:6). The Song of Deborah portrays the clans of Reuben as cowardly for failing to join her and Barak in their fight against the Canaanites (Judg. 5:15–16). More difficult to explain is why a tribe of so little effect would ever have had the prestigious status of firstborn. Perhaps that former preeminence stems from old memories that go back to the early Aramean origins of the clans that first began to confederate into the people Israel.

Chagall's Reuben window is a rich blue of sky and water filled with living things, suggestive both of the virility and the instability of Reuben. The blue is broken by a flaming red patch of flowers that perhaps recall the mandrakes Reuben collected for his mother, Leah (30:14).

Simeon and Levi are lumped together for anathema (vv. 5–7). They are portrayed by Jacob as violent, angry men, perhaps because of the incident at Shechem when they led the brothers to kill Hamor, the prince of that place, his son Shechem, and every male of the city in revenge for the rape of their sister Dinah (chap. 34). Jacob rebuked them at that time for making him "odious to the inhabitants of the land" (34:30). Now Jacob demotes them from preference too, along with Reuben. This reduction in status corresponds in part to subsequent history. Simeon is mentioned neither in the tribal ode of Moses (Deut. 33) nor the victory Song of Deborah (Judg. 5), and texts such as Joshua 19:1–9 indicate that

that clan was absorbed into Judah. Levi, on the other hand, later attains the status of priestly sanctity (see Num. 18:20–24 and Deut. 10:8). Because the tribe of Levi has no allotment of land, they will live on the public dole (Deut. 14:27–29). The negative assessment of Levi by Jacob thus does not correspond with subsequent history. This suggests that the sentences about Levi in his song reflect different, perhaps much earlier, traditions about Levi than what became normative.

Marc Chagall's Levi window picks up the later sacerdotal function of the Levitical priests, so his interpretation departs almost completely from Genesis 49:5–7. Emblazoned on two tables of the Torah is a verse about Levi from Moses' farewell speech: "They shall teach Jacob your ordinances, and Israel your law; they place incense before you, and whole burnt offerings on your altar" (Deut. 33:10). Flanking the tablets are candles and various symbols of Judaism and the synagogue, including a *kiddush* cup and a Star of David.

In contrast, the Judah window by Chagall is triumphant. Its wine red background thrusts forward the bejeweled ruler's crown being lifted up by priestly hands, the city of Jerusalem guarded by a lion, and a Hebrew inscription bearing the text of Genesis 49:8a. The crown recalls the promise of verse 10, "The scepter shall not depart from Judah," as well as the fact that the Davidic house established in Jerusalem in the land of Judah was descended from Judah through Tamar's son, Perez.

These themes emerge in Jacob's tribute to his fourth son, whom he elevates to preeminence over his brothers by saying, "Your father's sons shall bow down before you" (v. 8c). The imagery of the lion (v. 9), subject peoples (v. 10), abundance (v. 11), and physical beauty (v. 12) all serve to glorify Judah and perhaps reflect the emergence of that tribal group into political and economic dominance from the time of Saul and David onward. After all, we believe that the book of Genesis was collected and set down in writing in Judah, beginning in the time of the United Monarchy.

The fifth of the six sons of Leah to be addressed by Jacob is Zebulun (v. 13), who was actually the sixth in order of birth. He gets short shrift here, though he is praised in the Song of Deborah as a people who scorned death in the fight against the Canaanites (Judg. 5:18). The geographical location of the son/tribe is flawed, for the maritime placement near the Phoenician border (= Sidon) does not correspond to the boundaries of Zebulun given in Joshua 19:10–16. The area given here to Zebulun is given to Asher in the postconquest tradition. One has the sense that the balladeer had little real information about Zebulun, probably because the clan no longer had a separate existence, but that the name had a firm traditional place on the twelve-tribe list.

Undeterred by these critical caveats, Chagall symbolizes Zebulun with a window centered on a beautiful crimson sunset over the (Mediterranean) sea. Handsome fish leap in the foreground of the sun and swim in the water. A ship, the usual symbol of Zebulun, also rides the waves.

No one is surprised to see one of Chagall's technicolor donkeys prominently featured in his Issachar window (49:14). The blue face of the beast blends pleasantly with the verdant spring green of the background. Leah's child of the mandrakes (see 30:14–18), Issachar was allotted territory in the fertile plain of Esdraelon, near Mount Tabor in Galilee. The vines, trees, birds, and village of the window all suggest "that the land was pleasant" (v. 15). The reference to the forced labor required of Issachar might be a play on his name (taking the *sachar* element to mean "hire" or "wages" as Genesis 30:18 does), or it might reflect documented practices of forced labor by the Canaanite city-states in that region.

[16–21] Jacob turns now to his four sons by his two concubines, speaking first about Dan, son of Bilhah (vv. 16–17). Subsequent history gives us very little about Dan. The tribe was known principally for having migrated to the north from the cities (no territorial boundaries are listed) on the coastal plain allotted to it after the conquest (Josh. 19:40–48). Immediately following the story of Samson, himself a Danite, Judges 18 tells the story of Dan's brutal conquest of the city of Laish (Leshem), in the extreme northeast corner of Canaan. The tribe created a cult center there complete with its own idol and a Levitical priest from Bethlehem, all of which they had stolen along the way. This reputation for violence may account for the snake/viper imagery that Jacob now uses about Dan. Perhaps the little prayer, "I wait for your salvation, O LORD" (v. 18), expresses Jacob's prescient anxiety about the fate of Dan, which by postexilic times is no longer listed among the tribes. (1 Chron. 7:12 makes no mention of Dan and gives his only son Hashum or Hushim to the tribe of Benjamin.)

Like the other tribes descended from the concubines of Jacob, Zilpah's son Gad merits little attention either in these last words or in subsequent history (vv. 19–20) The text itself involves a wordplay on the proper name *Gad* ("good luck"; see 30:11), the verb *gadad* ("go in a throng"), and the noun *gedud* ("raiders"). Gad's territory was east of the Jordan; the meager biblical evidence suggests it was frequently involved in wars against its neighbors Ammon and Moab. In the farewell address of Moses, it is said that "Gad lives like a lion" (Deut. 33:20). In short, the militant image of Gad conveyed here seems to fit with what little we know.

Chagall's Gad window is a scene of apocalyptic warfare, in which a crowned and shielded eagle drives back terrible beasts. This window itself is assembled out of shattered glass fragments. Bloody red colors flow over a dark green background.

Zilpah's other son, Asher, is characterized with agricultural, even gastronomic images (v. 20). This corresponds well to the postconquest situation of the tribe on the coastal plain between Mount Carmel and Lebanon, even today one of the most fertile and lovely parts of Israel. Deborah criticizes Asher for staying by the seaside instead of taking part in the decisive struggle against the Canaanites (Judg. 5:17).

The Asher window by Chagall at the Hadassah Hospital is one of his loveliest. A joyous crowned eagle rises over a large menorah candelabrum, the ancient symbol of Yahweh and of Judaism. Everything about the window suggests the opulence and fruitfulness of the well-watered seacoast.

Bilhah's other son, Naphtali, also rates but a single verse. The Hebrew is obscure, but both the NRSV and various alternatives give the man a tender portrayal. Ancient Israelites admired the female deer, just as we do, for her agility (Ps. 18:33) and her grace and beauty (Prov. 5:19). The doe figures in the naturalistic imagery of wisdom texts such as the Song of Solomon (2:7; 3:5) and Job (39:1). In short, the brief portrait of Naphtali is flattering, but we really do not know why.

[22–28] Joseph merits a lengthy and genuinely beautiful address by his father. These verses have the true character of a blessing. Some of the Hebrew terms pose difficulties, yet the overall effect of the undoubtedly natural images is to present Joseph as a strong, fruitful, and honored son—all attributes that he has earned in the pages of the Joseph novella.

The NRSV rightly flags verse 22 as uncertain in meaning. How true that is can be seen by comparing its vine and enclosed well imagery with that of Sarna's translation: "Joseph is a wild ass,/ A wild ass by a spring/—Wild colts on a hillside.") We have no record of any attack on Joseph by archers (v. 22), nor of his own prowess with the bow (v. 23). The notion that he was strengthened and upheld by God, however, informs the entire Joseph novella.

In short order God is given five titles: "Mighty One of Jacob," "Shepherd," "the Rock of Israel," "the God of your father," and "the [God] Almighty" ([El] Shaddai). (1) The first of these epithets is used nowhere else in Genesis and only four times elsewhere in the Old Testament. The association with Jacob might link this divine name to the Bethel sanctuary that he is credited with founding and with the God-language of that place. (2) The image of God as shepherd, in contrast, is a biblical commonplace. It suggests providential protection and nurture. (3) The third title, "Rock of Israel," occurs nowhere else in the exact Hebrew wording found here (literally: "stone of Israel"), though the image of God as a rock is quite common. Sarna (344) suggests that the memorial stone that Jacob erected in Bethel (see 28:18, 22; 35:14) might be in mind here, given all the other allusions to Bethel in the series of epithets. (4) The very common title, "God of your father," also occurs at Bethel in its fuller form (28:13). (5) We have encountered the last of these epithets several times before, first in connection with Abraham, subsequently spoken to or by Jacob, and usually in Priestly contexts (see commentary on 17:1; also note 28:3; 35:11; 43:14; 48:3). Two of these occurrences are part of God's self-identification at Bethel (35:11; 48:3), which might suggest that that sanctuary used this God-language as well. The overall impression left by verses 24b–25a is that Jacob has Bethel on his mind.

Beginning with verse 25b, Jacob uses the verb "bless" once and the noun "blessings" four times. Now he really does invoke this powerful divine force upon his favorite son, calling upon the Almighty to enrich Joseph with the bounty of sky and sea and human reproduction (v. 25b). His own paternal blessings will surpass and outlast nature itself (v. 26a); he makes explicit that this wreath of empowerment adorns Joseph like no other brother (v. 26b).

Chagall's Joseph window seems to have imbibed the joy that infuses the text of Jacob's blessing (49:22–26). A golden background, the color of ripe grain, is embellished with many symbols of fruitfulness, including sheep and baskets of produce. Spirals of color suggest the "fruitful bough" Joseph is said to be (see also the praise of his fruitfulness in Moses' speech in Deut. 33:13–16). It was he, after all, who provided Egypt and all the world with food during seven years of famine. A mighty bird holds the taut bow of verse 24. The dignity and lasting significance of Joseph is stressed by a pair of hands holding a ram's horn (*shofar*) at the top of the picture. Located in the place of the appearance of deity, this symbol also suggests the high holy days of Judaism.

Compared with the favored son, Joseph, the beloved youngest son, Benjamin, gets short shrift (v. 27). The description of this son/tribe as a "ravenous wolf" fits with nothing we have learned from the Jacob cycle or the Joseph novella, so it must reflect conditions of a later era. The postconquest Benjamin allotment located the tribe in a narrow east-west strip between the hilly spine of Judah on the south and Ephraim on the north. Commerce and military ventures passed through Benjamin from both directions. Perhaps because of this physical situation, the tender boy of the Jacob cycle emerges in history, especially in the book of Judges, as quite militaristic. Benjamin fought with Deborah and Barak against the Canaanites (Judg. 5:14). The Benjaminite men of Gibeah (the hometown of Saul, also a Benjaminite) rape and kill a Levite's concubine (Judg. 19:22–30). In revenge, the rest of the tribes kill 25,000 arms-bearing Benjaminite men (Judg. 20:46) and put a ban on intermarriage with the remainder. However, the prospect of the total loss of one of the tribes leads the rest of Israel to a novel if crude solution. They abduct four hundred young virgins of the town of Jabesh-Gilead and give them to the Benjaminites so that they might get a fresh start (Judges 21).

[29–33] The words of the farewell speech are not quite Jacob's last. In the prose paragraph that follows, Jacob asks his sons to bury him in the cave of Machpelah at Mamre/Hebron in Canaan, the ancestral necropolis. The inventory of tombs stands at five—we learn for the first time in verse 31 that Jacob had buried Leah there and that his mother Rebekah was also interred there with Isaac. Jacob's burial there will be the sixth and last.

THE HAPPY ENDING OF THE JOSEPH STORY
Genesis 50:1–26

The fiftieth chapter should not be neglected because it offers a key to the meaning of the book of Genesis and perhaps of the Pentateuch as a whole. That key emerges in the dialogue that takes place between Joseph and the brothers beginning with verse 15. Before that grief processing and reconciliation can take place, however, the wish of the old man to be buried in Canaan has to be honored.

[50:1–14] Embalming is mentioned only twice in the Old Testament, both in the Egyptian setting of Genesis 50. Ancient Israel, like most of its neighbors, did not embalm corpses, partly because of its antipathy toward anything that smacked of a cult of the dead. At the end of the Old Testament period and in New Testament Christianity, a belief in the resurrection of the dead also tended to render embalming unnecessary. Lazarus stank after four days in the grave (John 11:39) but was whole after his resurrection. Jesus was buried with one hundred pounds of spices not as an embalming technique, but presumably in order to control the stench (John 19:39–40).

The Egyptians were the ancient people whose belief in the need to preserve the dead and their effects for the afterlife drove them to perfect the art of embalming. There is evidence that the dead of Egypt were crudely embalmed even before the cult of Osiris, a god of death and regeneration, became widespread in the Old Kingdom period (2700–2250 B.C.). However, by New Kingdom times (ca. 1567–1070 B.C.—about right for Jacob and Joseph), the practice had advanced greatly. The mummified bodies of Seti I and Rameses II have come down to this day from that period. The embalmers were not "physicians" as Genesis 50:2 would have it, but priests of the jackal-headed god of mummification, Anubis.

(Embalmers sometimes wore masks of Anubis while they worked; all of their work had a religious character.) The periods of forty days for embalming and seventy days for mourning mentioned in verse 3 conform quite well to Egyptian practices as recorded in Egyptian texts. (The Greek historian Herodotus thought the embalming itself took seventy days [*History*, 2.86].)

In the tradition of the Pentateuchal writers, the narrator has Joseph repeat Jacob's parting charge to "the household of Pharaoh" in its entirety (vv. 4–5); then, with Pharaoh's permission, they go up to Canaan with the remains of Jacob. Quite an impressive party makes the trip—not only the entire adult community of Israel, but also Pharaoh's household and assorted Egyptian elders and chariots (vv. 7–9). (Children and flocks are left behind; the family will only be away for a short time.) The local Canaanites are impressed by the size and sorrow of "the Egyptians" who pause for seven days of public mourning at the threshing floor of Atad "beyond the Jordan" (vv. 10–11). Because the phrase "beyond the Jordan" can mean either side of the river, depending upon the viewpoint of the speaker, many commentators locate their stopping point (renamed Abel-mizraim, "Mourning of Egypt") along the most direct route between the Nile Delta/Rameses area and Hebron, perhaps along the Gaza road. Remarkable human-shaped clay coffins on display in the Israel Museum in Jerusalem were found in an Egyptian Late Bronze Age cemetery at Deir el-Balah, about six miles southwest of Gaza. They reinforce the ample evidence that Egyptians and their sympathizers were a major presence in Canaan during the ostensible time of Joseph.

With Jacob buried, the family returns to Egypt (vv. 13–14). Then the plot thickens one last time. Source critics assign these remaining verses of the book to the Elohist.

50:15 **Realizing that their father was dead, Joseph's brothers said, "What if Joseph still bears a grudge against us and pays us back in full for all the wrong that we did to him?"**

After all the shock, ceremonies, and travel are over, the brothers mull things over and, as human beings will do, begin to experience anxiety. They say, "What if Joseph still bears a grudge against us . . . ?"

It is a sobering thought. But why would the brothers have assumed that Joseph wanted revenge? According to the terms of the story, Jacob was not really the protector of the brothers against Joseph, nor does anything in the story suggest that Joseph held back his rage only out of respect for Jacob. The brothers' fear has to be understood more in terms of the culture of the Near East. That culture permits a certain level of personal revenge. We saw that fact manifested earlier in Genesis 27:41: "Now Esau hated Jacob because of the blessing with which his father had blessed him, and Esau said to himself, 'The days of mourning for my father are approaching; then I will kill my brother Jacob.'" In the cultural setting of these stories, family feuds had to put all hostility on hold until the mandatory mourning period for a deceased person was over. Once that period was over, all bets were off. The brothers are thinking, "If Joseph has revenge in mind, the time is rapidly approaching when that fact will manifest itself." Only if the conversation reported in verses 16–17 really did take place at some point do we have reason to think that Jacob too might have worried about what powerful Joseph might do after his death.

> 50:16 **So they approached Joseph, saying, "Your father gave this instruction before he died,** 17 **'Say to Joseph: I beg you, forgive the crime of your brothers and the wrong they did in harming you.' Now therefore please forgive the crime of the servants of the God of your father." Joseph wept when they spoke to him.** 18 **Then his brothers also wept, fell down before him, and said, "We are here as your slaves."** 19 **But Joseph said to them, "Do not be afraid! Am I in the place of God?** 20 **Even though you intended to do harm to me, God intended it for good, in order to preserve a numerous people, as he is doing today.** 21 **So have no fear; I myself will provide for you and your little ones." In this way he reassured them, speaking kindly to them.**

If Jacob actually spoke the words of verse 17 at some time, we have no record of it. Perhaps this reveals the often-noted fragmentary or supplementary character of the Elohistic source—the words of supplication were once there in that narrative but got lost when sources were combined.

When he hears their plea, the ever lachrymose Joseph weeps. Robert Alter does not regard this as one of the three weepings that mark the stages of Joseph's emotional development (see commentary on 42:24). It is, however, associated with the approaching moment of truth about how Joseph really thinks. One possible reason why Joseph weeps here would be his pain that his brothers would have imagined him to be so heartless and cruel. Of course, they had some cause. He had put them through some pretty serious suffering, planting the cup in Benjamin's sack of grain, holding Benjamin as hostage, concealing his identity. In Genesis 45:1–2, their suffering was so intense that Joseph, who had earlier turned aside to weep so that his brothers could not see him (43:30), wept in front of them so loudly that he was heard by the Egyptians. Perhaps now he weeps that the brothers persist in their practice of prevarication: They feel they have to lie about what their father said in order to protect their own skins.

Verse 18 presents a slight textual problem. The Hebrew text says "the brothers *came*" or "*went* to him" The NRSV has eliminated the potential problem of where they were when they were speaking to him in verses 16–17 by emending the Hebrew to read, "the brothers also *wept.*" (The new reading requires only an exchange of one consonant of the Hebrew word with another consonant that looks very much like it.) This correction is based on a modern scholarly supposition and not on any variant among Hebrew manuscripts or any reading in a non-Hebrew version of antiquity; however, for better or for worse, it is now how many Americans will receive this tiny piece of the story. Luckily, nothing of faith is endangered thereby!

In chapter 37 Joseph the dreamer saw sheaves of wheat and heavenly bodies doing obeisance to himself. Now in the prostrations of the brothers in Genesis 50:18 all comes to pass exactly as he dreamt it would. We are not told that the brothers recall this offensive incident of the past (the very thing that caused them to sell Joseph into slavery), nor does Joseph bring it up in order to say "I told you so." He does not have to; we readers know. Far from gloating, Joseph says, "Do not be afraid! Am I in place of God?" (v. 19; see commentary on 42:18). By implication, God is the one to "fear" (that is, hold in deep esteem and awe), for God alone can bring about wonderful results out of human failings. Surely, Joseph's question focuses the entire novella exactly where the Pentateuchal writers wanted it focused: on the mysterious, hidden workings of God woven in and through the fabric of human moral and immoral behavior. The divine presence in history disqualifies any of the human players from playing God.

In verses 19–20 the issue of the fear of God, a unifying motif of the Elohistic writer, comes to the fore (see especially 22:12, but also 15:1; 21:17; 28:17; and 35:17). When the brothers offer to come back into the fellowship of Joseph as slaves, they only project onto him what they or we might do to rascally brothers if we could. What can and will God do with them? God can do more than Joseph or any human being can. God can weave them and their treachery into the history of salvation. This is the meaning of verse 20 and of the entire Joseph novella. Von Rad puts it this way:

> Joseph's meaning here is that, in the remarkable conduct of this whole story, God himself has already spoken. He has included the guilt, the brothers' evil, in his saving activity and thus justified them. Were Joseph to condemn them now, he would be setting a negative statement beside the one God had already spoken and would thus be putting himself "in the place of God." (von Rad, 427)

God kept them safe, God brought them to this day, in and through their sins, for God's own purpose—that through them and their descendants the promise of blessing through Israel (12:3b) might move on toward fulfillment. (See "Further Reflections on Genesis 50:20" below.)

Joseph's character has developed in all of this too. When his brothers actually do bow down to him as in the dream, he points away from himself to God. In verse 20 he says essentially what the hymn says, "So to [God] I leave it all." Among the many things that scripture means when it speaks of the fear of God is this. It means refusing to put my plans or your plans or even Pharaoh's plans in the place of God's plan.

Verse 21 does not conflict with this reading of the text. God has brought them through safely, but Joseph still has a role to play in providing them nurture and political safekeeping. One might say that Joseph is the agent of God in salvation but not the agent of God in judgment. That enables him to reassure them and speak kindly to them (v. 21b).

[22–26] The Elohistic narrator spends the last verses of the book of Genesis tidying up the story of Joseph and preparing for the most constitutive event in the history of Israel—the Exodus. Everyone stays in Egypt now, and Joseph sees his own great-grandchildren or possibly great-great-grandchildren (if "Ephraim's children of the third generation" means Ephraim's great-grandchildren). In fact, the children of Machir ben Manasseh were "born on Joseph's knees." (Was it an adoption rite? See the commentary on 48:12; note also 30:3. Machir is associated with Gilead in trans-Jordan in several texts.)

On his deathbed Joseph addresses his brothers. First (v. 24), he passes on to them directly for the first time the land promise that had not even been passed on to him until Jacob did so in Genesis 48:4. For the first time, the names of all three of the prior patriarchal recipients of the promise are linked to God's promise. In verse 25 the narrator uses the phrase "sons of Israel" or "Israelites" for the first time in a narrative context (excluding the mention of the term in two Priestly genealogies [36:31; 46:8] and in a scribal gloss [32:32]). In an abbreviated version of Jacob's last words in Genesis 49:29–32, Joseph makes them pledge to carry his "bones" with them when they return to Canaan (a promise fulfilled initially on the night of the exodus [Ex. 13:19] and finally when his remains are buried at Shechem [Josh. 24:32]). The narrator is not crisp about what will be in the coffin that is finally buried, a skeleton or a mummy (for the text says that Joseph was embalmed). The narrator is clear, though, that Joseph was 110 years old at his death. Life spans had dropped from father to father, and they keep dropping after Joseph. Among major biblical figures, only Job (140; see Job 42:16), the priest Jehoiada (130; see 2 Chron. 24:15),

Aaron (123; see Num. 33:39) and Moses (120; see Deut. 34:7) live longer than Joseph in the years that follow. Joshua ties his record at 110 (see Josh. 24:29).

FURTHER REFLECTIONS ON GENESIS 50:20

"Even though you intended to do harm to me, God intended it for good." Let that remarkable theological claim simmer in your mind while you conjure up pictures of the slave trade and the Indian wars, Auschwitz, and atomic explosions. The exact nuance of the Hebrew term *hashab* is key to the meaning of the Joseph story. Usually it means simply "think," but the NRSV "intend" works better here. Semantics leads to the larger issue posed by the narrative. Can it be that the brothers have the same intention in the events of their making that God does? Can the same events be governed by different intentions? Who starts this circle anyway, and in the end, who is responsible?

We get all tangled up in the possibility of double causation here. Can one and the same event be both evil and, in God's hands, good? The brothers have an evil scheme to get rid of Joseph. God also has a plan. It is to bring this people safely to Egypt in their time of need so that they might one day return to claim their inheritance in the land of promise. If God's plan is a fixed and preordained one, then all of the brothers' shenanigans are mere stage play. On the other hand, if God's activity is a work in progress, then God is free to make countermoves in response to the moves of the brothers, Potiphar, Pharaoh, and Joseph himself. However, the notion of an evolving divine plan seems to sacrifice God's foreknowledge and omnipotence on the altar of flexibility.

God does not want the brothers to do what they do. God does not order them to do what they do. Yet when they do it, God does not walk away and leave Joseph alone. With God's own initiative concealed in the obedient decisions Joseph makes, the two of them muddle through to victory. The same facts that could have led to further and further escalation of evil were used by God, through the agency of Joseph, to bring forth good. As Joseph puts it, "God sent me before you to preserve for you a remnant on earth. . . . So it was not you who sent me here, but God" (45:7–8). God seizes hold of their reprehensible act of selling Joseph into slavery to effect good. Is that double causation? Surely not. Double causation would render human moral behavior meaningless. Human responsibility in decision making is not subject to complete overturn by unseen forces of God. The human beings in this story are fully responsible as moral agents and are fully responsible for their evil. There is no tricky transmutation here. There is no denial here. Joseph truly did suffer exile and alienation. His brothers' deeds truly were violent and evil.

Yet God is not defeated by what they do. They do it; God uses it. The message of this text is this: In every terrible situation wrought by the evil schemes of human beings, God sees an opportunity, and by wiggling and adapting God comes to exercise sovereignty over it. The Joseph novella illustrates that process. So does the whole of the book of Genesis. Though it has to contend with perfidy and perversion, prevarication and pretense, God stands by the promise that in the descendants of Abraham all the nations of the world will find a blessing—and God sees it through.

The notion that God can muddle through with the raw material given God by human foibles is a deeply significant notion even today. This is especially true in the realm of pastoral care and guidance. When the task is to refuse to let people off the hook for their folly and sin, and yet equally to refuse to admit that God is defeated by these things, the teaching, "You meant it for evil but God meant it for good" is an invaluable notion. How good it is to know that God can weave our deeds, even ones motivated by evil intentions, into an improvisation of salvation!

The cross is illuminated by Joseph's summary statement. God did not plan the death of Jesus, inevitable as it may have been, but God wove it powerfully into the history of salvation. Perhaps the word "shape" also describes God's intentionality. Using the flawed material of history that we create, God shapes a different future than the one that we are making for ourselves.

What ought we then to do? Fear God and leave the ultimate outcome in God's hands. This is not an invitation to quietude, a temptation to sit on our hands. Our hands ought to be busy in the service of God's purpose. Joseph's were. We ought to do our best to conform our intention to God's intention, as far as we can discern it. God's intention in history is not that hard to discern: It always has to do with justice, care for the vulnerable and marginal, love, and peace.

"Even though you intended to do harm to me, God intended it for good." Learn from this text that we have to start right where we are, without pretending that the terrible atrocities of the past and present never happened.

Learn also from this text what it is that God wants for everyone. God wants people to survive.

Learn also from this text what it is that God wants from each of us. God wants us to be instruments of the divine purpose, busy heading off bloody tragedy, smart as whips when it comes to salvaging positive new directions out of breakdowns in the moral order, ever ready to broker peace.

Works Cited

Alter, Robert. *The Art of Biblical Narrative.* New York: Basic Books, 1981.

Barbour, Ian. *Religion in an Age of Science.* New York: Harper & Row, 1990.

Barr, James. *Biblical Chronology: Legend or Science?* London: University of London Press, 1987.

Bonhoeffer, Dietrich. *Creation and Fall.* Translated by John C. Fletcher. London: SCM Press, 1959.

Brueggemann, Walter. *Genesis.* Interpretation: A Bible Commentary for Preaching and Teaching. Atlanta: John Knox Press, 1982.

Burnham, Frederic. "Maker of Heaven and Earth: A Perspective of Contemporary Science." *Horizons in Biblical Theology* 12/2 (1990): 1–18.

Calvin, John. *Commentaries on the First Book of Moses Called Genesis.* Translated by John King. Grand Rapids: Wm. B. Eerdmans Publishing Co., 1948.

————. *Institutes of the Christian Religion.* Translated by Henry Beveridge. London: James Clarke & Co., n.d.

Charles, R. H., ed. *The Apocrypha and Pseudepigrapha of the Old Testament,* Vol. 2. Oxford: Clarendon Press, 1913.

Charlesworth, James H., ed. *The Old Testament Pseudepigrapha,* 2 vols. Garden City, N.Y.: Doubleday, 1983–85.

Coats, George W. *Genesis.* The Forms of the Old Testament Literature, vol. 1. Grand Rapids: Wm. B. Eerdmans Publishing Co., 1983.

Cross, Frank M. *Canaanite Myth and Hebrew Epic.* Cambridge: Harvard University Press, 1973.

Dabney, Robert L. *A Defence of Virginia.* Harrisonburg, Va.: Sprinkle Publications, 1977. (Reprint of the original 1867 edition.)

Dubos, René. *Beast or Angel? Choices That Make Us Human.* New York: Charles Scribner's Sons, 1974.

Fretheim, Terence. The book of Genesis. In *The New Interpreter's Bible*, edited by Leander E. Keck, et al. Vol. 1. Nashville: Abingdon Press, 1994.

Ginzberg, Louis. *The Legends of the Jews*. New York: Simon & Schuster, 1961.

Gottwald, Norman. *The Hebrew Bible: A Socio-Literary Introduction*. Philadelphia: Fortress Press, 1985.

Grene, David. *The History of Herodotus*. Chicago: University of Chicago Press, 1987.

Hall, Douglas John. *Imaging God: Dominion as Stewardship*. Grand Rapids: Wm. B. Eerdmans Publishing Co., 1986.

Hanson, Richard S. *The Serpent Was Wiser*. Minneapolis: Augsburg Press, 1972.

Hawking, Stephen. *A Brief History of Time*. New York: Bantam Books, 1988.

Koehler, Ludwig. *Old Testament Theology*. Translated by A. S. Todd. Philadelphia: Westminster Press, 1957.

Lipton, Diana. *Revisions of the Night: Politics and Promises in the Patriarchal Dreams of Genesis*. Sheffield: Sheffield Academic Press, 1999.

Luther, Martin. *Luther's Commentary on Genesis*. Translated by J. Theodore Mueller. Grand Rapids: Zondervan Publishing House, 1958.

McKane, William. *Studies in the Patriarchal Narratives*. Edinburgh: Handsel Press, 1979.

McKim, LindaJo., ed. *The Presbyterian Hymnal*. Louisville, Ky.: Westminster/John Knox Press, 1990.

Mann, Thomas. *Joseph and His Brothers*. Translated by H. T. Loew-Porter. Vol. 4, *Joseph the Provider*. New York: Alfred A. Knopf, 1944.

Mann, Thomas W. "All the Families of the Earth." *Interpretation* 45 (1991): 341–353.

Miller, Arthur. *The Creation of the World and Other Business*. New York: Viking Press, 1973.

Moyers, Bill. *Genesis: A Living Conversation*. New York: Doubleday, 1996. (Companion to Moyers's ten-part PBS series on the book of Genesis.)

Napier, B. Davie. *Come Sweet Death: A Quintet from Genesis*. Revised edition. New York: Pilgrim Press, 1981.

Rad, Gerhard von. *Genesis: A Commentary*. Translated by John H. Marks. The Old Testament Library. Philadephia: Westminster Press, 1961.

Riemann, Paul A. "Am I My Brother's Keeper?" *Interpretation* 24 (1970): 482–91.

Sarna, Nahum M. *Genesis: The Traditional Hebrew Text with New JPS Translation/Commentary.* The JPS Torah Commentary. Philadelphia: Jewish Publication Society, 1989.

Steinbeck, John. *East of Eden.* New York: Viking Press, 1952.

Steinberg, Naomi. *Kinship and Marriage in Genesis: A Household Economics Perspective.* Minneapolis: Fortress Press, 1993.

Teubal, Savina J. *Hagar the Egyptian: The Lost Tradition of the Matriarchs.* San Francisco: Harper & Row, 1990.

The Torah: The Five Books of Moses. Philadelphia: Jewish Publication Society of America, 1962.

Trible, Phyllis. *God and the Rhetoric of Sexuality.* Philadelphia: Fortress Press, 1978.

de Vaux, Roland, O.P. *Ancient Israel: Its Life and Institutions.* New York: McGraw-Hill, 1961.

Westermann, Claus. *Genesis 1–11, A Commentary.* Translated by John J. Scullion, S.J. Minneapolis: Augsburg Publishing House, 1984; *Genesis 12–36,* 1985; *Genesis 37–50,* 1986.

Wolff, Hans Walter. "The Kerygma of the Yahwist." In *The Vitality of Old Testament Traditions,* by Walter Brueggemann and Hans Walter Wolff. Atlanta: John Knox Press, 1975.

FOR FURTHER READING

Buechner, Frederick. *Son of Laughter.* San Francisco: HarperSanFrancisco, 1993.

Campbell, Antony F., and Mark A. O'Brien. *Sources of the Pentateuch.* Minneapolis: Fortress Press, 1993.

Carter, Jimmy. *The Blood of Abraham.* Boston: Houghton Mifflin, 1985.

Fox, Everett. *The Five Books of Moses.* The Schocken Bible, vol. 1. New York: Schocken Books, 1995.

Freedman, David Noel, ed. *The Anchor Bible Dictionary.* 6 vols. New York: Doubleday, 1992.

Gunkel, Hermann. *The Legends of Genesis.* Translated by W. H. Carruth. New York: Schocken Books, 1964.

Into the Word, Into the World. Disciple Program (includes Genesis). Nashville: Graded Press, 1991. Video and manual.

Kierkegaard, Søren. *Fear and Trembling.* Translated by Robert Payne. Oxford: Oxford University Press, 1939.

Noth, Martin. *A History of Pentateuchal Traditions.* Translated by Bernhard W. Anderson. Englewood Cliffs, N.J.: Prentice-Hall, 1972.

Pritchard, James B., ed. *Ancient Near Eastern Texts Relating to the Old Testament.* 3d ed. Princeton, N.J.: Princeton University Press, 1969.
————. *The Harper Atlas of the Bible.* New York: Harper & Row, 1987.
Rice, Tim, and Andrew Lloyd Webber. *Joseph and the Amazing Technicolor Dreamcoat.* New York: Holt, Rinehart & Winston, 1982.
Sharpless, F. Parvin. *The Myth of the Fall: Literature of Innocence and Experience.* Rochelle Park, N.J.: Hayden Book Co., 1974.
Teubal, Savina J. *Sarah the Priestess: The First Matriarch of Genesis.* Athens, Ohio: Swallow Press, 1984.
Wellhausen, Julius. *Prolegomena to the History of Ancient Israel.* Cleveland: World Publishing Co., 1957. German original, 1883.
Westermann, Claus. *Handbook to the Old Testament.* Translated by Robert H. Boyd. Minneapolis: Augsburg, 1967.